6744

American Literary Publishing Houses, 1638-1899
Part 1: A-M

Dictionary of Literary Biography

Documentary Series

Yearbooks

Dictionary of Literary Biography • Volume Forty-nine

American Literary Publishing Houses, 1638-1899
Part 1: A-M

6744

Edited by
Peter Dzwonkoski
University of Rochester

A Bruccoli Clark Book
Gale Research Company • Book Tower • Detroit, Michigan 48226

Manufactured by Edwards Brothers, Inc.
Ann Arbor, Michigan
Printed in the United States of America

Library of Congress Cataloging-in-Publication Data

American literary publishing houses, 1638-1899.

(Dictionary of literary biography; v. 49)
"A Bruccoli Clark book."
Includes index.
Contents: pt. 1. A-M—pt. 2. N-Z.
1. Literature—Publishing—United States—History—
Dictionaries. 2. American literature—Publishing—United
States—History—Dictionaries. 3. Publishers and pub-
lishing—United States—History—Dictionaries. 4. Book in-
dustries and trade—United States—History—Dictionar-
ies. I. Dzwonkoski, Peter. II. Series.
Z479.A448 1986 070.5'0973 86-18409
ISBN 0-8103-1727-3 (set)

Project Associates

Associate Editors: David Dzwonkoski

                                                           Martha A. Bartter
                                                        University of Rochester

                                                         Elizabeth Hoffman
                                                        University of Rochester

Graphics Editor: Mary M. Huth
                                                        University of Rochester

Research Assistants: Ruth H. Bennett
                                                         Theodora Mills

For the Reference Department of the University of Rochester Library, the books and the people

Contents

Contents

Plan of the Series

. . . Almost the most prodigious asset of a country, and perhaps its most precious possession, is its native literary product—when that product is fine and noble and enduring.

Mark Twain*

The advisory board, the editors, and the publisher of the *Dictionary of Literary Biography* are joined in endorsing Mark Twain's declaration. The literature of a nation provides an inexhaustible resource of permanent worth. It is our expectation that this endeavor will make literature and its creators better understood and more accessible to students and the literate public, while satisfying the standards of teachers and scholars.

To meet these requirements, *literary biography* has been construed in terms of the author's achievement. The most important thing about a writer is his writing. Accordingly, the entries in *DLB* are career biographies, tracing the development of the author's canon and the evolution of his reputation.

The publication plan for *DLB* resulted from two years of preparation. The project was proposed to Bruccoli Clark by Frederick G. Ruffner, president of the Gale Research Company, in November 1975. After specimen entries were prepared and typeset, an advisory board was formed to refine the entry format and develop the series rationale. In meetings held during 1976, the publisher, series editors, and advisory board approved the scheme for a comprehensive biographical dictionary of persons who contributed to North American literature. Editorial work on the first volume began in January 1977, and it was published in 1978.

In order to make *DLB* more than a reference tool and to compile volumes that individually have claim to status as literary history, it was decided to organize volumes by topic or period or genre. Each of these freestanding volumes provides a biographical-bibliographical guide and overview for a particular area of literature. We are convinced that this organization—as opposed to a single alphabet method—constitutes a valuable innovation in the presentation of reference material. The volume plan necessarily requires many decisions for the placement and treatment of authors who might properly be included in two or three volumes. In some instances a major figure will be included in separate volumes, but with different entries emphasizing the aspect of his career appropriate to each volume. Ernest Hemingway, for example, is represented in *American Writers in Paris, 1920-1939* by an entry focusing on his expatriate apprenticeship; he is also in *American Novelists, 1910-1945* with an entry surveying his entire career. Each volume includes a cumulative index of subject authors and articles. The final *DLB* volume will be a comprehensive index to the entire series.

With volume ten in 1982 it was decided to enlarge the scope of *DLB* beyond the literature of the United States. By the end of 1985 twenty-one volumes treating British literature had been published, and volumes for Commonwealth and Modern European literature were in progress. The series has been further augmented by the *DLB Yearbooks* (since 1981) which update published entries and add new entries to keep the *DLB* current with contemporary activity. There have also been occasional *DLB Documentary Series* volumes which provide biographical and critical background source materials for figures whose work is judged to have particular interest for students. One of these companion volumes is entirely devoted to Tennessee Williams.

The purpose of *DLB* is not only to provide reliable information in a convenient format but also to place the figures in the larger perspective of literary history and to offer appraisals of their accomplishments by qualified scholars.

We define literature as the *intellectual commerce of a nation*: not merely as belles lettres, but as that ample and complex process by which ideas are generated, shaped, and transmitted. *DLB* entries are not limited to "creative writers" but extend to other figures who in this time and in this way influenced the mind of a people. Thus the series encompasses historians, journalists, publishers, and screenwriters. By this means readers of *DLB* may be aided to perceive literature not as cult scripture in the keeping of cultural high priests, but as at the center of a nation's life.

*From an unpublished section of Mark Twain's autobiography, copyright © by the Mark Twain Company.

DLB includes the major writers appropriate to each volume and those standing in the ranks immediately behind them. Scholarly and critical counsel has been sought in deciding which minor figures to include and how full their entries should be. Wherever possible, useful references will be made to figures who do not warrant separate entries.

Each *DLB* volume has a volume editor responsible for planning the volume, selecting the figures for inclusion, and assigning the entries. Volume editors are also responsible for preparing, where appropriate, appendices surveying the major periodicals and literary and intellectual movements for their volumes, as well as lists of further readings. Work on the series as a whole is coordinated at the Bruccoli Clark editorial center in Columbia, South Carolina, where the editorial staff is responsible for the accuracy of the published volumes.

One feature that distinguishes *DLB* is the illustration policy—its concern with the iconography of literature. Just as an author is influenced by his surroundings, so is the reader's understanding of the author enhanced by a knowledge of his environment. Therefore *DLB* volumes include not only drawings, paintings, and photographs of authors, often depicting them at various stages in their careers, but also illustrations of their families and places where they lived. Title pages are regularly reproduced in facsimile along with dust jackets for modern authors. The dust jackets are a special feature of *DLB* because they often document better than anything else the way in which an author's work was launched in its own time. Specimens of the writers' manuscripts are included when feasible.

A supplement to *DLB*—tentatively titled *A Guide, Chronology, and Glossary for American Literature*—will outline the history of literature in North America and trace the influences that shaped it. This volume will provide a framework for the study of American literature by means of chronological tables, literary affiliation charts, glossarial entries, and concise surveys of the major movements. It has been planned to stand on its own as a vade mecum, providing a ready-reference guide to the study of American literature as well as a companion to the *DLB* volumes for American literature.

Samuel Johnson rightly decreed that "The chief glory of every people arises from its authors." The purpose of the *Dictionary of Literary Biography* is to compile literary history in the surest way available to us—by accurate and comprehensive treatment of the lives and work of those who contributed to it.

The *DLB* Advisory Board

Foreword

American Literary Publishing Houses, 1638-1899 is the second volume in the *Dictionary of Literary Biography* on American book publishing firms. Entries in the present volume concern trade publishing firms which were founded prior to 1900. *DLB 46* dealt with trade and paperback firms founded in the twentieth century. Some firms which began prior to 1900 and maintained their identities into the twentieth century—Macmillan, Putnam, and Scribner, for example—have their entire histories traced in this volume. For other companies with more complicated histories, it may be necessary to consult both this volume and *DLB 46* in order to get the complete story. Henry Holt and Company is covered in this volume from its founding as Leypoldt and Holt in 1866 down to its merger with Rinehart and Company and the John C. Winston Company in 1960 to form Holt, Rinehart and Winston; the separate histories of Rinehart, Winston, and Holt, Rinehart and Winston (which resumed the name Henry Holt and Company in 1985) are traced in *DLB 46*. Similarly, the history of the Bowen-Merrill Company is covered in this volume, while that of Bobbs-Merrill—the firm that resulted from the reorganization of Bowen-Merrill in 1903—is treated in *DLB 46*. D. Appleton and Company and The Century Company are both discussed in this volume, while the result of their merger—Appleton-Century-Crofts—is covered in *DLB 46*. Even in the case of firms which are dealt with entirely within one volume, it may be necessary to read more than one entry in that volume to get the full history. Although the Houghton Mifflin Company is in a sense the continuation of Hurd and Houghton, the two firms are distinct enough that they have been given separate entries in this volume.

This method of organization has been made necessary by the nature of the subject matter. American book publishing history is a history of mergers, acquisitions, split-ups, divestitures, reorganizations, and name changes. This trend is especially evident in the twentieth century, but it was also the case in earlier times. Use of the table of contents, the cumulative index, and headnotes ("See also the [name of firm] entry in *DLB 46*, *American Literary Publishing Houses, 1900-1980: Trade and Paperback*") in this volume should enable the reader to thread his way through these labyrinths. Also, a third volume in this series, which will deal with academic, reference, and small presses, will contain an index to all three volumes which will list all firms and individuals connected with them.

As was explained in the foreword to *DLB 46*, the entries in these volumes are restricted to firms that have had some *literary* impact on American culture: publishers of fiction, poetry, drama, and criticism, as well as publishers of literary biographies and reference works. Publishers of general nonfiction, atlases, directories, and so on have been excluded unless a significant portion of their activity was, at some time in their history, literary or literature-related. Even among firms defined as literary publishers, it was necessary to limit coverage to those which, in the judgment of the editors, have had significant influence on the literature consumed by the American reading public. As was also explained in the foreword to *DLB 46*, the terms *literary* and *literature* have been taken in a broad sense to include not only works of art but also the "literature" of the masses, such as dime novels and other forms of light reading.

Beginning with the Cambridge Press, which was brought to the Massachusetts Bay Colony from England in 1638 and published the *Bay Psalm Book* in 1640, the history of book publishing in America has had about it much of the sweep and variety of the American saga. Reflecting the chief preoccupation of the earliest settlers, the first American presses turned out religious works—prayer books, hymnals, collections of sermons, works of biblical exegesis—to the exclusion of most other kinds of books. Although the vast majority of these early products of the press are no longer read, certain titles—some of the works of Cotton and Increase Mather and the sermons of Jonathan Edwards, for example—survive at least in college literature anthologies. The proportion of religious to secular publishing has steadily decreased over the centuries; nevertheless, America has never been without its religious presses, and many firms have published notable literature that is also religious. During the early and middle 1800s the American Sunday-School Union and the American Tract Society attempted, on an unprecedentedly large scale, to cast bland spiritual and moral instruction in palatable literary forms, so that generations of nineteenth-century children might grow up to become strong Christians. Smaller commercial firms, such as Mahlon Day and Kiggins and Kellogg, published similar material but expanded the horizon of children's publishing by offering books of a more secular cast.

In modern America, publishing, printing, and bookselling are discrete functions not normally performed, except in the smallest of operations, by the same firm. Commercial publishers today select works to be published, negotiate with authors, make arrangements for the physical production of books, and finally either distribute them themselves or arrange for their distribution to booksellers. The publishing house may have little or nothing to do with the making of the physical book—printing, binding, and so on. Although a few old houses, such as Doubleday, Harcourt Brace Jovanovich, and Barnes and Noble, still maintain retail bookselling operations, most American bookstores are independent organizations. By contrast, early American printers frequently functioned as publishers and booksellers as well. For example, Isaiah Thomas, who published in Boston and Worcester, Massachusetts, from 1770 to 1802, was both a printer and a publisher. Mathew Carey of Philadelphia began as a printer-bookseller but established a firm that, between 1785 and 1838, became one of the first American publishing houses in the modern sense of that term. In New York from 1816 to 1844 Mahlon Day printed, published, and sold the children's books for which he became so well known.

One impediment to the growth of American literary book publishing, or at least to the publication of books by Americans in America, was the lack of an international copyright law. Many popular British novelists—Charles Dickens was perhaps the most extreme case—saw their works pirated royalty-free by American firms eager to profit from the absence of regulation. Their American counterparts—among them Ralph Waldo Emerson, Henry Wadsworth Longfellow, and Samuel Langhorne Clemens—complained angrily that so much American publishing energy was given over to British rather than American writing. Texts of the latest British novels were often on their way to American shores before the ink was dry on the first British editions and appeared in American bookstores amazingly soon thereafter. It took Harper and Brothers only twenty-one hours to set up, print, bind, and distribute Sir Walter Scott's *Peveril of the Peak* in 1823. Ninety percent of Harper's catalogue for 1833 consisted of reprints of English books. Not every American publisher took advantage of the lack of an international copyright agreement: Henry Holt and Company paid Thomas Hardy full ten

percent royalties. Even Harper ultimately paid large sums to British publishers and authors, almost $250,000 by 1875. Passage in 1891 of the Platt-Simonds Act, which made foreign authors eligible for copyright protection, marked the end of wholesale literary piracy in America.

For American book publishing the nineteenth century was a period of growth (as the twentieth has been a period of mergers). Although one could not, in the first half of the century, speak meaningfully of a national literature in America, the means for making such a literature available to the public was already in place. What F. O. Matthiessen called the American Renaissance in literature was paralleled and supported by a publishing industry that was also coming into full flower. Small, family-owned enterprises gradually became big businesses, a trend documented in the frequent changes in the addresses of many firms as they expanded and moved to larger quarters. By the middle of the nineteenth century several houses with names instantly familiar to American readers today—Harper, Scribner, Lippincott, Houghton Mifflin, Appleton, and Putnam—had begun to publish books and were in some cases already well established. The great house of Harper and Brothers began in New York in 1817 as a printing establishment; by 1830 it was the largest book printer in America, and by 1875 it was firmly established as a leader in the publication of books and periodicals. The name of J. B. Lippincott first appeared in a publisher's imprint in Philadelphia in 1836, though Lippincott was earlier associated with a bookstore and printing firm. The house of Appleton began formally in 1838 and survived as a family operation until 1933, when it merged with The Century Company, which later became Appleton-Century-Crofts. G. P. Putnam's Sons, another great family enterprise, began in 1848, although Putnam had been a partner in Wiley and Putnam since 1837.

As always in American enterprise, many small publishing houses rose hopefully to brief promise only to die within a few years or decades. Lamson, Wolffe and Company began in Boston in 1895 and ceased operations four years later; nevertheless, this partnership produced about seventy volumes whose fine printing and binding are admired today. The George M. Hill Company (1896?-1902) is little known today—except by admirers of L. Frank Baum, as the first publisher of *The Wonderful Wizard of Oz* (1900)—yet this firm employed Frank Kennicott Reilly and Sumner C. Britton, who later formed the Madison Book Company, which became the Reilly and Britton Publishing Company, which became the Reilly and Lee Publishing Company, which endured until 1957 as one of the best-known American publishers of juvenile fiction.

Many of the smaller firms which rose and fell in the nineteenth century were known as "cheap reprinters." As the name implies, they reprinted in inexpensive format, and without paying royalties, works first published by other firms, and then undersold the original publishers. These cheap reprinters, whose ranks included W. L. Allison and Company, DeWolfe, Fiske and Company, Estes and Lauriat, Hurst and Company, and Pollard and Moss, were the bane of the large, established publishers. Finally, competition among the reprinters grew so intense that one of their number—John W. Lovell—organized many of them into a trust to prevent their mutual ruin. The result, the United States Book Company, lasted only from 1890 to 1893 as competition continued from companies outside the trust and even from some within it. As unfair as the activities of these firms may have been to the publishers and authors whose works they appropriated, the importance of the cheap reprinters lies in the fact that they brought good literature within the financial grasp of vast numbers of Americans for the first time and thereby helped to increase the size of the reading public. Contributing to the same result were the publishers of dime novels, "five-cent libraries," and "railroad litera-

ture," such as Beadle and Adams and F. Gleason's Publishing Hall. Although the output of these firms could scarcely be described as "good literature"—it consisted for the most part of hastily written, formula adventure stories, westerns, and romances, often lurid in nature—they, too, helped to develop the reading habit in many Americans and thereby to broaden the market for the products of more "respectable" firms. The explosion of cheap literature in the nineteenth century was in many respects an anticipation of the "paperback revolution" of the twentieth century, which is chronicled in *DLB 46*.

As in *DLB 46*, publishing firms are listed in this volume according to the imprints that appeared on their books. Where a firm's name changed during the course of its history—and this was the case more often than not—its most important name is given in the main heading and the other names are listed in subheadings. The city in which the firm had its main office and the dates of founding, dissolution, and name change are given in parentheses below each heading. Since many firms have been inconsistent in regard to spelling out the word *and* in their names or replacing it by the ampersand, we have adopted the convention of using *and* in all cases.

—*Peter Dzwonkoski*

Acknowledgments

This book was produced by BC Research. Karen L. Rood is senior editor for the *Dictionary of Literary Biography* series. Philip B. Dematteis was the in-house editor.

Art supervisor is Patricia M. Flanagan. Copyediting supervisor is Patricia Coate. Production coordinator is Kimberly Casey. Typesetting supervisor is Laura Ingram. The production staff includes Rowena Betts, David R. Bowdler, Joseph Matthew Bruccoli, Deborah Cavanaugh, Mary S. Dye, Kathleen M. Flanagan, Joyce Fowler, Ellen Hassell, Pamela Haynes, Judith K. Ingle, Judith E. McCray, Joycelyn R. Smith, and Lucia Tarbox. Jean W. Ross is permissions editor. Joseph Caldwell, photography editor, and James Adam Sutton did photographic copy work for the volume.

Walter W. Ross and Rhonda A. Marshall did the library research with the assistance of the staff at the Thomas Cooper Library of the University of South Carolina: Lynn Barron, Daniel Boice, Connie Crider, Kathy Eckman, Michael Freeman, Gary Geer, David L. Haggard, Jens Holley, Marcia Martin, Dana Rabon, Jean Rhyne, Jan Squire, Ellen Tillett, and Virginia Weathers.

Special acknowledgment is given to the editors of *Publishers Weekly* for their generous assistance in providing material for illustrations for this volume. Unless otherwise credited, all advertisements reproduced here were taken from the pages of that magazine; many photographs of individuals were also derived from that source.

The editor would also like to thank the project associates for the *DLB* volumes on American literary book publishing and the many others who have been involved in this work. One of the associate editors, David Dzwonkoski, should be singled out for special praise. He has written many entries, revised and sometimes rewritten others, edited hundreds, and coordinated many aspects of a complicated enterprise. A former member of the University of Rochester Library staff, Barbara Salvage, helped with general editing. An indispensable mainstay of the research staff has been Theodora Mills. Formerly a reference librarian at the University of Rochester Library, Ms. Mills has written, rewritten, checked, fact-found, substantiated, and generally dug around in library caverns in aid of the project. A gifted researcher, she has helped and trained others in their work for these volumes.

Another member of the research staff, Ruth H. Bennett, long an editor and researcher with the University of Rochester's Ralph Waldo Emerson project, brought solid experience, careful attention to detail, and a quick intelligence to the project.

Administrative Assistant Marguerite Barrett coordinated the day-to-day work of the project for five years. She typed, filed, kept track of contributors, and devised and maintained a flow chart for nearly 800 entries. She was indispensable in the maintenance of order and morale and in countless other ways.

This has been very much a Rochester project, more specifically a University of Rochester project, more specifically still a University of Rochester Library project. Two of the project editors and more than ten major contributors are full-time members of the University of Rochester Library staff. Faculty members in the Department of English as well as many graduate students in English have also contributed. Special recognition is due the late Professor Rowland L. Collins. Some entries are the work of helpful people in the Rochester community not connected with the university. Other contributors have come from many of the major eastern universities, including the State Universities of New York at Albany, Binghamton, and Buffalo; the Universities of Pennsylvania, Pittsburgh, Virginia, North Carolina, South Carolina, and Florida; Duke University; Indiana University; Kent State University; Syracuse University; Cornell University; and Yale University.

Other individuals who have helped the project in various ways include Pauline Anderson, Phyllis Andrews, Thomas Berger, Albert Bergeron, John Bidwell, James Brunner, Dale Carrithers, Christie Chappelle, Peter Conn, Robert Creeley, Chris Drzyzga, Hoyt Duggan, Frances Dzwonkoski, William Ewert, Lois Frankforter, Donald Gallup, Philip Gerber, John Hench, Tom Hickman, Thomas T. Hill, Howard C. Horsford, Sidney Huttner, Desirée Johnson, William Joyce, Gail Junion, Dean H. Keller, Eugene Robert Kintgen, Jr., Tamara Knight-Anttonen, Anuradha Mookerjee, Jean Murphy, Linda Quinlan, Gail Reisman, Shirley Ricker, Bernard Rosenthal, Justin G. Schiller, Kellie Sheldon, Rollo Silver, Alison Tanner Stauffer, Madeleine B. Stern, Paul Strohm, Ling Ling Sun, John Tebbel, Paul F. Theiner, Robert A. Tibbetts,

Robert Torry, and Anne Whelpley. Margaret Becket and Kathleen McGowan of the University of Rochester Library reference staff were unfailingly ready to help, instruct, write, and advise.

In its final stages the project has relied heavily on the careful and steady work of several editorial assistants who performed the arduous and time-consuming task of checking for accuracy the thousands of bibliographical references included in the entries and of checking many other facts, as well. These volunteers are Dorothy Harper, Peggy Look, Anne Ludlow, Bob Rugg, Nancy Sleeth, and Lyndon Wells.

The editor owes special thanks to his supervisors at the University of Rochester Library. Past Director of University Libraries Alan Taylor per-mitted him to accept the general editorship in the knowledge that it would make demands upon his time and that of other library staff members. Mr. Taylor's successor, James Wyatt, has also supported the project, and, before she left Rochester for a new position, Assistant Director Margaret Perry did, too. Her successor, Janice Holladay, has been most patient and supportive. Grady W. Ballenger, Daniel H. Borus, Timothy D. Murray, Vincent L. Tollers, and Everett C. Wilkie, Jr., also merit special thanks.

Finally, no bibliographic project can hope to succeed without the support of an appropriate library or collection. The many bibliographical strengths and research facilities of the University of Rochester's Rush Rhees Library have made these volumes possible.

American Literary Publishing Houses, 1638-1899
Part 1: A-M

Dictionary of Literary Biography

Abbey Press
(New York: 1899?-1903)

Abbey Press was located at 114 Fifth Avenue in New York, with offices in London and Montreal. Although the firm's dates of operation are uncertain, the company is listed in *Trow's Business Directory of Greater New York* from 1900 through 1903; in the latter year it filed for bankruptcy.

Abbey Press published a wide range of titles, from success books to literary criticism. Wilkie Collins, Henry Drummond, Douglas M. Flattery, and Charles Kent were some of the authors published by Abbey; the company also produced editions of works by Dickens, Tolstoy, and Stevenson. Abbey sought especially to appeal to the reading public's desire to learn of romantic and faraway places. A staple of the company's list was the historical romance, including *A Continental Cavalier* (1899) by Kimball Scribner and *A Slaveholder's Daughter* (1900) by Belle Kearney. Abbey also catered to the public's interest in genteel society with social guides by Lady Constance Howard and personality sketches such as Charles Rideal's *The Cross of Honor* (1900).

—Bill Oliver

J. S. and C. Adams
(Amherst, Massachusetts: 1827-1856)
Carter and Adams
(Amherst: 1825-1827)

Not until 1825, when Amherst College finally obtained a state charter, was there a printer in Amherst, Massachusetts. Four young men—Samuel C. Carter, bookbinder; John Sidney Adams, printer; Adams's younger brother Charles; and Mark H. Newman, son of an Andover bookseller—obtained a Ramage press from the Boston Type Foundry and set themselves up as Carter and Adams, "printers, publishers, and booksellers." Two years later Carter left the firm, and the firm became J. S. and C. Adams. Newman also eventually moved away.

The sermons and addresses of Amherst College president Heman Humphrey and his successor Edward Hitchcock accounted for many of the firm's publications. In 1826 Carter and Adams published a revision of Jonathan Edwards's famous sermon *Sinners in the Hands of an Angry God*, Simeon Cotton's *Masonry Founded on the Bible*, and Humphrey's *The Good Pastor*. Beginning in 1833 the firm published many editions of *The Family Expositor* by Philip Doddridge.

The religious and educational preferences of the time did not encourage the publication of literature, although exceptions were made in 1839 and 1840 for poems read at gatherings of the Amherst literary societies. In 1834 Adams published Mrs. Lydia Howard Sigourney's *Sketches*. A travel book that approximated fiction, *The Story of Aleck, or Pitcairn's Island*, by Nathan Welby Fiske, was published in 1829 and an enlarged second edition titled

Aleck, the Last of the Mutineers; or, The History of Pitcairn Island appeared in 1845.

As business declined in the 1840s the Adams house sought the printing work of neighboring educational academies; in 1844 it started a weekly newspaper, the *Hampshire and Franklin Express*. The *Express* prospered, and, as the *Amherst Record*, still lives.

After Noah Webster's death in 1843, his heirs sold the unbound sheets of the 1841 edition of his dictionary to the Adams firm. Finding that the two-volume work was too much for them to handle, the brothers sold the sheets and all rights to G. and C. Merriam of Springfield, Massachusetts, thus beginning the Merriam firm's long association with Webster's dictionary.

The Adams brothers continued to handle the printing needs of Amherst until 1855, when they sold the business to William Faxon. For a few months in the spring of 1856 the firm was returned to the Adamses before John H. Brewster took over printing for Amherst.

Reference:

Newton Felch McKeon and Katharine Conover Cowles, *Amherst, Massachusetts, Imprints, 1825-1876* (Amherst, Mass.: Amherst College Library, 1946).

—*Everett C. Wilkie, Jr.*
Theodora Mills

Advance Publishing Company

(Chicago; Oak Park, Illinois: 1867-circa 1920)

Advance Publishing Company was the book publishing arm of *Advance* magazine, a Chicago-based Congregationalist church weekly founded in 1867. Like other religious periodicals in the latter part of the nineteenth century, *Advance* ventured into book publishing.

Almost all Advance publications were sermons or religious tracts. James Brand's *To What Extent Are Christians Responsible for Sabbath Desecration* (1892) and *The Young Christian and the Card Table* (1892) and William E. Barton's *What Has Brought Us Out of Egypt?: A Sermon* (1900) are typical Advance pamphlets. The firm also published catechisms and other instructional texts for youth, and religious fiction which was intended to have a moral impact on its readers. Many of these works were first published in the *Advance*. Modern morality tales such as Joseph Hocking's *The Scarlet Woman* (1900) and *"Lest We Forget": A Romance of the Fateful Period* (1900), in which the immoral actions of the characters lead to their downfall, served as examples of what could happen to even the most conscientious Christian if he were not careful.

In history, too, writers could find exemplary figures to hold up to their readers as ideals of spiritual and moral integrity. The recently deceased Queen Victoria inspired James Alonzo Adams (writing under the pseudonym "Grapho") to write *Victoria: Maid—Matron—Monarch* (1901); Adams

was editor of the *Advance* for many years. Barton's *Abraham Lincoln* (1920), *Theodore Roosevelt* (1920), and *George Washington* (1920) held each of these prominent Americans up for emulation and were reprinted several times.

Perhaps the best known of all Advance titles was Charles M. Sheldon's novel *In His Steps* (1897). Sheldon, the founder of the Central Congregationalist Church of Topeka, Kansas, believed that Christians should be actively involved in social reform. In order to boost attendance at the services at which he espoused this ideal, Sheldon developed the "serial sermon": each week he added a new installment to his sermon, usually a modern parable concerned with social reform. Sheldon became so popular that his congregation soon swelled. The *Advance* serialized the stories, including *In His Steps* in 1896.

In His Steps, subtitled *"What Would Jesus Do?,"* tells the story of a young minister who asks the members of his congregation to pledge themselves to live for a year as Jesus might. Those who take the pledge go on to effect many social reforms, thus putting into action Sheldon's ideas about Christian social responsibilities. Advance Publishing Company brought out *In His Steps* in book form in 1897; by 1899 five different editions were in print. That year, however, other publishers discovered that the copyright for *In His Steps* had been improperly registered. In the next few years at least seventeen publishers brought out editions of *In His Steps,* causing the book to become the best-selling work of its time.

Through most of its operating years, Advance Publishing Company was located at 215 West Madison Street in Chicago, but Advance publications of 1920 show Oak Park, Illinois, on their title pages. The Advance Publishing Company imprint does not appear later than about 1920. *Advance* magazine went through mergers with other religious magazines, resulting in several name changes. When the American Congregationalist church merged with the Evangelical and Reformed church in 1957, the two groups combined their magazine and publishing operations into *A.D. Magazine* and A.D. Publishing Company. Thus, while Advance Publishing no longer exists, it lives on in its descendant, A.D. Publications, 475 Riverside Drive, New York 10115.

—Timothy D. Murray

Robert Aitken
(Philadelphia: 1773-1813)

Robert Aitken, bookseller, stationer, and bookbinder, was established opposite the London Coffee House on Front Street in Philadelphia from 1773 to 1802. Aitken emigrated from Scotland and began his publishing career in 1773 with *Aitken's General American Register and Calendar for the Year 1774.* The same year he also published *The Grave* by Robert Blair, bound with Gray's *Elegy Written in a Country Church-yard.* In 1777 he published the first American edition of *The Fables of Aesop and Others,* translated by Samuel Croxall. His fame mainly derives from his publication of the first complete Bible in English in America in 1782.

Upon his death in 1802, his daughter Jane took over the business. In 1808, when the firm was located at 71 North Third Street, Jane Aitken pub-lished, in four volumes, the first American translation of the *Septuagint* by Charles Thomson. In 1813 operations ceased as a result of indebtedness, not related to the company, that Jane Aitken had inherited from her father.

References:

Victor H. Paltsits and P. Marion Simms, "The First American Bible in English," *Colophon,* new series 1 (1935-1936): 455-456;

Willman and Carol Spawn, "R. Aitken: Colonial Printer of Philadelphia," *Graphic Arts Review,* 24 (January 1961): 11-12, 14; (February 1961): 16, 18.

—Theodora Mills

John B. Alden
(New York: 1879-1908)
American Book Exchange
(New York: 1879-1881)
Useful Knowledge Publishing Company
(New York: 1882-1883)
Alden Publishing Company
(New York: 1883-1892)
Elzevir Publishing Company
(New York: 1893-1894)
John B. Alden Publisher
(New York: 1895-1905)
Alden Brothers Publishers
(New York: 1905-1908)

In 1874 John B. Alden moved from Chicago to New York with fifty old books and about seventy dollars in capital to start a used-book store, the American Book Exchange, at 55 Beekman Place. In 1879 the American Book Exchange moved into publishing pocket-sized cloth-bound books that sold for thirty-five and fifty cents apiece.

The books that Alden published were largely pirated from British and American authors, a common practice during that era of inadequate copyright laws. Authors whose works were published by the American Book Exchange included Bunyan, Byron, Carlyle, Cooper, Defoe, Dickens, George Eliot, Hawthorne, Irving, Macaulay, Poe, and Thackeray. The firm also published the literary journals *Library Magazine* and *Good Literature*.

Alden's practices of selling cheap books and dealing directly with customers rather than through booksellers—practices he termed his "Literary Revolution"—earned him the hostility of the book trade, which accused him of using devious business practices. By 1880, when he moved to 154 Nassau Street, he employed 500 people and was producing 4,000 books a day, but his profit margin was small because of the low prices of his books. In order to raise capital he sold stock in the enterprise in 1881, the same year he moved the firm to 764 Broadway. Although many people invested, the American Book Exchange went into receivership in December 1881.

Alden then formed the Useful Knowledge Publishing Company, a bookselling operation, at 18 Vesey Street. He returned to publishing in 1883 with the Alden Publishing Company, which he moved to 393 Pearl Street the following year. In addition to cheap editions of the classics, Alden published fiction by lesser-known authors of the day. He liked to publish novels dealing with the antebellum South, such as Charles W. Hutson's *The Story of Beryl* (1888); novels written by and concerning women, such as *The Woman's Story as Told by Twenty American Women* (1889), an anthology of stories by Harriet Beecher Stowe, Marietta Holley, Louisa May Alcott, Ella Wheeler Wilcox, and other women writers; and novels set in particular locations, such as William Averitt's *Stories and Poems of Western Texas* (1890).

In 1893 Alden began the Elzevir Publishing Company, Booksellers, at 57 Rose Street. Alden listed himself as president and treasurer of the firm. The Elzevir Company was the only part of the business that Alden could salvage from the defunct Alden Publishing Company. Alden was unable to equal the success of his earlier pirating days, and in the spring of 1894 he made an assignment of the firm to Frank Tracy, leaving total liabilities of $30,000 and assets of a larger, unstated amount.

Alden formed another business, John B. Alden Publisher, at 12 Vandewater Street in 1895, moving to 440 Pearl Street in 1897 and to the corner of Ninth Street and Fourth Avenue in 1900. He changed the name of the firm to Alden Brothers Publishers in 1905 and retired in 1908. By that time his relations with the rest of the book trade were more friendly than they had been in his early years. Alden died in 1924 at age seventy-seven.

References:
Ralph Admari, "The Literary Revolution," *American Book Collector*, 6 (1935): 138-140;
"John B. Alden [obituary]," *New York Times*, 6 December 1924, p. 15.

—*Mary Mahoney*

Alden, Beardsley and Company
(Auburn, New York: 1853-1857)
Alden, Markham and Company
(Auburn: 1852-1853)

Alden, Markham and Company was founded in Auburn, New York, in 1852 and soon became Alden, Beardsley and Company. James M. Alden and his brother-in-law John E. Beardsley were most active in the firm. Alden, Beardsley published about 100 titles, including seven fictional works. Among these were Sarah Elizabeth Bradford's *Lewie; or, The Bended Twig* (1853) and *Ups and Downs* (1854); Hugh De Normand's *Julienne, The Daughter of the Hamlet* (1854) and *The Brigand Captive* (1855);

and Julia Griffiths's edition of *Autographs for Freedom*, second series (1854). The firm went out of business in the Panic of 1857.

Reference:
Karl Sanford Kabelac, *Book Publishing in Auburn, New York, 1851-1876, an Introduction and an Imprints Bibliography* (Aurora, N.Y., 1969).

—*Karl Kabelac*

Charles Wesley Alexander
(Philadelphia: 1861-1878?)

Charles Wesley Alexander was a small publisher at 224 South Third Street, Philadelphia. Alexander wrote more than twenty books, most of them crime confessions and historical fiction. These were published anonymously or under the pseudonym Wesley Bradshaw by Alexander or by other Philadelphia publishers such as Old Franklin or Barclay and Company. Typical of his own works were *Maud of the Mississippi* (1864), *General Sherman's Indian Spy* (1865), and *Brigham Young's Daughter* (1870). His firm also put out a broadside, *Jeff Davis' Confession! A Singular Confession Found on the*

Dead Body of a Rebel! (1861). In 1867 Alexander published an edition of Mrs. E. D. E. N. Southworth's *The Coral Lady*. An exception to his usual list of sensational fiction was *Alexander's Family Friend* (1867), published in German and English. This volume was a compendium of handy information from cooking recipes to instruction in making artificial flowers and methods of detecting counterfeit money. Alexander appears to have gone out of business around 1878. He died in 1927 at the age of ninety.

—*Theodora Mills*

John Allen and Company
(Boston; New York: 1834-circa 1849)
Allen and Ticknor
(Boston: 1832-1834)

In 1832 John Allen formed a bookselling partnership with William D. Ticknor in Boston. The two men took over the retail department of Carter and Hendee, booksellers and publishers, at the Old Corner Book Store at 135 Washington Street. Besides bookselling, Allen and Ticknor engaged in publishing in a small way. Allen had previously published some books for the Swedenborgian Society and a few issues of the *New Jerusalem* magazine. He also owned a large circulating library.

The first Allen and Ticknor book was a translation from the German of Anselm von Feuerbach, *Caspar Hauser: An Account of an Individual, Kept in a Dungeon* (1832). The following year the firm published *Sayings and Doings at the Tremont House* by Zachary P. Vangrifter. Perhaps Allen and Ticknor's most significant title was Longfellow's translation from the Spanish of *Coplas de Don Jorge Manrique* (1833). Warren S. Tryon and William Charvat identify this work as Longfellow's "first genuinely literary effort in book form." Allen and Ticknor also published juveniles by Samuel G. Goodrich under his pen name Peter Parley: in 1833 the firm reprinted *A Present from Peter Parley to All His Little Friends*, followed in 1834 by *Peter Parley's Short Stories for Long Nights*. Jerome Smith's *Natural History of the Fishes of Massachusetts, Embracing a Practical Essay on Angling* came out in 1833. Around the same time the partners republished an anonymous juvenile, *The Black Velvet Bracelet* (1833); the author was identified in 1949 as Lucy Hiller Cleveland.

In 1834 Allen withdrew from the business; Ticknor went on eventually to form Ticknor and Fields with James T. Fields. Allen continued for a few years as a Boston publisher under the imprint of John Allen and Company. In 1835 he published his first adult novel, *The Unveiled Heart*, written anonymously by Cleveland. During the Panic of 1837 Allen relocated in New York.

In New York Allen reprinted *The Quod Correspondence* (1842), by John Treat Irving under the pen name of John Quod, and published two original books by Charles Frederick Briggs: *Bankrupt Stories* (1843) and *Working a Passage* (1844). In 1844 Allen formed a connection with Timothy Shay Arthur, the author of nearly 100 moral tracts and tales. Five Arthur titles came out in that year: *The Martyr Wife, Cecilia Howard, Hiram Elwood, Hints and Helps for the Home Circle*, and *The Lady at Home*. John Allen and Company went out of business around 1849.

Reference:

Warren S. Tryon and William Charvat, eds., *The Cost Books of Ticknor and Fields and Their Predecessors, 1832-1858* (New York: Bibliographical Society of America, 1949).

—Vincent Prestianni

W. L. Allison
(New York: 1869-1892)

William L. Allison was one of the many cheap-book publishers who flourished in New York in the last quarter of the nineteenth century. Before moving to New York City from Orange County, New York, Allison edited the *Newburgh Gazette* and published the *Working Farmer*. The W. L. Allison firm was founded in July 1869 as a successor to T. O'Kane and Company; during the 1880s its address was 93 Chambers Street. The firm published several reference works, including *Allison's Webster's Counting-House Dictionary of the English Language, and Dictionary of Electricity, Electrical Terms and Apparatus* (1883), and nonfiction such as Samuel M. Schmucker's *Arctic Explorations and Discoveries during the Nineteenth Century* (1886).

Although its library publications, such as the Arundale Edition, are considerably less well known than George Munro's Seaside Library or Harper's Franklin Square Library, Allison dealt in the same commodity—reprints of literary works produced and sold at the lowest possible prices. Typical of Allison publications was an undated, single-volume edition of the works of Jonathan Swift, printed on cheap paper. In 1890 Allison was one of the companies that sold its plates to John Lovell's United States Book Company. Lovell's failure in 1892 marked the end of W. L. Allison. Allison died in 1893.

Reference:
"William L. Allison [obituary]," *Publishers' Weekly*, 43 (11 March 1893): 425.

—*John H. Laflin*

Henry Altemus and Company
(Philadelphia: 1842-1936)

Henry Altemus and Company grew out of a bookbindery established in Philadelphia as early as 1790 by Joseph T. Altemus. The company began publishing in 1842, using the imprint Henry Altemus and Company. Its plant was at Fourth and Race Streets, with editorial offices at 806 Market Street by 1874 and at 28 South Fourth Street by 1890. The firm moved to 1326 Vine Street in 1914 and to 24 South Orianno Street in 1935. Chiefly a reprint house, Altemus published some original fiction and poetry and developed a full line of juveniles. The firm's most influential member was Henry Altemus, Jr., who decided which titles to reprint and which bindings to use.

By 1886 Altemus was able to manufacture over 5,000 books a day, both its own and those of other publishers. The firm specialized in the production of elaborate yet inexpensive bindings, often decorated or stamped cloth with imitation vellum spines. The popularity of the firm's bindings—as well as their low cost—was partially responsible for the development of new audiences for finer literary works.

In the early years, Altemus published Bibles in a variety of bindings; large, costly ones were especially popular. In 1889 the firm began reprinting standard literary works. The first three reprints, each featuring illustrations by Gustave Doré, were Milton's *Paradise Lost*, Dante's *Inferno, Purgatory, and Paradise*, and Coleridge's *The Rime of the Ancient Mariner*. By 1897 Bibles were no longer advertised in the company's catalogue, although they were supplied upon request.

The list of reprints soon grew to 250 titles, each available in an assortment of bindings. The Altemus Library series began with the works of à Kempis, Bacon, Emerson, Goldsmith, Hawthorne, Charles and Mary Lamb, and Ruskin. Prices ranged from 75¢ for cloth binding to $1.50 in half levant and $1.75 for half English calfskin. The Laurel series, added in 1893, consisted of boxed, two-volume sets of works of standard authors, priced from

$1.00 to $4.00 per set. The following year the Altemus Vademecum series began, featuring English literary classics priced at 25¢ to 75¢. In 1895 the firm began the Altemus Representative Poets, which included the works of Longfellow, Byron, Scott, Tennyson, and Moore. A Devotional series was also begun at this time, as well as Altemus's Young People's Library. How-to books, foreign-language dictionaries, and picture books also bore the firm's imprint.

In 1897 Altemus became the first publisher to pirate Henryk Sienkiewicz's *Quo Vadis.* The book became a major money-maker, as did Charles Sheldon's *In His Steps,* which the firm reprinted in 1899. At the turn of the century Altemus increased its publication of children's books. Titles in its many series for boys included Harrie Irving Hancock's *Dick Prescott's First Year at West Point: or, Two Chums*

in the Cadet Gray (1910) in the West Point series and *Uncle Sam's Boys as Sergeants; or, Handling Their First Real Command* (1911) in The Boys of the Army series. Other series were The High School Boys series and the Annapolis series. By 1928 the company's catalogue contained solely works for young people. The firm closed in 1936; its assets were sold to other publishers, including Platt and Munk.

References:

"Henry Altemus [obituary]," *Publishers' Weekly,* 70 (27 October 1906): 1155;

"Platt & Munk Company Inc. Has Bought from the Henry Altemus Company the Entire Series of Juveniles Called *Wee Books for Wee Folks,*" *Publishers' Weekly,* 129 (28 March 1936): 1333.

—Linda Quinlan

American News Company
(New York: 1864-1969)
Ancorp National Services
(New York: 1969-   )

For almost a century the American News Company was America's leading distributor of periodicals, newspapers, and books. Organized in 1864 at 119-121 Nassau Street, New York, through a union of the interests of H. Dexter, Hamilton and Company, and Tousey and Company, the preeminent news distributors of the day, the firm quickly gained a virtual monopoly on periodical distribution which went largely unchallenged until after the turn of the century.

Sinclair Tousey was the new company's president; the other major officers were Henry Dexter, vice-president; Solomon W. Johnson, treasurer; and John Hamilton and Patrick Farrelly, superintendents. It was the combined experience and reputations of these men, all pioneers in the news agency business, which established the American News Company as leader in its field. The firm grew rapidly: during its first year it conducted business amounting to $2 million. In 1875 it began publishing the trade journal *American Bookseller.* The company moved in March 1877 to larger quarters at 39-41 Chambers Street. By the early 1880s its annual business had risen to $17 million. Through a system of local branches which eventually grew to

400, the American News Company served the needs of thousands of magazine retailers nationwide with an efficiency with which the independent distributors could not compete.

The firm also captured a substantial portion of the paperback book distribution market. In the last decades of the nineteenth century, the American News Company was the primary distributor of popular dime novels and cheap reprint "libraries," among them Beadle and Adams's Erastus Beadle's Dime Novels, Frank Leslie's Home Library of Standard Works by the Most Celebrated Authors, and George Munro's Seaside Library. The firm also distributed books for Norman L. Munro, Street and Smith, and Frank Tousey.

Although the American News Company primarily was a jobber, it also published novels, including Robert St. Clar's *The Metropolites; or, Know Thy Neighbor* (1864), William H. Bushnell's *Ah-Meek, the Beaver; or, The Copper-Hunters of Lake Superior* (1867), Olive Logan's *Olive Logan's Christmas Story: Somebody's Stocking* (1867) and *The Good Mr. Bagglethorpe* (1869), and Mrs. Sarah Ann Wright's *The Gem of the Lake* (1868). The company also published *Mark Twain's Sketches. Authorized Edition* (1874). One of the firm's most prolific writers was Laura Jean Libbey; the title of her *A Forbidden Marriage; or, Love with a Handsome Spendthrift* (1888) indicates the nature of her material. Another frequent contributor was Richard Henry Savage, whose *The Masked Venus: A Story of Many Lands* appeared in 1893. The company's output of fiction declined during the twentieth century, but included a reprint of James Lane Allen's *The Choir Invisible* (1902). The American News Company also published works by Charlotte Turnbull, Mrs. Mary H. Huntington, Harriet Newall Lewis, Anthony Gould, and Ingersoll Lockwood.

On 1 July 1909 the firm moved to 11-15 Park Place. By 1925 the company was handling over a million paperbacks a month as only a part of its operations and again needed new quarters. On 5 January 1925 the American News Company moved to 131 Varick Street. In later years the firm held exclusive distribution rights for Dell Books, Popular Library, and Graphic Books.

As independent distributors gained strength and proved their efficiency, first the smaller and then the larger magazine and paperback publishers began to abandon the American News Company. Although the management of the American News

Company had anticipated this trend and had built up the firm's hardcover book department, the company remained heavily dependent on periodicals. The decisive blow came in 1957 when Dell Publishing Company transferred its magazine and book franchises to independent distributors, a move involving $30 million of Dell's $45 million in annual retail sales. Almost simultaneously, the American News Company liquidated more than 300 of its branches, retaining only those needed to handle its hardcover books. In 1969 the American News Company changed its name to Ancorp National Services, Incorporated. Its address is 21 East Fortieth Street, New York 10017.

References:

Covering a Continent: A Story of Newsstand Distribution and Sales (New York: American News Co., 1930);

Serving the Reading Public (New York: American News Co., 1944);

"Sketches of the Publishers: The American News Company," *Round Table,* 3 (7 April 1866): 218; (14 April 1866): 234-235; (21 April 1866): 250.

—*Donna Nance*

American Publishing Company
(Hartford, Connecticut: 1865-1903)

The American Publishing Company was founded in Hartford, Connecticut, on 10 April 1865 with seven stockholders. The first president was William N. Matson, but the man most responsible for the company's fortunes was Elisha Bliss, Jr., who joined as secretary in 1867 and later became president. After Bliss's death in 1880, his son Frank managed the company through its remaining years. The firm also published under at least five subsidiary imprints at various times, the most important being the Mutual Publishing Company and the Columbian Book Company.

The American Publishing Company was one

of the most successful subscription publishing houses in the late half of the nineteenth century. Subscription books were sold exclusively by canvass. Publication of a new title involved the recruitment of up to 3,000 rural agents who would invade the countryside carrying from door to door a book prospectus made up of selected sheets and sample bindings designed to attract unsophisticated customers, who often placed as much value on the size and appearance as on the content of the books they purchased. The effectiveness of this technique is suggested by the sales figures for two of the company's earliest books, a reprint of *The*

Great Rebellion (1865) by J. T. Headley and *Beyond the Mississippi* (1867) by Albert D. Richardson; both reached 150,000 copies.

In 1868 Bliss signed a contract with Samuel Langhorne Clemens (Mark Twain), who at that time was the author of only a slim volume of sketches but who had recently returned from a highly publicized excursion to Europe and the Middle East. The resulting *The Innocents Abroad* (1869) made Clemens famous and paid him $28,000 in royalties. For the following decade the American Publishing Company published all of Clemens's major works: *Roughing It* (1872), *The Gilded Age* (1873), *Mark Twain's Sketches: New and Old* (1875), *The Adventures of Tom Sawyer* (1876), and *A Tramp Abroad* (1880). The aggregate sales of these volumes through 1881 exceeded 300,000 copies. In 1881, after Bliss's death, Clemens left for another publisher, James R. Osgood; later he started his own subscription house, Charles L. Webster and Company, on the model of the American Publishing Company.

The American Publishing Company published works by several other authors of contemporary note. Marietta Holley's best-known book, *Josiah Allen's Wife* (1877), was followed by *The Lament of the Mormon Wife* (1880), *My Wayward Pardner* (1880), and *Miss Richards' Boy, and Other Stories* (1883). First published in London, Joaquin Miller's *Unwritten History: Life among the Modocs* was published by the American Publishing Company in 1874. Humorist Henry Wheeler Shaw, better known as Josh Billings, had *Twelve Ancestrals Sighns in the Billings' Zodiac Gallery* published by the company in 1873, followed, a year later, by *Everybody's Friend*. Bret Harte's only novel, *Gabriel Conroy*, was published by the firm in 1876.

By the 1890s subscription books were no longer selling well in relation to books offered through stores. Though many subscription houses failed before 1900, the American Publishing Company survived on the strength of Clemens's early books, which it continued to reprint until after 1900. The firm also published sets of collected works, including Clemens's in 1899, and two new subscription titles—*The Tragedy of Pudd'nhead Wilson* (1894) and *Following the Equator* (1897)—which Clemens brought to the company following the failure of his own firm. The American Publishing Company was bought out in 1903 by Harper and Brothers.

References:

Hamlin L. Hill, Jr., *Mark Twain and Elisha Bliss* (Columbia: University of Missouri Press, 1964);

Hill, "Mark Twain's Book Sales, 1869-1879," *Bulletin of the New York Public Library*, 65 (1961): 371-389;

Hill, ed., *Mark Twain's Letters to His Publishers, 1867-1894* (Berkeley: University of California Press, 1967).

—Joseph W. Warnick

American Stationers' Company

(Boston: circa 1837-1838)

The American Stationers' Company was a publishing firm located in Boston during the late 1830s. It published the first edition of Nathaniel Hawthorne's second book, *Twice-Told Tales* (1837). Since the late 1820s, Hawthorne had been having his tales published in gift books and periodicals with the idea of someday collecting them in a book. In 1836 Samuel Goodrich, who had published some of the author's stories in his gift book *The Token* (1831), made arrangements with John B. Russell, the agent for the American Stationers' Company, to publish Hawthorne's works in book form; and Hawthorne's first collection of tales was published on 6 March 1837. In the same year the American Stationers' Company published *Peter Parley's Universal History,* commissioned by Goodrich and written by Hawthorne and his sister Elizabeth under Goodrich's pseudonym.

Other than Hawthorne's books, the firm published little. In 1838 it published *Peter Parley's Common School History* by Goodrich. This book was republished by various firms in many editions.

—Elizabeth Hoffman

American Sunday-School Union

(Philadelphia: 1824-1974)

On 13 May 1817 representatives of several Philadelphia Sunday schools and adult religious schools met to form a society to cultivate unity among the different denominations. The aims of the Philadelphia Sunday and Adult School Union were to determine the amount and quality of instruction in Christian schools, to promote the establishment of such schools, and to communicate advice and experience among the schools. The growth of the society was extraordinary: it began with 43 Sunday schools educating 5,970 pupils; by 1824 the membership had grown to 720 schools with 55,000 pupils. In the latter year the society joined with other societies to form the American Sunday-School Union. Officers of the earlier society were continued into the later one: Alexander Henry served as president, George B. Claxton and John C. Perkins as secretaries, and Hugh De Haven, Jr., as treasurer.

In the 1820s the American Sunday-School Union began to publish "Select" or "Limited" Bible lessons; one lesson consisted of ten to twenty Bible verses for every week in the year. The lessons included the major stories and incidents of the Bible and were graded to suit different levels of maturity.

No books were published by the American Sunday-School Union without the sanction of the Committee of Publication, which consisted of fourteen members representing the Baptist, Methodist, Congregational, Episcopal, Presbyterian, Lutheran, and Dutch Reformed churches. Not more than three members could be of the same denomination and each had veto power.

Tales, history, biography, travel, poetry, songs, and didactic works carried the union imprint. Between 1817 and 1830 the Committee of Publication published six million copies of its various titles, many of which were for children. Works by Mary Martha Sherwood included *The Infant's Progress* (1827), *The Broken Hyacinth* (1828), and *The Errand-Boy* (1830?). Titles by other authors during the 1820s included Margaret Whyte's *The Story of the Kind Little Boy* (1825) and Obadiah Jennings's *The History of Margaretta C. Hoge* (1827). Charles Robert Leslie and Thomas B. Welch were two of the notable artists whose works illustrated the publications of the American Sunday-School Union. Augustus Kollner, a Philadelphia engraver and lithographer, often worked for the organization.

Nonfiction works published by the American Sunday-School Union included Anna C. Reed's highly popular biography *The Life of George Wash-*

ington (1829), which was translated into more than a dozen foreign languages and achieved a wider circulation than any other life of the first president, and the anonymous *The Early Saxons; or The Character and Influence of the Saxon Race, Illustrated in a History of the Introduction of Christianity into England* (1842). Later fiction titles included Lucy Ellen Guernsey's *Irish Amy* (1854) and *Cousin Deborah's Story* (1869) and Margaret Murray Robertson's *The Little House in the Hollow* (1868).

Popular series in which the union published its works included The Village and Family Library, The Silver Library, and Life in the Nursery. The Choice Library of Books was first published by the American Sunday-School Union in 1838. This series, which was sold for thirty-three dollars a set, comprised 121 books in uniform bindings, encased in a paneled wooden box which was to be fastened to the wall of the schoolroom or private library. Another series was The Child's Cabinet Library, begun in 1849 and comprising seventy-five titles in fifty volumes. The Juvenile, Sunday-School, and Family Library consisted of 100 volumes, 72 to 252 pages each, bound in muslin, at ten dollars for the set. *The Shepherd of Salisbury Plain* was the first title in the series, which also included *Dr. Cotton Mather, Mahomed Ali Bey,* and *The Harvey Boys, Illustrating the Evils of Intemperance and Their Remedy.* The union usually disseminated its literature at cost, enabling small communities and Sunday schools to enjoy free circulating libraries financed through voluntary contributions. The scheme proved successful in creating a taste for reading and in promoting popular education.

During the nineteenth century the union pursued a vigorous program of publishing periodicals. Starting in July 1824 it published the monthly *American Sunday-School Magazine.* For younger children, the union in 1823 purchased the *Teachers' Offering,* a periodical which had been begun in New Haven, Connecticut. Under the new title *Youth's Friend and Scholars' Magazine* the magazine's circulation quickly reached 13,000 copies. It was continued until 1842, when it was superseded by a larger and more impressive biweekly, the *Youth's Penny Gazette.* For the youngest children, the union published the *Infant's Magazine* from 1829 to 1834.

In response to a call for a newspaper the union prepared the weekly *Sunday-School Journal and Advocate of Christian Education,* which first appeared on 24 November 1830. This periodical carried news of the progress of Sunday schools throughout the country, with accounts of experimental plans and methods. It also included explanations of the Select Uniform Limited Lessons used by teachers in Christian schools, as well as reports of conventions and other events. In 1835 the paper became biweekly. In 1859 it was succeeded by the *Sunday-School Times,* which was followed by the *Sunday-School World.*

Frederick Adolphus Packard was editor of publications from 1828 to 1867; he also wrote *The Teacher Taught* (1839) and *Life of Robert Owen* (1866). Edwin Wilbur Rice was editor of publications from 1870 to 1915, and his *The Sunday-School Movement, 1780-1917, and the American Sunday-School Union, 1817-1917* (1917) is the standard reference work on publications of the union. Rice was succeeded by the Reverend James McConaughy.

During the twentieth century the publication department issued periodicals, aids to lessons, and vacation Bible school materials. The chief union periodical in this century was *Sunday School World,* a magazine for teachers. The American Sunday-School Union was succeeded in 1974 by the American Missionary Fellowship, which has no publishing program.

References:

Murray Frank McDonald, "An Analysis of the American Sunday School Union Publications in the Old Juvenile Collection in the Brooklyn Public Library," M.A. thesis, University of North Carolina, 1963;

Edwin Wilbur Rice, *The Sunday-School Movement, 1780-1917, and the American Sunday-School Union, 1817-1917* (Philadelphia: American Sunday-School Union, 1917);

Ellen Shaffer, "The Children's Books of the American Sunday-School Union," *American Book Collector,* 17 (October 1966): 20-28.

—Earl R. Taylor

Elisha Bliss

Alexander Henry, first president of the American Sunday-School Union

Frederick A. Packard, editor of the Sunday-School Union's publications from 1828 to 1867

S. V. S. Wilder, first president of the American Tract Society

American Temperance Union

(Philadelphia: 1836-1865)

The purpose of the American Temperance Union was to effect social and religious reform by persuading the nation to abstain from alcohol. Its Permanent Temperance Documents stated: "Let all do the same, and drunkenness will universally and for ever cease. Pauperism, crime, sickness, insanity, wretchedness, and premature death, will, to a great extent, be prevented. Health, virtue and happiness will be increased; human life be prolonged; the gospel, through grace, be more widely extended, and generally embraced; God be more highly honored, and souls in greater numbers be illuminated, purified, and saved."

The American Temperance Society, the union's parent organization, was founded on 13 February 1826. Headquarters for the union were established in Philadelphia in 1836, and Dr. John Marsh, former secretary of the American Temperance Society, was appointed editor and corresponding secretary. Union publications were mostly brochures, pamphlets, tracts, the union's two periodicals—*Youth's Temperance Advocate* and *The Journal of the American Temperance Union*—the annual temperance almanac, and annual reports. Union publications were available generally and at cost, but special efforts were made to reach immigrant families, missionaries, and philanthropists. The union attracted a wide readership. The anonymous *Confessions of a Reformed Inebriate* (1844), for example, required a second edition four years later, and Marsh's novel *Hannah Hawkins, the Reformed Drunkard's Daughter* (1844) went through nine editions before the end of the decade. Such literary publishing as the union undertook had, of course, a strong temperance bias.

By midcentury, the significance of the American Temperance Union as the nation's center of temperance activity had diminished and its publishing operation had declined. The union was gradually eclipsed by other movements and societies which it had helped to foster and, in 1865, was absorbed by the National Temperance Society.

—Gregory M. Haynes

American Tract Society

(New York; Oradell, New Jersey; Garland, Texas: 1825-   )

The American Tract Society is less noteworthy for its contribution to original American belles lettres than for its attempt to counteract popular fiction by creating an audience for an alternative religious literature. The society was founded in New York on 11 May 1825 in order to oppose the "injurious moral tendency," as its annual report put it in 1836, of novelists such as Maria Edgeworth and Sir Walter Scott. In his paper "The Evils of an Unsanctified Literature," presented at a public meeting in October 1842, the Reverend James W. Alexander described the society's enterprise as the creation of "a thoroughly Christian literature" such as no country had yet had, in order to eradicate the evil influences of imported plays, novels, and romances.

The American Tract Society was the product of a merger between the two major tract publishers in the country—the New England Tract Society, formed in Boston in 1814, and the New York Religious Tract Society, established in 1812—as well as at least forty other small evangelical publishers active since 1803. The organization elected as its first president S. V. S. Wilder, a successful businessman and Paris agent for Boston and New York mercantile houses, who had found time to associate with twenty-one religious or charitable societies.

Primarily Presbyterian and Congregationalist in membership, the society formed a Publishing Committee with representatives from each participating denomination. With this group continually reviewing society publications, the organization had already approved 185 tracts (proselytizing religious pamphlets) and printed 697,900 copies before moving into headquarters at 87 Nassau Street in May 1826. During its second year the house turned out more than three million copies, a figure which doubled in the year ending in May 1829.

The society's tracts were not imaginative literature but tools for saving souls. Although the organization defended its publications against what its seventh annual report called "the general indiscriminate charge that Tracts are fiction," to counteract the effects of popular fiction the American Tract Society created a kind of subliterature designed to spread the gospel. Tracts in the form of sermons, treatises, and question-and-answer expositions of doctrine were joined by dialogues, allegories, narratives, and devotional works intended to persuade the reader through an imaginative appeal. The descriptive list of the Principal Series of Tracts of 1859 defends such works as being "narratives of facts, though not always in the order of their occurrence." The entries are characterized as "entertaining," "pleasing," and "amusing" narratives. For example, Tract No. 87, *Conversation in a Boat, Between Two Seamen*, is "sustained throughout with interest, in a sailor's style"; No. 136, *The Two Old Men*, contrasts character types through dialogues between a "lukewarm formalist" and a "humble evangelical disciple." In Tract No. 586, *Margaret, the Bayman's Wife*, Rev. J. H. Ingraham encouraged long-suffering wives by telling a story of "female influence on a hardened transgressor." Of the 611 tracts on the society's list in 1859, almost one-fourth re-created the story of sin and redemption.

In 1828 the society expanded its publishing to include books. It began that year with Philip Doddridge's *Rise and Progress of Religion in the Soul*, followed by a reprint of Richard Baxter's *The Saints'*

Everlasting Rest (1830), John Pike's *Persuasives to Early Piety* (1830), and the three-volume *Twelve Sermons to the Soul* (1830) by George Burder. Also in 1830 the society issued the first of its many reprints of Bunyan's *The Pilgrim's Progress*. First published by the society in 376 pages, it was reprinted periodically as part of the organization's Evangelical Family Library, Christian Library, and Youth's Christian Library. In 1846 new plates were cast for an edition of 464 pages with new engravings. At the end of the 1840s *The Pilgrim's Progress* swelled to 603 pages, with new engravings and selections from Bunyan's *Grace Abounding*. At a dollar a copy, this edition was the society's most expensive publication to date. The society also produced the work in four foreign-language editions: one in French in 1840, two in German the following year, and one in Welsh in 1845. A few years later the society could boast of having published this classic in twenty-five languages; total sales reached nearly half a million in 1894. This religious allegory continued to be reprinted by the American Tract Society into the mid twentieth century.

In its first few years the house had chiefly issued reprints of British authors obtained from the Religious Tract Society of London. For example, Tract No. 49 was William Cowper's account of his brother's conversion. As time passed, eminent American writers of religious literature began to fill the lists with their works—Cotton Mather; Timothy Dwight; John Witherspoon; Dr. Benjamin Rush, whose treatise on "ardent spirits" was the source of a temperance tract; and Mason L. Weems, from whose *The Drunkard's Looking Glass* (1813) was extracted the discourse for another temperance message.

The writings of Jonathan Edwards provided a steady source for the society's publishing ventures. An abridgment of Edwards's account of the conversion of Abigail Hutchinson in the Great Revival of 1740 became Tract No. 78 in 1825. In the following year came Tract No. 144, Edwards's memoirs of his own conversion and religious exercises. Subsequent publications of Edwards's writings included a rewritten version of *The Treatise on Religious Affections* in 1832; an abridged edition of *The Life of David Brainerd* the next year; *A History of the Work of Redemption* in 1839; and in 1845 a volume entitled *Treatises on Revivals* containing abbreviated versions of his *Narrative of Surprising Conversions* and *Thoughts on the Revival of 1740*.

The society offered premiums and prizes of $50 and $100 for outstanding treatments of assigned topics, thereby enticing contributions from the underpaid faculties of New England colleges. For Tract No. 317, *Call and Qualifications for the Christian Ministry,* a $100 premium was awarded in 1835 to Ralph Waldo Emerson.

The American Tract Society became a leader in publishing for a juvenile audience, beginning with printers' plates and engravings inherited from the New York Religious Tract Society. At the annual meeting in 1828 production of 239,000 copies of a series of sixty-five children's tracts was reported. These tracts were produced as toy books, illustrated with woodcuts, printed in different shapes and sizes, and bound in multicolored paper. New titles were added yearly: the annual report for 1850 listed 207 titles of tracts for children. At that time, the society was turning out more than one million toy books in English, German, French, and Spanish.

Until 1832 the society's publications for children were confined mostly to tracts. The ninth annual report, however, announced expansion into publishing standard-sized books for children: "While on the one hand, the Committee wish to issue publications rich in the glorious truths of salvation, and to do what they can to counteract the prevailing thirst in the rising generation for the mere entertainment of high wrought fiction ... they are aware, on the other hand, that the young demand something more entertaining than mere didactic discussion." Writers were solicited to produce children's works exclusively for the society, and for the first time the organization entered into competition with other publishers to secure the talents of successful authors. One writer it signed was Jacob Abbott, a Congregational clergyman and pioneer educator of young women. The first of his books to be published by the society was *The Young Christian* (1832), an international favorite which went into four British editions. Abbott continued with *The Corner Stone* in 1834. In 1833 he joined his brother, John Abbott, a Congregational clergyman and historian, to write *The Child at Home* and *The Mother at Home,* works which enjoyed a considerable international vogue. Another author signed by the society was Thomas Gallaudet, a popular religious writer and founder of the American Asylum for the Deaf and Dumb. From 1834 to 1843 he contributed seven volumes with titles such as *The History of Joseph* (1834) and *The History of Josiah* (1837) to form the series Scripture Biography for the Young. Gallaudet continued to add titles to the Youth's Biographical Series and Youth's Narrative Series, which were combined with Scripture Bi-

ography for the Young in 1843 to form the Youth's Christian Library in forty volumes.

By midcentury the society's list of juvenile books had grown to sixty-nine volumes, more than one million copies of which were in print. By that time the house had produced more than seven million tracts for children in several languages. Production and sales in this area expanded in the second half of the century. Magazines for children were organized, such as *Child's Paper* (1852-1897), *Child at Home* (1863-1873), and *Apples of Gold* (1871). By 1894 *Songs for Little Ones at Home* had sold more than a third of a million copies.

The society's literary works for both adults and children followed the traditional formulae for simple didactic narrative. The writers kept the plots simple, abbreviating any action in the mundane and sinful world. They allowed none of the ambiguities of complex characterization; their narratives focused upon the extreme personality changes caused by the influence of sin and the intervention of divine grace. The writers designed their works to clarify crucial religious issues, such as the doctrinal cornerstone of Protestant fundamentalism—that man is saved by God's grace through faith, not through works. Set speeches constituted the climaxes of many society narratives, and reactions of first-person, eyewitness narrators insured the proper response of the reader. In the closing lines, such a narrator often directly exhorted the reader to believe and be saved.

These narratives tried to appeal to both the pious and the profane; accordingly, they drew from two stock character types. One was the person poor in what the world values but rich in religious piety, domestic fidelity, and divine grace. He endures a life of hardship, influences those around him, and reaps his final reward in heaven. An example is the anonymous *The Village Funeral,* Tract No. 36, probably published during the society's first year. The other pattern for characterization was the Prodigal Son, the wayward child of indulgent Christian parents, who undergoes the humbling process from debauchery to deathbed repentance.

The society's efforts to reach all segments of the growing nation contributed to the expansion of the American reading public. Small pockets of the population usually ignored by commercial publishers were cultivated: a special line of publications for the blind was begun; arrangements were made to put society literature into the hands of sailors on whalers, canalboats, ferryboats, cruise ships, and freighters. The society supplied reading matter to prisons, orphanages, and poorhouses. When more

Americans began to travel by water and rail, the society made tracts and books easily available to passengers. When the nation moved westward, the society distributed its literature to homesteaders and prospectors. As the influx of immigrants increased, books and tracts were designed for publication in the major European tongues, as well as in Gaelic, Portuguese, and Danish. Publication for German immigrants was particularly extensive: in 1850 the society listed 147 tracts, 42 books, and 17 children's tracts in that language alone. At the end of the century, two of the society's six periodicals were in German. At that time, its foreign publication program also aimed at the Hungarian, Finnish, and Polish arrivals to American shores. The society has also distributed its publications free to American soldiers in each war the country has fought, beginning with the Mexican War in 1846.

The society made a substantial contribution to literacy by providing many frontier families with the only reading matter they possessed, and hence the only books with which to teach their children to read. By publishing its literature in their various dialects, the society directly aided the education of Indians.

The creation of a wider reading public would not have been possible without the society's efficiency in book production and its innovative methods of promotion and distribution. The directors minimized overhead by centralizing publishing activities at the New York headquarters at 87 Nassau Street, where each floor served its function of printing, binding, storage, or sales. Daniel Fanshaw, a prominent New York printer, started the house's production with presses powered by mules that were lifted up through a portal of the printing floor. By 1832 production outgrew the headquarters. In order to install new six-roller presses, the original building was demolished and promptly replaced in 1847 by a new structure containing seventeen presses which by May 1848 had produced over eight million books and tracts—a daily average of 27,000 publications. Between 1848 and 1850 fifteen million tracts rolled off the presses, a total of 529 separate titles. In 1855 *Norton's Literary Gazette* noted that the society's production outranked that of all other religious publishing houses in the country. These were the years of its peak production. By the society's fiftieth anniversary in 1875, the publishing department had produced 9,679 separate publications, including 1,732 books. To accommodate this unparalleled output, on 24 March 1894 the society moved its offices and presses to 10 East Twenty-third Street; five years later it returned to

yet a newer, twenty-one-story building at the site of its first headquarters.

None of these publications reached their audiences through conventional book-trade outlets. Wilder engineered methods of mass distribution that could reach more people than the sales channels of popular literature. He established outlets in the larger cities—for example, at 153 Wabash Avenue in Chicago and with Lockwood, Brooks and Company, the society's chief Boston agency—and founded circulating libraries which offered special discounts on purchases. He also deployed corps of agents who systematically divided up sales areas and canvassed door to door. On the frontier, more than 600 colporteurs, armed with detailed instruction booklets issued by the Executive Committee, evangelized among the Indians and set up distribution outposts. Perhaps Wilder's most influential promotional innovation was his Tract-of-the-Month Club, which circulated a descriptive sales magazine every month and offered free tracts as dividends. The club was a forerunner of twentieth-century subscription book clubs.

The directors knew that one of the best promotional techniques for enticing American audiences away from the snares of secular literature was to print publications which were better made and more attractive than anything else on the market. Consequently, the American Tract Society gained fame for the high quality of its works, which surpassed the products of commercial publishers. Records reflect the firm's continual effort to improve its physical product. In the mid-1840s, for example, the society upgraded its line of children's toy books, improving the quality of illustrations and paper, changing the format, and using more legible type.

The society's annual report for 1848 noted that the Publishing Committee wanted illustration "in the first style of the art." The society attracted the best artists and engravers of the day, appointed management to organize their output, and purchased more sophisticated equipment to reproduce their work. The result was a revolution in American book illustration which set the standard for other publishers in the second half of the nineteenth century. Alexander Anderson, whom the English printer W. J. Linton praised as "the first engraver on wood in America," produced engravings for the society for many years until his death in 1870. Notable for the style that Linton called "pure white line," Anderson contributed some of the eight full-page engravings in the 1832 *Pilgrim's Progress* and produced two more for *The Life of David Brainerd* the next year. His distinguished pupil Joseph A. Adams came to the firm in the late 1830s to embellish Gallaudet's Scripture Biography for the Young. In 1847 one of Adams's pupils, Robert Roberts, accepted the job of supervising all engraving work. B. F. Childs replaced Roberts after his death in 1850, leading a host of well-known artists and engravers whose work enhanced the appeal of the society's Christian literature in competition with the literature of the marketplace.

Though the commissioned artwork necessitated price increases, the society was able to undersell all competitors by offering its books and tracts at cost; owning its presses enabled it to cut those costs by twenty-five percent. The 1832 *Pilgrim's Progress*—376 pages bound in full sheep, with engravings by Anderson and William Mason—could be purchased for thirty-seven and one-half cents.

The twentieth century brought relocation in midtown Manhattan before the society moved to a one-story building in Oradell, New Jersey, in 1962 and to Garland, Texas, in 1978. The firm ceased book publication in 1948; its periodicals, almanacs, and Bibles were also discontinued; and instead of maintaining its own translators for domestic ethnic groups, it now supports foreign tract publishers. Yet the organization publishes more than thirty million tracts annually, gives away millions of complimentary copies, and continually reviews and improves the style of these publications for widest appeal to contemporary audiences. Its directors plan to diversify once again into popular commu-nications forms such as greeting cards, posters, and electronic media in order to spread its message most effectively.

The American Tract Society has accomplished more than any religious publishing house in the nation. Its impact on the American literary scene was greatest in the nineteenth century, when its efforts at evangelism were expressly literary. As a means of leading the new nation to God, these writers and divines sought to erect a new canon of literary taste. The great achievement of the American Tract Society was to foster a wide reading public by perpetuating the Anglo-American heritage of religious writing. It is currently headed by Dr. S. E. Slocum, Jr.; its address is 1624 North First Street, Garland, Texas 75040.

References:

Seth Bliss, *A Brief History of the American Tract Society, Instituted at Boston, 1814, And Its Relations to the American Tract Society at New York, Instituted 1825* (Boston: T. R. Marvin, 1857);

The Publications of the American Tract Society, II (New York: American Tract Society, 1827);

G. L. Shearer, "The American Tract Society," *Century Magazine* (June 1892): 313-314;

Lawrance Thompson, "The Printing and Publishing Activities of the American Tract Society from 1825 to 1850," *Papers of the Bibliographical Society of America*, 35 (1941): 81-114.

—Gregory M. Haynes

Alexander Anderson, renowned as the father of American wood engraving, produced many illustrations notable, in the words of W. J. Linton, for their "pure white line" to illustrate Society publications

Daniel Appleton

CRUMBS

FROM

THE MASTER'S TABLE;

OR,

SELECT SENTENCES,

Doctrinal, Practical, and Experimental.

BY W. MASON.

NEW-YORK:

D. APPLETON,

Clinton-Hall.
Stereotype Edition.
1831.

Title page for Appleton's first book. It measured three inches square.

The Appleton building at 346-348 Broadway in 1854 (courtesy of the New-York Historical Society)

Silas Andrus and Son
(Hartford, Connecticut: 1844-circa 1855)
Andrus and Judd
(Hartford: 1833-1839)
Silas Andrus
(Hartford: 1820-1833)

One of the first subscription book publishers, Silas Andrus started as a Hartford, Connecticut, binder and bookseller in 1815. Five years later he became a publisher, offering piracies of books out of copyright as well as Bibles. Among the latter was the first folio-sized stereotyped Bible produced in America, printed in 1829. Another title was Susanna Rowson's 1790 novel *The History of Charlotte Temple*, which Andrus reprinted in the 1820s and 1830s.

By 1833 the firm was known as Andrus and Judd. Andrus went bankrupt in 1839 but formed a new partnership with his son about five years later. Silas Andrus and Son published Isaac Mitchell's *Alonzo and Melissa* (1844)—another reprint—and John Pierce Brace's *Tales of the Devils* (1846). The firm continued publishing as late as 1855.

Andrus's brother William, a traveling auctioneer for the company, established the firm of Mack and Andrus at Ithaca, New York, in 1824. Everard Peck, who helped Andrus in his early days as a printer, later founded E. Peck and Company of Rochester, New York. Another associate, David F. Robinson, went on to found D. F. Robinson and Company in Hartford; this firm later evolved to become The Baker and Taylor Company.

Reference:
Newton Case Brainard, ed., *The Andrus Bindery: A History of the Shop, 1831-1838* (Hartford, Conn.: Case, Lockwood & Brainard, 1940).

—David Dzwonkoski

Henry F. Anners
(Philadelphia: 1842-1850)

The firm of Henry F. Anners was located at 48 North Fourth Street in Philadelphia between 1842 and 1850. Anners reprinted many books by Timothy Shay Arthur, most of whose work had moralizing themes: *The Ruined Gamester; or, Two Eras in My Life. An Autobiographical Romance* (1842); *Married and Single; or, Marriage and Celibacy Con-* trasted, *in a Series of Domestic Pictures* (1847); *The Maiden: A Story for My Young Countrywomen* (1848); and Arthur's first book of importance, *Six Nights with the Washingtonians. A Series of Original Temperance Tales* (1849), which had originally been published in 1842.

—Kathleen R. Davis

D. Appleton and Company
(New York: 1838-1933)
D. Appleton
(New York: 1831-1838)

1890-1900	*1900*	*1918*

See also the Appleton-Century-Crofts entry in *DLB 46, American Literary Publishing Houses, 1900-1980*.

Daniel Appleton opened a dry goods store in Haverhill, Massachusetts, around 1813. In 1817 he moved to Boston and in 1825 to New York, where he established a general store at 16 Exchange Place. The book department soon became the most successful part of the business, and in 1831 Appleton sold off the rest of his merchandise and opened a bookstore in Clinton Hall, 3 Beekman Street. Later that year he published his first book, *Crumbs from the Master's Table,* a three-inch-square, 192-page volume of Bible verses. In the next few years other religious and practical works were published, and the business grew. In 1838 Appleton's son William Henry Appleton was made a junior partner after two successful buying trips to Europe. The new firm of D. Appleton and Company moved to 200 Broadway the following year.

Appleton entered the children's book field with Harriet Martineau's *The Crofton Boys* (1842). After the success of this book the firm quickly developed a line of juveniles selling for thirty-eight cents a volume. In the 1840s Appleton also began publishing readers, textbooks, scientific and technical books, and fiction in Spanish; by the end of the Civil War the firm had a virtual monopoly on the South American trade. Appleton also published texts for the study of Spanish and Portuguese in the United States, including Alberto de Tornos's *The Combined Spanish Method* (1867), reprinted many times, and Arturo Cuyas's English-Spanish dictionary (1903). In the 1840s Appleton published the writings of the British Tractarian movement led by John Henry Newman. There was a strong reaction against these publications from Protestant religious quarters. In 1847 Appleton published *Appleton's Railroad and Steamboat Companion*, the first of a series of profitable travel guides that included the famous *Appleton's European Guide Book Illustrated* (1870), which went into twenty-nine editions by 1896.

Edward L. Youmans met William Henry Appleton in 1846 and began an association that made Appleton the most respected trade publisher of science books. Youmans soon joined the firm as an editorial adviser, and Appleton published his *Class-Book of Chemistry* (1851) and *Chemical Atlas* (1854). Youmans was instrumental in Appleton's publication of the first American edition of Charles Darwin's *On the Origin of Species* (1860). He persuaded the Darwinian philosopher Herbert Spencer to let Appleton publish his works; in 1860 the firm published *Education,* four years later *First Principles,* and eventually Spencer's entire Synthetic Philosophy series. Appleton published *Man's Place in Nature* (1863) and *Lay Sermons and Addresses* (1870) by Darwin's disciple Thomas Henry Huxley. These scientific publications, which supported the theory of evolution, were condemned by the religious press, but Appleton argued that the publisher's imprint on a book did not constitute endorsement of its contents. In 1872 Appleton began its International Scientific series, another of Youmans's projects, with John Tyndall's *Forms of Water*. Appleton's policy of making royalty payments to foreign authors enabled the firm to obtain the latest works by some of the most important scientific writers in Europe. The series included Walter Bagehot's *Physics and*

23

The Appleton factory in Brooklyn, 1868

William Worthen Appleton; Daniel Sidney Appleton, Jr.; William Henry Appleton; Robert Appleton; and Colonel Daniel Appleton. The photograph was taken in 1894 at about the time of William Henry Appleton's retirement as president of the firm (courtesy of the Wave Hill Center for Environmental Studies).

Politics (1873), Spencer's *The Study of Sociology* (1882), and John W. Draper's *History of the Conflict between Religion and Science* (1903), which was condemned by the pope.

Appleton's early periodicals included the *Popular Science Monthly,* which the firm sold to McClure, Phillips and Company in 1900, and *Appleton's Journal of Popular Literature, Science and Art,* begun in 1869. *Booklovers Magazine,* which had been started by another firm in Philadelphia in 1903, was purchased by Appleton in 1904. It became *Appleton's Magazine* in 1906 and published short stories, serials, and topical articles by Henry James, Joseph Conrad, Booth Tarkington, and Rex Beach. The magazine proved unprofitable and was discontinued in 1909.

Daniel Appleton retired in 1848. The firm was reorganized with William Henry Appleton as president; two other sons, Daniel Sidney and John Adams, were admitted as partners. The "D." was retained in the company name at the request of their father, who died on 27 March 1849.

Appleton entered the medical book field with John Appleton Swett's *Treatise on the Diseases of the Chest* (1852). In 1888 Appleton published Arpad G. Gerster's *Aseptic and Antiseptic Surgery,* the first book with photographs of actual operations being performed. William Osler's *Principles and Practice of Medicine* (1892), revised periodically, eventually sold several hundred thousand copies. In 1894 Appleton published L. Emmett Holt's *Care and Feeding of Children,* a successful medical work for a popular audience. Appleton also published G. Stanley Hall's monumental *Adolescence* (1904) and *Senescence* (1922). The *New York Medical Journal* was published by Appleton from 1868 to 1895.

The publication in 1846 of a series of quality readers and spellers edited by Albert D. Wright was followed by the Cornell Geographies in 1853 and other series of arithmetics, histories, and readers. In 1855 Appleton published Noah Webster's *Elementary Spelling Book,* the famous "Blue-Back Speller." It is said that one of Appleton's largest presses ran continuously printing only this book. Selling tens of millions of copies and remaining in print until 1950, the speller was one of Appleton's most lucrative publications.

In 1856 Appleton published *Appleton's Cyclopaedia of Biography* and in 1858 *Appleton's New American Cyclopaedia,* edited by Charles A. Dana and George Ripley, a new volume of which was issued every few months for six years; the *New American Cyclopaedia* was sold door-to-door as well as on the installment-subscription plan. A revised edition was published from 1872 to 1876. Begun in 1861, *Appleton's American Annual Cyclopaedia,* edited by W. J. Tenney, was published in various formats until 1902. In 1887 Appleton published the *Appleton's Cyclopaedia of American Biography* in six volumes.

In 1854 Appleton moved to 346-348 Broadway, where it opened one of the best bookstores in America. D. Appleton and Company was reorganized in 1856, with William Henry Appleton, Daniel Sidney Appleton, and Samuel Francis Appleton taking on editorial responsibilities; John Adams Appleton confined himself to business affairs.

The first adult novel published by Appleton was probably *The Adventures of Margaret Catchpole,* an obscure work reprinted sometime in the 1840s. Daniel Appleton did not like fiction, and little was published except the works of standard British authors. When William Henry Appleton became president, the house began to publish more fiction, especially romantic and sentimental novels. Appleton published Eliza Ann Dupuy's *The Conspirator* in 1850, and in 1853 *Tempest and Sunshine* by Mary Jane Holmes, one of the most successful women writers of the nineteenth century. Appleton also published Holmes's *English Orphans* (1855) and *Lena Rivers* (1856). Printed in Mobile during the Confederacy, Louisa Mühlbach's *Joseph II and His Court* was discovered by William Worthen Appleton, William Henry's son, and reprinted by Appleton in 1867. Appleton subsequently published her other works.

Lewis Carroll's *Alice's Adventures in Wonderland* was to have been published by Macmillan in London in 1865, but Carroll and the illustrator John Tenniel were disappointed with the printing of the wood engravings and demanded cancellation of the entire first pressrun. Macmillan printed a new edition which was completed toward the end of 1865 and appeared with the date 1866. In London at this time, William Worthen Appleton read the work and, with Carroll's consent, secured the rejected first printings. Appleton issued the work with a new title page in 1866.

In 1867 the building at 346-348 Broadway burned and Appleton moved to 443-445 Broadway. The firm moved to 90-94 Grand Street in 1869. William Worthen ("Mr. Willie") Appleton was made a junior partner in 1868.

Gen. Adam Badeau's three-volume *Military History of General Grant* was published in 1868 and *Memoirs of General William T. Sherman* appeared in 1875. Also in 1875, Appleton signed a contract with

Jefferson Davis to publish his account of the war, *The Rise and Fall of the Confederate Government* (1881).

Appleton moved to 549-551 Broadway in 1872. The next year it published *Picturesque America; or, The Land We Live In*, edited by William Cullen Bryant. This was the first in a distinguished series of expensively produced and profitable art books developed under the guidance of George S. Appleton, who became a partner in 1865. The three-volume *Picturesque Europe*, edited by Bayard Taylor, was published in 1875; the two-volume *Picturesque Palestine, Sinai, and Egypt*, edited by Sir Charles William Wilson, appeared in 1881. Appleton financed an expedition to obtain material for the latter work, but it did not sell as well as the other two. Appleton also published other lavishly produced art books, such as *Artistic Houses* at $300 a set. The firm moved to 1-5 Bond Street in 1880.

Bryant had begun his association with Appleton in 1854 when the firm published at his request two new editions of his poems, one of them with illustrations. Appleton published the Roslyn Edition of Bryant's later poems in 1876, and an edition of Bryant's complete works was published posthumously in 1884.

J. C. Derby, then an Appleton representative, read the poems and sketches of Joel Chandler Harris in the *Atlanta Constitution* and bought the rights to his work. In December 1880 Appleton published *Uncle Remus: His Songs and His Sayings*, but dissatisfied with illustrations by F. S. Church and W. Moser, Harris had his subsequent books published by other firms. In 1895 Appleton published a new edition of *Uncle Remus: His Songs and His Sayings* with drawings by Harris's favorite illustrator, A. B. Frost.

The American Book Company was formed in 1890 by the merger of the textbook divisions of four major houses, including D. Appleton and Company. The firms agreed not to publish competing textbooks for at least five years, after which Appleton returned to publishing its own textbooks.

The Appletons had always felt strongly about the need for an international copyright and had always paid royalties to European authors. The American Publishers' Copyright League was formed in 1887 with William Henry Appleton as its first president. An international copyright law was finally passed by Congress in 1891. In 1894 William Henry resigned as president of Appleton and William Worthen Appleton succeeded him. Also in 1894 Appleton moved to 72 Fifth Avenue.

Appleton began the Town and Country Li-

brary of fiction in 1888 with *The Steel Hammer* by Louis Ulbach. A new title was published every month, selling for fifty cents in paper and a dollar in hardcover. Appleton published many novels in the 1890s and early 1900s, among them *The Deemster* (1888) by the best-selling Hall Caine; it was followed by *The Manxman* (1894), *The Christian* (1897), and *The Eternal City* (1901). Appleton published Rudyard Kipling's short-story collection *Many Inventions* (1893) and his volume of poetry *The Seven Seas* (1896). Appleton rejected George Moore's *Esther Waters* in 1894, published his *Evelyn Innes* in 1898, but rejected the sequel, *Sister Teresa*, in 1901. In 1906 the firm published Moore's *The Lake* and *Memoirs of My Dead Life*, with the famous preface "Apologia Pro Scriptis Meis." Appleton had insisted that some scenes be deleted, and Moore agreed, on the condition that he be allowed to write a preface denouncing censorship. From 1911 to 1914 Appleton published his three-volume *Hail and Farewell*.

In 1894 Stephen Crane, lacking money to complete the typing of *The Red Badge of Courage*, showed it to Hamlin Garland, an Appleton author. Garland referred Crane to Appleton, and the firm unenthusiastically agreed to publish the book in 1895. It was a success, and Appleton published Crane's *The Little Regiment* (1896) and *The Third Violet* (1897).

In 1896 Appleton published Joseph Conrad's *An Outcast of the Islands*, Arthur Conan Doyle's *Exploits of Brigadier Gerard*, and Gilbert Parker's *The Seats of the Mighty*. Although Appleton did not publish Edward Bellamy's *Looking Backward*, which had been published by Ticknor in 1888, it did publish the sequel, *Equality*, in 1897. Also in that year Appleton published Robert W. Chambers's *The Mystery of Choice*. Chambers left Appleton for Harper, but returned in 1906 with *The Fighting Chance*, the first of many more successful novels with Appleton. Edward Noyes Wescott's *David Harum* (1898) was the firm's all-time best-seller. Appleton also published many books for boys by three popular authors, Ralph Henry Barbour, William Heyliger, and Joseph A. Altsheler.

Appleton had tied up too much capital in the selling of books on the installment plan, and after the failure of Harper in 1899, banks were reluctant to renew Appleton's notes. In March 1900 the firm went into receivership; late in April Appleton resumed publishing, and by October it had paid all of its debts and had filed articles of incorporation. In 1902 Appleton moved to 436 Fifth Avenue. On 3 June 1904 Joseph H. Sears became president of the company and William Worthen Appleton moved to the board of directors.

David Graham Phillips's *The Second Generation* was published in 1907. Other titles of this popular novelist published by Appleton were *The Hungry Heart* (1909), *Old Wives for New* (1910), and *The Price She Paid* (1912). Considered controversial, his *Susan Lennox: Her Fall and Rise* was completed in 1908 but was not published until 1917, six years after his death. It was condemned by the secretary of the Society for the Suppression of Vice; the publicity, as always, spurred sales. Appleton moved to 35 West Thirty-second Street in 1908 and in that year published the first of Joseph C. Lincoln's many novels, *Cy Whittaker's Place*.

Appleton had made several ventures into music book publishing: in 1845 the firm had published *Rudimental Lessons in Music* by James F. Warner; in 1883 Appleton acquired the *Normal Music Course*, but it proved unsuccessful and was sold. In 1915 the firm initiated its music department with the Whole World series of music books, known in the trade as Appleton's Green Books.

Despite the financial difficulties of the turn of the century, Appleton continued to sell widely by subscription; in fact, the firm opened its entire list to subscription purchase and extended the plan to retail booksellers as well as subscription agents. By 1917 financial difficulties had forced another major reorganization. In 1919 John W. Hiltman succeeded Sears as president of the company.

In 1920 the firm announced that Harold Bell Wright had become an Appleton author; he was so popular that Appleton had to establish a separate department to handle publication and distribution of his books. In 1921 Edith Wharton's *The Age of Innocence* (1920) won the Pulitzer Prize for fiction. Appleton had also published her *The Reef* (1912), *Summer* (1917), and *The Marne* (1918) and went on to publish her later works, including *Old New York* (1924). Another Appleton author, Zona

Gale, won the Pulitzer Prize for drama in 1921 for *Miss Lulu Bett* (1921).

In 1924 Appleton took over Stewart Kidd, specialists in drama books, including the series Stewart Kidd Little Theater Plays and The Stewart Kidd Modern Plays and outdoor books. The Dollar Library was launched by Appleton in 1927 with twenty titles, among them *David Harum*, Gilbert Murray's *A History of Ancient Greek Literature,* and Herbert Spencer's *Education.*

On 1 June 1933 D. Appleton and Company merged with the Century Company to form the D. Appleton-Century Company. Century brought its dictionary, a hymnbook department, and textbooks. Appleton had a respected line of medical books, and both houses had strong trade lists. The new firm was divided into trade, education, medical, dictionary, hymnbooks, music, and Spanish departments. Century moved from its Fourth Avenue offices to Appleton's headquarters at 35 West Thirty-second Street. Hiltman became chairman of the board of directors, and W. Morgan Shuster, president of Century, became president of D. Appleton-Century.

References:

"Contributions to Trade History: D. Appleton and Co.," *American Bookseller,* new series 19 (1886): 139-141, 161-163;

House of Appleton (New York, 1927);

The House of Appleton-Century (New York: Appleton-Century, 1936);

Grant Overton, *Portrait of a Publisher and The First Hundred Years of the House of Appleton 1825-1925* (New York & London: Appleton, 1925);

"William Henry Appleton [obituary]," *New York Times,* 20 October 1899, p. 7;

"William Worthen Appleton [obituary]," *New York Times,* 28 January 1924, p. 15;

Gerard R. Wolfe, *The House of Appleton* (Methuen, N.J. & London: Scarecrow Press, 1981).

—*George E. Tylutki*

The Arena Publishing Company
(Boston: 1890-1896)

In 1889 Benjamin Orange Flower founded a monthly magazine, the *Arena: A Periodical of Protest,* with its office in the Pierce Building, Copley Square, Boston. In *Progressive Men, Women and Movements of the Past Twenty-Five Years,* Flower explained the philosophy behind the magazine's establishment: "One of the chief purposes of the management of 'The Arena' was to present great vital movements and theories of the hour, giving emphasis to the sides and views which, because of their conflicting with entrenched privilege or the rising tide of reaction, or on account of their being too new and unconventional to be popular, were for prudential and financial reasons denied a free hearing in current periodical literature." In 1890 The Arena Publishing Company published its first book, Helen H. Gardener's *Is This Your Son, My Lord?*

The *Arena* attracted writers who had previously found a small market for their works of social protest. One such writer was Hamlin Garland, whose *Main-Travelled Roads: Six Mississippi Valley Stories* was published by Arena in 1891. Years later, Garland described his distress at the public reaction to his first book: "The discussion which this little volume provoked was astounding. I was saddened as well as irritated. In regions where I had expected appreciation I received almost nothing but abuse. I had been false to the spirit of the Western boom. I had put heat and cold and dirt and drudgery into my book."

Flower, on the contrary, was delighted with the controversy created by *Main-Travelled Roads* and asked Garland to follow it up with a novel about the Farmers' Alliance, an agrarian movement then at its height. Garland went to Kansas, Georgia, and Colorado to study the activities of the alliance. The product of these travels was *A Spoil of Office,* published by Arena in 1892. *Jason Edwards, an Average Man* (1892) was Garland's last contribution to Arena's list.

The following year Elbert Hubbard, who later wrote the famous "A Message to Garcia" (1899), moved to Boston and accepted a position in the Arena office. The company soon published his first two novels: *One Day: A Tale of the Prairies* (1893) and *Forbes of Harvard* (1894).

Many of the 206 books published by Arena during its six years as a book publisher reflected Flower's liberal political and social views; women's issues were particularly well represented. On the other hand, many of the books dealt with such subjects as astral projection, transmigration of souls, palmistry, hypnotism, and astrology. The explanation for this anomaly seems to be that Arena functioned as a vanity press and would publish almost any work if its author paid the full cost of production. Ambrose Bierce once submitted a book to the firm and was outraged when he was informed of this policy. Among the novels published by the company were Walter Thomas Cheney's *An Apocalypse of Life* (1893), Sarah M. Gardner's *The Fortunes of Margaret Weld* (1894), Sigmund B. Alexander's *A Moral Blot* (1894), Albert Bigelow Paine's *Mystery of Evelin Delorme: A Hypnotic Story* (1894), Will Allen Dromgoole's *The Heart of Old Hickory, and Other Stories of Tennessee* (1895), Mary Clay Knapp's *Whose Soul Have I Now?* (1896), and Carlton Waite's *A Silver Baron* (1896). Arena books were published in both cloth and paperback editions.

The Arena Publishing Company went bankrupt in late 1896 and was reorganized in 1897. Flower left the firm, which continued to publish *Arena* magazine but ceased publishing books. Flower died in 1918.

References:

"Benjamin O. Flower [obituary]," *New York Times*, 25 December 1918, p. 15;

Benjamin O. Flower, *Progressive Men, Women and Movements of the Past Twenty-Five Years* (Boston: New Arena, 1914);

Hamlin Garland, "Roadside Meetings of a Literary Nomad," *Bookman*, 70 (January 1930): 514-528;

Roger E. Stoddard, "Vanity and Reform: B. O. Flower's Arena Publishing Company, Boston, 1890-1896. With a Bibliographical List of Arena Imprints," *Papers of the Bibliographical Society of America*, 76 (1982): 273-337.

—Carol Ann Wilkinson

Authors' Publishing Company
(New York: 1873-1880)

AUTHORS' PUBLISHING COMPANY.

A cooperative publishing venture, the Authors' Publishing Company was the first concerted effort by authors in the United States to publish their own works for their own profit, bypassing the control of publishing houses. The company published more than ninety titles; most of them were literary efforts, the remainder expositions of or polemics on causes close to their authors' hearts, ranging from political economy to apologetics to scientific grammar.

The Authors' Publishing Company was founded at 27 Great Jones Street in New York in 1873; it moved to 30 Bond Street in 1874, to 13 Bond Street in 1875, and to 27 Bond Street in 1876. For a time there was also an office at 18 North Third Street in Harrisburg, Pennsylvania. At its inception the company had $100,000 in capital and seventy-eight stockholder-members in eighteen states, the District of Columbia, and Mexico. William B. Smith served as president, J. S. Whitworth as vice-president, C. C. Adams as secretary, and E. B. Barnum as treasurer. Smith was the most ex-

perienced in New York publishing. The company had an International Committee "specially charged with looking after the interest of members abroad, of foreign authors who desire assistance in the publication, translation, or protection of their works in this country, and with the advocacy of the passage of an International Copyright Law." Most of the twenty-one members of the committee were editors of newspapers or religious journals; a few were lawyers or clergymen.

The Authors' Publishing Company became publicly active in 1874, when it announced a competition for prizes in several categories of writing. The winners, published in the Authors International Prize series, were announced in a full-page advertisement in *Publishers' Weekly* for 29 August 1874. Company director Rev. William I. Gill's *Evolution and Progress: An Exposition and Defence* (1875) was acclaimed as the best manuscript on any subject and designated the "Company's First Book." *Irene; or, Beach-Broken Billows* (1875) by Mrs. B. F. Baer won the award for best fiction; the novel was the first literary work the firm published. The third winner was Gill, for *Analytical Process; or, The Primary Principle of Philosophy.*

Indicative of *Publishers' Weekly*'s attitude toward the Authors' Publishing Company was the remark which concluded a brief notice of the results of the prize competition: "The Authors' Publishing Company, we fear, is not founded on a rock in taking up the superstition of a natural enmity between authors and publishers. The latter are only too glad to get good books." The point at issue, from the authors' point of view, was not merely access to publication channels, but also appropriate compensation and control over their creations.

Novels were the company's stock in trade; hardcover titles included *Her Waiting Heart* (1875) by Lou. Capsadell (pseudonym of Henrietta H. Hammond), *Shadowed Perils* (1876) by M. A. Avery, *Deacon Cranky, the Old Sinner* (1878) by George Guirey, and *Summer Boarders* (1880) by Mrs. Adéle M. Garrigues. Paperback novels came out in the Satchel series, which featured *Egypt Ennis; or, Prisons Without Walls* (1876), written pseudonymously by Smith; *Spiders and Rice Pudding* (1879) by Sarah G. Barbour; and *Our Smoking Husbands and What to Do with Them* (1879) by Harriet P. Fowler. There were also a few slender volumes of verse. The Enchanted Library for Young Folks, which the APC

endeavored to promote as readers in the schools, included *Linda; or, Ueber das Meer* (1878) by H. L. Crawford, *The Queer Little Wooden Captain* (1879) by Sydney Dayre, and *Harry Ascott Abroad* (1879) by Matthew White, Jr. In nonfiction, M. R. Pilon, a member of the International Committee, wrote several books on political economy, among them *The Yanko-Sequor on Free Trade, Valuation of Commodities, Fundamental Principles of the Grangers, Demonetization of Gold, and Free Banks* (1875); E. E. Riggs compiled *The Mystic Key: A Poetic Fortune Teller* (1878); and Henry Kiddle edited *Spiritual Communications* (1879). Other subjects included spelling reform, proposed changes in clothing, and advice on feminine beauty.

The Author's Publishing Company's sole distinction was in being the first of its kind. The company had scant influence on the American publishing scene or on literary history. The firm was dissolved in 1880.

References:

"Authors International Prize Series," *Publishers' Weekly*, 6 (19 August 1874): 222;

"Literary and Trade News," *Publishers' Weekly*, 6 (5 September 1874): 247.

—*Sharon Ann Jaeger*

John Babcock
(Hartford, Connecticut: 1795-1802)
John Babcock and Son
(New Haven, Connecticut: 1811-1824)

By 1795 John Babcock had become involved in the publishing, printing, and bookselling business of his father, Elisha Babcock, in Hartford, Connecticut, and his name appeared in the firm's imprint. Seven years later, John moved to New Haven. In that year another family-owned firm, Sidney's Press, was established in New Haven; John was no doubt associated with it. In 1811 he reestablished his own publishing and bookselling operations under the imprint John Babcock and Son. During the next thirty years, the Babcock family set up branch offices in Massachusetts, New York, Louisiana, and South Carolina. The firm also published under the imprints Sidney Babcock, and Sidney and William Babcock.

Under the imprint of John Babcock, the firm published a variety of children's books. One of its first offerings was *Instructive and Entertaining Emblems* by "Miss Thoughtful" in 1795; it was republished in 1796 and 1798. Another popular seller was Charles F. P. Masson's *Elmina; or, The Flower That Never Fades*, published in 1799 and 1800. Biblical stories for children also appeared on the firm's list during this time.

In 1799 Babcock published *The English Hermit; or, The Adventures of Philip Quarll* by Peter Longueville. The following year, its children's literature included *The New Robinson Crusoe* by Joachim Heinrich von Campe (pseudonym of Richard Johnson), *A New History of Blue Beard* by Charles Perrault, *The Life and Death of Tom Thumb*, and an edition of juvenile poems. Babcock's firm was also the original publisher of *Wisdom in Miniature: Or, The Young Gentleman's and Lady's Magazine*. First issued in 1796, it appeared every other year until 1818, although Babcock ceased publishing it in 1804.

Children's literature also composed a significant part of the list of John Babcock and Son. In 1818 the firm published Mrs. Mary Sherwood's *The History of Little Henry and His Bearer* and in 1819 John Aiken and Anna L. (Aiken) Barbauld's *The Farm-Yard Journal, Also The History of the Marten*, Maria Edgeworth's *The Basket-Woman, and the Orphans*, William Godwin's *Baldwin's Fables: Ancient and Modern*, Charles and Mary Lamb's *Poetry for Children*, and Elizabeth Somerville's *Maria, or The Ever-Blooming Flower*. *The Story of Ali Baba and the Forty Thieves* was published in 1820. Most of these books contained woodcut illustrations, some designed by Dr. Alexander Anderson.

Moral literature for both children and adults included an edition of Susanna Rowson's *The History of Charlotte Temple* (1801) and the second American edition of John Bunyan's *Christian Pilgrim* (1802). One of the last titles on Babcock's list was William F. Sullivan's *Pleasant Stories; or, The Histories of Ben the Sailor, and Ned the Soldier*. This book was published jointly with Sidney Babcock in 1824. After this date, John Babcock's name no longer appears to have been used in the imprint.

—*Elizabeth Hoffman*

Richard G. Badger and Company

(Boston: 1896?-1932)

See also the Bruce Humphries, Incorporated entry in *DLB 46, American Literary Publishing Houses, 1900-1980*.

Richard G. Badger and Company was founded in the mid-1890s at 157 Tremont Hall, Boston. By 1900 it had moved to 194 Boylston Street. The firm is best remembered today as a forerunner of the modern vanity press. Eugene O'Neill, Willa Cather, and Edwin Arlington Robinson paid the firm to publish their first books.

Badger's output consisted mostly of nonfiction, with an emphasis on science and social science; the firm's literary publications were drama, verse, and, occasionally, novels. Early Badger poetry includes Robinson's *The Children of the Night* (1897) and Cather's *April Twilights* (1903). Badger also published such fiction as John Uri Lloyd's *The Right Side of the Car* (1897), Helen Leah Reed's *Miss Theodora: A West End Story* (1898), and Harriet Prescott Spofford's *Old Madame, & Other Tragedies* (1900).

O'Neill had been writing plays for a year when he approached Badger about publishing *Thirst* in 1914. The $450 cost of publishing the 1,000 copies of the first edition was financed by O'Neill's father. *Thirst* was one of the earliest volumes published under Badger's main imprint, The Gorham Press. The Poet Lore Plays, more than eighty titles by authors including Maeterlinck, Chekhov, Gorki, Schnitzler, Sudermann, Andreyev, D'Annunzio, and Hebbel, were published as individual numbers of *Poet Lore* magazine under the imprint of The Poet Lore Company but were printed at Badger's Gorham Press. August Strindberg's *Advent* (1914), another Poet Lore play, was one of the first translations of Strindberg's work in America. Badger also published the American Dramatists series, which consisted of reprints from Badger's backlist of plays. The Contemporary Dramatists series featured works by foreign playwrights, including Hugo von Hofmannsthal's *Death and the Fool* (1913) and José Echegaray's *The Great Galeoto* (1914).

Badger's list stagnated during the 1920s, and few new works of literature appeared. His reputation suffered when he was convicted in 1923 of publishing obscene literature. Badger's Rational Sex series included sex manuals and psychoanalytic works by William Stekel. *Publishers' Weekly* commented, "It is hoped that booksellers who have thought they could handle this material and still keep their self respect as merchants will see the light. . . ." Around 1922 Badger moved to 100 Charles Street. Six years later, he purchased the business of Arthur Vinal of New York. In 1932 the Badger firm was sold to Bruce Humphries, Incorporated.

—David Dzwonkoski

Francis Bailey
(Lancaster, Pennsylvania; Philadelphia: 1772-1797)
F. and R. Bailey
(Philadelphia: 1797-1808)
Lydia R. Bailey
(Philadelphia: 1808-1861)

Although occasionally employed since 1745 as an assistant to Peter Miller at Ephrata, Pennsylvania, Francis Bailey waited until 1771 before launching his first publishing venture, the *Lancaster Almanac,* in Lancaster, Pennsylvania. After a brief partnership with Stewart Herbert, Bailey opened his own shop at Spring Street in Lancaster in 1772, with assistance from his brother Jacob and his sister Abigail. His early printings there included the fourth edition of Thomas Paine's *Common Sense* (1776) and *The Articles of Confederation* (1777).

Upon moving to Market Street in Philadelphia in 1778, Bailey joined with Hugh Henry Brackenridge to publish twelve monthly issues of the *United States Magazine.* After his 1781 publication of *The Constitutions of the Several Independent States,* a volume containing the United States Constitution, the Declaration of Independence, and the Paris Treaty, Bailey was appointed official printer to the United States Congress and the State of Pennsylvania. In 1784 he issued, on type cast by Justus Fox, the first printing of the laws of Pennsylvania. Bailey also published the weekly *Freeman's Journal,* which featured articles by Jonathan Sergeant, George Osbourne, and George Bryan. Verse by Philip Freneau, the Revolutionary War poet, occasionally appeared, and in 1788 Bailey published *The Miscellaneous Works of Mr. Philip Freneau; Containing His Essays and Additional Poems.*

By 1797 Bailey owned presses at Sadsbury and Octoraro, Pennsylvania. With the addition of his son Robert to the business, the firm became F. and R. Bailey, at Yorick's Head, 166 High-Street, Philadelphia. Among its publications was John Swanwick's *Poems on Several Occasions* (1797). With Francis Bailey's gradual retirement and his son's death in 1808, control of the firm passed to Robert Bailey's widow, Lydia R. Bailey.

One of the first woman printers of Philadelphia, Lydia Bailey published a third edition of Freneau's *Poems Written and Published During the American Revolutionary War* (1809) but was primarily a printer of children's books. From her office at 84 Crown Street, she often printed for Johnson and Warner and the Philadelphia Female Tract Society. Eventually, her son, Robert William, who had assisted since his childhood, took over her duties. Upon her son's death in 1861, Lydia Bailey retired. She died eight years later.

References:

"Mrs. Lydia R. Bailey, the Printer," *Typographic Advertiser,* 14 (1868-1869): 397;

William Peden, "Jefferson, Freneau, and the Poems of 1809," *New Colophon,* 1 (1948): 394-400.

—*David Dzwonkoski*

The Baker and Taylor Company

(New York; Hillside, New Jersey; Bridgewater, New Jersey: 1885-)

D. F. Robinson and Company
(Hartford, Connecticut: 1828-1834)

Robinson, Pratt and Company
(Hartford; New York: 1834-1843)

Pratt, Woodford and Company
(New York: 1843-1860)

Farmer, Brace and Company
(New York: 1860-1861)

Pratt, Oakley and Company
(New York: 1861-1862)

Blakeman and Mason
(New York: 1862-1864)

Oakley and Mason
(New York: 1864-1872)

Mason, Baker and Pratt
(New York: 1872-1874)

Baker, Pratt and Company
(New York: 1874-1885)

The Baker and Taylor Company began in Hartford, Connecticut, in 1828 as D. F. Robinson and Company, a bookbinding, bookselling, and publishing firm set up by David F. Robinson. Robinson, who had learned his trade from Silas Andrus of Hartford, published America's first successful physics textbook, John Lee Comstock's *A System of Natural Philosophy* (1830).

The firm went through a confusing series of name changes during the next fifty-seven years. It became Robinson, Pratt and Company after Henry Z. Pratt acquired a partnership in 1834. The following year the firm moved to 259 Pearl Street in New York. Robinson's nephew, O. P. Woodford, became a partner when Robinson retired in 1843, and the firm was renamed Pratt, Woodford and Company. It moved to 4 Cortlandt Street in 1848. During this time the firm was publishing textbooks, as well as jobbing books for other publishers.

Pratt, Woodford and Company acquired two more partners, Elijah P. Farmer and T. K. Brace; and in 1860 the firm's name was changed to Farmer, Brace and Company. Within about a year, however, it became Pratt, Oakley and Company, reflecting the addition of another partner, James S. Oakley. By 1862, Birdseye Blakeman and Albert Mason had joined the firm, and it became Blakeman and Mason. Blakeman departed two years

later, and the name was changed to Oakley and Mason. The firm stopped publishing at this time and concentrated on its wholesaling of books and stationery.

James Shaw Baker had joined the firm in 1859; when Oakley retired in 1872, Baker became a partner and the name was changed to Mason, Baker and Pratt; two years later it was changed again, to Baker, Pratt and Company.

In 1885 William T. Pratt—Henry Z. Pratt's nephew—left the firm; Nelson Taylor formed a partnership with Baker, creating The Baker and Taylor Company at 9 Bond Street. Baker and Taylor began a publishing division that year, and the firm published a few books each year until 1914—as many as twenty-one in 1911. Among its publications were Richard Le Gallienne's *How to Get the Best out of Books* (1904), John Macy's *A Child's Guide to Reading* (1909), W. Somerset Maugham's *The Explorer* (1909), and Owen Johnson's *The Humming Bird* (1910) and *The Varmint* (1910). Other authors whose works were published by the firm were Josiah Strong, John Bigelow, Russell Sturgis, B. E. Stevenson, Daniel Gregory Mason, Mary E. Bennet, Enoch F. Burr, Frank S. Child, Frederick H. Cogswell, William J. Flagg, and Juliet W. Thompkins.

Herbert S. Baker became president of the

firm in 1912—James S. Baker had died in 1904—and in 1914 he discontinued all publishing activities. Baker and Taylor's religious books were turned over to Revell and the rest of its list to Doubleday, Page.

Herbert Baker died in 1934. He was succeeded as president by William A. Hunter. Baker and Taylor moved to Hillside, New Jersey, in 1948. Jack D. Willis assumed the presidency in 1965.

Since the 1940s The Baker and Taylor Company has been one of the largest book wholesalers in the United States. It is currently a division of W. R. Grace and Company. August Umlauf is president of Baker and Taylor. The firm's address is 625 E. Main Street, Bridgewater, New Jersey 08807.

References:

"Herbert S. Baker [obituary]," *Publishers' Weekly*, 126 (22 December 1934): 2218;

"James Shaw Baker [obituary]," *Publishers' Weekly*, 66 (3 December 1904): 1552-1553.

—Theodora Mills
Philip B. Dematteis

Walter H. Baker Company ("Baker's Plays")
(Boston: 1892-   )
Herbert Sweet and Company
(Boston: 1845-1872)
George M. Baker and Company
(Boston: 1872-1892)

The Boston firm Walter H. Baker Company—familiarly known as Baker's Plays—is the second oldest publisher of plays in the United States after Samuel French. It began as Herbert Sweet and Company in 1845; the firm was sold to William H. Spencer in 1851 and to Lee and Shepard in 1871. After a fire at the Lee and Shepard offices in 1872, the play division was sold to George M. Baker, who renamed the firm George M. Baker and Company. Baker's inventory consisted of seventy plays. Some of the plays were English; many had been written by Baker himself; and some were dramatizations of popular contemporary fiction, such as Mrs. Henry Wood's *East Lynne* (1894), a melodrama which Baker's Plays continues to keep in print.

Baker's brother Walter managed the firm un-

til 1892, when he formed a partnership with Frank E. Chase, a Boston journalist, and renamed the firm the Walter H. Baker Company. When Chase died in 1920, his interest passed to Theodore Johnson, who became president after Walter Baker's death in 1929. Johnson was succeeded in 1951 by M. Abbot Van Mostrand.

In the 1920s the firm opened a religious department, offering plays for church groups. In the 1930s and 1940s the company expanded its lists of choral readings, one-act plays, and European plays. In 1964 Baker's Plays acquired Harper and Row's drama department, a leader in the publication of plays for junior and senior high schools.

Baker's Plays' 1982 catalogue reflects a diversified playlist that includes holiday plays, melodramas, minstrels, and musicals. Of the more than

*Herbert S. Baker, president of The Baker and Taylor
Company from 1912 until his death in 1934*

Hubert Howe Bancroft

2,200 plays offered, the selection of religious dramas and pageants remains especially strong, but the greatest concentration is among general one-act and three-act plays. Included are Eugene O'Neill's *Ah, Wilderness!* (1933), Thornton Wilder's *Our Town* (1938), James Thurber and Elliott Nugent's *The Male Animal* (1940), Archibald MacLeish's *J. B.* (1958), William Saroyan's *The Cave Dwellers* (1958), Arthur Kopit's *Oh Dad, Poor Dad, Mama's Hung You in the Closet and I'm Feelin' So Sad* (1960), Woody Allen's *Don't Drink the Water* (1967), Edward Albee's *All Over* (1971), John Guare's *The House of Blue Leaves* (1972), and David Rabe's *Sticks and Bones* (1972).

Largely through mail orders, Baker's Plays has served amateur groups in dramatic schools, little theaters, elementary and high schools, churches, radio stations, and women's clubs. One of the firm's all-time best-sellers since it was first produced in 1919 has been *Aaron Slick of Punkin' Crick* by Lt. Beale Cormack. Baker's Plays is located at 100 Chauncy Street, Boston 02110.

Reference:

"Baker's Plays Marks Centenary Year," *Publishers' Weekly*, 148 (8 September 1945): 966-969.

—Phyllis Andrews

A. L. Bancroft and Company
(San Francisco: 1869-1897)

H. H. Bancroft and Company
(San Francisco: 1856-1869)

The Bancroft Company
(San Francisco: 1887-1898)

The History Company
(San Francisco: 1887-1892)

Bancroft-Whitney Company
(San Francisco: 1887-1919)

Hubert Howe Bancroft, a native of Ohio who had been a bookseller in Buffalo, New York, and in California, and George L. Kenney founded H. H. Bancroft and Company, booksellers and publishers, on Montgomery Street in San Francisco in 1856. Bancroft's brother Albert arrived in California in 1858 and was soon installed as bookkeeper in the firm, where he exhibited excellent managerial skills. By 1860 he had a half interest in the company. It was under Albert Bancroft's direction that the stationery, bookselling, and printing departments of H. H. Bancroft and Company became profitable. Recognizing his brother's business sense, Hubert felt that he could safely leave the company in Albert's hands while he pursued his research into the history of the Pacific Coast of North America.

Books published by H. H. Bancroft and Company included titles in law, medicine, and education. Among literary works published by Bancroft were *The Giant Judge* (1859) and *Esther, the Hebrew-*

Persian Queen (1859) by William Anderson Scott; *The California Hundred* (1865), a poem by J. Henry Rogers in memory of J. Sewell Reed and his gallant volunteer band; *Anselmo, a Poem* (1865) by George R. Parburt; and *The California Scrapbook* (1869), edited by Oscar Shuck, which contains over 200 articles, most of them by California writers. In 1868 Bancroft published an edition of Edward Rowland Sill's *The Hermitage and Other Poems,* which appeared in the same year under a New York imprint.

In 1869 A. L. Bancroft and Company was formed, and H. H. Bancroft and Company was phased out. As Hubert became more preoccupied with his book collecting and literary pursuits, Albert continued the firm's publishing program, in which legal publications predominated. It is estimated that in its first seven years, A. L. Bancroft and Company produced over 350,000 copies of various pamphlets and books. Literary works were mostly poetry, including *Songs of the Sand Hills* (1873) by Walking Hiller (pseudonym of Joseph

Ross), *Madame Jane Junk and Joe* (1876) by Oraquill (pseudonym of Mary Bornemann), *Behind the Arras* (1877) by Constance M. Neville, and *Apache-land* (1878) by Charles Debrille Poston. Between 1856 and 1886 the output of the Bancroft firms far surpassed that of any other California publisher.

In October 1882 A. L. Bancroft and Company published the first six volumes of Hubert's history of the Pacific states, *The Works of Hubert Howe Bancroft;* volumes one through five had been published originally in New York by Appleton between 1874 and 1876. Although only Hubert's name appeared as the author of the history, the work was actually written by about a dozen scholars and assistants. Of the eventual total of thirty-nine volumes, it is estimated that Hubert wrote about ten and one-half, although he supervised and edited the entire work. Between October 1882 and October 1890, one additional volume of *The Works of Hubert Howe Bancroft* appeared every three months.

In April 1886 the Bancroft building was consumed by fire and many of the plates for Hubert Bancroft's history were destroyed, along with the completed volumes awaiting shipment. Because A. L. Bancroft and Company could rely on other printing plants, the firm could continue printing the *Works;* all of the history in manuscript had been saved, and paper was already on its way from the east. One week after the fire the law department of A. L. Bancroft was transferred to the new Bancroft-Whitney Company, with Albert and Sumner Whitney as partners. After a fraternal quarrel, Albert continued only the bookselling activities of A. L. Bancroft and Company; his brother formed The History Company, which published the remaining nineteen volumes of the *Works*. The twenty volumes published by A. L. Bancroft and Company before the fire were republished with the imprint of The History Company.

Several other companies were established by members of the Bancroft family after the fire. Will B. Bancroft, a nephew of Hubert and Albert formerly in charge of the printing plant of A. L. Bancroft and Company, set up a printing business under his own name. Hubert soon persuaded Will to become a partner in The Bancroft Company, a printing, publishing, and bookselling firm organized in 1887 which carried on Hubert's publishing program, except for the thirty-nine-volume his-

tory. Perhaps the most notable book produced by The Bancroft Company was Hubert Bancroft's *The Book of the Fair*, published to coincide with the Columbian Exposition in Chicago in 1893; the book was printed at the Blakely Printing Company in Chicago. The Bancroft Company also published literary works, including *Zanthon, a Novel* (1891) by James Doran, *Helen Duvall, a French Romance* (1891) by James L. Young, and *The Bride of Infelice* (1892) by Ada L. Halstead (pseudonym of Laura E. Newhall). The Bancroft Company continued in business until 1898. Three cousins, Charles, George, and Harlow Bancroft, established Bancroft Brothers, a schoolbook and supply house in San Francisco. This company also remained in business until 1898. The History Company ceased operations in 1892; in order to put its assets out of the reach of a former employee who was suing The History Company for breach of contract, Hubert Bancroft established the California Book Company. Nothing was ever published by the California Book Company.

By 1892 A. L. Bancroft and Company had become only a music store, and by 1897 it had ceased to function altogether. Albert Bancroft continued as president of Bancroft-Whitney Company, a major publisher of law books, until the early 1890s, when he sold his stock to invest in an ill-fated land and water company. He left San Francisco around 1895 and died in 1914. Hubert Howe Bancroft died in 1918, after selling his vast collection of Western Americana to the University of California at Berkeley, where it formed the basis of the Bancroft Library. The Bancroft-Whitney Company was merged into the Lawyers Co-operative Publishing Company in 1919.

References:

John Walton Caughey, *Hubert Howe Bancroft: Historian of the West* (Berkeley & Los Angeles: University of California Press, 1946);

Harry Clark, *A Venture in History: The Production, Publication, and Sale of the Works of Hubert Howe Bancroft* (Berkeley: University of California Press, 1973);

"Hubert Howe Bancroft [obituary]," *New York Times*, 3 March 1918, p. 23.

—Bruce L. Johnson

E. E. Barclay and Company
(New York; Cincinnati; Philadelphia: 1840-1891)

In the early 1840s a few sensational fiction titles appeared under the imprint of E. E. Barclay of New York. In 1847 and from 1855 to 1857, Barclay books came from Cincinnati, but for most of the time from 1848 to 1891, the firm of E. Elmer Barclay was located in Philadelphia. Five street addresses are known: 734 Market Street from 1858 to 1862; 56 North Sixth Street from 1863 to 1865; 602 Arch Street from 1866 to 1868; 610 Arch Street from 1869 to 1870; and 21 North Seventh Street from 1871 until the firm went out of business in 1891.

The house specialized in thrillers—"true" stories of suffering, adventure, crime, and passion that were often exaggerations of contemporary news stories. Representative titles, all anonymous, include *The Startling Confessions of Eleanor Burton: A Thrilling Tragedy from Real Life Exhibiting a Dark Page in the Manners, Customs, and Crimes of the "Upper Ten" of New York City* (1852); *The Lady Lieutenant: A Wonderful, Startling and Thrilling Narrative of the Adventures of Miss Madeline Moore, Who, in Order to be Near Her Lover, Joined the Army, Was Elected Lieutenant, and Fought in Western Virginia under the Renowned General McClellan* (1862); *The Rebel Cousins: or, Life and Love in Secessia* (1864); *The True Narrative of the Five Years' Suffering & Perilous Adventures by Miss Barber, Wife of "Squatting Bear," a Celebrated Sioux Chief* (1872); and *The Great Wrongs of the Shop Girls* (1879).

Not all Barclay works were anonymous. The publisher-author Charles Wesley Alexander brought to Barclay his tale *Pauline of the Potomac; or, General McClellan's Spy* (1862). The firm also published an edition of the popular drama *The Black Crook* (1866). George Lippard Barclay wrote *The Great Fire of Chicago!* (1872), *The Kelsey Outrage!* (1873), and *All Honor to Stanley! Dr. David Livingstone's Discoveries in Africa* (1873). In 1875 the firm published *Nasby on Inflation* by Petroleum V. Nasby (D. R. Locke).

The Barclay list for 1877 included books on wine-making, spiritualism, and astronomy. The prices were low, usually twenty-five cents; all the books were illustrated; and some titles were offered in German.

Reference:
Thomas M. McDade, "Lurid Literature of the Last Century: The Publications of E. E. Barclay," *Pennsylvania Magazine of History and Biography*, 80 (1956): 452-464.

—*Theodora Mills*

C. W. Bardeen
(Syracuse, New York: 1880-1922)
Davis, Bardeen and Company
(Syracuse: 1874-1880)

Charles William Bardeen was a partner in the Syracuse, New York, firm of Davis, Bardeen and Company from 1874 to 1880, then the owner of its successor firm, C. W. Bardeen, from 1880 until 1922. The firm published works for teachers and classroom use. Its few literary titles had school-related themes and were mainly authored by Bardeen. Titles by him include *Roderick Hume: The Story of a New York Teacher* (1878) and its sequel *Commissioner Hume: A Story of New York Schools* (1899), *Fifty-five Years Old, and Other Stories about Teachers* (1904), and *Ruby Floyd's Temptation, and Other Stories about Schools* (1915).

Reference:
"Obituary: Bardeen of Syracuse," *Publishers' Weekly*, 106 (30 August 1924): 658.

—*Karl Kabelac*

A. S. Barnes and Company

(Hartford, Connecticut; Philadelphia; New York; San Diego: 1838-   )

Barnes and Burr

(New York: 1859-1865)

After an apprenticeship with D. F. Robinson and Company, twenty-one-year-old Alfred Smith Barnes founded his own publishing firm in Hartford, Connecticut, in 1838. His partner was Charles Davies, a mathematics professor at Trinity College. The company, which became a leader in educational publishing, began with a series of mathematics texts written by Davies. In 1840 the partners moved to Minor Street in Philadelphia; five years later they established the company at 51 John Street in New York. Here they began to publish the National Series of Standard School Books, which included Davies's *Arithmetic* (1838), James Monteith's *First Lessons in Geography* (1855), and Richard Green Parker and James M. Watson's *The National Fifth Reader* (1858).

In 1848 Davies sold his interest in the company to Edmund Dwight; Dwight resold it the next year to Barnes's brother-in-law, Henry L. Burr. In 1859 the company's name was changed to Barnes and Burr. The firm expanded its line to include physical education books. The *Plymouth Collection of Hymns and Tunes* (1855), compiled by Henry Ward Beecher, was the first of many hymnbooks published by Barnes.

The firm resumed the name of A. S. Barnes and Company when Burr died in 1865; it moved that year to larger offices at the corner of John and William Streets. The following year Alfred Cutler Barnes, son of Alfred Smith, became a partner; he was made president at his father's death in 1888. Two years later the American Book Company, a firm set up by Barnes and four other publishers, took over the educational books published by A. S. Barnes and Company, which then moved to 751 Broadway and expanded its list of noneducation titles. A few years later the company relocated to

56 East Tenth Street and then to 156 Fifth Avenue; there, under the leadership of another of A. S. Barnes's sons, Henry B. Barnes, it ventured into the publication of fiction. Among the earliest fiction works published by Barnes were Annie Eliot Trumbull's *A Christmas Accident, and Other Stories* (1897), *A Cape Cod Week* (1898), *Rod's Salvation* (1898), and *Mistress Content Craddok* (1899). The firm's greatest successes in fiction were Joseph C. Lincoln's popular stories of life on Cape Cod: *Cap'n Eri* (1904), *Partners of the Tide* (1905), *Mr. Pratt* (1906), and *"The Old Home House"* (1907). The company's fiction list also included Gouverneur Morris's *The Pagan's Progress* (1904), Henry C. Rowland's *The Mountain of Fears* (1905), and works by Alfred Henry Lewis and S. R. Crockett.

Ripley Hitchcock, the firm's new literary adviser, immediately saw the value of a science book by Robert Kennedy Duncan, *The New Knowledge* (1905). A year after it published this important text, the firm acquired the educational books and periodicals of E. L. Kellogg and Company and once again became a publisher of schoolbooks. It moved that year to 11-15 East Twenty-fourth Street.

A. S. Barnes and Company was incorporated in 1909 with Henry Burr Barnes as president and John Barnes Pratt, Alfred S. Barnes's nephew, as vice-president. Pratt became head of the company when Barnes died in 1911. John and Wayne Laidlaw became partners in the firm in 1918 but withdrew after a year and went on to form Laidlaw Brothers. By then Barnes was publishing only in its most profitable areas: hymnals and books on physical education, sports, and dance. In 1951 Rinehart and Company acquired an interest in A. S. Barnes but sold it four years later. During the 1950s A. S. Barnes, under the leadership of John

The History Company building, built by Hubert Howe Bancroft after the A. L. Bancroft and Company building was destroyed by fire

Alfred Smith Barnes

John Barnes Pratt became president of A. S. Barnes and Company in 1911 following the death of his uncle

Barnes Pratt's son John Lowell Pratt, became the world's largest publisher of sports books. Thomas Yoseloff purchased the company in 1958; in 1980 it was acquired by Leisure Dynamics, Incorporated and began to diversify its list to include general nonfiction, cinema, art, and history, as well as sports and recreation. In 1982 A. S. Barnes and Company was merged with Oak Tree Publications, a wholly owned subsidiary of Leisure Dynamics, and is now an imprint of that company. In 1985 Leisure Dynamics, Incorporated was acquired by Coleco Industries. Oak Tree Publications is located at 9601 Aero Drive, San Diego, California 92123.

References:

"Barnes Celebrates 100th Anniversary," *Publishers' Weekly,* 133 (26 February 1938): 1015-1017;

John Barnes Pratt, *A Century of Book Publishing, 1838-1938: Historical and Personal* (New York: Barnes, 1938);

Pratt, *Personal Recollections: Sixty Years of Book Publishing* (New York: Barnes, 1942);

Seventy-five Years of Book Publishing (New York: Barnes, 1913).

—Carol Ann Wilkinson

Beacon Press
(Boston: 1902-   )
American Unitarian Association
(Boston: 1854-1902)

Founded in Boston in 1854, the press of the American Unitarian Association did not officially become Beacon Press until 1902. The firm, noted for its liberal social and religious leanings, was established to publish books on ethical, sociological, religious, and philanthropic subjects.

Beacon's list consists largely of nonfiction titles, though during the late 1950s there was a flurry of novels. These included a reprint of André Malraux's 1929 novel *The Conquerors* (1956), the first American edition of Italo Calvino's *The Path to the Nest of the Spiders* (1957), and George P. Elliott's first novel, *Parktilden Village* (1958). Other publications include the Best Short Plays series, edited by Margaret Mayorga and published annually between 1955 and 1961, and a series of paperback fiction. The press has also maintained a list of juvenile works since its beginning. Beacon presently publishes a reprint series of women's fiction and twentieth-century black women's novels.

The firm's extensive list of books on literary history and criticism has included works by some of the twentieth century's most respected critics, such as Lionel Trilling's *A Gathering of Fugitives* (1956), Eric Bentley's *What Is Theatre?* (1956), and works by Katherine Mansfield and Hugh Kenner. In 1963 Beacon published the first U.S. edition of *The Historical Novel* by the Hungarian critic György Lukács.

Beacon's nonfiction publications have sometimes advanced controversial political positions. Notable examples were two books by Paul Blanshard, *American Freedom and Catholic Power* (1949) and *The Right to Read* (1955). The firm's all-time best-seller is Philip Slater's *The Pursuit of Loneliness* (1970), with half a million copies sold by 1984.

Beacon published Herbert Marcuse's *Negations: Essays in Critical Theory* (1968) and Hans Hofmann's *Discovering Freedom* (1969). The firm also offered "cause-oriented" books, such as Daniel Berrigan's *The Trial of the Catonsville Nine* (1970) and *The Pentagon Papers* (1971-1972), edited by Sen. Mike Gravel. Mary Ann Lash succeeded Wells Drorbaugh, Jr., as director and editor in chief in 1978; Lash was replaced in 1983 by Wardy Strothman. In May 1984 Beacon Press celebrated its 130th anniversary. It is still located at its original address: 25 Beacon Street, Boston, Massachusetts 02108.

Reference:

"Beacon Press Celebrates 130 Years of Quiet Furor," *Publishers Weekly,* 225 (1 June 1984): 20-21.

—Gary R. Treadway

Beadle and Adams
(Buffalo, New York; New York: 1856-1860,
1872-1898)
Beadle and Vanduzee
(Buffalo: 1851-1853)
Beadle and Brother
(Buffalo: 1853-1856)
Irwin P. Beadle and Company
(New York: 1860)
Beadle and Company
(New York: 1860-1872)

The firm of Beadle and Adams was, under one of its earlier names, the first to publish dime novels in series. The forerunner of the mass-market paperback, the dime novel was published in paper wrappers, usually illustrated with scenes of high action, romance, or glamour. Poorly printed on the cheapest paper, these publications were aimed at young audiences, railroad travelers, light readers, and male readers of action stories. They ranged from standard, square sixteenmos to comic-book sizes. Usually, individual volumes were numbered parts of longer series in the same format. The dime novel had declined sharply by the 1930s, to reappear in the 1940s as the modern fiction paperback.

The Beadle brothers were born in Pierstown, New York: Erastus Flavel in 1821, Irwin Pedro in 1826. Erastus began his career in 1838 as an apprentice with H. and E. Phinney, booksellers and publishers of schoolbooks in Cooperstown, New York; in 1847 he was hired as a stereotyper by Jewett, Thomas and Company, which published the *Buffalo Commercial Advertiser*. In 1850 Erastus and Irwin, who had trained as bookbinders, formed a printing partnership, Beadle and Brother's Buffalo Stereotype Foundry, at 6 West Seneca Street in Buffalo. Two years later Erastus and Benjamin C. Vanduzee, an engraver, began publishing a children's magazine, *Youth's Casket,* under the imprint of Beadle and Vanduzee. When Vanduzee left the firm in 1853, Irwin became a partner, and the imprint became Beadle and Brother. Irwin left after about a year. Erastus ran the firm under his own imprint until Robert Adams, his stereotyper, became a partner in 1856, at which time the imprint became Beadle and Adams. Adams, an Irishman from Londonderry, was only nineteen when the partnership was formed. Beadle and Adams immediately began a second magazine, *The Home. A Fireside Companion and Guide for the Wife, the Mother,* *the Sister, and Daughter.*

In 1858 the Beadle brothers and Adams moved to New York, where Erastus continued to publish *The Home* at 333 Broadway, while also sharing an interest in Irwin P. Beadle and Company, which was started by Irwin and Adams at 141 William Street. In 1859 Irwin P. Beadle and Company began publishing series of dime nonfiction works. Its first three titles were *Beadle's Dime Song Book* and Mrs. Metta V. Victor's *Dime Cook-Book; or, Housewife's Pocket Companion* and *Dime Recipe Book. A Directory For the Parlor, Nursery, Sick Room, Toilet, Kitchen, Larder, etc.*, all in 1859. When Erastus stopped publishing *The Home* in 1860, he joined Irwin P. Beadle and Company.

In July of that year the firm issued the first number in the Beadle's Dime Novels series, Ann S. Stephens's *Malaeska: Indian Wife of the White Hunter*, in orange wrappers, 6 5/8 inches by 4 1/2 inches and 128 pages in length. The novel had originally been serialized in *The Ladies Companion* in 1839. Nine more numbers in the series, all published in 1860, bore the Irwin P. Beadle and Company imprint; these included *The Privateer's Cruise, and the Bride of Pomfret Hall. A Sea Tale of '76* by Charles Jacobs Peterson under the pseudonym Harry Cavendish (No. 2), *Myra, the Child of Adoption. A Romance of Real Life* by Stephens (No. 3), and *Seth Jones; or, The Captives of the Frontier* by Edward Sylvester Ellis (No. 8). *Malaeska* and *Seth Jones* were best-sellers. Late in 1860, with number eleven in the series, Mary Andrews Denison's *The Prisoner of La Vintresse; or, The Fortunes of a Cuban Heiress*, the imprint became Beadle and Company, but there were no changes in the organization of the firm. An English branch, Beadle's American Sixpenny Publishing House, was opened in 1861 at 44 Paternoster Row, London, to stop English pirating of the books; the dime novels appeared there as Beadle's American Library. The English branch was

Erastus Flavel Beadle, Robert Adams, and Irwin Pedro Beadle in 1862

Cover for Beadle and Company's first dime novel (courtesy of the Rare Book Division, New York Public Library, Astor, Lenox and Tilden Foundations)

sold to George Routledge and Sons in 1866. In addition to further works by Stephens and Ellis, Beadle's Dime Novels included Victor's *The Backwoods Bride: A Romance of Squatter Life* (1860), Augustine Joseph Hickey Duganne's *The Peon Prince; or, The Yankee Knight-errant* (1861), Harry Hazelton's *The Silver Bugle; or, The Indian Maiden of St. Croix* (1864), Roger Starbuck's *The Golden Harpoon; or, Lost Among the Floes. A Story of the Whaling Grounds* (1865), and Prentiss Ingraham's *Captain of Captains; or, "The Broom of the Seas." A Story of the Moorish Corsairs* (1873).

Around July 1862 Erastus and Adams purchased Irwin's share and continued the Beadle and Company imprint at 118 William Street; Irwin founded a second Irwin P. Beadle and Company with George Munro in December 1862. Irwin P. Beadle and Company competed with Beadle and Company in the dime novel field, but Irwin sold out to Munro in February 1864. Munro remained a strong competitor of the Beadles for many years.

Irwin started his third Irwin P. Beadle and Company at 51 and 53 Ann Street in 1865 with *Irwin P. Beadle's New No. 1 Comic and Sentimental Song Book for the People* and, in October 1865, the first number of Irwin P. Beadle's American Novels series. This series included James Fenimore Cooper's *O-i-chee: A Tale of the Mohawk* (1865), which had previously been published in *Home Weekly* magazine, as well as titles by Ellis (who wrote under various pseudonyms about a third of all the novels Irwin published), Edwin Evans Ewing, P. Hamilton Myers, and Julius Warren "Leon" Lewis (who used the pseudonym Illion Constellano). In 1866 the firm, relocated to 102 Nassau Street and renamed Irwin and Company, began a short-lived series called Irwin's Six Penny Tales while continuing to publish the American Novels series, forty-eight numbers of which appeared before it was discontinued in December 1868. Irwin left the firm around 1867. Before his death in 1882, he was in business for some years as a bookbinder.

Erastus and Adams's Beadle and Company became successful during the Civil War, when thousands of the firm's dime novels, either purchased by the army or donated by Beadle, were shipped to the troops. Several titles boosted patriotism with stories of the Revolutionary War, among them N. C. Iron's *Stella, the Daughter of Liberty: A Tale of the War of '76* (1861) and Mary Andrews Denison's *Captain Molly; or, The Fight at Trenton, Christmas, 1776* (1865). Other titles may have offered subtle comments on the Confederacy's disloyalty to the Union, for they dealt with treason—

for example, Iron's *Gideon Godbold: A Tale of Arnold's Treason* (1862)—and Toryism—as in Duganne's *The King's Man: A Tale of South Carolina in Revolutionary Times* (1862). From 1861 to about 1898, these and other stories were edited by Orville J. Victor, who had begun as an author of some of the earliest Beadle publications. In 1856 he had married Metta Victoria Fuller, who as Mrs. Metta V. Victor wrote many successful Beadle novels, including one of the better-known Beadle's Dime Novels, *Maum Guinea and Her Plantation Children; or, Holiday Week on a Louisiana Estate. A Slave Romance* (1861), a popular abolitionist novel that was admired by Abraham Lincoln.

Much of the success of Beadle and Company after the Civil War was probably due to the 1864 arrangement between the firm and Sinclair Tousey's American News Company for the sale and distribution of Beadle's publications. The American News Company imprint appeared on the first forty-four numbers in the American Tales series, with the Beadle and Company imprint replacing it on number forty-five.

Beadle and Company published many other series. Number three in its Dime Book of Fun series was the first book publication of Mark Twain's *Jim Smiley's Frog* (1866), an abridged version of "The Celebrated Jumping Frog of Calaveras County." The octavo Fifty Cent Books series, published from 1866 to 1869, featured romance stories, as did most of the twenty-five numbers of the Cheap Editions of Popular Authors series, which were published from 1875 to 1877 and sold for twenty-five cents.

In 1872 the name of the firm was changed back to Beadle and Adams, but the Adams family was now represented by Robert Adams's brothers, William and David; Robert had died in 1866. In 1875 the Beadle and Adams Twenty Cent Novels were launched. As with the Cheap Editions of Popular Authors series, the thirty-two numbers of the Twenty Cent Novels were all reprints from Beadle's weekly story paper, the *Saturday Journal*, started in 1870. The *Journal*, renamed *Beadle's Weekly* in 1882 and *Banner Weekly* in 1885, published a total of 685 serialized stories by authors including Joel Chandler Harris, "Oliver Optic," Margaret E. Sangster, and Frank H. Converse.

By 17 November 1874, 321 numbers of the Beadle Dime Novels had appeared. Between that date, when it was renamed the New Dime Novels series, and its discontinuation in 1885, 309 numbers, including several reprints from the earlier series, were published. Though the stories may often have been old material, they appeared in new, bright, multicolored pictorial wrappers. Rivaling the New Dime Novels in success and importance was the Dime Library, which had begun in 1877 as Frank Starr's New York Library and was briefly called Beadle's Dime Library during 1878 before receiving its final name in 1879.

The Dime Library made a major contribution to the popular mythology of the American West. One of the first numbers in the series was *Kit Carson, Jr., the Crack Shot of the West* (1878) by Buckskin Sam (Samuel S. Hall). There were stories by William Frederick Cody (Buffalo Bill), including *Death Trailer, the Chief of Scouts; or, Life and Love in a Frontier Fort* (1878), *The Wizard Brothers; or, White Beaver's Red Trail* (1886), and *The Dread Shot Four; or, My Pards of the Plains* (1897), as well as stories about him by Ingraham, such as *Buffalo Bill's Body Guard; or, The Still Hunt of the Hills* (1892) and *Buffalo Bill's Flush Hand; or, Texas Jack's Bravos* (1893). Ingraham also wrote *Wild Bill, the Pistol Dead Shot; or, Dagger Don's Double* (1882), a tale of Wild Bill Hickok. Most of the veteran Beadle writers contributed to the series, along with newer authors including Joseph E. Badger, Philip S. Warne, Oll Coomes, Albert W. Aiken, Frederick Whittaker, and Thomas Chalmers Harbaugh. More than 1000 numbers of the American Library were published in its thirty-two-page octavo format.

Deadwood Dick unsuccessfully sought Calamity Jane's hand in marriage in Edward L. Wheeler's *Deadwood Dick, the Prince of the Road; or, The Black Rider of the Black Hills* (1877), the first number of the juvenile Half-Dime Library. It was followed by Harbaugh's *Old Frosty, the Guide; or, Niokana, the White Queen of the Blackfeet* (1879), Wheeler's *Fritz, the Bound-Boy Detective; or, Dot Leetle Game mit Rebecca* (1881), and William R. Eyster's *The Sport in Velvet; or, Big Burk's Bluff* (1895). For young ladies, Beadle and Adams began the Waverly Library of romances in 1879. Another boys' series, Beadle's Boy's Library, started in 1881, consisted mainly of reprints from earlier series.

In addition to dime novels, Beadle and Adams published song books, biographies, self-help guides, and baseball annuals. Among the firm's nine periodicals was *Beadle's Monthly: A Magazine of Today,* a genuine effort at a literary review that ran from 1865 to 1866. Only the *Saturday Journal* became a lasting success.

Having reached a peak of popularity in the 1870s, dime novels began to lose favor during the 1880s. Beadle and Adams concentrated on reprints, but occasionally published new titles until William Adams's death in 1896. Erastus Beadle had died in 1894, David Adams in 1886. In February 1898 the firm's assets were sold to M. J. Ivers and Company of New York. The Dime Library, the Half-Dime Library, and the Beadle Boy's Library were continued by Ivers until that firm's demise in 1905. The assets of the Ivers Company were purchased by the Arthur Westbrook Company of Cleveland, which kept some of the Beadle dime novels in print until it went out of business in 1937.

References:

"The Beadle Collection of Dime Novels Given to The New York Public Library by Dr. Frank P. O'Brien," *Bulletin of The New York Public Library,* 26 (1922): 555-628; 27 (1923): 561;

Albert Johannsen, *The House of Beadle and Adams and Its Dime and Nickel Novels: The Story of a Vanished Literature,* 3 volumes (Norman: University of Oklahoma Press, 1950-1962);

Frank Luther Mott, "The Beadles and their Novels," *Palimpsest,* 30 (1949): 173-189;

Louis George Pecek, "The Beadle Story Papers, 1870-1897: A Study of Popular Fiction," Ph.D. dissertation, Ohio State University, 1959;

John T. Winterich, "The Bonanza Boys from Buffalo; or, the Beadles and Their Books," *Publishers' Weekly,* 157 (20 May 1950): 2134-2138.

—David Dzwonkoski

Belford, Clarke and Company

(Chicago and New York: 1875-1892)

The key figure behind Belford, Clarke and Company, Alexander Belford, was born in Ireland on 6 May 1854 and moved with his family first to America and, shortly after, to Toronto, Canada. Both his parents died there when he was nine. Within three years this child prodigy was business manager of the *Toronto Evening Telegraph*. At the same time, he founded the Canadian News Company; he had also published a few books. In 1872 Belford began a publishing partnership, Belford Brothers, in Toronto with his older brothers Charles and Robert; James Clarke joined three years later. Soon after, Charles died, and Alexander Belford and Clarke formed Belford, Clarke and Company at the corner of Congress and Wabash in Chicago. The firm continued Belford Brothers' practice of specializing in inexpensive sets of the complete works of established authors, particularly Mark Twain.

"Aleck" Belford outraged the established publishing community with what were then unorthodox bookselling tactics. He opened bookstalls in department stores and eventually expanded Belford, Clarke retail departments to most major cities, all of them selling pirated reprints at cut rates. He also retaliated against uncooperative bookstores by persuading nearby retailers to stock his books at his own risk. The firm was soon doing over a million dollars a year in business; in 1879 it opened a New York branch, managed by Robert Belford, at 384-386 Broadway.

The practice of pirating—producing cheap, unauthorized reprints of books originally published by other firms—caused Belford, Clarke and Company some problems. In 1884 courts in New York and Chicago granted injunctions against the firm for republishing one of Estes and Lauriat's *Chatterbox* books. But with the financial backing of Lyman C. Gage, a Chicago banker, Belford prospered. One of his great financial successes was *Peck's Bad Boy and His Pa* (1883) by Gov. George W. Peck of Wisconsin. This book—and six others by Peck—sold well for years. Belford, Clarke also published Norman C. Perkins's *A Man of Destiny* (1885) and Albion W. Tourgée's *The Veteran and His Pipe* (1886). Another notable success came with an agreement with A. and C. Black of Edinburgh for a long-term option to publish an American edition of the *Encyclopaedia Britannica*, which Belford,

Clarke had already successfully reprinted. The encyclopedia was sold on the installment plan through newspapers. Clarke then went to London and introduced the same sales method there, in partnership with the *Times*.

The firm's literary output reached its peak in the late 1880s. Perhaps the most significant literary title during this period was Gertrude Atherton's first book, *What Dreams May Come* (1888). Belford, Clarke also occasionally published poetry, but most of the firm's publications were popular fiction titles: adventure tales, such as James William Buel's *Life and Marvelous Adventures of Wild Bill, the Scout* (1880); and romances such as Madeline Dahlgren's *Divorced: A Novel* (1887), Laura Daintrey's *Eros* (1888), Mary Dallas's *The Devil's Anvil* (1889), and Edgar Fawcett's *How a Husband Forgave* (1890). Belford, Clarke also published humorist Edgar Wilson Nye's *Bill Nye and Boomerang; or, The Tale of a Meek-Eyed Mule* (1881), Edgar Everston Saltus's *Eden: An Episode* (1888), and Ernest De Lancey Pierson's *The Black Ball: A Fantastic Romance* (1889).

The firm began to fail when its building in Chicago was destroyed by fire early in 1886. Belford attempted to carry on by transferring half the stock from the New York branch to Chicago. The New York branch split off in 1888 as The Belford Company. Clarke left the firm, moving to New York to publish the *Century Dictionary and Cyclopedia*. In 1892 the Chicago branch merged with several other publishers to form the Werner Company; Belford was the second largest stockholder and managed the publishing department in the new firm.

In 1897 Belford and George Middlebrook left the Werner Company to form their own publishing firm, Belford, Middlebrook and Company, in Chicago. Two years later it was operating as Alexander Belford and Company at 277 Dearborn Street, but by 1901 it was out of existence. Belford retired to Los Angeles, where he died in September 1906.

Reference:
"Alexander Belford—In Memoriam," *Publishers' Weekly*, 70 (20 October 1906): 1098-1099.

—David M. Niebauer
David Dzwonkoski

Robert Bell

(Philadelphia: 1768-1784)

Robert Bell, born in Glasgow, Scotland, in 1724, came to Philadelphia about 1767 and opened a bookshop on Third Street, selling books at retail and by auction. He published his first books in 1768, among them the first American edition of Samuel Johnson's *The History of Rasselas, Prince of Abissinia*. Bell's plan was to reprint English books at reduced prices, and his publications included Laurence Sterne's *A Sentimental Journey* (1770), Sir William Blackstone's *Commentaries on the Laws of England* (1771), Edward Young's *Night Thoughts* (1777), and James Thomson's *The Seasons* (1777). In January 1776 he published the pamphlet *Common Sense* by his former clerk Thomas Paine, and in 1777 he published in two volumes the first American edition of *Paradise Lost*. Bell was one of the most successful book auctioneers of his day, and died in Richmond, Virginia, in 1784 while on an auction trip. With his death the Robert Bell imprint ceased to appear.

References:

Robert Bell, *Illuminations for Legislators, and for Sentimentalists* (Philadelphia: Printed and sold by Robert Bell, 1784);

Carl and Jessica Bridenbaugh, *Rebels and Gentlemen: Philadelphia in the Age of Franklin* (New York: Reynal & Hitchcock, 1942);

Ruth Shepard Granniss, "The First American Edition of *Paradise Lost*," *Literary Miscellany*, 2 (1909): 4-9;

Robert F. Metzdorf, "The First American *Rasselas* and Its Imprint," *Papers of the Bibliographical Society of America*, 47 (1953): 374-376.

—*Kathleen McGowan*

Benziger Brothers
(New York: 1853-1972)
Benziger Publishing Company
(New York; Encino, California: 1972-   )

Benziger Brothers was founded at 311 Broadway in New York in 1853 as the American branch of the Swiss publishing firm established in Einsiedeln in 1792 by Joseph Charles Benziger. In 1860 the American firm became an independent company managed by the founder's grandsons, J. N. Adelrich Benziger and Louis Benziger. In 1867 the firm was named Printers to the Holy Apostolic See, which gave it the exclusive right to publish official liturgical texts of the Roman Catholic church. Benziger Brothers moved to 36 Barclay Street, in New York's Catholic publishing center, during the 1870s.

Early Benziger Brothers lists are dominated by devotional and prayer books; missals; lives of saints and other religious figures; and educational materials, including the Catholic National Series of Readers. From 1898 until 1921 the firm published *Benziger's Magazine*, an illustrated monthly, and for many years it also published the annual *Catholic Home Almanac*.

The firm's scope gradually broadened to in-

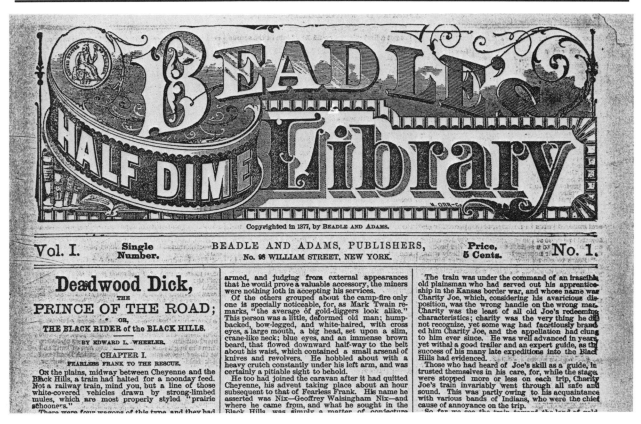

Page one of the first issue

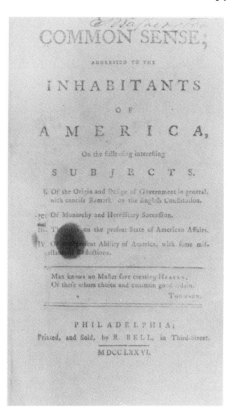

Thomas Paine, author of this anonymous work, had been a clerk
for Robert Bell

Joseph Charles Benziger

clude history, travel, philosophy, and fiction. Novels of manners, historical romances, and similar light fiction became an important part of the firm's listings during the late 1890s. Most of the novels published by Benziger had religious themes, including William Henry Anderdon's *The Catholic Crusoe; Adventures of Owen Evans* (1881) and titles in the American Author Series of Catholic Novels such as Walter Lecky's *Mr. Billy Buttons* (1896) and *Père Monnier's Ward* (1898). The firm also published novels by Maurice F. Egan, Leila Hardin Bugg, and Henryk Sienkiewicz. In 1913 Benziger inaugurated its Standard Fifty Cent Library series of novels by popular writers. By the middle of the twentieth century, Benziger Brothers had published more than 2,500 titles, the majority of which were religious or educational.

Benziger's early years were prosperous, and the firm opened several branches. The first, established at 217 Vine Street, Cincinnati, in 1860, moved to 143 Main Street in 1877. A St. Louis branch was founded in 1875 at 204 North Fifth Street. The Chicago branch opened in 1887 at 222 West Madison Street and moved to 214-216 West Monroe Street in 1912; the building was destroyed by fire in 1920 and the Chicago branch then moved to 205-207 West Washington Street. Branches were also opened in San Francisco in 1929 and Boston in 1937. In 1894 Benziger Brothers established a plant in Brooklyn to manufacture devotional objects and religious art. The firm also opened studios in Pietrasanta, Italy, for the production of marble art objects, and in 1926 established a plant in Bridgeport, Connecticut, to produce church brasses.

In 1932 the New York office moved to 26-28 Park Place. The company moved to 12 West Third Street and then to 6-8 Barclay Street in the 1950s and in 1960 to 7 East Fifty-first Street where it opened a retail store and sold books and church goods.

In 1968 Benziger Brothers was acquired by Crowell-Collier and Macmillan. In 1972 the firm became part of Crowell-Collier and Macmillan's educational subsidiary, Benziger Bruce and Glencoe, Incorporated and the name was changed to Benziger Publishing Company. Benziger's president, Jack E. Witmer, was elected president of the new company. Each of the three firms that made up the subsidiary continued to publish under its own imprint, with Benziger assuming responsibility for educational materials for elementary and secondary schools. Benziger's major series included the Benziger Readers, The Word is Life series of religious education books, and the environmental series, The Web of Life. The Bruce Publishing Company published titles in vocational education, and Glencoe Publishing Company published college textbooks. Later, the Bruce Publishing Company was discontinued and Benziger was made an imprint of the Glencoe Publishing Company. Glencoe's address is 17337 Ventura Boulevard, Encino, California 91316.

Reference:

"Famous Catholic House Has Diamond Anniversary: Benziger Bros., 1853-1928," *Publishers' Weekly*, 113 (18 February 1928): 673.

—*Judith Bushnell*

R. G. Berford Company
(Philadelphia and New York: circa 1840-1844)

During the early 1840s, the R. G. Berford Company was located in Publishers' Hall at 101 Chestnut Street, Philadelphia. Berford also published a small number of books in New York, mostly romances and temperance novels such as Timothy Shay Arthur's *The Seamstress: A Tale of the Times* (1843) and *Family Pride; or, The Palace and the Poor House* (1844). Other novelists whose works were published by the firm include George Lippard, whose *Herbert Tracy; or, The Legend of the Black Rangers* appeared in 1844, and Edward Judson.

—Judith Bushnell

Drexel Biddle
(Philadelphia: 1897-1904)
Drexel Biddle and Bradley
(Philadelphia: 1895-1897)

A member of a socially prominent Philadelphia family, Anthony Joseph Drexel Biddle attended private schools in Philadelphia and Meidelberg, Germany, then joined the staff of the *Philadelphia Ledger* as a reporter. In 1893 he began to contribute free-lance articles to magazines and newspapers.

In 1895 Biddle went into partnership with his brother-in-law Alexander Bradley to form the publishing company of Drexel Biddle and Bradley. The firm revived the *Philadelphia Sunday Graphic* with Biddle as editor, but the venture lasted only one year. Three of Biddle's own works, *The Madeira Islands, An Allegory and Three Essays,* and *The Froggy Fairy Book,* were published by the company in 1896. The partnership was dissolved in 1897, and Biddle went on alone as Drexel Biddle in the Drexel Building. In 1899 the firm moved to 228 South Fourth Street, with offices at 67 Fifth Avenue, New York, and The Strand, London.

Biddle continued to publish his own works,

including *Shantytown Sketches* (1897), *Word for Word and Letter for Letter: A Biographical Romance* (1898), and *The Second Froggy Fairy Book* (1898).

Other Drexel Biddle publications include *La Strega* (1899) by Ouida (Marie Louise de la Ramée), a translation of Guy de Maupassant's *Strong as Death* (1899), and Mrs. Mary Louisa Molesworth's *The Laurel Walk* (1899). "Three American Beauties" were advertised in 1903: Alfred Henry Lewis's *Peggy O'Neal* (1903); Jessie Carden in Frederick Upham Adams's *John Burt* (1903)—"a rattling good story of great force"; and "The Howard Chandler Christy girl, Indiana Stillwater" in Martha Morton's *Her Lord and Master* (1902). At this time the company's address was 415 Locust Street.

Biddle was well known in Philadelphia not only as an author, publisher, corporate executive, and traveler, but as an amateur boxer and sportsman. In 1904 he sold his publishing interests to the R. F. Fenno Company of New York and turned his attention to physical culture. He preached a creed of "athletic Christianity" and formed a Sunday school class to promote his beliefs. Drexel Biddle Bible Classes spread across the country and abroad, with some 300,000 members by 1910.

In World War I Biddle started a training camp for young Philadelphians, featuring calisthenics, gymnastics, and instruction in military maneuvers, and carried on this expertise as an officer in the Marines. During World War II, although nearly seventy, he was recalled from retirement to serve as a Marine instructor in hand-to-hand and bayonet fighting. Biddle died in 1948.

Reference:

"Col. A. J. Biddle Sr. Dead at Age of 73," *New York Times*, 28 May 1948, p. 23.

—Ruth H. Bennett

John Bioren
(Philadelphia: 1797-1835)
Bioren and Madan
(Philadelphia: 1795-1797)
Mountford, Bioren and Company
(Philadelphia: 1794-1797)

Born in 1772, John Bioren began his publishing career with the firm of Mountford, Bioren and Company in Philadelphia in 1794 and in April 1795 joined Patrick Madan in a partnership which lasted until January 1797. After that, he published under his own name. During his early partnerships Bioren oversaw the printing of *The Works of William Shakespeare* in eight duodecimo volumes. Three volumes appeared in 1795 and five in 1796. The American editor of the *Works* is believed to have been Joseph Hopkinson, a prominent Philadelphia lawyer, judge, and patron of the arts. Although the Bioren and Madan edition is largely reprinted from Dublin, Edinburgh, and London editions, including end notes by Samuel Johnson, the preface contains the first Shakespearean criticism to appear in America.

Bioren's other publications included a two-act play by Charles Kemble, *Plot and Counterplot, or The Portrait of Cervantes . . . as Performed at the Philadelphia Theatre* (1808), and many grammar texts and children's books. Among the children's books was an edition of *The Prize for Youthful Obedience* (1807), illustrated by Alexander Anderson, known as the father of wood-engraving in the United States. Other Bioren titles were *Plain Tales, for the Improvement of Youth* (1802), Elizabeth Somerville's *The Village Maid* (1802), and Thomas G. Condie's *The Juvenile Port-Folio, and Literary Miscellany* (1813).

Bioren's firm was located near the Customs House in the center of Philadelphia's business district. He was involved in many cooperative publishing arrangements, including a sixteen-year association with Mathew Carey, and often printed books and pamphlets for other publishers. Bioren died in 1835.

Reference:

Marian S. Carson and Marshall W. S. Swan, "John Bioren: Printer to Philadelphia Publishers," *Papers of the Bibliographical Society of America*, 43 (1949): 321-334.

—Deborah L. Brandt

Anthony Joseph Drexel Biddle

John Bioren

Presley Blakiston, cofounder with Robert Lindsay of Lindsay and Blakiston Company (courtesy of McGraw-Hill Publishing Company, Inc.)

Kenneth M. Blakiston became president of the firm following his father's death in 1898 (courtesy of McGraw-Hill Publishing Company, Inc.)

The Blakiston Company
(Philadelphia; New York: 1939-1954)
Lindsay and Blakiston Company
(Philadelphia: 1843-1882)
P. Blakiston Son and Company
(Philadelphia: 1882-1898)
P. Blakiston's Son and Company
(Philadelphia: 1898-1939)

Robert Lindsay and Presley Blakiston founded the Lindsay and Blakiston Company in 1843 at Fourth and Chestnut Streets in Philadelphia. The firm published a small, general list, with theological titles predominating until the late 1840s, when literary books became equally prominent. The company published Timothy Shay Arthur's *The Ruined Gamester; or, Two Eras in My Life* (1844) and a reprint of his *Family Pride; or, The Palace and the Poor House* (1844), Mrs. Tuthill's *Mirror of Life* (1847), David Bates's *Eolian* (1849), Mrs. Mary Robson Hughs's *May Morning; or, A Visit to the Country. For Little Boys and Girls* (1849), and Fanny Foley's *Romance of the Ocean* (1850). In 1851 the firm moved to 25 South Sixth Street. The company published H. H. Weld's *Star of Bethlehem; or, Stories for Christmas* (1851), Hannah Townsend's *History of England, in Verse* (1852), Bates's *Poems* (1853), T. Muegge's *Afraja: A Norwegian and Lapland Tale* (1854), and reprinted James Montgomery's *Poetical Works* (1852) and Mary Howitt's *Dial of Love, a Book for the Young* (1854). The firm later published Harriet B. McKeever's *Edith's Ministry* (1860) and *Woodcliff* (1865). Lindsay and Blakiston began to specialize in medical textbooks in the mid 1860s. In 1880 the company moved to 1012 Walnut Street. Two years later Lindsay retired and the firm was renamed P. Blakiston Son and Company. When Presley Blakiston died in 1898, his son Kenneth M. Blakiston became president and altered the firm's name slightly to P. Blakiston's Son and Company. In 1906 Blakiston became the official publisher for the American Red Cross.

Kenneth Blakiston died in 1937 and was succeeded by Horace G. White. The firm was reorganized in 1939 and became The Blakiston Company. During World War II Blakiston received the highest quotas for paper because of the demand for its *American Red Cross First Aid Textbook* (1940). The acquisition of the firm by Doubleday, Doran in 1944 allowed Doubleday access to a greater supply of paper while it gave Blakiston the opportunity to reenter the general publishing field.

Soon after becoming a Doubleday subsidiary, Blakiston published series of popular novels under the Triangle Books imprint. These Blakiston "Specials" were budget books, printed on cheap paper, and included reprints of *The Fountainhead* (1943) by Ayn Rand, *The Captain from Castile* (1945) by Samuel Shellabarger, and *China Flight* (1945) by Pearl Buck. Blakiston also reprinted works by Faith Baldwin and Kathleen Norris and published several series of nonfiction books. There were seven titles in the Harvard Books on Astronomy series, while the New Home Library provided original editions of informational guides for a dollar each.

In the summer of 1952 Blakiston moved all but its shipping department to 575 Madison Avenue, New York. In October 1954 McGraw-Hill Book Company purchased The Blakiston Company and the firm became the Blakiston Division, part of the McGraw-Hill Health Education Department. The Blakiston imprint was discontinued in 1967.

References:

"Blakiston Rounds Out 100 Years as Medical Publishers," *Publishers' Weekly*, 145 (8 January 1944): 117-119;

"Kenneth Blakiston [obituary]," *Publishers' Weekly*, 131 (30 January 1937): 537;

"McGraw Hill Announces Purchase of Blakiston,"

Publishers' Weekly, 166 (16 October 1954): 1635-1636;

One Hundred Years, 1843-1943 (Philadelphia: Blakiston, 1943);

"Presley Blakiston [obituary]," *Publishers' Weekly*, 53 (4 June 1898): 906-907;

"Robert Lindsay [obituary]," *Publishers' Weekly*, 42 (24 September 1892): 373-374.

—*Elizabeth Hoffman*

Blelock and Company
(New York: 1864-1869)

Located at 19 Beekman Street in New York and, as a wholesale bookseller, at 130 Canal Street in New Orleans, Blelock and Company published a modest number of books between 1864 and 1869, mostly titles on the wartime South and novels by women. Five Southern women had their first novels published by Blelock and Company. These included *Our Refugee Household* (1866) by Mrs. Louise Clack, *Ingemisco* (1867) by Marian C. L. Reeves, *Not a Hero* (1867) by Mrs. E. L. Pugh, *Cragfont* (1867) by Mrs. Emma L. Wynne, and *Albert Hastings* (1868) by Mrs. Mary Whitaker. In 1869 A. Eyrich of New Orleans succeeded Blelock and Company.

—*Theodora Mills*

E. Bliss and E. White
(New York: 1821-1826)
White and Bliss
(New York: 1821)
E. Bliss
(New York: 1826-1833)

The bookselling and publishing firm of Elam Bliss and Elihu White was located at 128 Broadway in New York from 1821 to 1826. White's name disappeared from the imprint after 1826, but Bliss continued to publish books until 1833, when difficult economic times and the dissatisfaction of his most famous author, William Cullen Bryant, ended his publishing career.

In 1821, under the imprint White and Bliss, there appeared, in pamphlet form, a speech given by the writer Gulian Crommelin Verplanck to the New York Historical Society in December 1818. Renamed E. Bliss and E. White, the firm published *A New-England Tale; or, Sketches of New-England Character and Manners* (1822), *Redwood* (1824), and *The Travellers; A Tale, Designed for Young People* (1825), all by Catharine Maria Sedgwick.

On 10 August 1822 Bliss and White were first listed as publishers of the *Minerva; or, Literary, Entertaining and Scientific Journal.* This four-column, eight-page weekly was first published on 6 April 1822 by the editor, G. L. Birch, at 44 Maiden Lane, "and at the office of the Long Island Patriot, Brooklyn." In the forty-eighth issue in March 1823, George Houston was listed as editor; in October 1823 the poet James G. Brooks became the literary and poetry editor. In 1824 the format of the magazine was changed to double-column, larger type, and sixteen pages. The last issue of the magazine was dated September 1825.

While publishing the *Minerva*, Bliss and White became interested in starting a journal that would develop and encourage American writers. The *Atlantic Magazine*, an eighty-page monthly, appeared in May 1824, with Robert Charles Sands as editor. Sands left after six months, and the journal continued under the editorship of Dr. Henry James Anderson.

In the same month that the *Atlantic Magazine* first appeared, fifty-eight New Yorkers interested in the arts and sciences formed the Athenaeum Society. The members discussed with Bliss and White the possibility of publishing a magazine that would express the interests of the society. Because the society wanted a general magazine and the publishers a literary review, a compromise was effected in April 1825 with the transformation of the *Atlantic Magazine* into the *New York Review and Athenaeum Magazine*. Bryant was hired to edit the publication.

The combined review-magazine published contributions from Bryant, Anderson, Sands, Fitz-Greene Halleck, Henry Wadsworth Longfellow, N. P. Willis, George Bancroft, and the elder R. H. Dana. Nevertheless, it was hard to find contributions, and the *New York Review and Athenaeum Magazine* was merged in July 1826 with the older Boston journal, the *United States Literary Gazette*. In October the name was changed to *United States Review and Literary Gazette*, and the magazine was from then on published in Boston by Bowles and Dearborn and in New York by G. and C. Carvill.

After these magazine publishing ventures, Bliss devoted himself to book publishing. Among his publications were George Tucker's fantasy satire *A Voyage to the Moon* (1827), Mrs. L. Larned's *The Sanfords* (1830), Hannah F. Lee's *Grace Seymour* (1830), and James Lawson's *Tales and Sketches, by a Cosmopolite* (1830). The outstanding books of the firm's last years were the three numbers of the gift annual *The Talisman* (1828-1830) and Bryant's *Poems* (1832). *The Talisman* was a joint production of three friends—Bryant, Sands, and Verplanck—who used the pseudonym Francis Herbert. George Palmer Putnam described these "elegant" little books as "the father of American 'annuals' and a good deal better than some of the children." Because the authors were too busy with other things and not all in New York City, it was discontinued; but Bliss republished it in 1833 as *Miscellanies First Published under the Name of the Talisman*. The *Poems* of 1832 was the first collection of Bryant's poetry since 1821. The book sold well for the first half of the thousand-copy run in spite of the rather high price of $1.25, but by the end of the year Bliss still had 100 unsold copies.

References:

Henry W. Boynton, *Annals of American Bookselling 1638-1950* (New York: Wiley, 1932), p. 168;

Charles H. Brown, *William Cullen Bryant* (New York: Scribners, 1971), pp. 127, 129, 164, 170, 182-183, 196, 217.

—*Theodora Mills*

Robert Bonner's Sons
(New York: 1887-1903)

Robert Bonner's Sons was established in 1887 to continue the *New York Ledger*, a successful story paper, and to publish in book form the popular literature from the *Ledger*. Combining the characteristics of newspapers and magazines, the story papers reached the masses of new readers. These papers, usually weeklies, were the forerunners of dime novels. Subtitled *A Journal of Choice Literature, Romance and Useful Information*, Bonner's *New York Ledger* was one of the most widely read of these papers.

Robert Bonner was born near Londonderry, Northern Ireland, on 28 April 1824. He came to the United States in 1839 and settled near Hartford, Connecticut, where he was soon employed on the *Hartford Courant* as a printer's devil. His printing skill was fabled: it is reported that he set 25,500 ems of solid type in twenty hours and twenty-eight minutes.

Bonner soon began to write for newspapers. His correct, lucid, and entertaining style appealed to the common reader. In 1844 he went to New York, where he was a correspondent for several newspapers and a proofreader and assistant foreman on N. P. Willis's *Evening Mirror*. He also came into contact with favorite writers of the day.

Bonner soon became the printer for the *Merchant's Ledger*, a publication for the dry goods trade. In 1851 he purchased the paper for $500. He gradually began to print stories in the obscure *Merchant's Ledger*, which he renamed the *New York Ledger* in 1855. It became a story paper, filled with serials, short stories, poetry, editorials, and humor columns.

From the start the fledgling publisher determined to pay whatever was necessary to secure leading writers. In 1855 he approached Sara Payson Parton, who, under the pseudonym Fanny Fern, was an author of light fiction and essays then at the height of her popularity. He first offered her twenty-five dollars per column, then fifty and seventy-five dollars. The writer balked at having her work appear next to business news but finally agreed to $100 per column. Consequently, for her ten-column story "Fanny Ford," she received the unprecedented amount of $1,000. This startling payment generated excellent publicity. Despite generous fees to authors and the absence of advertising, Bonner was able to sell his weekly cheaply and still make a profit from circulation alone. A subscription in 1855 was a dollar per year.

Although he carried no advertising in his paper, Bonner showed a remarkable faculty for arranging displays and advertising in other publications. Advertising boosted the circulation of his paper to nearly half a million. Bonner's theory was to catch the eye and lure the mind by manipulation of type, by repetition, and by innovative techniques. He would, for example, purchase a whole page in other newspapers and fill it with a reiteration of such short sentences as "Read the *New York Ledger*." He originated the trick of beginning a story in another paper and then ending it abruptly with the announcement that it would be continued in the *Ledger*.

Bonner continued to purchase the work of popular writers. He secured a series of short articles from the orator and essayist Edward Everett by pledging $10,000 toward the purchase and preservation of Mount Vernon. He paid Charles Dickens $5,000 for "Hunted Down," the only story Dickens ever wrote for an American publication. Tennyson received the same amount for a poem, and Longfellow got $3,000 for some short poems. Henry Ward Beecher received $30,000 for *Norwood*, which appeared serially in 1866 before Scribners published it in book form the following year; at the head of the title page of the Scribners edition was "*From The New York Ledger*." Other noted writers who contributed to the *Ledger* included Harriet Beecher Stowe, William Cullen Bryant, Horace Greeley, Timothy Shay Arthur, Louisa May Alcott, George Bancroft, N. P. Willis, George L. Raymond, Emerson Bennett, and Lydia H. Sigourney. Two of Bonner's most frequent and popular contributors were Mrs. E. D. E. N. Southworth and Sylvanus Cobb, Jr.

After years of success Bonner retired in 1887. The business passed into the hands of his sons, Andrew Allen, Robert Edwin, and Frederick, all three of whom had been part of the paper for the previous ten years. Robert Bonner's Sons, with offices at William and Spruce Streets, soon began to publish *Ledger* stories in book form.

Cobb had formed an association with the *Ledger* in 1856 which lasted for the remainder of his life. Bonner had lured Cobb from a Boston story paper, *The Flag of Our Union*. It was probably

Robert E. Bonner, founder of the New York Ledger

Front page of an issue of Bonner's popular and successful story paper

Cobb who helped most to make the *Ledger* dominant in the popular field. In thirty-one years he contributed 122 novelettes, 862 short stories, and 2,143 sketches. Cobb is said to have been the first to mass produce popular fiction. His stories have been described as "at once moral and sensational, romantic and naive, pious and sentimental." His *The Gunmaker of Moscow* (1888) was tremendously popular and often reprinted. At least nineteen books by Cobb were published under the Bonner imprint.

Mrs. Southworth wrote more than sixty romances, which sold millions of copies for various publishers. Her melodramatic and sentimental plots were full of catastrophes and deliverances, a formula which Bonner encouraged. She first appeared under the Bonner imprint in 1889 with *A Leap in the Dark, Nearest and Dearest, Unknown,* and *The Hidden Hand*. A Bonner ad, quoting the *Passaic Herald,* gives at once an idea of the popularity of the company's wares, the role of advertising, and the serial-to-book sequence: "The most valuable and popular story ever published in the *New York Ledger* was Mrs. Southworth's *The Hidden Hand*. So great was the demand for it that it was republished in the *Ledger* three times! The cry came from everywhere: 'Publish this great story in book form!' And now it is published in book form and is eagerly read by thousands of admirers." Altogether, the firm published sixteen titles by Mrs. Southworth during the latter part of her career.

Bonner published six books by Harriet Newell Lewis; the first, *Her Double Life* (1888), was among the earliest of the company's books. Other Bonner authors are today equally obscure. Three of Laura Jean Libbey's tearfully sentimental books were pub-

lished by Bonner in 1890: *Ione, A Mad Betrothal,* and *Parted by Fate*. Four novels by Jean Kate Ludlam appeared in the early 1890s, along with works by Robert Grant, John Habberton, William Henry Peck, and Maurice Thompson. Typically, these books sold for a dollar each in cloth, half that in paper.

In 1890 the house brought out two novels by Anna Katharine Green, *The Forsaken Inn* and *A Matter of Millions*. The firm published *A Son of Old Harry* (1891) by Albion W. Tourgee and *The Return of the O'Mahony* (1892) by Harold Frederic. Amelia E. Barr wrote competent, wholesome historical fiction with Texas, New York City, and the English countryside as backgrounds. The firm published *Mrs. Barr's Short Stories* (1891) and four other books by her.

In 1898 the weekly *Ledger* became the *Ledger Monthly*. Robert Bonner died on 6 July of the following year. In 1901 the *Ledger* was sold, and in 1903 it ceased publication. It was also in 1903 that Robert Bonner's Sons was dissolved. Street and Smith purchased the plates of the firm's books and republished many of the novels in its ten-cent line.

References:

Ralph Admari, "Bonner and *The Ledger*," *American Book Collector*, 6 (1935): 176-193;

Stanwood Cobb, *The Magnificent Partnership* (New York: Vantage, 1954);

Elisha Jay Edwards, "Robert Bonner," *Review of Reviews*, 20 (1899): 161-165;

"New York Ledger," *Fourth Estate*, 10 (6 October 1898): 1-2.

—Vincent Prestianni

Book Supply Company

(Chicago: 1895-1920)

Elsbery W. Reynolds founded the Book Supply Company, a mail-order house at 266-268 Wabash Avenue, Chicago, in 1895. Incorporated in 1899, the firm continued inconspicuously until Reynolds met Harold Bell Wright, who was preaching at a revival meeting. From this encounter came Wright's first novel, *That Printer of Udell's* (1903). The Book Supply Company advertised the book heavily and successfully; reprinted in 1911, it sold more than 450,000 copies. The firm published Wright's *The Shepherd of the Hills* in 1907 and *The Calling of Dan Matthews* in 1909, and sales continued to rise. Months before a new Wright novel was ready, the Book Supply Company would begin its relentless advertising campaign in newspapers of many cities and in *Publishers' Weekly. The Uncrowned King* was published in 1910, *The Winning of Barbara Worth* in 1911, and *Their Yesterdays* in 1912. The Book Supply Company moved to 220-222 West Monroe Avenue in 1910 and to 231-233 West Monroe the following year. By 1913 the firm claimed to have sold over four million copies of Wright's books, although his works were held in contempt by critics. In certain regions of America Wright's works, with their emphasis on homespun morality and the virtues of rugged, independent living, are still in demand.

In 1916, with the publication of *When a Man's a Man*, the Book Supply Company described itself as "publishers of Harold Bell Wright's books." He may by then have been the firm's sole author. In 1919 *The Re-Creation of Brian Kent* appeared, and early the following year the last advertisement of the Book Supply Company was carried in *Publishers' Weekly*. Wright's later works were published by better-known houses.

—*Arlene Shaner*

Bowen-Merrill Company

(Indianapolis: 1885-1903)

See also the Bobbs-Merrill Company entry in *DLB 46, American Literary Book Publishers, 1900-1980: Trade and Paperback.*

In 1838 Samuel Merrill and E. H. Hood opened a bookstore in Indianapolis. In 1851 Merrill bought out Hood and expanded the bookstore operation to include publishing. Merrill's early efforts were directed toward publishing law books, and by 1859 his company had gross sales of over $10,000 per year in this area. Merrill's son, Samuel Merrill, Jr., gradually took over the business, and after his return from Civil War service directed the firm through a variety of consolidations and name changes—Merrill, Field and Company; Merrill, Hubbard and Company; and Merrill, Meigs and Company.

The first important Merrill, Meigs literary publication was James Whitcomb Riley's *The Old Swimmin' Hole and 'Leven More Poems* (1883). This book had been published earlier by G. C. Hitt, another Indianapolis publisher; but it was after Merrill, Meigs acquired the rights and published its edition that the book achieved tremendous success.

In 1853 William Stewart, a Maryland bookseller, bought a one-third interest in the Indianapolis firm of H. West and Company. In 1854 Stewart, along with Silas T. Bowen, purchased the entire West business and renamed it Bowen, Stewart and Company. Bowen, Stewart was not involved in book publishing; instead, it concentrated exclusively on the retailing and wholesaling of books and stationery supplies.

In 1885 Bowen, Stewart merged with Merrill, Meigs to form the Bowen-Merrill Company at 18 West Washington Street in Indianapolis, the plant of Bowen, Stewart. Already employed with Bowen, Stewart at this time were two men who soon came into prominence with the new firm: William Conrad Bobbs became head of the law book department; John Jay Curtis served successively as retail department manager, secretary, and vice-president. Both men later became presidents of the firm. Merrill retired in 1890. Following the success of

1912 advertisement. The company published Wright's first novel in 1903 and by 1913 claimed to have sold over four million copies of his books.

The Old Swimmin' Hole, by 1898 Bowen-Merrill was offering thirteen Riley titles. As Riley became the most popular poet of his time, the firm reaped enormous profits from the sales of his books.

Around the turn of the century Bowen-Merrill's literary lists were dominated by fiction, which achieved even greater success than did the poetry of Riley. Like many other publishing houses, Bowen-Merrill found that historical fiction was particularly popular with American readers. Included on the firm's lists were Charles Major's *When Knighthood Was in Flower* (1898), published under the pseudonym Edwin Caskoden; Maurice Thompson's *Alice of Old Vincennes* (1900); Charles Frederic Goss's *The Redemption of David Corson* (1900); and Emerson Hough's *The Mississippi Bubble* (1902). But the firm's best-selling title during this period—indeed, its most popular title ever—was L. Frank Baum's *The Wonderful Wizard of Oz* (1902), to which Bowen-Merrill obtained the rights after a Chicago publisher, George L. Hill, had brought out a moderately successful edition in 1900. By the time *The Wonderful Wizard of Oz* went out of copyright in the 1950s more than three million copies had been sold.

Most of Bowen-Merrill's turn-of-the-century popular novels are now forgotten. During their own time, however, these books achieved phenomenal success, due largely to the innovative advertising and marketing techniques developed by Curtis. He used mass advertising to market the firm's books, a remarkable break with tradition at the time. Curtis also introduced the colored book jacket and the jacket blurb. He established a New York office for Bowen-Merrill in 1898.

Bowen-Merrill continued to publish a strong list of law books, primarily on Indiana State law. In 1898 the firm purchased the Houghton Mifflin law list, which included over twenty works by some of the best-known legal minds of the time.

In 1903 Bowen-Merrill became the Bobbs-Merrill Company when Bobbs, who had become president of Bowen-Merrill when Bowen died in 1895, officially replaced Bowen in the partnership.

References:

Edwin H. Cady, ed., "Studies in the Bobbs-Merrill Papers," *Indiana University Bookman,* 8 (1967): 1-116;

John Jay Curtis, "Reminiscences of a Publisher," *Publishers' Weekly,* 117 (10 May 1930): 2419-2420;

The Hoosier House (Indianapolis: Bobbs-Merrill, 1923);

"John Jay Curtis, 1857-1931," *Publishers' Weekly,* 120 (1 August 1931): 409-410;

Jack O'Bar, "A History of the Bobbs-Merrill Company 1850-1940: With a Postlude through the Early 1960s," Ph.D. dissertation, Indiana University, 1975;

"William C. Bobbs, 1861-1926, Old Indianapolis House Loses Its Chief," *Publishers' Weekly,* 109 (20 February 1926): 604-606.

—Timothy D. Murray

John Bradburn
(New York: 1861-1866)

John Bradburn was born in Ireland in 1805 and came to America in 1820. He became a bookseller at 122 Fulton Street, New York, during the 1850s and published nearly fifty books from 1861 through 1866. His imprints give his address as 49 Walker Street, and sometimes further identify him as "successor to M. Doolady," although Doolady was publishing independently at the same time.

Bradburn's publications are remarkable for their diversity. They include two titles about the sea, both translations from French. On slavery and the Civil War he published for the tastes of both sides, while favoring the South. The oddest of his books on these themes was *Subgenation: The Theory of the Normal Relation of the Races, an Answer to "Miscegenation"* (1864) by John H. Van Evrie.

Literature predominated among Bradburn's publications and included reprints of English classics such as Dickens's *Our Mutual Friend* (1865) and translations from Victor Hugo and Spanish and German authors. The bulk of the literature he published was American, mostly by minor authors such as Virginia Frances Townsend, Margaret Hosmer, and Leonard Kip. Bradburn's preference for the cause of the South was illustrated by his publication of *Macaria; or, Altars of Sacrifice* by Mrs. Augusta Jane Wilson in 1864, the same year the Richmond publishers West and Johnson published it. The volume was such a powerful defense of the Confederate cause that it was banned by a Union Army officer. Bradburn also published two editions of the popular Mrs. Wilson's first book, *Inez; A Tale of the Alamo*, in 1864 and 1865.

—Theodora Mills

Ira Bradley and Company
(Boston: circa 1876-1890)
Bradley and Woodruff
(Boston: 1890-1893)
A. I. Bradley
(Boston: 1893-1900)

Located at 162 Washington Street in Boston during the late nineteenth century, Ira Bradley and Company published literary works on a small scale. One of the firm's more interesting publications was a novel called *Gwendolen* (1878), which was advertised as an anonymous sequel to George Eliot's *Daniel Deronda* and published so as to resemble Eliot's novel.

In 1890 the firm's imprint changed to Bradley and Woodruff and the address to 234-236 Congress Street. In February 1893 the partnership dissolved and Bradley continued under the name of A. I. Bradley and Company. Among the firm's fiction publications during its twenty-four-year history were Amelia E. Barr's *The Preacher's Daughter* (1892), three works by Mary Denison, and one by John Habberton. The firm also published juveniles, particularly by the prolific British writer Evelyn E. Green, and religious books. On 26 March 1900 a fire in the upper stories of the building on Congress Street badly damaged the stock. Bradley moved temporarily to 56 Summer Street, where he intended to carry on the business. Nothing more was heard of the firm.

—Theodora Mills

J. W. Bradley and Company
(Philadelphia: circa 1849-1887)
Bradley and Company
(Philadelphia: 1887-1888)

J. W. Bradley and Company was first located at 48 North Fourth Street in Philadelphia and moved to 66 North Fourth Street. Perhaps the earliest Bradley publication was the 1849 first edition of *Sketches of Life and Character* by Timothy Shay Arthur. Bradley was one of Arthur's main publishers, often sharing the imprint with some other house: thus, the first edition of *Ten Nights in a Bar-Room* (1854), Arthur's best-known work, bears the imprint "Philadelphia: Lippincott, Grambo and Co.; J. W. Bradley." Bradley published or had a hand in publishing at least sixteen titles by the prolific temperance novelist.

Bradley published works of history, biography, and travel, but fiction accounted for more than half of the firm's output. Titles included John Townsend Trowbridge's *The Deserted Family; or, Wanderings of an Outcast* (1853), Martha Russell's *Sibyl; or, Out of the Shadow into the Sun* (1857), and Emerson Bennett's *Intriguing for a Princess: An Adventure with Mexican Banditti* (1859). Other novelists whose works were published by Bradley include Peregrine Herne, George Canning Hill, Virginia Francis Townsend, and Daniel Pierce Thompson. By 1887 the firm's name had changed to Bradley and Company. The firm ceased publishing in 1888.

—Judith Bushnell

Frederic A. Brady
(New York: 1858?-1873?)

The Frederic A. Brady publishing house opened around 1858 at 126 Nassau Street, New York. Within a year or so the firm moved to 24 Ann Street; late in 1864 it moved to 22 Ann Street. Brady publications mainly catered to popular taste for tales of adventure, crime, mystery, and fallen women. The most famous of Brady's dime novelists was Ned Buntline, the pseudonym of Edward Zane Carroll Judson, who wrote more than twenty novels for Brady, including *Clarence Rhett; or, The Cruise of the Privateer* (1866). John Hovey Robinson wrote about fifteen novels for Brady. Justin Jones, who signed his works as Jack Brace, and Joseph Holt Ingraham also wrote for Brady. Brady published several novels by Mary O. Francis under her pen name Margaret Blount, and Mrs. May Agnes Francis Fleming wrote half a dozen novels for Brady under the names May Carleton and M. A. Earlie. Brady also published satire, including *Comic Lectures on Everything in General and Nothing in Particular* (1860?) by Deacon Snowball and Diedrich Lager-Bladder and *War Letters of a Disbanded Volunteer, Embracing His Experiences as Honest Abe's Bosum Friend and Unofficial Advisor* (1864) by Joseph Barber.

After 1862 the firm turned chiefly to reprinting novellas that had appeared in magazines, especially the *New York Mercury*. Buntline's *The Rattlesnake; or, The Rebel Privateer* (1865) first appeared in the *Mercury* in 1862.

Brady advertised some of Blount's newly published novels in the *American Literary Gazette* and exchanged novels with U. P. James of Cincinnati and with T. B. Peterson and Brother of Philadelphia. Brady paperback octavos sold for ten, fifteen, twenty-five, or fifty cents. After 1867 Brady published infrequently and ceased operations by 1873.

—Joseph J. Hinchliffe

Samuel Merrill

Ned Buntline (Edward Zane Carroll Judson), who wrote more than twenty novels for Frederic A. Brady (photograph by Sarony)

Charles H. Brainard
(Boston: 1843-1845)

Charles H. Brainard of 82 Washington Street, Boston, published sensational novels in cheap editions between 1843 and 1845. These included two titles each by Boston writers Francis A. Durivage and Augustine J. H. Duganne, and *Ellen Merton, the Belle of Lowell* (1844), an unattributed romance.

Brainard also published *Fialto, or The Chain of Crime* (1843), based on Eugene Sue's *Mathilde, Memoires d'un Jeune Fille.*

—*Theodora Mills*

Brentano's
(New York: 1885-1933)

August Brentano, an Austrian immigrant, began as a news dealer in 1856 at Broadway and Houston Street in New York. Moving up Broadway, the store reached Union Square, where it remained until 1907; then it moved north to 225 Fifth Avenue, where it reached the pinnacle of its success. Two nephews, August and Arthur Brentano, came to work for their uncle in 1873, followed the next year by their brother Simon; and in 1877 the brothers purchased the interests of their uncle, who wanted to retire. August Brentano died in 1886.

The firm began publishing in a small way in 1885. In 1887 the brothers formed a corporation capitalized at $300,000 and opened stores in Chicago, Washington, London, and Paris; the latter two stores were independent corporations. In 1892 a devastating fire in New York did not interrupt business for more than a day, and by 1894 the brothers, again as a partnership, moved into a store built for them at Sixteenth and Broadway. The eldest, August, died in 1899; Simon and Arthur managed the business during the depression of the 1890s. Simon became the president and the principal director of the business; Arthur was vice-president, with rare books his speciality; Charles E. Butler was secretary; and Claude Mecklen served

as treasurer. Simon Brentano died in 1915, leaving his majority interest in the company to his widow and sons, Lowell and August.

Lowell, his wife, his cousin Arthur Brentano, Jr., and Butler continued to expand both the publishing and retail parts of the business. In the 1920s Arthur Brentano, Jr., added a new main store at 1 West Forty-seventh Street to the old store at 225 Fifth Avenue; he also established three other Manhattan branches and stores in Philadelphia, Pittsburgh, and Cleveland. He was also active in the American Booksellers Association, where he was a leader in the opposition to book clubs, especially the Literary Guild of America, which undercut bookstores.

The firm published reprints, foreign-language textbooks and literary translations, art books, some game books in the early days, light fiction, and popular and even controversial nonfiction, such as works by Margaret Sanger. These publications were often grouped in series. The drama series included Harvard Plays of the 47 Workshop and the Dramatic Club; Modern English Dramatists, which featured the plays of Eden Philpotts; and contemporary works in the British Drama League Plays. Works of George Bernard

Shaw were the most important publications of the house, but there were other collected works, such as those of Edgar E. Saltus.

The variety of Brentano's publications is suggested in titles ranging from *Baby's Biography* (1891), a gift book for new parents, to *The Life of Benvenuto Cellini* (1906), translated by John Aldington Symonds. Translations were published in the Lotus Library of Continental Masterpieces, which included Stendhal's *The Red and the Black* (1898), Flaubert's *Madame Bovary* (1919), and Barbey D'Auervilly's *Story without a Name* (1919). The Wayside series ranged from the *Rubáiyát of Omar Khayyám* (1907) to Kipling's *Soldier Tales* (1909). The Wisdom series offered *Wisdom of Benjamin Franklin* (1906), *Wisdom of Oscar Wilde* (1906), *Wisdom of Ralph Waldo Emerson* (1911), and *Wisdom of the Egyptians* (1923). Reprints predominated in Brentano's lists, but the firm was the first publisher of *Eight More Harvard Poets* (1923), edited by Foster Damon and Robert Hillyer, and *Thalassa* (1906)

and *A Dull Girl's Destiny* (1907), two of Mrs. Gertrude M. Reynolds's many titles.

When the stock market crash came in October 1929, Brentano's was especially vulnerable because of its rapid expansion. In February 1933 the publishing business was sold to Coward-McCann except for the rights to Shaw's publications, which went to Dodd, Mead. The firm survived as a bookseller by going into receivership and involuntary bankruptcy, and reorganizing.

References:
"August Brentano [obituary]," *Publishers' Weekly*, 55 (13 May 1899): 785;

"Obituary Note: Charles E. Butler," *Publishers' Weekly*, 105 (23 February 1924): 609;

"Obituary Notes: Simon Brentano," *Publishers' Weekly*, 87 (20 February 1915): 580-581;

"The Will of Simon Brentano," *Publishers' Weekly*, 87 (6 March 1915): 670.

—Theodora Mills

Job Buffum

(Boston: 1850-circa 1861)

Job Buffum, originally from Nashua, New Hampshire, was a publisher in Boston until the Civil War. Between 1850 and 1853 he published four small selections of English poetry edited by John Stowell Adams, a minor American writer interested in spiritualism and music. In 1855 he published *Town and Country,* a book of short stories by

Adams. This volume was republished by Buffum in 1856, and in 1858 G. W. Cottrell put it out with the title *Half-Hour Stories of Choice Reading. Lucretia, the Quakeress,* an antislavery novel by Mrs. Phebe Ann Hanaford, was published in 1853.

—Theodora Mills

Bunce and Brother
(New York: 1852-1856)

Bunce and Brother was established in 1852 at 134 Nassau Street in New York. Its founder, Oliver Bell Bunce, was a moderately successful novelist and dramatist who turned to publishing largely to find a more lucrative outlet for his literary talents. The attempt failed: Bunce and Brother went out of business four years later.

The company's first publication was *The Romance of the Revolution* (1852), a collection of revolutionary anecdotes compiled by Bunce. During the next four years, Bunce published several novels, including Stuart Godman's *The Ocean-Born* (1852), Frederick Chamier's *Jack Adams, the Mutineer* (1853), Ann Sophia Stephens's *Fashion and Famine* (1854) and *The Old Homestead* (1855), John Brougham's *A Basket of Chips* (1855), and the anonymous *Blanche Dearwood* (1855), "a new romance of American life." By 1855 Bunce and Brother had moved to 126 Nassau Street, where Bunce's drama *Fate; or, The Prophecy* was published in 1856. The firm ceased operations that year.

After Bunce and Brother failed, Bunce became manager of the publishing house of James G. Gregory; he later served a brief period with Harper and Brothers before becoming literary manager of D. Appleton and Company in 1867. He stayed with Appleton for the remainder of his life, editing *Appleton's Journal* and conceiving and executing such enormously successful projects as Appleton's *Picturesque America* (1872-1874), of which nearly a million sets were sold.

Reference:
"Oliver Bell Bunce [obituary]," *New York Times,* 17 May 1890, p. 649.

—Donna Nance

Burgess, Stringer and Company
(New York: 1843-1848)
Burgess and Garrett
(New York: 1848-1850)
Garrett, Dick and Fitzgerald
(New York: 1850-1851)

Wesley Burgess and James Stringer founded Burgess, Stringer and Company in New York in 1843. Located at 222 Broadway under P. T. Barnum's American Museum, the firm sold books and published periodicals, music, and low-priced fiction. In the 1840s technological, political, and social factors led to the establishment of cheap book production in both hardcover and paperback, and a whole new reading public emerged. Burgess and Stringer exploited this revolution, selling huge quantities of paper-covered volumes at twenty-five cents each, and became one of America's largest producers of inexpensive books during this "cheap-publishing era."

The most prominent writer on the Burgess, Stringer list was James Fenimore Cooper, whose works the company reprinted in thirty-three volumes, some of which were illustrated by F. O. C. Darley. The series included *Mercedes of Castile* (1845), as well as such better-known works as *The Pilot* (1845), *The Red Rover* (1845), *The Spy* (1845), and *The Redskins* (1846). The company sold large quantities of the Cooper novels and reprinted them frequently. Burgess, Stringer also published several works by William Gilmore Simms, then regarded as one of the foremost Southern men of letters. His *Castle Dismal; or, The Bachelor's Christmas* was published in 1844 and reprinted the following year. Simms's *Helen Halsey; or, The Swamp State of Conelachita* was published in 1845.

During the cheap book boom of the 1840s publishers began to draw heavily upon American writers, who, as a result, proliferated rapidly. Burgess and Stringer published works by many of these new American authors, including the political satirist Seba Smith's *May-Day in New York* (1845) and Anna Sophia Stephens's *High Life in New York* (1845), published under the pseudonym Jonathan Slick. The firm published Joseph Holt Ingraham's *The Cruiser of the Mist* (1845) and reprinted Joseph Clay Neal's *Charcoal Sketches; or, Scenes in a Metropolis* (1848). Burgess, Stringer also published works by Timothy Shay Arthur, Lewis Gaylord Clark, and Henry William Herbert.

Stringer left Burgess, Stringer and Company in 1848 to found Stringer and Townsend, also at 222 Broadway. He was replaced as Burgess's partner by Ransom Garrett, and the firm became Burgess and Garrett. Burgess sold his interest in 1850 to Garrett, William Brisbane Dick, and Lawrence R. Fitzgerald; the company's name then changed to Garrett, Dick and Fitzgerald and finally, in 1851, to Dick and Fitzgerald.

—*Gary R. Treadway*

A. L. Burt Company
(New York: 1902-1937)
A. L. Burt
(New York: 1883-1902)

In 1883, after more than thirty years as a salesman, Albert L. Burt opened an office at 105 John Street, New York, and published *The National Standard Dictionary*, which was offered as a premium by mail order houses. Burt specialized in printing classics and standard works in sets at prices from twenty-five cents to one dollar per volume. After moving to 65 Beekman Street in 1890, Burt initiated his best-known series, Burt's Home Library (of Classics from the World's Best Books). This set of well-printed, clothbound classics was begun with twenty-five titles, among them Goldsmith's *The Vicar of Wakefield*, Irving's *The Sketch-Book*, and *Discourses of Epictetus*. Burt moved to 97-101 Reade Street in 1894 and to 52-58 Duane Street in 1899.

The firm was incorporated as the A. L. Burt Company in 1902 and began to compete with Grosset and Dunlap for reprint rights to popular fiction. Burt's series included American Copyright Novels, Burt's Copyright Fiction, and Burt's Reprint Copyright Fiction. Burt died on 28 December 1913. His sons Harry P. Burt (president and treasurer), Frederick A. Burt (secretary), and Edward F. Burt (assistant treasurer) carried on the business. The following year the A. L. Burt Company moved to 114-120 East Twenty-third Street.

One of the first areas that Burt entered was children's fiction. Books for girls were published in the Wellesley, Fireside, and Little Women series; books for boys, in the Rugby and Little Men series; other series included the Mother Goose series, the Jules Verne series, the Fairy Library, and the Alger series. Howard R. Garis's books comprised the Uncle Wiggily Bed Time series, and forty books by G. A. Henty made up the Henty series. Burt was the first to offer the Tarzan books of Edgar Rice Burroughs, including *Tarzan of the Apes* (1914) and *The Son of Tarzan* (1918), in popularly priced editions. In 1925 Burt took over the children's books of Elsie Dinsmore and with aggressive promotion brought them to renewed popularity; hundreds of thousands of copies were sold at fifty cents apiece in the 1930s.

Zane Grey self-published his first novel, *Betty Zane* (1903), but it sold poorly. In 1906 Burt published Grey's second novel, *The Spirit of the Border*, which eventually sold well. Burt published Grey's *The Last Trail* in 1909 before Grey signed with Harper. In 1911 Burt made arrangements to publish fifty-cent editions of Harold Bell Wright's books. Burt reprinted E. Phillips Oppenheim's *The Great Impersonation* (1920) and P. G. Wodehouse's *Jeeves* (1925), both of which had steady sales. Burt also reprinted works by Arthur Conan Doyle, O. Henry, Joseph C. Lincoln, Edgar Wallace, Rex Beach, Kathleen and Charles Norris, Sax Rohmer, and Robert W. Chambers. Although A. L. Burt published Burt's Foreign Dictionaries, the Crescent Library, Burt's Standard Reference Books, and other nonfiction, it is best known for its reprints of fiction.

In August 1930 George Sully and Company was liquidated and the plates and copyrights were sold to Burt. Sully's stock included anthologies, cookbooks, and guides to opera, etiquette, speechmaking, letter-writing, and games.

By 1933 Burt was the second largest reprint house in the United States, after Grosset and Dunlap, and in 1936 only Grosset and Dunlap, Macmillan, Doubleday, and Oxford published more books than A. L. Burt. When Blue Ribbon Books bought A. L. Burt in February 1937 there were 2,000 titles by 450 authors on Burt's reprint list.

References:

"A. L. Burt & Company Bought by Blue Ribbon Books," *Publishers' Weekly,* 131 (6 March 1937): 1117-1118;

"Burt Celebrates Fiftieth Anniversary," *Publishers' Weekly,* 124 (15 July 1933): 163-164;

"Obituary Notes: Albert L. Burt," *Publishers' Weekly,* 85 (3 January 1914): 21.

—*George E. Tylutki*

E. H. Butler and Company
(Philadelphia: 1837-1898)
Butler, Sheldon and Company
(Philadelphia and New York: 1898-1903)

E. H. Butler and Company was founded by E. H. Butler in Philadelphia in 1837. Beginning as a publisher of educational works, in the 1840s Butler became a major force in the gift book trade. At the height of the popularity of gift books between 1845 and 1855, E. H. Butler and Company annually published *Leaflets of Memory* (1844-1855), *The Snow Flake* (1849-1855), *Christmas Blossoms and New Year's Wreath* (1849-1854), and *Friendship's Offering* (1852-1855). *Leaflets of Memory,* edited by Reynell Coates, contains original work by G. H. Boker, H. B. Hirst, Alice B. Neal, and Thomas B. Read.

Besides gift books, Butler published other anthologies, including *The Female Poets of America* (1849), edited by Read; *The Female Prose Writers of America* (1852), edited by John Seely Hart; and *A Gallery of Distinguished English and American Poets* (1858) and *A Gallery of Distinguished English and American Female Poets* (1860), both edited by Henry

Coppée. In the 1860s Butler published editions of many British poets, including Oliver Goldsmith, Robert Burns, William Wordsworth, and Elizabeth Barrett Browning.

In 1873 Butler's sons took over the firm, moved it from 611 Market Street to 723 Chestnut Street, and phased out literary works in favor of textbooks. In 1891 E. H. Butler and Company absorbed Joseph B. Cowperthwait and Company, another Philadelphia textbook house, and moved to 220-222 South Fifth Street. Seven years later Butler consolidated with Sheldon and Company, a New York firm, and became Butler, Sheldon and Company of Philadelphia and New York. In 1903 the house was acquired by the American Book Company.

—*Dorsey Kleitz*

H. M. Caldwell Company

(New York and Boston: 1896-1914)

On 11 April 1896 Herbert M. Caldwell announced in *Publishers' Weekly* that the reprint firm H. M. Caldwell Company was opening with a long list of illustrated, carefully printed, and beautifully bound books in an assortment of designs at various prices. The firm was located at 9-11 East Sixteenth Street in New York. A year and a half later the advertisements of the house included a Boston address, 208-218 Summer Street. Books published by the house ranged from classics to current fiction, from children's books to American, British, and European essays and poetry. Caldwell's advertisements offered commonly read literature in bindings that would suit any decor. In 1910 the Boston firm of Dana Estes and Company bought a controlling interest in H. M. Caldwell, continuing to use the design and sales skills of its founder. In April 1914 Estes sold out to the Page Company and accepted the purchase offer of the Dodge Publishing Company in New York for the plates and stock of the Caldwell Company.

References:

"Dodge Publishing Company Absorbs H. M. Caldwell Company," *Publishers' Weekly*, 85 (4 April 1914): 1154;

"Herbert M. Caldwell Announces the Organization of the H. M. Caldwell Co. to Publish Books," *Publishers' Weekly*, 49 (11 April 1896): 1.

—*Theodora Mills*

Cambridge Press

(Cambridge, Massachusetts: 1638-1692)

The first press in British North America, the Cambridge Press was brought to the Massachusetts Bay Colony from England by Rev. Jose Glover late in 1638. When Glover died en route, a locksmith, Stephen Day, whom Glover had hired to establish an ironworks, set up the press. The first Cambridge publication was a 222-word broadside, *The Oath of a Free-man*, printed in 1638 or early 1639. Day and his son Matthew produced Harvard theses, pamphlets on local Indians, almanacs, and books of laws and liberties. The most important—and earliest surviving—work printed by the Days was *The Whole Booke of Psalmes* (1640), popularly known as the *Bay Psalm Book*.

In 1641 the printing works were moved to Harvard College following Mrs. Glover's remarriage to Henry Dunster, the president of Harvard. The press was operated by Samuel Green, beginning around 1649. Green printed religious treatises, Harvard theses, and translations. With the help of Marmaduke Johnson, Green printed John Eliot's translation of the Bible into the Algonquin language in 1663. *The Eliot Indian Bible* was the first Bible in any language to be published in the colonies.

Green also made works by some of the most important religious men of the time, including Richard Mather, John Cotton, and Thomas Shepard, available to the settlers. Shortly after the publication of Cotton Mather's *Ornaments for the Daughters of Zion* in 1692, Green retired and his son Bartholomew moved the press to Boston.

Reference:

Robert Roden, *The Cambridge Press, 1638-1692: A History of the First Printing Press Established in English America* (New York: Dodd, Mead, 1905).

—*Chris M. Anson*

M. Carey and Company
(Philadelphia: 1785)
Carey, Talbot and Spotswood
(Philadelphia: 1786-1787)
Mathew Carey and Company
(Philadelphia: 1787-1789)
Carey, Stewart and Company
(Philadelphia: 1790-1791)
M. Carey
(Philadelphia: 1792-1816)
M. Carey and Son
(Philadelphia: 1817-1821)
M. Carey and Sons
(Philadelphia: 1821)
H. C. Carey and I. Lea
(Philadelphia: 1822-1827)
Carey, Lea and Carey
(Philadelphia: 1827-1829)
Carey and Lea
(Philadelphia: 1829-1832)
Carey, Lea and Blanchard
(Philadelphia: 1833-1838)
Lea and Blanchard
(Philadelphia: 1838-1850; 1865)
Blanchard and Lea
(Philadelphia: 1851-1865)
Henry C. Lea
(Philadelphia: 1865-1879)
Henry C. Lea's Son and Company
(Philadelphia: 1880-1884)
Lea Brothers and Company
(Philadelphia: 1885-1907)
Lea and Febiger
(Philadelphia: 1908-   )

See also the Mathew Carey entry in *DLB 37, American Writers of the Early Republic.*

Mathew Carey established the first modern American publishing company. The business was continued by his son and son-in-law, who made it the publisher of choice for some of the best American writers of the 1820s and 1830s. After various changes of name the firm survives in the twentieth century, although as early as the 1840s it began to focus on its present specialty of medical publishing.

Carey was born in Dublin on 28 January 1760.

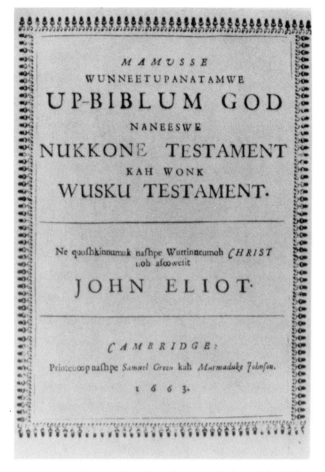

Algonquian title page for John Eliot's translation of the Bible, the first Bible in any language to be published in the colonies

Mathew Carey

His father had prospered as an army contractor and was able to provide for the education of his six sons. Mathew took to books and study with enthusiasm and at the age of fifteen announced a desire to become a printer and bookseller. His father felt that this was an inappropriate, undependable trade and refused to find a master to whom his son could be apprenticed, but Mathew took matters into his own hands and began learning the trade with a printer named McDonnel. Along with his passion for books and printing, Carey developed an interest in politics, particularly in the issue of England's sovereignty over Ireland. In 1779 he wrote and printed an anonymous pamphlet exhorting the Catholics of Ireland to rebel against the British Penal Code. A reward was posted for his arrest, and it became expedient for him to leave the country.

He went to France, where he met Benjamin Franklin, who was then the American minister to the French court, and became an assistant in Franklin's hobby printing office at Passy. He soon went on to work full time in the shop of the Didots, the great French printing family. During his year in France, he met many of Franklin's friends, including the Marquis de Lafayette. When he felt it was safe, Carey returned to Dublin, where he edited a revolutionary weekly, the *Freeman's Journal*. Beginning in October 1783 he brought out a paper of his own, the *Volunteer's Journal*, whose tone he later described as "enthusiastic and violent." Within the year he was brought before the House of Commons on a criminal libel charge. After a month in the Dublin Newgate Prison, he was freed but, facing further prosecution, he immigrated to Philadelphia, where he arrived on 1 November 1784.

Lafayette, who was then visiting George Washington, learned of Carey's arrival and sent him a draft for $400, a sum which Carey repaid (without interest) when Lafayette next visited America in 1824. Carey used the money to buy a press formerly used by Robert Bell, and on 25 January 1785 he began to publish the *Pennsylvania Evening Herald*. He also began to publish books at this time, first under the imprint M. Carey and Company, then—starting in March 1786—in partnership with Christopher Talbot and William Spotswood as Carey, Talbot and Spotswood. Later in 1786 he was involved in a duel with Col. Eleazer Oswald. The duel, occasioned by his writing and publishing *The Plagi-Scurriliad: A Hudibrastic Poem. Dedicated to Colonel Eleazer Oswald* (1786), resulted in a leg wound for Carey that took months to heal and which may have been a factor in the discon-

tinuation of the *Herald*. Nevertheless, in October 1786 he was one of six partners who started the *Columbian Magazine*, the first numbers of which Carey both printed and edited. But he soon withdrew from the *Columbian* to start his own magazine, the *American Museum*. In February 1787 his imprint was changed to Mathew Carey and Company.

The *American Museum* first appeared in January 1787 and became the first successful magazine published in America. By mid-1789 the list of subscribers had climbed to 1,696, including many of the most influential men of the time; and the contents were equally distinguished. Even though Carey did not intend to publish much original material, the *American Museum* contained selections from the best American writers on politics, economics, education, science, morals, and literature. On the issue of the new constitution Carey published material by Washington, Franklin, Noah Webster, Alexander Hamilton, John Jay, Fisher Ames, Tench Coxe, Francis Hopkinson, John Dickinson, Roger Sherman, Oliver Ellsworth, David Ramsay, Elbridge Gerry, Richard Henry Lee, Benjamin Rush, James Wilson, and Edmund Randolph. Relatively little fiction appeared in the *American Museum*, but no other American magazine of the eighteenth century published so much poetry; and almost all of the selections were by American poets. Philip Freneau held a prominent place, and generous helpings were offered from the works of Hopkinson, John Trumbull, David Humphreys, and Timothy Dwight. Of particular note were the thirty-five poems by the recently deceased Joseph Brown Ladd of Charleston, South Carolina: Ladd's poems breathed with the spirit of a new generation brought up on Ossian and Chatterton and suspicious of the strictures of Dr. Johnson. By the time the *American Museum* ceased publication in 1792, none of its readers could doubt that the new nation had a literature of its own.

Meanwhile, Carey's firm had become Carey, Stewart and Company at the beginning of 1790, and it was under that imprint that it published the book that brought Carey into prominence as a publisher: the Catholic Douay Bible (1790), the first quarto Bible published in America. On 1 January 1792 the firm's name was changed to M. Carey. The following year Carey moved the firm from Front Street, where it had occupied various addresses since its founding, to 118 High Street (the present Market Street). The company moved to 122 High Street in 1803, to 121 Chestnut Street in 1814, and to 124-126 Chestnut Street in 1816.

Carey was the most enterprising publisher of

his time, and he pioneered many techniques of modern publishing. He exploited the advantages of publishing both books and a literary journal. Publication of Freneau's poems, for example, encouraged the sale of Carey's edition of Freneau's *Select Poems on Various Occasions* (1787). He used his magazine to advertise his books, and he put together a string of agents from Halifax to Savannah, more than fifty by 1790, to obtain subscriptions and distribute the *Museum*. These agents—booksellers, printers, and merchants—were also able to distribute his books. In the beginning he himself went on the road to sell books, solicit subscriptions, and collect accounts, but eventually he hired travelers who, equipped with sample copies and subscription forms, penetrated the backwoods to settlements beyond the reach of established booksellers. His most celebrated agent was Mason Locke Weems, the famous Parson Weems who invented the story of George Washington and the cherry tree, and Weems with his biographies of Francis Marion (1809), Franklin (1818), and William Penn (1822) was one of the firm's more profitable authors as well. From 1792 until his death in 1825 Weems covered the South, selling Carey's famous quarto Bible and his own pious tracts but also obtaining orders for other books on the Carey list.

A bookseller in Raleigh, North Carolina, wrote in 1800, "Nothing sells better here than modern law," and a year later requested that "Mr. Carey will be so obliging as to send as many of the Novels as he can procure, it will be mutually our interest to keep a good collection, as the good folks here love *light* reading." Readers snapped up Carey's editions of Susanna Haswell Rowson's *The Inquisitor* (1794) and *Charlotte, A Tale of Truth* (1794)—later reprinted with its more famous title *Charlotte Temple* (1797)—and Eugenia De Acton's *Plain Sense: or the History of Henry Villars and Ellen Mordaunt* (1799). He rarely missed a chance to anticipate the wishes of potential customers. In the 1790s he reprinted plays being performed by the Old American Company at the theater in Southwark as well as the most popular songs from these productions, and playgoers could purchase these works from what Carey called "itinerant stationers" as they left the theater. Along with Isaac Bickerstaffe's *The Romp* (1792) and *Love in a Village* (1794), John O'Keeffe's *The Farmer: A Comic Opera* (1792) and *Wild Oats* (1793), he published *Don Juan; or, The Libertine Destroyed* (1792), which may or may not have been recognizable to its alleged author, Mozart.

Beginning in the 1790s, the volume of his business drove Carey to move beyond the old role of a printer-bookseller who produced an entire book in his own shop to develop specialists in the various aspects of book production. A generation earlier, Isaiah Thomas had expanded his business by setting up partnerships with other printers throughout New England, each partnership functioning as a separate establishment but able to benefit by exchanges with other shops in the Thomas empire. Carey improved on Thomas's system by commissioning other firms to do part or all of the printing, contracting with binders, and employing—perhaps for the first time in America—men such as Samuel Lewis who specialized in proofreading. By the time Carey needed to put out an edition of a new Sir Walter Scott novel almost overnight, the system was so well organized that he could place parts of the book with nearly every printer in Philadelphia and have the finished product on the way to New York booksellers in under thirty hours. Carey began as a printer, but he became a publisher in the modern sense: an organizer of workers in a host of trades subsidiary to the production of books.

Early American booksellers sometimes traded their books for books owned by competitors, in order to maintain fuller stocks. As Carey's business expanded, he found that merely exchanging titles with other booksellers did not solve the problem of several editions of the same work competing with each other. When printers supplied only local markets, this situation had created no difficulties; but as other firms, such as Thomas and Andrews of Boston, who were once sufficiently remote enlarged their operations, the trade became more confused. In 1801 Carey issued circulars pointing to the success of book fairs in Leipzig and Frankfurt and proposing similar meetings in America to be held alternately in New York and Philadelphia. When the publishers met in New York on 1 June 1802, Carey drew up a constitution for the American Company of Booksellers, an organization designed to facilitate the exchange of books among booksellers and also intended to function in a way similar to the London Stationers' Company by serving notice of a printer's interest in a foreign title. The book fairs were a great success for a few years, but the rudimentary attempt at a copyright system for foreign books never worked. When small, back-country printers used the exchange system to flood the country with large editions of popular titles printed on cheap paper with worn type, the larger publishers withdrew and the company collapsed.

Carey had always written a few of his own publications. *A Short Account of the Malignant Fever*

(1793), on the yellow fever epidemic in Philadelphia, was a best-seller, and he jousted with William Cobbett in *A Plumb Pudding for the Humane, Chaste, Valiant, Enlightened Peter Porcupine* (1799) and *The Porcupiniad* (1799). *The Olive Branch; or, Faults on Both Sides, Federal and Democratic* (1814) addressed the internal dissension exacerbated by the War of 1812 and sold 10,000 copies in Carey's editions; since he did not copyright it, in order to spread its ideas, there were substantial printings in several other places as well. After publishing *The Olive Branch* he became more and more interested in writing on political and economic issues, particularly in advocating protectionist legislation, and he began to turn the firm over to his son and son-in-law so that he might pursue these interests. On 1 January 1817 his son, Henry Charles Carey, became a junior partner in the firm, which was renamed M. Carey and Son. On 24 April 1821 Isaac Lea, who had married Mathew Carey's daughter, Frances Anne, entered the business, which was then renamed M. Carey and Sons. On 1 January 1822 the younger generation completed the takeover by buying out Mathew and renaming the firm H. C. Carey and I. Lea.

Born in 1793, Henry Charles Carey had sold books at the 1802 New York book fair, and at the age of twelve he had managed his father's branch store in Philadelphia. Trained thus for the publisher's profession, Carey also inherited his father's energy and ingenuity, and under his direction Carey and Lea became the leading publisher in the nation. Without giving up its position as probably the country's largest general publisher, Carey and Lea became the most significant publisher of English and American literature in the United States before 1840.

The groundwork for this achievement as a distinguished publisher of fiction was laid in the competition to publish the works of Scott. Beginning with *Waverley* in 1814, there was a craze for the works of "the great unknown of the North" unlike anything ever seen before in the American bookselling trade. Since Scott's works enjoyed no copyright protection in the United States, they could be reprinted by anyone, and the demand was so tremendous that a whole printing could be sold off in twenty-four hours if it were the first on the market. The winners in this competition could make a large sum of money very quickly; losers could be stuck with a slow-moving stock. The Carey firm had been out in front with *Waverley* and had its share of both winners and losers thereafter. By 1822 Carey and Lea was buying advance sheets

from Thomas Wardle of Philadelphia, who got them from a mysterious British source which transmitted them by way of Hurst, Robinson and Company of London. The uncertainties of this scheme became apparent in early 1822, when the firm lost out in the races to reprint *The Pirate* and *The Fortunes of Nigel* and was subsequently criticized for printing texts that differed from the Edinburgh edition. The textual problems were in part a result of hasty printing but were also a reflection of Scott's habit of making last-minute revisions not included with the advance sheets. Carey and Lea's problems were compounded in June 1822, when a letter arrived from Archibald Constable and Company, Scott's Edinburgh publishers, accusing the Philadelphia firm of printing stolen sheets. Henry Carey's prompt response satisfied Constable about the Philadelphia publisher's honesty—apparently the Constable firm itself had supplied the sheets that reached Wardle—and also enabled Carey to make an agreement to purchase advance sheets directly from Edinburgh. Beginning with *Peveril of the Peak* and *Quentin Durward* in 1823, this new arrangement bore fruit, and Carey and Lea effectively controlled the American market until Scott's death in 1832.

In 1817 Carey had written to Longman's in London requesting early copies of "such new works that come out as may be likely to bear publication in this country." Longman referred the firm to John Miller, who became its London agent until 1861. Miller was authorized to make arrangements for priority to titles by G. P. R. James, Theodore Hook, Benjamin Disraeli, and Edward Bulwer-Lytton. In 1832 and 1833 the firm published the first American editions of Jane Austen's novels, but it was Charles Dickens who provided the next reprint bonanza; 11,000 copies of *The Posthumous Papers of the Pickwick Club* (1836) were sold by January 1838, and the firm had similar success with *Sketches by Boz* (1836-1837) and *Oliver Twist* (1837). On 24 June 1837 Carey broke with all tradition by sending unsolicited remuneration to an English author. His letter to "Mr. Saml. Dickens" brought an equally surprising reply when Dickens refused the money, asking instead for copies of the Carey and Lea editions of his works.

From 1822 through September 1838 nearly a third of Carey and Lea's titles were fiction, 290 out of 930. Furthermore, an increasing number of these titles were by Americans; the *National Gazette* pointed out on 13 May 1824 that "of seventeen new works which Messrs. Carey and Lea have in press and announce, *eleven* are American; which shows a remarkable increase of the number of domestic

*Henry Charles Carey, who became a junior partner of
M. Carey and Son in 1817*

*Isaac Lea, a partner in M. Carey and Sons. In 1822 he and
Henry Carey bought out Mathew Carey and formed the firm of
H. C. Carey and I. Lea*

*Henry Charles Lea, a partner in Blanchard and Lea following
his father's retirement in 1851*

*Christian Carson Febiger, who joined the firm of Henry C. Lea's
Son and Company in 1880*

productions in literature and science." Publishing American fiction was riskier than reprinting British novels, since the publisher had to pay the author for his copyright. In 1822 Carey published John Neal's *Logan,* a Byronic extravaganza whose "interminable" dream world was, according to Neal himself, "without moral or design—but alive with tremendous apparitions." When the 750-copy edition of *Logan* moved slowly, Carey and Lea declined to publish any more novels by Neal, but the firm continued its efforts to create a list of fiction by American authors. It made overtures to James Fenimore Cooper, who had published *The Spy* (1821) and *The Pioneers* (1823) on his own, selling them through Charles Wiley of New York. Carey and Lea eventually persuaded Cooper that the firm could bring him greater returns by getting his books into places unreachable by the usual methods of distribution. The new relationship began with *The Last of the Mohicans* (1826), purchased for $5,000 with rights to the work for four years, and continued for nearly two decades, although as Cooper's popularity declined in the 1830s, payments for his new works declined as well.

At about the same time the firm approached Cooper, Carey and Lea offered to become Washington Irving's publisher; Henry suggested to Irving's brother Ebenezer, his literary agent, that if Carey and Lea could "make arrangements for the Copy Right of the Sketchbook," its sale "might be rendered 5 times greater than it now is." It published *Tales of a Traveller* in 1824, but not until 1829 did the firm come to handle all of Irving's productions. This agreement lasted until after Carey's retirement in 1838 and brought to the firm some of Irving's best work: *A Chronicle of the Conquest of Granada* (1829), *The Alhambra* (1832), *A Tour on the Prairies* (1835), *The Crayon Miscellanies* (1835), *Astoria* (1836), and *Adventures of Captain Bonneville* (1837). Carey and Lea also kept Irving's earlier works in print, to the profit of both parties.

By the 1830s Carey and Lea's reputation was such that authors approached the firm. John Pendleton Kennedy submitted his first novel, *Swallow Barn* (1832), which did not sell well; but when Kennedy offered *Horse Shoe Robinson* (1835) in 1834, Carey had enough confidence in the work to print 2,500 copies. The firm began to put the book to press before Kennedy had completed it, but problems developed as Kennedy wrote on and on. Carey and Lea requested a speedy finale and the cutting of about a hundred pages lest the price have to be raised; Kennedy cut forty pages. The book's great success vindicated Carey's judgment; it went into

four printings by the end of 1836. Unfortunately, Kennedy turned out not to be as prolific as Irving and Cooper, and his third and last novel, *Rob of the Bowl* (1838), did not attain the popularity of *Horse Shoe Robinson.* Robert Montgomery Bird followed up *Calavar* (1835) with *The Infidel* (1835), *The Hawks of Hawk-Hollow* (1835), and *Nick of the Woods* (1837). The increasing size of the pressruns, from 2,000 copies for *Calavar* to 3,000 for *The Hawks of Hawk-Hollow* and *Nick of the Woods,* along with the appearance of second editions of *Calavar* and *The Infidel* in 1835, attest to the success of Bird's work. In addition to these authors Carey and Lea also published fiction by Catharine Maria Sedgwick, John Treat Irving, and Ralph Ingersoll Lockwood.

Concerned that their publications were not receiving adequate attention in the Boston-based *North American Review,* the leading intellectual journal of the time, Carey and Lea decided to start their own magazine. Immediately after they took over the firm, they began corresponding with Robert Walsh, a well-known and respected critic whom they wished to appoint as editor, but it was not until 1827 that the *American Quarterly Review* appeared. Circulation of the *American Quarterly Review* went as high as 4,000 copies, then settled down at about 2,500. Besides Walsh's own contributions, the journal regularly published work by Cooper, James Kirke Paulding, Henry D. Gilpin, George Bancroft, and George Ticknor, and it presented scholarly, scientific, and political contributions from Peter Duponceau, Albert Gallatin, Dr. Robley Dunglison, and Dr. John D. Godman. In 1831, during a period of retrenchment, the *American Quarterly Review* was sold off, but it continued to publish works by Carey and Lea authors and kept their names in the public eye.

A more important venture was the publication in 1826 of the *Atlantic Souvenir; A Christmas and New Year's Offering,* America's first literary annual. In 1824 Carey and Lea had become American agents for the *Forget-Me-Not,* the English forerunner of the well-illustrated and sumptuously bound gift books which became popular items for almost half a century, but Carey became convinced that a similar volume filled with American writing and American illustrations would be even more salable. The first annual was printed in an edition of 2,000 copies, and by 1831 the pressrun was over 10,000. Under Gilpin's editorship the *Atlantic Souvenir* published prose by Paulding, Irving, Sedgwick, Charles Sealsfield, and W. L. Stone, as well as poetry by Longfellow, Bryant, Bancroft, Fitz-Greene Halleck, Mrs. Sigourney, James G. Percival, Grenville

Mellen, N. P. Willis, and James Nelson Barker. In 1832 both Nathaniel Hawthorne and Edgar Allan Poe offered to write for the *Atlantic Souvenir,* but by that time Carey and Lea was making plans to sell it to Samuel G. Goodrich, who combined it with his *Token.* The *Atlantic Souvenir* was a showcase of book production and artwork, a testament to the technical achievements of American publishing, but more important was the literary phenomenon it began. The gift books became a place where beginning writers could display their work in the company of established authors.

In 1827 Carey's younger brother Edward became a junior partner, and H. C. Carey and I. Lea became Carey, Lea and Carey. In 1829 the younger Carey withdrew from the partnership, taking with him the firm's retail book business, and began publishing in partnership with Abraham Hart as Carey and Hart. The original firm took Carey and Lea as an imprint until 1833, when it added a new partner, William A. Blanchard, and began publishing as Carey, Lea and Blanchard. As had Mathew Carey before them, both Henry C. Carey and Isaac Lea had substantial interests outside publishing which eventually called them away from the business. In the 1830s Carey became interested in political economy, a field in which he is still remembered. His *Essay on the Rate of Wages* (1835) appeared under the firm's imprint, and when his three-volume *Principles of Political Economy* began to appear in 1837 he was ready to retire. On 1 October 1838 the partnership dissolved, with the business continuing as Lea and Blanchard. Lea became a widely respected natural scientist, author of almost 280 papers on conchology, mineralogy, and geology; but he stayed with the firm until 1851.

By the time of Carey's retirement, the center of American publishing was shifting to New York; only the superior organization of the firm and Carey's energy enabled Carey, Lea and Blanchard to withstand the challenge of the Harper brothers for publishing supremacy. After 1839 Lea and Blanchard steadily declined as a major literary publisher. The firm developed a new specialty which enabled it to survive, although it underwent several further name changes. Second only to the quantity of fiction in the list of titles published between 1822 and 1838 was the number of medical titles. Supplementing these books was the *American Journal of the Medical Sciences,* evolving in 1827 out of the firm's earlier *Philadelphia Journal of Medical and Physical Sciences;* from this background the company responded to changes in the publishing scene by becoming a major publisher of medical texts.

Lea and Blanchard's shift away from literary publishing is evident in its dealings with Poe. The firm agreed to publish 750 copies of Poe's *Tales of the Grotesque and Arabesque* (1840), granting Poe the copyright and twenty copies and itself the profits, if any. When Poe, seeking better terms, sought to sell the firm the copyright, it declined. Nevertheless, Cooper's novels continued to appear under the Lea and Blanchard imprint for a few more years, *Ned Myers* (1843) being the last, and the firm briefly experimented with fiction by William Gilmore Simms, publishing *The Kinsmen* (1841), *Confession; or, The Blind Heart* (1841), and *Beauchampe; or, The Kentucky Tragedy* (1842). Carey and Lea continued its successful reprinting of the works of Dickens, but although it sent relatively generous royalties, it was unable to strike a bargain for advance sheets, as it had with Scott. It was the only American reprinter that stereotyped its editions; but when Lea retired in 1851, the firm sold the plates to T. B. Peterson and Company of Philadelphia and gave up the Dickens business.

Lea's share in the firm passed to his son, Henry Charles Lea, and the company name was changed to Blanchard and Lea. In 1865 Blanchard retired and the firm became Lea and Blanchard for a few months, then was renamed Henry C. Lea. The same year it moved from Fourth Street to a new building at 706-708 Sansom Street. By 1880 the firm was the largest publisher of medical books in the world. That year Lea's son Henry, Henry M. Barnes, and Christian C. Febiger became partners in the business, and its name was changed to Henry C. Lea's Son and Company. The elder Lea retired in 1885 and his youngest son, Arthur H. Lea, became a partner, with the firm's name changing to Lea Brothers and Company. When Barnes retired in 1879 the firm received its present name, Lea and Febiger. The descendant of Mathew Carey's publishing business now offers medical, dental, veterinary, and health-related books only. Its address since 1924 has been 600 South Washington Square, Philadelphia 19106-4198.

References:

Richard L. Bonnell, "The Press of Mathew Carey, 1785-1851," M.A. thesis, Drexel Institute of Technology, 1953;

Earl L. Bradsher, *Mathew Carey, Editor, Author and Publisher: A Study in American Literary Development* (New York: Columbia University Press, 1912);

Joseph Jackson, "The First Catholic Bible Printed in America," *Records of the American Catholic*

Historical Society of Philadelphia, 56 (1945): 18-25;

David Kaser, *Messers. Carey & Lea of Philadelphia: A Study in the History of the Book Trade* (Philadelphia: University of Pennsylvania Press, 1957);

Kaser, ed., *The Cost Book of Carey & Lea, 1825-1838* (Philadelphia: University of Pennsylvania Press, 1963);

George MacManus, "Mathew Carey: American Bookseller and Publisher," *Mountain-Plains*

Library Quarterly, 9 (Fall 1964): 3-5, 7-11;

Helen M. McCadden, "The Father of the American Book Fair," *Catholic World,* 144 (1936-1937): 547-551;

Rollo G. Silver, "Mathew Carey, 1760-1839," *Antiquarian Bookman,* 25 (1 February 1960): 355;

Silver, "Mathew Carey's Proofreaders," *Studies in Bibliography,* 17 (1964): 123-133.

—*Frank Shuffelton*

Carey and Hart
(Philadelphia: 1839-1849)
E. L. Carey and A. Hart
(Philadelphia: 1829-1839)
A. Hart
(Philadelphia: 1849-1854)

When Carey, Lea and Carey, the firm started by Mathew Carey in 1785 and headed by his son Henry C. Carey, divided its business in November 1829, Edward L. Carey, Henry's younger brother, took the retail trade and formed a partnership with eighteen-year-old Abraham Hart, whose skill at selling books at his mother's fancy goods shop had attracted the Careys' attention. Born in 1806, Carey had worked in the family firm since boyhood, serving as its agent in England in 1822, as head of the firm's bookstore from 1824 to 1827, and as a junior partner with Isaac Lea in Carey, Lea and Carey from 1827 to 1829.

Working closely with the parent firm Carey and Lea (which became Carey, Lea and Blanchard in 1833), whose offices adjoined theirs at Chestnut and Fourth, Carey and Hart began publishing in September 1830. The firm reprinted foreign works, including medical texts such as its first publication, Thomas P. Teale's *A Treatise on Neuralgic Disease* (1830), but it soon built an impressive list of quality reprints of British and Continental literature.

Unlike many American firms, E. L. Carey and A. Hart was not wary of publishing native writers. *A Narrative of the Life of David Crockett,* a tremendous success in 1834, encouraged the firm to publish copyrighted works by Americans, particularly frontier humor and sporting books. The Crockett book went through nineteen printings in two years, partly because Carey and Hart arranged for a publicity tour to promote the work in New England and the North. Later, when *An Account of Col. Crock-*

ett's Tour to the North and Down East (1835) was selling poorly, Carey persuaded Richard Penn Smith to put together *Col. Crockett's Exploits and Adventures in Texas* (1836), which capitalized on Crockett's heroic death at the Alamo. By selling well, it also helped to clear the shelves of the *Tour.* Through such forceful marketing, the firm became well known nationally. It had agents in major cities from Boston to Cincinnati and New Orleans, and from 1833 to 1836 it also maintained offices at Charles and Baltimore Streets in Baltimore.

Carey and Hart was equally ingenious and energetic in marketing its reprinted English works. In 1836 Harper and Brothers published *Stories of the Sea* by Capt. Frederick Marryat, an author customarily handled by E. L. Carey and A. Hart. The Philadelphians, with the support of Carey, Lea and Blanchard, sought revenge by paying a large price for an advance copy of *Rienzi* (1836) by Edward Bulwer-Lytton, whose works Harpers usually reprinted. E. L. Carey and A. Hart received its copy from the same ship that brought a copy to Harper and Brothers, rushed it to Philadelphia, and divided it among twelve printers. It was printed and collated overnight and bound the next morning. All seats on the afternoon stage were reserved for Hart and 500 copies of *Rienzi.* The E. L. Carey and A. Hart edition, as a result, went on sale in New York a full day before Harpers' rival edition, a crucial head start in the competitive reprint market. *Rienzi* proved a great success, selling 125,000 copies within a decade.

When Marryat visited America, Carey and

Hart, thanking him for *Peter Simple* (1833), *Jacob Faithful* (1834), and other novels the firm had successfully reprinted, sent him a check for $2,000 as a "compliment" and an "encouragement." Asserting that he had thought that all American publishers were "pirates," Marryat visited Carey and Hart and offered them his latest work, *Snarleyyow; or, the Dog Fiend* (1837). Although Hart, in particular, vigorously opposed an international copyright, the firm offered Marryat one of the first payments by an American publisher to a foreign author. (In an exchange of letters with George Putnam, published in *Norton's Literary Gazette* in 1853, Hart defended the reprinting of English works as a "legitimate and honorable trade" but added, "I am in favor of compensating and have generally compensated Foreign authors without any obligation on my part to any existing Copyright Law.")

Although it offered the inexpensive Carey's Library of Choice Literature from 1835 to 1836, during the 1830s E. L. Carey and A. Hart specialized in quality books, usually selling for one or two dollars in well-printed cloth editions. The firm was the first in England or America to publish a book by William Makepeace Thackeray, whose *The Yellowplush Correspondence* appeared in 1838. The following year, the firm's imprint became simply Carey and Hart. It published Thomas Macaulay's *Critical and Miscellaneous Essays* (1842-1844), which was compiled in five volumes from an earlier Boston reprint and British periodicals. In 1844 it reprinted for the first time Chapman and Hall's English edition of Charles Dickens's *A Christmas Carol*, with the original illustrations by John Leech.

The firm's most important contribution to American literature was its support of regional writing, particularly frontier humor. In addition to *The American Joe Miller* (1840), the first of many jest books bearing the illiterate comedian's name, Carey and Hart also published Joseph C. Neal's *Charcoal Sketches* (1838), which was reprinted eleven times by 1844, and William Tappan Thompson's *Major Jones' Courtship* (1844), which quickly went through six printings. William T. Porter, the editor of the *Spirit of the Times*, compiled a volume of humorous sketches from his popular sporting journal. In *The Big Bear of Arkansas* (1845) Porter brought together twenty-one sketches from writers including Thomas Bangs Thorpe, Johnson Jones Hooper, Sol Smith, and Henry Clay Lewis. When an initial printing of 4,000 copies quickly sold out, Porter put together thirty-three more sketches in *A Quarter-Race in Kentucky* (1847). He also introduced several of his writers to Carey and Hart, who read-

ily published collections of their sketches. These volumes of regional humor were a great success for the firm. Hooper's *Some Adventures of Captain Simon Suggs,* for example, rapidly sold out an edition of 3,000 copies in 1845. Within months the company published another 5,000 copies with four more illustrations, and by 1850 it had printed more than 12,000 copies.

Carey retired in 1838 and died in 1845. In a tribute to Carey, whom he often visited in Philadelphia, William Gilmore Simms wrote in the *Southern and Western Magazine:* "In business, he was enterprising and liberal; in private life, modest, manly, and affectionate." Carey's nephew, Henry Carey Baird, inherited his share of the firm; its imprint remained Carey and Hart until 1849, when it became A. Hart.

In 1846 Carey and Hart republished its most popular works of southwestern and regional humor and began publishing new titles in a paperback series, the Library of Humorous American Works. By 1849 eighteen volumes had appeared, most published jointly with Burgess and Stringer, who distributed Carey and Hart books in New York. Felix O. C. Darley illustrated most of these works. His sketches for Neal's *Peter Ploddy* (1844) were among his first book illustrations. His comic drawings, which also decorated the uniform wrapper of these volumes, did much to make them a popular success.

Carey, Hart, and Baird all had shrewd business sense. For every loss, such as *Elinor Wyllys* (1846) by Amabel Penfeather (James Fenimore Cooper), the firm could show a financial success. Mrs. E. D. E. N. Southworth's *The Curse of Clifton* (1853) sold over 225,000 copies in the decade after its publication. The company offered a deluxe illustrated edition of Longfellow's poetry (1845) at the same time it was actively marketing cheap publications like its Library of Humorous American Works and Library for the People in paper covers at fifty cents a volume.

Carey and Hart also did a thriving business in literary annuals. *The Gift,* edited for several years by Elizabeth Leslie, in 1845 included works by Emerson, Longfellow, N. P. Willis, Poe, and Simms and featured plates by John Cheney and J. T. Pease of paintings by W. S. Mount and Asher Durand. In five years *The Gift* sold over 40,000 copies. In 1840 the firm printed 7,500 copies.

In addition to *Poets and Poetry of Europe* (1845), which Carey had persuaded Longfellow to edit, the firm published works edited by the most famous American anthologist of the time, Rufus W. Gris-

Edward L. Carey

Abraham Hart

*Henry Carey Baird, Edward L. Carey's nephew, inherited a
share in the firm upon his uncle's death in 1845*

George Washington Carleton

wold. Griswold's *Poets and Poetry of America* (1842) quickly went through ten editions; he subsequently compiled *Poets and Poetry of England* (1845), *Prose Writers of America* (1847), and *The Female Poets of America* (1849). In 1847 Carey and Hart published Griswold's *Washington and the Generals of the American Revolution,* a two-volume work with material by such authorities as Simms and E. D. Ingraham; the same year, a work of "fictional history," J. T. Headley's *Washington and His Generals,* was published by Baker and Scribner. The rivalry led to a scandal when Headley accused Carey and Hart of paying for the publication of an unfavorable review of his book, written anonymously by Griswold.

Late in 1849 Baird established his own firm at Market and Fifth, using the imprint Henry Carey Baird and Company (Successor to E. L. Carey). Although he received the plates of some Carey and Hart publications and reprinted some of them, his firm became one of the first in the country to specialize in technical and scientific publications. Hart continued to publish as A. Hart (Successor to Carey and Hart). Fire destroyed a building he had just constructed at Chestnut and Sixth in 1851, but within months the firm had rebuilt at that address. In addition to reprinting titles from the Library of Humorous American Works, Hart offered eleven new volumes in that series, including works by Hooper and Simms. The most popular work in this second series was *Odd Leaves from the Life of a Louisiana "Swamp Doctor"* (1850) by Madison Tensas (Henry Clay Lewis). Hart also published romances by Mrs. Southworth and Caroline Lee Hentz, a "cheap and correct edition" of Scott's novels (1852),

and three anthologies of British poetry. The firm also continued to offer medical titles.

Hart retired in March 1854. According to J. C. Derby, he was known for his "urbane courtesy" and his "happy and persuasive powers" as a book salesman. His plates and stock were sold at auction. Parry and McMillan purchased many works, as well as the right to the title "Successors to A. Hart, late Carey and Hart." Plates from the original series of humorous works, which had been divided by Baird and Hart in 1849, were subsequently acquired by Getz and Buck of Philadelphia, but were passed on in 1854 to T. B. Peterson and Sons, where they formed the bulk of Peterson's Library of Humorous American Works.

After retiring, Hart became involved in various enterprises, such as the American Button-hole Machine Company, and, until his death in 1885, he was active in Jewish educational and charitable organizations in Philadelphia.

References:

J. C. Derby, *Fifty Years Among Authors, Books and Publishers* (New York: G. W. Carleton & Company, 1884);

Louis Ginsberg, *A. Hart: Philadelphia Publisher* (Petersburg, Va., 1972);

David Kaser, *Messrs. Carey & Lea of Philadelphia: A Study in the History of the Book Trade* (Philadelphia: University of Pennsylvania Press, 1957);

One Hundred and Fifty Years of Publishing (Philadelphia: Lea & Febiger, 1935).

—Grady W. Ballenger

G. W. Carleton
(New York: 1861-1871)
G. W. Carleton and Company
(New York: 1871-1886)

In 1857 George Washington Carleton formed a partnership with Edward P. Rudd and Rudd's father George to create the bookstore and publishing house of Rudd and Carleton at 310 Broadway in New York. Before going into business with the Rudds, Carleton had been employed as a clerk with the New York importing firm Burnham, Plumb and Company. His only contact with publishing had come through an avocation, drawing: Carleton had drawn humorous sketches and had sold them to some of the better humor magazines. In 1861 Edward Rudd died and George Rudd retired. Carleton changed the firm's name to G. W. Carleton and moved its offices to 413 Broadway. Carleton had discovered that, inverted, the Arabic symbol for books appeared to form his initials. This symbol, which became the G. W. Carleton trademark, had first appeared on the title page of Thomas Bailey Aldrich's *The Course of True Love Never Did Run Smooth,* which Rudd and Carleton published in 1858.

Aldrich, who later served as literary advisor to Carleton, was one of the authors—particularly humorists—who gathered at Carleton's bookshop and subsequently had books published by G. W. Carleton. Fitz-James O'Brien, R. H. Stoddard, Robert H. Nevell, Charles G. Halpine, and M. M. Pomeroy were members of the Carleton circle of humorists.

The two best-known humorists Carleton published were Artemus Ward and Josh Billings. Artemus Ward was the pseudonym of Charles Farrar Browne, one of the most popular humorists of the day both as an author and as a speaker. Browne was a practitioner of "phonetic humor," employing comical misspellings and non sequiturs to make his audience laugh. G. W. Carleton published Browne's first two books, *Artemus Ward, His Book* (1862) and *Artemus Ward, His Travels* (1865), as well as several other collections. Like Browne, Josh Billings—whose real name was Henry W. Shaw—achieved his humor through the use of exaggerated misspellings and other linguistic devices. It was

on Browne's advice that Carleton published Shaw's first book, *Josh Billings, Hiz Sayings* (1866). Carleton also brought out Shaw's most popular work, *Josh Billings' Farmer's Allminax* (1870), following it with annual supplements until 1879. But though Carleton was a shrewd judge of saleable humor, he was not infallible. In 1867, failing to heed Browne's advice, Carleton turned down Mark Twain's *The Celebrated Jumping Frog of Calaveras County,* one of the most popular humorous pieces of all time. The work was published that year by C. H. Webb of New York.

In addition to humor, G. W. Carleton maintained an extensive list of popular fiction. Mary Jane Holmes wrote more than twenty books for Carleton; though she is largely forgotten she was one of the most popular American authors in the latter half of the nineteenth century. Augusta Jane Evans Wilson's *St. Elmo* (1867) sold more than a million copies. Both Holmes's and Wilson's works consisted of heavy doses of mawkish sentiment and romance, along with a healthy measure of moral advice—one of the best-selling formulas in American publishing at the time. Other romance authors on Carleton's lists included May Agnes Fleming, Miriam C. Harris, Fanny Fern (Sara P. Willis Parton), and Marion Harland (Mary Virginia Terhune).

Equally as popular as the sentimental romance was the adventure novel, and Carleton published J. H. Robinson's wilderness tales, John Esten Cooke's historical romances, and Capt. Mayne Reid's frontier adventures.

Carleton increased his stock of popular fiction by acquiring the rights to reprint novels from Street and Smith's *New York Weekly.* His Best of the *New York Weekly* series included work by Edward Judson, J. H. Robinson, Bertha M. Clay, Cora Agnew, and Annie Ashmore. Carleton developed reprint agreements with other firms as well, enabling him to bring out uniform editions of the works of many of his most popular authors.

G. W. Carleton's popular fiction, together

with its humor titles, helped make the firm one of the most successful of its time. *Publishers' Weekly* noted in 1907 that "the firm is estimated to have brought out more sensational books by native writers than any publishing house in the country." But Carleton's interests were not limited to American writers. He was an avid reader of European literature, particularly the work of French novelists, and was determined to bring these works to American readers. Rudd and Carleton had brought out successful translations of Jules Michelet's *L'Amour* (1859) and *La Femme* (1860), and Carleton published a translation of Victor Hugo's *Les Misérables* (1862) in five volumes that was second only to *Uncle Tom's Cabin* in pre-Civil War book sales. Although Carleton's attempt to introduce the work of Balzac to the American reading public was a failure— Carleton abandoned his plans to publish a collected edition—he continued to publish works by Ernest Renan and Eugene Chavelle as well as books by Italian and Spanish authors. Carleton also maintained a line of reprints of English classics; his uniform edition of the works of Charles Dickens was especially popular.

In addition to literature and humor, G. W. Carleton published a full line of general trade books. The Carleton lists were filled with "how to" books, specialized encyclopedias, general reference works, and self-improvement books. Carleton also published three travel books written and illustrated by himself.

In 1869, during the height of Carleton's publishing success, the firm moved into luxurious offices in the Worth House in Madison Square on Fifth Avenue. In 1871 Carleton made his longtime clerk, George Dillingham, a partner, and the firm name changed to G. W. Carleton and Company. One year later the firm moved to still larger quarters under the Fifth Avenue Hotel at 192 Fifth Avenue. In 1883 G. W. Carleton dissolved its bookstore operation to devote itself entirely to publishing. That year the firm moved to 33 West Twenty-third Street. After Carleton retired in 1886, Dillingham continued the business as the G. W. Dillingham Company. Carleton died in 1901.

References:

"George W. Carleton [obituary]," *Publishers' Weekly*, 60 (19 October 1901): 857-858;

"Jubilee of G. W. Dillingham Company," *Publishers' Weekly*, 72 (10 August 1907): 345-347;

Madeleine B. Stern, "G. W. Carleton: His Mark," *Publishers' Weekly*, 150 (17 August 1946): 710-715.

—Timothy D. Murray

Robert Carter and Brothers
(New York: 1848-1890)
Robert Carter
(New York: 1834-1848)

Robert Carter immigrated to New York from Scotland in 1831. After teaching for a few years, in 1834 he leased a store at the corner of Canal and Laurens streets and with $600 in savings purchased the stock of a failed bookseller. Carter's bookselling business prospered, and he moved to larger quarters at 58 Canal Street. In 1836 Carter published his first book, William Symington's *On the Atonement and Intercession of Jesus Christ*. With this publication Carter countered the prevailing view of the New York publishing community, most of whom had turned the book down. The work sold well and went through several editions.

In 1841 Carter published a three-volume translation of Merle d'Aubigne's *History of the Great Reformation*, which he planned to sell for three dollars per set. But after another publisher brought out a cheap, one-volume edition of the book, Carter published a one-dollar edition and sold over 10,000 copies in a few months. The success of this book brought the firm into prominence.

In 1848 Carter moved to larger quarters at 285 Broadway, took his brothers Walter and Peter as partners, and changed the firm's name to Robert Carter and Brothers. Eight years later the firm moved to 520 Broadway.

Robert Carter and Brothers prospered, almost in spite of the fact that Robert Carter limited the firm's potential by publishing only books that were consistent with his religious and moral beliefs. The firm's publications included tracts and sermons, scholarly religious histories and theological treatises, and reprints of classic religious works, as well as poetry, fiction, and travel books with religious themes or moral messages.

By 1875 Robert Carter and Brothers had published more than 1,500 titles. Some of the more popular and prolific authors—known today only to scholars—whose work Carter published were Andrew Alexander Bonar, Thomas Chalmers, Thomas Boston, John A. Clark, Catherine Sinclair, Jane Taylor, and "Old Humphrey" (George Mogroff).

Among the firm's better-known fiction titles were Lydia Howard Sigourney's *Water-Drops* (1848); James Bridges's *The Collier's Tale* (1853); Mrs. Jane Elizabeth Hornblower's *Vara; or, The Child of Adoption* (1854), *Nellie of Truro* (1856), and *"The Julia"* (1859); Stephen Higginson Tyng's *The Captive Orphan: Esther the Queen of Persia* (1860); and Mrs. Georgiana A. McLeod's *Sea Drifts* (1864). Susan Bogert Warner wrote at least eight titles for the firm, including *Melbourne House* (1864), *My Desire* (1879), *The Letter of Credit* (1882), and *Daisy Plains* (1885).

The firm was especially successful with its books for youth. In the latter half of the nineteenth century Robert Carter and Brothers published more children's books and Sunday school texts than any other American publishing house; by 1875 the firm had published more than 500 juvenile titles. Among the more prolific children's authors who wrote for Carter were Emma Marshall, Susan Warner, Julia Mathews, and Joanna H. Mathews. Most of the firm's juveniles had a strong moralistic and religious flavor.

Robert Carter became one of the most respected members of the American publishing community. During his later years Carter spent most of his time with religious and social concerns, leaving the operation of the firm to his brothers and to his son, Robert Carter, Jr., who had joined the business in 1874 when Walter Carter left to open his own bookstore. After his death in 1889, however, Carter's brother and son were unwilling to carry on without him. They put the firm up for sale, and on 23 September 1890 the assets of Robert Carter and Brothers were sold at auction.

References:

Peter Carter, "Reminiscences of Robert Carter and His Work," *Publishers' Weekly*, 37 (7 June 1890): 767-768;

Carter, "Some Recollections of the Book Trade," *Publishers' Weekly*, 15 (22 March 1879): 354-355; (10 May 1879): 538-539;

Annie Cochran, *Robert Carter: His Life and Work. 1807-1889* (New York: Randolph, 1891);

"Robert Carter [obituary]," *Publishers' Weekly*, 37 (4 January 1890): 11-12.

—*Timothy D. Murray*

Carter and Hendee
(Boston: 1828-1830; 1831-1832)
Carter, Hendee and Babcock
(Boston: 1830-1831)
Carter, Hendee and Company
(Boston: 1832-1836)

Timothy Harrington Carter came to Boston in 1815 and worked as a clerk for the printing and publishing firm of Jacob A. Cummings and William Hilliard. As the business prospered, he assumed management and brought in additional clerks, all of whom went on to become publishers: Charles Little, John Hubbard Wilkins, Harrison Gray, and his brother, Richard Bridge Carter. Carter was soon made a partner and the firm's name was changed to Cummings, Hilliard and Company. Carter acquired the Boston Type Foundry in 1822 and arranged to buy stereotyping apparatus from New York, creating the first stereotyping plant in Boston. In 1827, having made a modest fortune, Carter left Cummings, Hilliard and sold the stereotype foundry. In 1828 Carter leased a property at 135 Washington Street. He extensively renovated the building, making it into a bookshop, which later became the famous Old Corner Bookstore. He erected additional buildings on the property, in one of which he installed several printing presses. When the business was under way, he sold a one-third interest to his brother Richard and a one-third interest to Charles Hendee, a clerk, and the firm was called Carter and Hendee.

Carter and Hendee published the first American editions of George Combe's *The Constitution of Man Considered in Relation to External Objects* (1829) and Lydia Maria Child's best-selling cookbook, *Frugal Housewife* (1829). Among the firm's fiction titles were William Tudor's *Gebel Teir* (1829), Fr. Claire de Durfort's *Ourika* (1829), and Silas Pinckney Holbrook's *Sketches, by a Traveler* (1830). In 1829 Carter and Hendee took over publication of the *American Journal of Education* (the title was changed several times in the following years) from Wait, Green and Company and S. G. Goodrich, and in April of the same year started the *School Magazine* as an adjunct of that journal. The firm published at least two books for children: *The Young Emigrants* (1830) by Susan Ann Livingston Sedgwick and *Peter Parley's Story of the Storm* (1830) by Samuel Goodrich.

Edwin Babcock joined the firm in December 1830, and the name was changed to Carter, Hendee and Babcock. The firm published Francis Greenwood's fiction annual *The Scrap Table, for MDCCCXXXI* (1830). James T. Fields (later of Ticknor and Fields) came to work for Carter, Hendee and Babcock in 1831. That year the firm took over from Putnam and Hunt publication of *Juvenile Miscellany*, edited by Child. Toward the end of 1831 Babcock withdrew from the firm and it again became Carter and Hendee. It published Francis Greenwood's annual, *Youth's Keepsake* (1831), which included two poems by Oliver Wendell Holmes.

In July 1832 Carter and Hendee bought the book stock and publishing interests of Richardson, Lord and Holbrook, then sold the retail side of the business and some miscellaneous publishing interests to John Allen and William Ticknor. Renamed Carter, Hendee and Company, the firm moved to 131 Washington Street and engaged in wholesale book sales and publishing. Allen and Ticknor and Carter, Hendee published several books under a double imprint in 1833, including Almira H. L. Phelp's *Lectures to Young Ladies*, Caleb Cushing's *Reminiscences of Spain*, and James S. Knowles's *Select Works*.

Between 1832 and 1836 Carter, Hendee published educational, religious, and medical works; annuals and gift books; juveniles; and some fiction. It published the first American editions of James Paxton's *An Introduction to the Study of Human Anatomy* (1832) and Sarah K. Trimmer's *The Ladder to Learning: A Collection of Fables* (1833). Child's *The Coronal: A Collection of Miscellaneous Pieces Written at Various Times* appeared in 1832 and her *Good Wives* in 1833. John Greenleaf Whittier's *Moll Pitcher, a Poem*, which he excluded from his collected works, was published in 1832. Other titles published by Carter, Hendee include *The Child's Own Book of Tales and Anecdotes about Dogs* (1832), B. H. Draper's *Bible Illustrations* (1832), Francis Greenwood's *A History of King's Chapel, in Boston* (1833), and Warren Burton's *The District School as It Was* (1833).

Carter, Hendee and Company remained at 131 Washington Street until the dissolution of the partnership in January 1836. Hendee continued as a bookseller and later as a publisher at 131 Washington Street. Richard Carter joined John H. Wilkins to form Carter, Wilkins and Company. Timothy Carter continued in business at 147 Washington Street as a bookseller and as a publisher of children's books, including *Little Reader* (1837) and *Grandmamma's Book of Rhymes, for the Nursery* (1842) under the imprint T. H. Carter. His name appears (retaining the copyright) on the title page of many of the Jacob Abbott books published by William Ticknor, including *Jonas's Stories: Related to Rollo and Lucy* (1839), *Jonas as a Judge* (1840), and *Jonas on a Farm in Summer* (1842). As T. H. Carter and

Company he published *Littell's Living Age* (1844-1845), edited by Eliskim Littell. Carter died on 11 July 1894 at age ninety-five.

References:

Robert W. Flint, "The Boston Book Trade 1836-1845," M.A. thesis, Simmons College, 1956;

Florence W. Newsome, "The Publishing and Literary Activities of the Predecessors of Ticknor & Fields," M.A. thesis, Boston University, 1942.

—George E. Tylutki

Cassell Publishing Company
(New York: 1860-1899)

Cassell Publishing Company of London, which was founded in 1833 by John Cassell, opened an office at 39 Park Row, New York, in 1860 and appointed John Robbins as manager. The office's main purpose was to sell family Bibles. It was closed when the Civil War began in 1861. In 1865 another office was opened by Walter Low at 596 Broadway. In 1868 Robert Turner was sent from London to take over the business; Turner returned to London in 1873, and Charles Geard managed the office for two years. Between 1865 and 1875 Cassell not only published books but also handled English-manufactured stationery and playing cards, and colored lithographs produced by the Paris house of Theo. Dupuy.

In 1875 an American, Oscar M. Dunham, became manager of the office. Dunham bought the company from Cassell in 1890 for $330,000, keeping the name Cassell Publishing Company. Dunham expanded the firm by acting as agent for London books other than those published by Cassell, as well as by publishing American books of a lighter nature than the books Cassell of London had published. Dunham continued Turner's policy of publishing illustrated works, including those of Gustave Doré.

In June 1893 Cassell was declared insolvent and placed in the hands of a receiver. Shortly afterwards, Dunham absconded with $180,000 in funds, and the Cassell Publishing Company was

taken over by one of its principal creditors, William L. Mershon, at 31 East Seventeenth Street. Cassell published the popular detective stories of Julian Hawthorne, the *Journal of Marie Bashkirtseff* (1890), Ambrose Bierce's *Can Such Things Be?* (1893), the novels of Arthur T. Quiller-Couch, and a perennial seller, Chauncey M. Depew's *Orations and After-Dinner Speeches* (1896). In addition, Cassell published some illustrated editions of J. M. Barrie's work.

Because Cassell of London had little control over its former subsidiary, it opened its own offices in 1898 at 7 and 9 West Eighteenth Street, New York. By the end of the year, this office was suing Mershon for various malpractices; Mershon's company went out of business in 1899. Cassell of London closed its American offices in 1913, and Funk and Wagnalls Company became the firm's agents. Although Funk and Wagnalls later divested itself of its position as Cassell's agents, it still handles Cassell dictionaries.

References:

"Contributions to Trade History: No. XX [through XXIII], Cassell & Company (Limited)," *American Bookseller*, new series 19 (1886): 7-8, 24-25, 45-48, 83-86;

Simon Nowell-Smith, *The House of Cassell: 1848-1958* (London: Cassell, 1958).

—Elizabeth Scott Pryor

The Century Company
(New York: 1881-1933)

See also the Appleton-Century-Crofts entry in *DLB 46, American Literary Publishing Houses, 1900-1980: Trade and Paperback.*

In 1870 Roswell Smith and Josiah Gilbert Holland founded *Scribner's Monthly,* a magazine published by Scribner and Company, a subsidiary of the Charles Scribner publishing house. Eleven years later Smith and Holland bought out the Scribner interests and formed The Century Company at 33 East Seventeenth Street, Union Square, New York. The name of the magazine was changed to the *Century Illustrated Magazine* and it became one of the most respected literary magazines in America. (From 1925 until its demise in 1929, it was called the *Century Monthly Magazine.*) Its contributors included Robert Louis Stevenson, William Dean Howells, Henry James, Mary Hartwell Catherwood, and James Whitcomb Riley. Also in 1881 Century purchased *St. Nicholas* magazine, perhaps the greatest American children's periodical, from the Scribner firm, which by then had become Charles Scribner's Sons. Holland died shortly after the founding of The Century Company.

The book publications of The Century Company were generally without lasting literary merit, although several of the titles sold well, and some became children's classics. Frank Stockton's *The Casting Away of Mrs. Lecks and Mrs. Aleshine* and its sequel, *The Dusantes,* appeared under the Century imprint in 1886 and 1888, followed in 1889 by Joel Chandler Harris's *Daddy Jake the Runaway.* The company published the first novel of Alice Hegan Rice, *Mrs. Wiggs of the Cabbage Patch* (1901), which sold almost 200,000 copies in a little more than a year. Other successful children's books include Palmer Cox's *The Brownies: Their Book* (1887), Eleanor Hollowell Abbott's *Molly Make-Believe* (1910), and Jean Webster's *Daddy-Long-Legs* (1912). The firm also published travel books, notably Edith Wharton's *Italian Villas and Their Gardens* (1904), Harry A. Franck's *A Vagabond Journey around the World* (1910), and Frederick O'Brien's *White Shadows in the South Seas* (1919). One of Century's most important nineteenth-century authors was S. Weir Mitchell, a Philadelphia physician who wrote, in addition to medical books, historical romances and other novels. Mitchell's most significant literary work, *Hugh Wynne: Free Quaker,* first serialized in the *Century Magazine,* was published in book form by the firm in 1897. Century published the Author's Edition of Mitchell's works in ten volumes in 1903.

Century's literary output during the twentieth century includes the first books of William Rose Benét and Alexander Woollcott, as well as most of the literary works of Donn Byrne. The firm published Benét's *Merchants From Cathay* in 1913 and Woollcott's *Mrs. Fiske* in 1917. After a brief career with Harper's, Byrne settled into a long relationship with Century. His most important works— *Messer Marco Polo* (1921), *Blind Raftery and His Wife Hilaria* (1924), *Brother Saul* (1927), and *Field of Honor* (1929)—bear the Century imprint.

The Century Company was well known for its reference works: *The Century Atlas of the World* (1887); *The Century Dictionary* (1889), which ran to 7,046 pages in six volumes and took seven years and over a million dollars to complete; and *The Century Cyclopedia of Names* (1894). Frank H. Scott succeeded Smith as president in 1890; he was replaced by W. W. Ellsworth in 1912. W. Morgan Schuster became president in 1915, the same year the firm moved to the Armory Building at 353 Fourth Avenue. In June 1933 The Century Company merged with D. Appleton and Company to become the D. Appleton-Century Company.

References:
Samuel C. Chew, *Fruit among the Leaves* (New York: Appleton-Century-Crofts, 1950), pp. 67-152;
William W. Ellsworth, *A Golden Age of Authors: A Publishers Recollection* (Boston: Houghton Mifflin, 1919);
The Story of the Century Co., 1870-1923 (New York: Century, 1923);
Two Score Years and Five: Quality (New York: Century, 1915).

—*Robert McNutt*

Robert Carter

Roswell Smith

*Josiah Gilbert Holland, cofounder of The
Century Company*

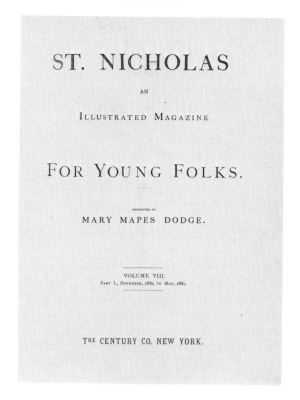

ST. NICHOLAS

AN

ILLUSTRATED MAGAZINE

FOR YOUNG FOLKS.

CONDUCTED BY

MARY MAPES DODGE.

VOLUME VIII.
PART I., NOVEMBER, 1880, TO MAY, 1881.

THE CENTURY CO. NEW YORK.

*Title page for the bound edition of the magazine The Century
Company purchased from Charles Scribner's Sons
in 1881*

William Charles
(New York; Philadelphia: 1808-1820)
Mary Charles
(Philadelphia: 1820-1823)

To escape prosecution in Edinburgh for caricaturing some city magistrates, William Charles came to New York in 1801. By 1807 he was an engraver at 195 Broadway. He published his first book, *Pompey the Little Who Was Tied to the Kettle,* in New York in 1808. Between then and 1815 he moved to Philadelphia and opened a bookstore and printing shop at 32 South Third Street. He published toy books (small illustrated books for young children), some of them in two styles—one with plain plates and a more expensive edition with colored engravings.

Nearly all of Charles's books were copied from English juveniles. Titles included *Pug's Visit to Mr. Punch* (1810), *The Lost Child: A Poetic Tale, Founded Upon a Fact* (1811), *Dame Trot and her Comical Cat* (1817), and *Little Nancy, or the Punishment of Greediness* (1817). Most of his thirty-eight known titles contain copperplate engravings although, as was the custom, they were unsigned. Many of his titles were sold by other Philadelphia firms, such as Morgan and Yeager, Morgan and Sons, and Johnson and Warner. These publishers printed their own names at the base of the front cover, but the title page usually had the Charles imprint, and the engraved plates and engraved text were his. After Charles died in 1820 his wife, Mary Charles, continued publishing toy books under her own name until her death in 1823.

Reference:

Harry B. Weiss, "William Charles, Early Caricaturist, Engraver and Publisher of Children's Books," *Bulletin of the New York Public Library,* 35 (1931): 831-840.

—*Kathleen McGowan*

The Christian Publishing Company
(St. Louis: 1870-1914)
The Christian Board of Publication
(St. Louis: 1914-1954)
Bethany Press
(St. Louis: 1954-1984)
CBP Press
(St. Louis: 1984-   )

The official publishing arm of the Disciples of Christ, The Christian Publishing Company was founded around 1870 at 1522 Lucas Place, St. Louis, Missouri. While stressing religious books and hymnals, the firm occasionally published religious fiction such as A. F. Smith's *Ernest Leighton* (1881), Barton Orville Aylesworth's *"Thirteen," and Twelve Others from the Adirondacks and Elsewhere* (1892), James Hiram Stark's *Hugh Carlin; or, Truth's Triumph* (1896), and John Augustus Williams's *Rosa Emerson; or, A Young Woman's Influence. A Story of the Lodge, the Church, and the School* (1897). One of the company's more prolific authors was John Breckenridge Ellis, whose *In the Days of Jehu* appeared in 1898, followed by *King Saul* (1898) and *Shem: A Story of the Captivity* (1900).

In 1903 the firm moved to 1522 Locust Street, and in 1907 to 2712 Pine Boulevard. The firm changed its name to The Christian Board of Publication in 1914. Eleven years later the imprint of the Bethany Press was created, and in 1954 this became the official name of the company. In 1984 the firm's name was changed to CBP Press. The firm has changed addresses several times over the years, but it has always remained on Pine Boulevard, currently at 2721. Its mailing address is Box 179, St. Louis, Missouri 63166.

—*David Dzwonkoski*

Robert Clarke and Company
(Cincinnati: 1858-1894)
The Robert Clarke Company
(Cincinnati: 1894-1909)

Born in Scotland in 1829, Robert Clarke immigrated to the United States in 1840 with his parents, who settled in Cincinnati. He entered the book trade in the early 1850s as an employee of Lyon and Patterson, a Cincinnati rare and second-hand book firm. When Lyon and Patterson was dissolved in 1854, Clarke bought an interest in the firm, which was then reorganized under the name of Patterson and Clarke with offices at 46 Sixth Street. Patterson and Clarke was never involved in publishing. In 1857 Clarke bought out Patterson's interest in the business. Under Clarke, the firm became the first bookstore in the Midwest to import books directly from Paris and London.

In 1858 Clarke and two partners, Roderick D. Barney and John W. Dale, purchased the law book publishing business of the Henry W. Derby Company, as well as that firm's distribution agencies for Harper and Brothers and Derby and Jackson. The three men formed Robert Clarke and Company and moved into the old offices of Henry W. Derby and Company at 55 West Fourth Street. Although the new firm retained Clarke's rare book and import business—it acted as agents for several English firms and maintained a London office—it was well on its way to becoming one of the most prominent publishing houses in the Midwest.

The Derby law list was one of the finest in the Midwest, and Derby titles formed a large percentage of Clarke's publications during the firm's first two decades. But by the late 1880s Clarke had established its own law list and had become one of the three or four largest legal publishers in the United States.

Although legal publishing made up a large percentage of its total sales, the firm is best remembered today for its historical publishing. Clarke had a strong interest in American history and archaeology, particularly of the Ohio and Missouri valley regions. Over the years he acquired thousands of books on Western Americana and history for his personal library. He eventually sold his Americana collection to Rutherford B. Hayes, and it now forms the nucleus of the Rutherford B. Hayes Memorial Library in Fremont, Ohio.

Clarke initiated his historical publishing with the Ohio Valley Historical Serial. The first volume, Dr. William Smith's *Historical Account of Bouquet's Expedition against the Ohio Indians, in 1764*, originally published in England in 1766, appeared in 1868. The remaining books in the series were *History of Athens County, Ohio* (1869) by Charles Walker, *Sketch of his Campaign in Illinois* (1869) by George Rogers Clark, *Pioneer Biography* (1869-1871) by James McBride, *An Account of the Remarkable Occurrences in the Life and Travels of Col. James Smith* (1870), *Pioneer Life in Kentucky* (1870) by Daniel Drake, and *Miscellanies* (1871). The firm's *Bibliotheca Americana*, a series of catalogues published between 1875 and 1893, have become classic reference sources. Other important historical titles published by Clarke include *Leith's Narrative* (1883); Thomas Marshall Green's *Historic Families of Kentucky* (1889); and two key works on the archaeology and pre-European settlement of the Ohio Valley, John Patterson MacLean's *The Mound Builders* (1879) and Warren King Moorhead's *Fort Ancient: The Great Pre-Historic Earthwork of Warren County, Ohio* (1890).

Robert Clarke and Company also developed a solid literary list, with a particular emphasis on criticism and poetry. Important critical works published by the firm include J. Appleton Morgan's *The Shakespearean Myth* (1881), David Philipson's *The Jew in English Fiction* (1889), and James Henry Cotter's *Shakespeare's Art* (1903). Nearly all of the poets on Clarke's list were regional authors, most of whom are not read or remembered today. Among the more prolific Clarke poets were Horace

Peters Biddle, an Indiana judge who wrote for the firm from 1870 to 1882; Coates Kinney; Laura G. Collins; and the Piatt family—John James Piatt, his wife, Sarah Morgan Piatt, and his father, Donn Piatt—who wrote nearly twenty books of poetry, romances, and other works for Clarke. Books by William Henry Venable, probably the most noteworthy poet Clarke published, include *June on the Miami and Other Poems* (1877) and *Melodies of the Heart* (1885). Venable's son Emerson edited the anthology *Poets of Ohio* (1909), the first major gathering of the work of poets from the region.

Although Robert Clarke and Company did not publish a large or significant body of original fiction, it reprinted the standard classics, as well as such contemporary works of regional interest as James Hall's western legends. In 1896 Clarke reprinted a work which has since become a minor classic, John Uri Lloyd's *Etidorhpa*, a science fiction novel which went through ten editions by 1900. Clarke's fiction list included Belle Bellville's *The Written Leaves* (1892), Katherine Cochran's *Posie; or, From Reveille to Retreat* (1896), and Nicholas Longworth's *The Marquis and the Moon* (1899) and *Silas Jackson's Wrongs: A Romance of Anderson's Ferry* (1889).

In 1891, due to a revision of Cincinnati street numbering, Robert Clarke and Company's address was changed from 55 West Fourth Street to 31-39 East Fourth Street. By then, the company had long since reached its zenith. Its law book publishing had begun to decline, and the firm continued its successful publishing of historical, literary, and general works into the first decade of the twentieth century at greatly reduced levels. In 1894 the firm underwent reorganization, incorporating as The Robert Clarke Company. The board of directors included all of the original partners; Clarke became the first president. The reorganization was made

largely in response to the economic climate resulting from the Panic of 1893 but also because Clarke was losing interest in publishing and preferred to spend his time on study and travel. In 1899 Clarke died and Roderick D. Barney assumed the presidency of the firm. On 26 February 1903 fire destroyed its offices, equipment, and stock. Although the firm was open for business the next day at 18 East Fourth Street, it never recovered from the catastrophe.

In 1905 Jay F. Lang, a law book publisher in Norwalk, Ohio, acquired a controlling interest in the company but published few new titles. Lang's failure to finance the reconstruction of his Norwalk plant, which had also been destroyed by fire in 1903, forced the company into receivership. In August 1909 the W. H. Anderson Company of Cincinnati purchased the firm's law books and copyrights, while W. K. Stewart, an Indianapolis bookseller, bought the equipment and the right to use the firm name. For twenty-six years Stewart and his partner, John G. Kidd, ran their business under the name of The Robert Clarke Book Store, while publishing under the Stewart Kidd Company imprint. In 1935 Kidd bought out Stewart's interest in the partnership, changing the bookstore's name to John G. Kidd and Son, Incorporated. The Stewart Kidd Company was purchased by Appleton in 1924.

References:

Charles Haynes McMullen, "The Publishing Activities of Robert Clarke & Co., of Cincinnati, 1859-1909," *Papers of the Bibliographical Society of America*, 34 (1940): 315-326;

William Henry Venable, "Robert Clarke—In Memoriam," *Publishers' Weekly*, 56 (16 September 1899): 361-362.

—Timothy D. Murray

Claxton, Remsen and Haffelfinger
(Philadelphia: 1868-1880)
E. Claxton and Company
(Philadelphia: 1880-1891)

George Remsen began working for the publishing firm of John Grigg in Philadelphia in 1828. Edmund Claxton joined them in 1833; Charles C. Haffelfinger apprenticed with the company, then Grigg and Elliott, in 1842 at the age of fourteen. In 1846 Claxton and Remsen were admitted as partners, and remained so after J. B. Lippincott purchased and reorganized the house in 1850 to form Lippincott, Grambo and Company. The firm became J. B. Lippincott and Company in 1855. In 1858 Haffelfinger was added as a partner. When the partnership expired in 1868, Claxton and Remsen decided to set up a new establishment and offered Haffelfinger an equal share in the business.

Soon outgrowing their first location at 819-821 Market Street, the partners decided to erect a complete bookmaking establishment that would be an ornament to the city of Philadelphia. The ground floor of the building, at 624-628 Market Street, was devoted to bookselling and offices, the second to the firm's stationery business, the third to book manufacturing, and the fourth to the display and sale of school furniture.

The house's reputation as a publisher was built by such mechanical and engineering works as John Cresson Trautwine's *Civil Engineer's Pocket Book* (1872), which sold 20,000 copies before J. Wiley took over its publication in its ninth edition in 1885. The firm also published religious, educational, and historical books and "fine editions" of Goldsmith's and Hazlitt's works. The *Avon Shakespeare* (1879) was called by *Publishers' Weekly* "the best, handsomest, and most legible type of any one-volume edition of its size on the market."

Claxton, Remsen and Haffelfinger undertook publication of a considerable amount of contemporary fiction. Before the Civil War, Philadelphia carried on a prosperous trade with the South, and Haffelfinger, while with the Lippincott firm, had

been particularly successful in garnering southern sales. Many of the new company's titles reflected that established audience. In 1869 the firm published, under her pseudonym "Filia," Sarah Ellis Dorsey's first novel, *Agnes Graham*, a story of slavery in New Orleans that had been serialized in the *Southern Literary Messenger* in 1863 and 1864. The book was a joint publication of Claxton, Remsen and Haffelfinger and J. A. Gresham, a New Orleans firm, as were Robert N. Ogden's *Who Did It?* (1870), a novel set in New Orleans, and Eliza Pugh's *In a Crucible* (1872), a story about Louisiana during the Civil War. Claxton, Remsen and Haffelfinger also published L. C. Hill's *Laure: The History of a Blighted Life* (1869), about the occupation of New Orleans by Union troops; Sarah Whittlesey's *Bertha the Beauty: A Story of the Southern Revolution* (1872); and Celina Means's *Thirty-Four Years: An American Story of Southern Life* (1878), published under the pseudonym John Marchmont.

Other fictional works published by Claxton, Remsen and Haffelfinger include Mary Nauman Robinson's *Sidney Elliott* (1869), *Twisted Threads* (1870), and *Clyde Warleigh's Promise* (1873) and Elsie Leigh Whittlesey's *Who Was She?* (1871), *Helen Ethinger* (1872), and *The Hemlock Swamp and a Season at the White Sulphur Springs* (1873). Together with A. Roman in San Francisco, the firm published Josephine Clifford McCrackin's *Overland Tales* (1877). McCrackin's first story had been published by Bret Harte in the *Overland Monthly*, and Harte had encouraged her to continue writing about her adventures as an army wife in the Southwest. *Overland Tales* was the first collection of these stories—many of them about women abandoned by brutal spouses and forced to make their own way—that had been published earlier in periodicals.

In 1876 Remsen retired from the company in ill health. When his capital was withdrawn upon his death in March 1880, the firm's financial situation—already disrupted by Jay Gould's manipulation of the gold and money markets—became desperate. In September 1880 Claxton announced the formation of E. Claxton and Company, a partnership with his son Robert. Immediately after the reorganization, on 1 October 1880, Claxton moved the business to 930 Market Street. Haffelfinger remained with the new firm as a salesman until a year before his death in April 1885.

E. Claxton and Company continued to issue the "useful" books, standard works, and novels for which Claxton, Remsen and Haffelfinger had been noted. Some of the new firm's titles reflect its long-established southern trade: Henry Flanders's *The Adventures of a Virginian* (1881); Emma Nelson Hood's *Bob Dean; or, "Our Other Boarder"* (1882), a story set in Texas from the Republic to the end of the Civil War; and Richard Penfield's story of the North Georgia gold fields, *Luelle: A Southern Romance* (1884).

Beleaguered by recalls of loans negotiated by the old firm, Claxton was forced to make an assignment in April 1884. According to *Publishers'* *Weekly*, Claxton ascribed the failure to the cheap publications of standard works, the dearth of "new and striking" literary works, and "the suicidal practice" of dry goods houses selling books at wholesale prices to draw in trade. If business were in "a normal condition," Claxton believed, the firm could have discharged its debts. Following the bankruptcy, Edward Meeks, a longtime associate, continued to handle the house's most important titles until shortly after Claxton died on 13 September 1891.

References:

"Claxton, Remsen & Haffelfinger," in "The Bookmakers. Reminiscences and Contemporary Sketches of American Publishers," *New York Evening Post*, 8 September 1875;
"Failure of E. Claxton & Co.," *Publishers' Weekly*, 25 (19 April 1884): 489;
"Obituary. Charles Carson Haffelfinger," *Publishers' Weekly*, 27 (25 April 1885): 491;
"Obituary. Edmund Claxton," *Publishers' Weekly*, 40 (29 September 1891): 364.

—*Susan K. Ahern*

P. F. Collier
(New York: 1874-1898)
P. F. Collier and Son
(New York: 1898-1918)
P. F. Collier and Son Company
(New York: 1918-1919)
P. F. Collier and Son Corporation
(New York: 1919-1960)
P. F. Collier, Incorporated
(New York: 1960-1961)
Collier Books
(New York: 1961-   )

Born in Ireland in 1849, Peter Fenelon Collier immigrated to the United States in the late 1860s. After a brief enrollment in St. Mary's Seminary in Cincinnati, he worked for Sadlier and Company, John E. Potter and Company, and P. J. Kenedy. After Kenedy rejected Collier's idea of selling books on an installment plan, Collier started his own firm in New York in 1874 to carry out his innovation by purchasing the plates to *Father Burke's Lectures*. He also sold Bibles on his deferred-payment plan. His first original publication was a biography of Pope Pius X in 1874, followed three years later by sets of Dickens and Shakespeare. The printing was contracted out until 1880, when Collier opened his own print shop.

With his expanding printing plant—with a capacity of 20,000 volumes a day—and a highly efficient subscription sales operation which divided the United States into thirty-two regions and ninety-six subregions, Collier became enormously successful. From the firm's beginning until 1909, Collier sold over fifty million volumes—mostly in-

expensive reprints—including almost six million volumes of Dickens and one and a half million volumes of James Fenimore Cooper. Encyclopedias accounted for about four percent of the Collier output. Collier also published sets of the works of Sir Walter Scott, William Makepeace Thackeray, and Edward Gibbon. In 1888 the firm established a magazine, *Once a Week;* in 1896 it was reorganized as *Collier's Weekly.* With the addition of Collier's son Robert J. Collier to the firm in 1898, the company became P. F. Collier and Son. Soon after—having had several earlier addresses—the firm settled at 416-424 West Thirteenth Street.

In 1909 Collier announced what became his most famous project, the Harvard Classics, popularly known as The Five-Foot Shelf. Edited by Charles W. Eliot and other Harvard professors, the collection offered the works of authors from Homer to Dickens in uniform editions of good quality. From 1909 to 1921, the firm sold 240,000 sets of fifty volumes each.

After P. F. Collier's death in 1910, Robert Collier assumed the presidency of the newly incorporated firm. When Robert died in 1918, the firm was reorganized as the P. F. Collier and Son Company, with George D. Buckley as president. A year later the firm was purchased by The Crowell Publishing Company, which had been founded in Springfield, Ohio, in 1877 as a magazine publisher. The parent firm became Crowell-Collier, with the imprint of the P. F. Collier and Son Corporation as a subsidiary. In 1921 Crowell-Collier acquired the subscription list of Harper and Brothers, gaining sets of the works of Hardy, Twain, Howells, and Conan Doyle, as well as Woodrow Wilson's *A History of the American People* (1902). Also by subscription, Crowell-Collier began publishing the Junior Classics series.

When Crowell-Collier acquired a controlling interest in The Macmillan Company in 1960 the Collier line became P. F. Collier, Incorporated. In the same year Crowell-Collier moved to 640 Fifth Avenue, where the Collier subsidiary had been located since 1951. In 1961 Crowell-Collier launched its own paperback line, Collier Books, which subsequently became part of Macmillan Publishing Company; as the primary Macmillan paperback imprint it publishes fiction and a wide spectrum of general interest categories.

The parent corporation became Crowell-Collier and Macmillan, Incorporated in 1965 and Macmillan, Incorporated in 1972. The Macmillan Publishing Company is the major trade subsidiary. The firm's address since 1967 has been 866 Third Avenue, New York 10022.

References:
"80 Years of Facts and Figures," *Library Journal,* 80 (1 April 1955): 732-733;
Kenneth McArdle, ed., *A Cavalcade of "Collier's"* (New York: Barnes, 1959).

—David Dzwonkoski

Peter Fenelon Collier

Isaac Collins in 1806 (courtesy of Grellet N. Collins, Chestertown, Maryland)

Collin and Small
(New York: circa 1873-circa 1876)

The New York publishing firm of J. B. Collin and George G. Small seems to have lasted only a few years, with publications appearing from 1873 to 1876 under the Collin and Small imprint. The imprint J. B. Collin appears in 1876 and that of Tousey and Small in 1878, with Small dropping out in 1880. Collin and Small evidently published fewer than a dozen fiction titles, most of them humorous. Some of these were written by Small, under the pseudonym Bricktop: *The Trip of the Porgie;* *or, Tacking up the Hudson* (1874); *My Mother-in-Law* (1875); and *"I Told You So"; or, The Beats and Baits of Society* (1876?). As The Bald-Headed Historian, Small wrote *A Bald-Headed History of America* (1876) for the firm. Some of the firm's other publications were written by John A. Harrington under the pseudonym John Carboy. Collin and Small books were slim volumes, averaging 60 pages and rarely exceeding 100.

—Ada M. Fan

Isaac Collins
(Burlington, New Jersey; Trenton, New Jersey; New York: 1770-1802)
Isaac Collins and Son
(New York: 1802-1805)
Collins, Perkins and Company
(New York: 1805-1808)
Collins and Perkins
(New York: 1808-1811)
Collins and Company
(New York: 1811-1817)
Collins and Hannay
(New York: 1817-1834)
B. and S. Collins
(New York: 1835-1836)
Collins, Keese and Company
(New York: 1836-1842)
Collins, Brother and Company
(New York: 1842-1847)
Collins and Brother
(New York: 1847-1884)
Charles Collins
(New York: 1884-1890)

Isaac Collins of Burlington, New Jersey, a Quaker printer known for the high quality of his work, became the printer for the colony of New Jersey in 1771. He also edited and printed the *New Jersey Gazette*, the first real newspaper in the colony, from December 1777 to November 1786, while printing, publishing, and selling almanacs, Quaker and non-Quaker religious works, medical books, history books, and antislavery publications. After moving to Trenton, he published in 1791 his most famous book, the second quarto edition of the Bible in English to be printed in America. (The first had been the Douay version printed by Mathew Carey in 1790.) It is still admired for its fine printing and scholarship.

In 1796 Collins moved to 189 Pearl Street in New York City, where his business enjoyed a modest prosperity under the name of Isaac Collins and

Son from 1802 to 1805. Benjamin Perkins became a partner in the firm in 1805, and its name was changed to Collins, Perkins and Company. With the death of his wife in 1805, Collins decided to retire; but he remained active until the completion of the second printing of the famous Bible in 1807. Perkins died in 1810, and the following year the name of the firm became Collins and Company. Two of Collins's sons, Benjamin and Joseph, stereotyped Lindley Murray's *English Grammar* in 1816 for one of the many editions published by the Collins house. The *English Grammar, Keys to the Exercises,* and other works by Murray were highly profitable for the Collins firm, though other publishers also brought out editions over the years.

In 1822 Benjamin Collins and Samuel Hannay moved the store to 230 Pearl Street, where the company was known as Collins and Hannay. Especially prior to 1834 the Collins firm—alone or in partnership with others—published literature as well as law, history, medicine, and science books. Chief among its literary offerings were editions of works by Shakespeare, Byron, Radcliffe, and Disraeli. A half-dozen titles by Sir Walter Scott were published by Collins and Hannay in the 1820s, including an abridgment of *The Life of Napoleon* in 1827, the same year that Carey and Lea published its three-volume edition. Carey and Lea had paid Scott £295; he received no money from Collins and Hannay.

Although it was then much easier and cheaper to reprint English works than to publish new American ones, Collins and Hannay put out five books by Americans from 1824 to 1826. Written by now-forgotten authors, the titles suggest an effort to select the popular: *The Christian Indian: or, Times of the First Settlers* (1825); *The Spirits of Odin; or, The Father's Curse* (1826). The firm's most important publication by an American author was a twenty-four-volume edition of James Fenimore Cooper's novels and tales that appeared from 1825 to 1832. The firm published no works of American literature after 1832.

In 1832 Benjamin Collins withdrew from the firm and was replaced by George B. Collins, the son of Charles Collins, Isaac's eldest son. In 1834 the firm went bankrupt. The following year Isaac Collins's grandsons Benjamin and Stacy began business as B. and S. Collins and, in 1836, John Keese joined them to form Collins, Keese and Company at 254 Pearl Street. Here the firm remained most of the time until 1884. At various times the firm was known as Collins, Brother and Company, Robert B. Collins in the 1850s, and later Collins and Brother. Charles Collins, the last of the family, discontinued the firm in 1884 but published a few educational books under his own imprint at 414 Broadway until 1885 and from the office of A. S. Barnes and Company until 1890.

References:

Richard F. Hixson, *Isaac Collins: A Quaker Printer in 18th Century America* (New Brunswick, N.J.: Rutgers University Press, 1968);

George C. Rockefeller, "The First Testaments Printed in New Jersey," *Papers of the Bibliographical Society of America,* 45 (1951): 148-151.

                                                      —Theodora Mills

S. Colman

(Portland, Maine; New York: 1830?-1846)

Samuel Colman began his career as a bookseller and publisher in Portland, Maine. Among the early Colman books were language texts by Henry Wadsworth Longfellow, including *Elements of French Grammar, Manuel de Proverbes Dramatiques,* and *French Exercises,* all in 1830. Colman moved to New York in the early 1830s to open a publishing house and bookstore at 8 Astor House, Broadway. Widely varied in genre and character, Colman's books were known for their beauty, being among the first in the United States to carry engraved illustrations. His bookstore was one of the showplaces of Manhattan in the late 1830s.

A strong nationalist, Colman dedicated himself to publishing works by American writers. He published a Library of American Poets series as well as a Dramatic Library, a Library of Romance, and Books for the Young—all exclusively by American authors. *Colman's Monthly Miscellany,* a literary review, ran from July to December of 1839, folding shortly before the publisher went bankrupt in the aftereffects of the Panic of 1837, which damaged many New York publishing houses. Colman eventually recovered and continued publishing until 1846. The bankruptcy tarnished his reputation because it prevented Colman from meeting the terms he had agreed to for Longfellow's *Hyperion* (1839), of which Colman was the first publisher. At the time, however, as Longfellow himself readily admitted, very few publishers would even look at American works, much less pay for them.

Before the bankruptcy Colman apparently offered generous terms, though the frequency with which he met them remains unclear. He paid N. P. Willis $300 for the play *Bianca Visconti* (1839) and, in the same year, agreed to advance $2,000 "on account" for Willis's *Romance of Travel* and *Tortesa the Usurer,* and also agreed to a twenty percent royalty on sales. Colman was the publisher of John Quincy Adams's speech *The Jubilee of the American Constitution* (1839) and the New York agent for Jared Sparks's twelve-volume *The Writings of George Washington* (1834-1837) and Samuel Goodrich's immensely popular Peter Parley series of books for home instruction.

—*George Hutchinson*

W. B. Conkey Company

(Chicago and Hammond, Indiana: 1877-1949)

The W. B. Conkey Company was founded in 1877 by Walter B. Conkey in a basement at 143 Monroe Street, Chicago, with two dollars in capital. The nineteen-year-old Conkey limited his operation at first to a small bindery. He later took on printing work, and in 1890 his company absorbed the Illinois Printing and Binding Company and moved into that firm's Chicago offices. In 1897 Conkey built his own plant at 617 Conkey Street, Hammond, Indiana, while maintaining an office at 332 South Michigan Avenue, Chicago. The firm eventually added a New York branch at 1 Madison Avenue. The Hammond plant was an immense structure with the capacity to handle all phases of book publishing and manufacture. Stressing excellence of craftsmanship, Conkey became renowned for the high quality not only of its own books but also of the books and catalogues it produced for other companies.

The Conkey lists for the late nineteenth and

early twentieth centuries reflect popular trends in American publishing during that period. In 1898 Conkey published the Harvard Series, the Yale Series, the Hammond Series, and the University Series, reprints of works by authors including Tennyson, Hawthorne, Conan Doyle, and Robert Louis Stevenson. Priced at twenty-five cents to a dollar each—only slightly higher than other publishers' reprint series of the time—the Conkey series were distinguished by their durability and their attractive bindings and design. Conkey also published poetry by Delia Austria, Edmund Vance Cooke, and Ida Celia Whittier. The more than twenty volumes of Ella Wheeler Wilcox's sentimental verse published by Conkey included *Poems of Passion* (1833), *Three Women* (1897), and *Poems of Power* (1901). Conkey also published contemporary American fiction by John Heber Flood, Herbert B. Robinson, and S. Ella Wood.

As a publisher of juveniles, Conkey produced series aimed at various age groups, from young children (the Precocious Piggy Series and the Old Mother Hubbard Series) to young adults (the Young Folks Standard Classics). By 1903 Conkey claimed to be "the largest manufacturing publishers in the world of toy books and board-covered juveniles."

Conkey's extensive humor list consisted for the most part of reprints and collected editions of popular humorists in the Humorous Series of Cloth Covered Books and the Franklin Series. Works by George Wilbur Peck became an important part of the Conkey list: Conkey reprinted *Peck's Bad Boy and His Pa* (1883) and collected Peck stories into anthologies such as *Peck's Bad Boy No. 2* (1894). Conkey reprinted more than ten of humorist Edgar Wilson (Bill) Nye's western tales in the last two decades of the nineteenth century.

Henry P. Conkey, Walter B. Conkey's son, took over the firm in 1923 and continued the Conkey emphasis on good books at reasonable prices. It was the firm's emphasis on quality—"building better books" as W. B. Conkey put it—and the manufacturing innovations it helped to bring about for which the company is best remembered. In 1949 the Rand McNally Company purchased the W. B. Conkey Company and added the Hammond plant to its own publishing operations.

References:
"Rand McNally Buys W. B. Conkey Press," *Publishers' Weekly*, 155 (8 January 1949): 129;
Where Better Books Are Built: A Picture Story of the Plant and Products of the W. B. Conkey Company (Hammond, Ind.: Conkey, 1940).

—*Timothy D. Murray*

John Conrad and Company
(Philadelphia: 1800-1816)
John Conrad
(Philadelphia: 1817-1822?)

John Conrad was a Philadelphia bookseller who built up connections with other bookstores in Baltimore and Washington and in Petersburg and Norfolk, Virginia. He published about a dozen books a year from 1800 to 1807; after that he published less frequently. John Conrad and Company was located at 30 Chestnut Street from 1800 to 1815 and at 66 and 68 Chestnut Street through 1816. From 1806 to 1816 Conrad also listed two addresses on Walnut Street and another at 205 Market Street. The "and Company" was dropped after 1816, and only the Chestnut and Sixth Street address was used.

Books published by Conrad included chemistry texts, atlases, almanacs, Supreme Court reports, and reprints of European and American literature. The firm published the *Literary Magazine and American Register*, founded by Charles Brockden Brown, from October 1803 to December 1807. Goldsmith, Defoe, Sheridan, Johnson, and Scott were among the British authors whose works Conrad published. The best-known—perhaps the only—American literary writers whose works were published by Conrad were Brown and Hugh H.

Brackenridge. In 1801 Conrad reprinted Brown's *Edgar Huntley* and published his *Jane Talbot* for the first time. Conrad reprinted Brackenridge's *Modern Chivalry* in 1804. Joel Barlow's epic poem *The Co-* *lumbiad* was published in 1807. Conrad's imprint disappeared around 1822.

—*Theodora Mills*

The Continental Publishing Company
(New York: circa 1896-circa 1906)

The Continental Publishing Company began in New York in the 1890s. From 1897 to 1901 it was located at 25 Park Place. A large percentage of the firm's output consisted of popular fiction such as Verner Zevola Reed's *Tales of the Sun-Land* and *Lo-to-kah* and Paul Tyner's *Through the Invisible.* These titles were published in 1897 and were followed the next year by Elizabeth Winthrop Johnson's *Orchard Folk: Two California Stories,* Eugenia Bacon's *Lyddy: A Tale of the Old South,* and Francis Eugene Storke's *Mr. De Lacy's Double.* Beulah Downey Hanks's *For the Honor of a Child* appeared in 1899, and one of the company's best-sellers, Leo Charles Dessar's *A Royal Enchantress: The Romance of the Last Queen of the Berbers,* was published the following year. Among the illustrators of these books were Charles Craig, L. Maynard Dixon, and John Aarts. From 1901 to 1906 the firm's address was 24 and 26 Murray Street, with offices also at 389 Fifth Avenue. The firm also had a London branch. It seems to have gone out of business around 1906.

—*David Dzwonkoski*

David C. Cook Publishing Company
(Chicago: 1875-1935)

Chiefly a reprint house and publisher of Sunday school books, the David C. Cook Publishing Company was located at 36 Washington Street in Chicago and distributed its books from Elgin, Illinois. According to one of its advertisements, the firm's intention was to produce "the best, cheapest and most complete Sunday school Library in the world." The literary publications of the firm had a religious and moral cast and included reprints of T. S. Arthur's perennial best-seller *Ten Nights in a Bar-Room and What I Saw There* and the popular *The Prince of the House of David* (1898) by Rev. J. H. Ingraham. Cook occasionally published original fiction; Florence M. Kingsley's *Titus, A Comrade of the Cross* (1895) won a $1,000 prize for the best biography of Jesus Christ and sold over a million copies. Many Cook publications were published in series such as The New Sabbath Library, which included Mary E. Bamford's *Out of the Triangle* (1895), Fannie E. Newberry's *The Wrestler of Philippi* (1896), and Becca Middleton Samson's *A Devotee and a Darling* (1898). Small quartos, Cook novels were published in pamphlet format at five cents and clothbound at twenty-five cents per copy. Books were sold by subscription. The firm ceased operation in 1935.

—*Peter Dzwonkoski*

Increase Cooke and Company
(New Haven, Connecticut: 1802-1813)

Increase Cooke was born on 15 March 1771 and graduated from Yale in 1793. In 1802 he started the bookselling and publishing firm of Increase Cooke and Company in partnership with John Babcock at 1810 Church Street, New Haven, Connecticut. The company eventually moved to Chapel Street, where it became a prolific publisher of children's books. Instructive "true histories" were published, including James Alexander Haldane's *The Vain Cottager; or, The History of Lucy Franklin* (1807) and *Early Instruction Recommended: In a Narrative of the Life of Catherine Haldane* (1812). The firm published editions of William Moseley's *The New Token for Children; or, a Sequel To Janeway's* (1806), *Aesop's Fables* (1807), William Godwin's *Fables Ancient and Modern* (1807), and Daniel Defoe's *Robinson Crusoe* (1807). *The Happy Family; or, Winter Evenings' Employment* was reprinted from the 1800 English edition in 1803, 1804, and 1807.

In 1806 Increase Cooke and Company published Hannah More's *The Shepherd Of Salisbury Plain*, the first and most famous of her Sunday School Tracts. Nonfiction published by Cooke included the third edition of Noah Webster's *Elements of Useful Knowledge* (1808). Other books included *Stories, Original and Selected, in Prose and Poetry* (1813) and *Original Poems* (1813) by Ann Gilbert and Jane Taylor. The company published no books after 1813. After a long period of ill health Cooke died on 3 April 1814.

—*George E. Tylutki*

George Coolidge
(Boston: circa 1840-circa 1889)

Primarily a publisher of almanacs and city directories, George Coolidge established his firm in Boston in the early 1840s. His earliest known address was 130 Washington Street, where he published William Russell's *Guide to Plymouth, and Recollections of the Pilgrims* in 1846. This volume contained reprinted selections by Washington Allston, William Cullen Bryant, Rufus Dawes, and Timothy Dwight. From 13 Tremont Row, Coolidge published Alice Cary's *Poems of Old Age* in 1861. During the 1860s and 1870s, when his firm was located first at 3 Milk Street and, by 1869, at 289 Washington Street, Coolidge published the *Lady's Almanac*. These annual publications usually featured poems or stories by Alice and Phoebe Cary and Thomas Bailey Aldrich. Coolidge continued printing and publishing into the late 1880s.

—*David Dzwonkoski*

Copeland and Day

(Boston: circa 1892-1899)

Led by William Morris at his Kelmscott Press, a revival in fine printing occurred in England in the late nineteenth century. Morris stressed imaginative typefaces, elaborate typographical designs, and superior paper and binding. Herbert Copeland and Frederick Holland Day wanted to promote a similar revival in America. Both men belonged to Boston's literary-artistic set. Day, a rich eccentric famous for his flowing hair, pointed black beard, pince-nez, and exotic garments (among them a fez and Turkish slippers), provided the financial backing and artistic direction for the enterprise. He had worked for the Boston branch of A. S. Barnes from 1884 to 1889. Copeland, a staff member of the *Youth's Companion* magazine, contributed his extensive literary contacts and did much of the administrative and editorial work.

The exact starting date of their partnership is unknown, but by December 1892 they were receiving proofs for their second book, Dante Gabriel Rossetti's *The House of Life*, which was not published until 1894. By August 1893 Copeland and Day had opened a small office at 69 Cornhill. The first published book of the firm was *The Decadent: Being the Gospel of Inaction* (1893) by American architect Ralph Adams Cram. Neither the Cram nor the Rossetti volume bears the Copeland and Day imprint; the first publication to do so was *The Hobby Horse*, published in three numbers in 1893 and 1894.

The firm produced ninety-six titles, nearly all of them literary works, including fifty-four books of poetry, twenty-three volumes of fiction, and eleven collections of essays. Some were new editions of works by contemporary British authors, including Richard Le Gallienne, Alice Meynell, Francis Thompson, and Oscar Wilde; others were translations from Italian, French, Yiddish, Greek, and Old French. Many of the firm's titles also bear the imprint of Elkin Mathews or John Lane in England.

The work of American writers formed most of the list. Copeland and Day published Gelett Burgess's first book, *Vivette* (1897), and M. A. DeWolfe Howe's first book, *Shadows* (1897), as well as Alice Brown's *Meadow Grass; Tales of New England Life* (1895) and Louise Imogen Guiney's *Nine Sonnets Written at Oxford* (1895) and *Patrins* (1897). Stephen Crane's first book of poetry, *The Black Riders and Other Lines*, appeared in 1895. Two Copeland and Day books were best-sellers in 1897: *Free to Serve* by Emma Rayner and *Harvard Episodes* by Charles Macomb Flandrau. Also extremely popular were Bliss Carman and Richard Hovey's *Songs from Vagabondia* (1894) and *More Songs from Vagabondia* (1896).

Series published by the firm included the Oaten Stop series, chapbooks of work by young American poets including Herbert Bates, Hannah Parker Kimball, and James Buckham. The English Love Sonnet series, featuring familiar works by Shakespeare and Elizabeth Barrett Browning, were prime examples of the new elaborate typographical style.

William Dana Orcutt worked on many of the Copeland and Day books as an apprentice printer at John Wilson and Sons in Cambridge. Later, he praised the visual style developed by Day: instead of imitating Morris, Orcutt explained, Day "absorbed" the sources and aesthetic principles Morris used and made a fresh interpretation of them. Day's most important designer, according to Orcutt, was the architect Bertram Grosvenor Goodhue, whose typographical decorations adorned many of the Copeland and Day showpieces, notably the English Love Sonnets.

Frederick Holland Day (photograph by Reginald Craigie; courtesy of Jean and Kahlil Gibran)

Herbert Copeland (Harvard University Archives)

Important artists of posters, book covers, and illustrations included Maxfield Parrish, John Sloan, and Will Bradley. Ethel Reed's pictures for Gertrude Smith's *The Arabella and Araminta Stories* (1895) helped to make this children's book a collector's item. Copeland and Day was one of the first American publishers to give the illustrator equal prominence with the author, both in advertising releases and on the title page.

Day's private income enabled him to compensate for any titles that made no profit. Apparently his changing interests, rather than money problems, brought Copeland and Day to an end. By 1898 Day had become deeply involved in portrait photography, and in 1899 the eighty Copeland and Day titles then in print were sold, most of them to Small, Maynard and Company. Copeland died in 1923; Day died ten years later. Orcutt summarized the achievement of Copeland and Day: "[they] gave the old, established firms a shock by demonstrating that there really was a public that recognized a well-made book."

References:

Joe Walker Kraus, "Messrs. Copeland & Day—Publishers of the 1890s," *Publishers' Weekly*, 141 (21 March 1942): 1168-1171;

Kraus, *Messrs. Copeland and Day, 69 Cornhill, Boston, 1893-1899* (Philadelphia: MacManus, 1979);

William Dana Orcutt, "Frederick Holland Day," *Publishers' Weekly*, 125 (6 January 1934): 51-52, 54.

—*Margaret Becket*

N. Coverly

(Boston; Chelmsford, Massachusetts; Concord, Massachusetts; Plymouth, Massachusetts; Middleborough, Massachusetts; Amherst, New Hampshire; Haverhill, New Hampshire; Medford, Massachusetts; Salem, Massachusetts: 1770-1803)

Nathaniel Coverly began publishing in Boston in 1770. In 1775 he moved to Chelmsford, Massachusetts, where he printed in conjunction with Elisha Rich. In 1776 Coverly moved to Concord; by 1778 he had returned to Boston, where he published until 1784, by himself and in partnership with Robert Hodge. The following year he went to Plymouth and published the *Plymouth Journal* from 19 May 1785 to 13 June 1786. Coverly published in Middleborough in 1787 and 1788, then he returned to Boston, where he published the *Gentlemen and Ladies Town and Country Magazine* from February 1789 to August 1790. In 1794 he was again in Concord, and the following year in Amherst, New Hampshire, where he published the weekly *Amherst Journal, and the New Hampshire Advertiser* with his son, Nathaniel, Jr., from 16 January 1795 to 9 January 1796. Coverly then moved to Haverhill, New Hampshire, and published the *Grafton, Minerva and Haverhill Weekly Bulletin* from March 1796 to January 1798. For the next few years he published in Medford and Salem, Massachusetts. Coverly left Medford in March 1800 and printed only in Salem until 1802, when he fled Salem and declared bankruptcy. In 1803 he went to Boston, where he remained until his death in 1816.

One of the first works published by Coverly was an edition of Mary White Rowlandson's *A Narrative of the Captivity, Sufferings and Removes of Mrs. Mary Rowlandson* (1770). Later, he published another "captivity" story, *A Surprising Account of the Captivity and Escape of Philip M'Donald* (1796). Among the educational titles printed (and often reprinted) by Coverly were *The New-England Primer, Improved* (1762), *The American Primer, Improved* (1776), William Perry's *The Only Sure Guide to the English Tongue* (1788), and James Murray's *An Impartial History of the War in America, between Great Britain and the United States* (1781-1784). He published Mercy Otis Warren's *The Motley Assembly, A Farce* (1779) and J. Horatio Nichols's *The New-England Coquette: From the History of the Celebrated Eliza Wharton. A Tragic Drama in Three Acts* (1802). Coverly published Bickerstaff's, Weatherwise's, and Farmer's almanacs between 1785 and 1798 in Boston, Plymouth, Medford, and Salem. Among the British titles reprinted by Coverly were Alexander Pope's *An Essay on Man* (1780), Joseph Addison's *Cato: A Tragedy* (1782), and Henry Fielding's *The Remarkable History of Tom Jones, a Foundling* (1799).

Most of Coverly's children's books were published during his various residences in Boston, a few in Plymouth and Salem. In 1775 he printed an edition of Isaac Watt's *Divine Songs Attempted in Easy Language for the Use of Children*. With Hodge he published *The Holy Bible Abridged ... For the Use of Children* (1782), and in 1783 he published *The History of Little Goody Two-Shoes*, the woodcut illustrations for which he used in several other books including a reprint of Defoe's *Robinson Crusoe* (1784). Coverly also reprinted John Wright's *Spiritual Songs For Children* (1784). *Nurse Truelove's New-Year's Gift; or, The Book of Books for Children* was published in Plymouth in 1787. *The House That Jack Built. Also, The History of Mrs. Williams, and Her*

Plumb Cake (1787) contains the earliest American printing of "Little Red Riding Hood." Coverly published *The History of Master Friendly* (1792), *The Puzzling Cap, A Choice Collection of Riddles, In Familiar Verse* (1793), Richard Johnson's *The History Of A Little Child Found Under A Haycock* (1794) and *Tom Thumb's Little Book* (1794), *Jacky Dandy's Delight* (1799), *Little Stories For Little Children* (1803), and *The Juvenile Budget, Being A New Collection of Entertaining Fables* (1803). Coverly apparently did not publish any books after 1803.

—*George E. Tylutki*

Thomas Y. Crowell Company
(New York: 1876-1979)

1945

designed in 1959

Born in 1836 in West Dennis, Massachusetts, Thomas Young Crowell went to sea when he was sixteen. After four years, during which he advanced from cabin boy to second mate, Crowell took a job with Benjamin Bradley, a Boston bookbinder, for four dollars a week. Taking classes in his spare time to complete his interrupted education, Crowell rose to general manager by 1862. After Bradley's death, Crowell went into partnership with Bradley's widow but eventually bought her out. In 1870 he established "Thomas Y. Crowell, Successor to Benjamin Bradley" at 57 Washington Street.

In 1875 Crowell purchased the plates, books, and sheet stock of Warren and Wyman, a New York religious publisher. The following year he started a small publishing firm at 744 Broadway, New York, and hired William W. Wyman, one of the

partners of the defunct company, as his manager. In July 1876 the first Thomas Y. Crowell Company catalogue, an eight-page list of sixty titles, was published.

Crowell's first real publishing success was the Red Line Poets series, which offered attractively printed and bound volumes at modest prices. Between a quarter- and a half-million copies each of the poems of Burns, Byron, Tennyson, and Browning were sold. By 1882 there were forty-five titles in the series.

The firm moved to Clinton Hall, the center of the New York publishing world, in 1881. Crowell was the first to recognize an American market for modern Russian literature. Beginning with Tolstoy's *My Religion* (1885) and following with *Anna Karénina* (1886) and a four-volume *War and Peace* (1889), he slowly expanded his firm's list of Russian authors. In 1886 Crowell published the first well-researched labor history, Richard T. Ely's *The Labor Movement in America*. Ely went on to become the editor of the successful Crowell's Library of Economics and Politics. Crowell never abandoned his interest in publishing religious books, such as James R. Miller's popular *Making the Most of Life* (1891). Crowell published more than forty of Miller's works, with total sales of more than two million.

During the 1890s Crowell offered a balanced list of titles ranging from popular pamphlets to literary classics. In 1899 the firm was fourteenth in American book production. By the turn of the century Crowell had moved to 426-428 West Broadway. A biographical sketch of Crowell published in 1926 notes that Crowell "had little interest in ephemeral books, light fiction, or in belles lettres. He preferred solid books and was chiefly interested in those that would inspire or be useful for reference, so that one editor was led to say that he 'never issued a book that one is not better for having read.' "

Crowell died in 1915 and was succeeded by his son T. Irving Crowell, who supervised the move to 393 Fourth Avenue. The company continued to add reference titles to its list, such as *Crowell's Dictionary of Business and Finance* (1923) and an edition of *Roget's International Thesaurus* (1932). Trade books included Frank Heller's translations of Gunnar Semer's *The Grand Duke's Finances* (1924) and *The London Adventures of Mr. Collin* (1924), and lines of children's, gift, and devotional books. In 1937 T. Irving Crowell became chairman of the board and was succeeded as president by his son Robert L. Crowell. T. Irving Crowell died in 1942.

In 1938 Elizabeth Riley, formerly a buyer for Macy's book department and Brentano's, joined Crowell and developed a successful children's line. The firm followed a policy of conservative growth through the 1940s and 1950s. The 1960s saw more additions to the company's already formidable list of reference books: *Crowell's Handbook of World Opera* appeared in 1961; *Crowell's Handbook of Classical Literature* in 1964; *Crowell's Handbook of Classical Drama* in 1967.

In the 1970s several new handbooks appeared, including one on classical mythology (1970) and another on Elizabethan and Jacobean literature (1974). Crowell was acquired by Dun and Bradstreet in 1968, but retained its identity. Robert Crowell retired in 1972 and was replaced by Lewis Gillenson. Two years later the firm acquired Abelard-Schuman, Chandler Publishing Company, Criterion Books, the John Day Company, and Intext Educational Publishers. In 1979 Crowell itself was taken over by Harper and Row. Its name survives as an imprint of that firm.

(The Crowell-Collier Publishing Company stems from a merger of P. F. Collier and Son Company with The Crowell Publishing Company, a firm unrelated to Thomas Y. Crowell.)

References:

Chester T. Crowell, "How I Found Myself: The Publisher's Story," *Saturday Evening Post,* 197 (7 March 1925): 49-50, 69;

Thomas Irving Crowell, *Thomas Young Crowell, 1836-1915: A Biographical Sketch* (New York: Crowell, 1926);

"T. Y. Crowell Centenary," *Publishers' Weekly,* 125 (31 March 1934): 1282-1283.

—Linda DeLowry-Fryman

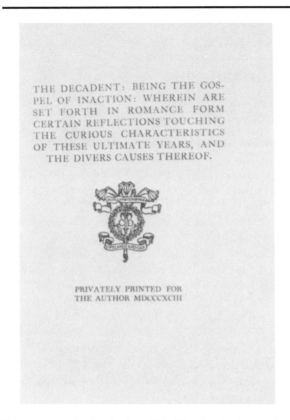

THE DECADENT: BEING THE GOS-
PEL OF INACTION: WHEREIN ARE
SET FORTH IN ROMANCE FORM
CERTAIN REFLECTIONS TOUCHING
THE CURIOUS CHARACTERISTICS
OF THESE ULTIMATE YEARS, AND
THE DIVERS CAUSES THEREOF.

PRIVATELY PRINTED FOR
THE AUTHOR MDCCCXCIII

*Title page for the first book published by Copeland and Day,
written by architect Ralph Adams Cram*

Thomas Young Crowell in 1882

*57 Washington Street, Boston, where Crowell established
"Thomas Y. Crowell, Successor to Benjamin Bradley"
in 1870*

*T. Irving Crowell, who succeeded his father as president of the
firm in 1915*

Cummings and Hilliard
(Boston: 1812-1823)
Cummings, Hilliard and Company
(Boston: 1823-1827)

In 1812 William Hilliard, a printer in Cambridge, Massachusetts, formed a partnership with Jacob Abbott Cummings, a Boston schoolteacher, to publish and sell textbooks at 1 Cornhill in Boston. Cummings and Hilliard published many of the reading texts required for entrance to Harvard University, among them Cummings's *Introduction to Ancient and Modern Geography* (1817). The firm also published Harvard professor Jacob Bigelow's three-volume *American Medical Botany* (1817); the work contained many engravings in color, an achievement rarely seen in books before.

Cummings and Hilliard published some literary works by American authors, including the first two books by Lydia Maria Child: *Hobomok* (1824) and *The Rebels; or, Boston before the Revolution* (1825); Timothy Flint's *Francis Berrian; or, The Mexican Patriot* (1826); and novels by Eliza L. Cushing,

Sarah Savage, and Nicholas M. Hentz. William Cullen Bryant's second book of poetry, *Poems*, was published under the Hilliard and Metcalf imprint in 1821 and sold by the Boston bookstore for 37 1/2¢.

When Cummings died in 1823, the firm's name was changed to Cummings, Hilliard and Company. Timothy Carter, who later founded Carter and Hendee, became a partner at this time. Carter persuaded Hilliard to enter the lucrative law book field. In 1824 Thomas Jefferson requested Hilliard's help in purchasing books and journals for the University of Virginia library, and Hilliard's company established a branch bookstore in Charlottesville, near the university. In 1827 Harrison Gray joined the firm, which became Hilliard, Gray and Company.

—*Theodora Mills*

Peter F. Cunningham
(Philadelphia: circa 1860-1873)
Peter F. Cunningham and Son
(Philadelphia: 1873-1908)

Peter F. Cunningham began his Philadelphia business around 1860, publishing Catholic theological and liturgical works almost exclusively. In the 1860s and early 1870s Cunningham published a few literary works, the earliest known being Mary L. Meany's *Grace Morton; or, The Inheritance: A Catholic Tale* (1864) and *The Confessors of Connaught* (1865). Most of Cunningham's other novels were "Catholic Tales" as well. These included Cora Berkley's *The Beauforts* (1866), Mary Miller Meline's *The Montarges Legacy* (1869), and Fannie Warner's *Beech Bluff* (1870). Several other titles were published anonymously.

After 1873, as Peter F. Cunningham and Son, the firm published few novels. Of these, Mrs. Clara M. Thompson's *Hawthorndean; or, Philip Benton's Family* (1873) is the best known. This was followed two years later by Joseph Riley Chandler's *The Beverly Family; or, Home Influence of Religion*. The firm also published The Young Catholic's Library during this period. By 1888 the company's address was 817 Arch Street. In 1908 P. J. Kenedy and Sons purchased the business.

—*David Dzwonkoski*

Cupples, Upham and Company
(Boston: 1883-1887)
Cupples and Company, Publisher
(Boston: 1887)
Cupples and Hurd
(Boston: 1887-1890)
J. G. Cupples Company
(Boston: 1890-1893)

Joseph G. Cupples and Henry M. Upham were partners in A. Williams and Company, a Boston bookselling and publishing firm at the Old Corner Book Store, 135 Washington Street. After Williams retired in April 1883 the firm was reorganized as Cupples, Upham and Company. The third partner was Charles L. Damrell, who had been with Williams longer than the other two and earlier with James Munroe and Company. In April 1887 Cupples left the Old Corner Book Store to Damrell and Upham and listed himself as Cupples and Company, Publisher, at 94 Boylston Street. Within a month A. D. Hurd, son of M. M. Hurd of Hurd and Houghton, became a partner in the firm, which became Cupples and Hurd. By February 1890 Hurd had left, and Cupples continued to publish and sell books under the name J. G. Cupples Company. The firm moved to 250 Boylston Street in 1892.

Fiction and poetry accounted for nearly half of the firm's titles. Cupples, Upham published twelve titles in fiction; Cupples and Hurd thirteen; and J. G. Cupples five. Women writers of fiction outnumbered the men; none are well known today.

Sarah Greene, whose most popular works were published by A. Williams, had two more published by the successors: *Some Other Folks* (1884) and *Lastchance Junction, Far, Far West* (1889). Two novels by Hannah Elizabeth Goodwin Talcott were published, *One among Many* (1884) and *Our Party of Four* (1887). William Wilberforce Newton's *The Priest and the Man* (1883) and William Henry Rideing's *A Little Upstart* (1885) and *Thackeray's London* (1885) were all published by Cupples, Upham. Cupples and Hurd published *Wit, Wisdom and Pathos* with selections from Heinrich Heine in 1888, and in 1892 J. G. Cupples added a volume of selections from Goethe. The firm's most famous title was Johanna Spyri's *Heidi* (1885). J. G. Cupples Company went out of business in 1893.

References:

"A Change in Boston Firm, Agreement of Mr. Cupples from the 'Old Corner,'" *Publishers' Weekly*, 31 (23 April 1887): 562;

"Cupples and Hurd," *Publishers' Weekly*, 31 (14 May 1887): 638.

—Theodora Mills

Robert L. Crowell became president of Thomas Y. Crowell Company in 1937, when his father became chairman of the board

Advertisement

Title page for an anonymous work showing Day's use of woodcuts and verse in his publications

James Cephas Derby

William S. Damrell
(Boston: 1835-1837; 1848-1861)
Ford and Damrell
(Boston: 1833-1835)
Whipple and Damrell
(Boston: 1837-1848)

A Boston publisher noted chiefly for his temperance tales, William S. Damrell began his career in partnership with John Ford under the name Ford and Damrell in 1833 at Wilson Lane. In 1834 the firm moved to 26 State Street. During its two-year existence, Ford and Damrell published Lucius Manlius Sargent's *I am Afraid There is a God! Founded on Fact* (1833) and *My Mother's Gold Ring* (1833), *The Moderate Drinker* (1834) by "A Friend of Temperance," Mary L. Fox's *The Ruined Deacon: A True Story* (1834), and the anonymous *Home; or, An Account of Charles Grafton, a Sailor* (1834).

By 1835 Ford and Damrell were publishing separately, with Ford continuing at the State Street address while Damrell moved to 3 Cornhill. Under the imprint William S. Damrell, Damrell published mainly the works of Sargent until 1837, when he joined with an obscure figure named Whipple to form Whipple and Damrell at 9 Cornhill. The new partners published Hannah Farnham Lee's *Three Experiments of Living: Living within the Means; Living up to the Means; Living beyond the Means* (1837), a best-selling moralistic novel. The novel's sequel, *Elinor Fulton,* and Lee's *The Contrast; or, Modes of Education* and *Rich Enough: A Tale of the Times* were also published in 1837. Whipple and Damrell published *The Lectures; or, Woman's Sphere* (1839) by Sarah Josepha Hale and *A History of the "Striped Pig"* (1838) and *Retrenchment; or, Ways and Means* (1841), both anonymous works. The firm also published or reprinted further works by Sargent before the partnership dissolved in 1848.

Resuming his own imprint, Damrell published Mrs. J. Thayer's *The Drunkard's Daughter* (1842) and Sargent's *Diary of the Rev. Solomon Spittle* (1847) before forming a partnership with Frank C. Moore in 1848. Under the name Damrell and Moore, the firm specialized in city directories, while occasionally publishing such fiction as Mrs. Gertrude Vingut's *Irene; or, The Autobiography of an Artist's Daughter* (1853). The firm was located at 16 Devonshire until its demise in 1861.

—Evelyn A. Walker

Mahlon Day
(New York: 1820?-1846)
Day and Turner
(New York: 1815-1820?)
Baker, Crane and Day
(New York: 1846-1848)

In the first quarter of the nineteenth century Mahlon Day established what in a few years became one of the most important and successful children's book publishing companies in New York. Many of the books that bore his imprint initiated the movement away from the stark didacticism and dry morality of the children's literature of the previous century toward more imaginative and entertaining forms.

Day was born in Morristown, New Jersey, on 27 August 1790. His education cut short by the death of his father, Day was apprenticed to a printer. He completed his apprenticeship in 1811 and left home to find work in New York. By 1815 he was married and had begun his own business as a printer in partnership with Charles Turner at 35 Beaver Street. Day and Turner published the *New York Shipping and Commerce List* from 1815 to 1819. It is not clear how long Day worked with Turner, but children's books published by the firm after 1821 bear only the Day imprint. Day moved his company to 84 Water Street in 1820 and to 372 Pearl Street in 1823. There were two subsequent Pearl Street addresses—376 in 1825 and 374 in 1835.

Day called his children's books "toys" and sold them for one to twelve and a half cents each. According to Harry B. Weiss's examination of 135 Day titles, fifty percent dealt with biography or natural history; twenty-five percent were moral tales and fables; fifteen percent were schoolbooks, readers, and primers; and ten percent were religious material, such as Bible stories and collections of hymns.

Much of Day's children's literature was published anonymously, either without attribution or with obscure references such as "by a Lady" or "by Frank and Harry." Many books were reprints of English originals, including Mrs. Mary Martha Sherwood's *Babes in the Wood* (1825) and *Little Robert and the Owl* (1830), Anna Letitia Barbauld's *Barbauld's Hymns* (1830) and *Barbauld's Lessons for Children* (1834), Mrs. Lucy Lyttelton Cameron's *Memory* (1834), and Jane and Anne Taylor's *Original Poems,*

for Infant Minds (1834) and *A Day's Pleasure* (1833). Most of Day's books for children were intended to be instructional or informative, such as *The History of Curious and Wonderful Beasts* (1833), *Black-Bird's Nest, an Instructive Tale* (1834), and *City Cries and London Sights* (1834). Some titles clearly suggest the blend of fiction with the expression of morality or virtue: *Blind Susan; or, The Affectionate Family* (1829), *Little Susan and Her Lamb* (1829), *The True and Wonderful Story of Paul Gasford, Who, When Only About Four Years Old Was Lost in the Woods, and by His Own Remarkable Contrivance and Wisdom, after Four Days' Travel, Got Safe to His Parents, at Niagara, 40 Miles from the Place Where He Was Lost* (n.d.), and Hannah More's *The Happy Waterman; or, Honesty the Best Policy* (1829). That idle fantasy was to be shunned is suggested in such titles as *Jack Halyard and Ishmael Bardus. Shewing the Folly of Reading Silly Rhymes and of Listening to Foolish Stories about Ghosts* (n.d.). The *Journal of Education,* the *New York Weekly Messenger,* and the *New York Evening Journal* commended Day's books for being amusing as well as for avoiding "bad influences."

Day's books were often heavily illustrated; sometimes a book consisted simply of woodcuts accompanied by a few lines of verse. Many illustrations, some in color, were by J. A. Adams; Alexander Anderson's engravings were used in *Book of Cuts, Designed for the Amusement and Instruction of Young People* (1823) and possibly in *Rhode Island Tales* (1833) by Avis C. Howland.

Other children's book publishers in New York at the time included Samuel Wood, whose books were so similar to those of Day that often only the imprints distinguished the work of one firm from that of the other; Solomon King; N. B. Holmes; Daniel Cooledge; and Kiggins and Kellogg. Of these competitors, Wood had the largest market. Day competed with Wood and others by using the covers of his books, and even some of the inner pages, for advertisements. Some books end with rhymes that publicize Day's name and the location of his store. *Rhode Island Tales,* for instance, closes with the following stanzas:

And here behold in fair array,
   A part of this her work,
Printed and sold by Mahlon Day,
   Who lives in famed New-York.
In Pearl-street stands his handsome store,
   The number we affix,
In figures marked above the door,
   Three hundred seventy-six.

The cover of *Simple Stories* (1833) reads:

Of all the Stores in New-York city,
   Day's is the one for Toys,
Many are there in prose or ditty,
   For either Girls or Boys.

Other minor publications of Day's firm include *Day's New-York Miniature Almanac*, books on rhetoric, lectures, an edition of *Pilgrim's Progress*, reckoners, Brown's *Bible Concordance*, drawing books, Testaments, twenty kinds of dictionaries, and thirteen catechisms.

After Day retired in 1846, his nephew Stephen M. Crane, his son, Edward M. Day, and George Baker, a former apprentice, took over the firm under the name of Baker, Crane and Day.

Edward had only a limited interest in publishing, however, and when he left New York for Rochester, Baker, Crane and Day collapsed.

In 1820 Day and his wife had become members of the Society of Friends, and they worked diligently for the society for many years. Day was also a member of the boards of the New York Institution for the Blind, the Society for the Reformation of Juvenile Delinquents, and the Association for the Benefit of Colored Orphans. On 27 December 1854 Day was returning from a trip abroad on the steamer *Arctic* when the ship struck another vessel in a dense fog. Day and his wife and daughter were killed in the accident.

References:
Margaret Toth, "Mahlon Day's Books for Children," *University of Rochester Library Bulletin*, 7 (1951-1952): 56-64;
Harry B. Weiss, "Mahlon Day, Early New York Printer, Bookseller and Publisher of Children's Books," *Bulletin of the New York Public Library*, 45 (December 1941): 1007-1021.

—Chris M. Anson

T. S. Denison and Company
(Chicago; Minneapolis: 1876-)

Founded in 1876 by Thomas Stewart Denison at 70 Metropolitan Block in Chicago, T. S. Denison and Company moved to 163 West Randolph Street, then to 152 West Randolph, and finally to 623 South Wabash Avenue. Denison died in 1911; he bequeathed the company to Eben Norris, who had worked his way up in the firm. When Norris died in 1943, the company was acquired by Lawrence M. Brings, who moved it the following year to Minneapolis.

Although the company has become exclusively a publisher of educational material, for most of its history it published plays, vaudeville sketches, comedies, dialogues, monologues, and poetry readings, many of them written, compiled, or adapted by the founder, who also wrote a few novels. The plays and other materials were distributed and advertised through catalogues and field agents. At one time, the company was probably the largest

distributor of such material in the United States. Cheaply printed, most of the plays sold for fifteen or twenty-five cents and were intended to be produced by school or church groups.

The company's materials were sold in series, such as the Amateur Series, The Amateur Stage, The Star Drama, The Alta Series, Friday Afternoon Series, Friday Afternoon Speaker, and Wide-Awake Dialogues. Wide-Awake Dialogues, introduced in 1903, sold 500,000 copies by 1906; and Friday Afternoon Series of Dialogues, introduced around 1880, sold 50,000 copies by 1910. Plays written by Denison include *Borrowing Trouble* (1878), *Hard Cider; A Temperance Sketch* (1880), and *The Danger Signal* (1883).

An advertisement in the December 1929 issue of *The Drama* for Denison's Popular Fall-Evening Plays includes Larry Edward Johnson's *Her Step Husband* (1925), *The Absent-Minded Bridegroom*

(1926), and *Back Seat Drivers* (1929); Neil E. Schaffner's *Ghost Bird* (1927); Maude Fulton's *Sonny; A Comedy Drama* (1929); and Florence Edna May's *Glorious Annabelle; A Farce* (1929).

T. S. Denison and Company is currently lo-cated at 9601 Newton Avenue South, Minneapolis 55431. Lawrence Brings is chairman of the board; Keith M. Brings is president.

—*Everett C. Wilkie, Jr.*

J. C. Derby and Company
(New York: 1853-1855)
Derby and Jackson
(New York: 1855-1861)

James Cephas Derby, the oldest of four brothers in the book trade, was born in Little Falls, New York. On 10 September 1833, shortly after his fifteenth birthday, he was apprenticed to the Auburn bookseller Henry Ivison. In 1840, supplied with Ivison's capital, Derby purchased the bookstore of Ulysses Doubleday and founded J. C. Derby and Company. Four years later Derby formed a partnership with his clerk, Norman C. Miller. Derby and Miller and its successor firms continued in Auburn until 1857, evolving a list of over 100 titles.

In December 1853 Derby sold his share of the partnership and established J. C. Derby and Company at 8 Park Place, New York. George Ripley, literary editor of the *New York Tribune*, was engaged as his reader. Following Ripley's recommendation, Derby became the first publisher of the work of Thomas Bailey Aldrich. Aldrich's *The Bells: A Collection of Chimes* appeared in 1855 and was followed in 1857 by *Daisy's Necklace*. The firm also hired Aldrich as a reader.

In 1855 Edwin Jackson, formerly of H. and E. Phinney of Cooperstown, became a partner in the firm, which was renamed Derby and Jackson. Derby and Jackson published more than 300 titles, including current American literature and standard English classics, the latter in handsome, uniform library editions. The firm also exploited the new market for costly subscription publications and earned a reputation for having pioneered this risky but profitable style of production. Frank Goodrich's lavishly illustrated *The Court of Napoleon* (1857) was one such subscription work. The firm published Henry Ward Beecher's *Star Papers* (1855) and *Notes from Plymouth Pulpit* (1859), Alice Cary's *Married, Not Mated* (1856) and *Pictures of Country*

Life (1859), Frederick S. Cozzens's *The Sparrowgrass Papers* (1856), and Harriet Beecher Stowe's *The Minister's Wooing* (1859). Fiction published by Derby and Jackson included Frances Miriam Whitcher's *The Widow Bedott Papers* (1856), John Esten Cooke's *The Last of the Foresters* (1856), Marion Harland's *Moss-Side* (1857) and *Nemesis* (1860), T. S. Arthur's *The Hand but Not the Heart* (1858) and *Steps towards Heaven* (1858), Miriam Fletcher's *The Methodist* (1859), and Miriam Coles Harris's *Rutledge* (1860).

In 1861 Derby and Jackson discontinued business, and Derby's friend William Henry Seward appointed him librarian of the State Department. In 1865, again through Seward, he became the United States dispatch agent in New York. Also in 1865, he was appointed United States general agent of the 1867 Paris Exhibition, a service for which he was decorated by Napoleon III.

From 1868 until 1872 Derby lived in retirement in Aiken, South Carolina. He then returned to New York to become manager of D. Appleton and Company's subscription department; in 1880 he became a New York literary scout and subscription agent for the new firm of Houghton Mifflin. His last publishing venture occurred in 1891, when he published the three-volume biography *William Henry Seward* by Frederick W. Seward over the Derby and Miller imprint. Derby died in 1892.

References:

James C. Derby, *Fifty Years among Authors, Books and Publishers* (New York: Carleton, 1884);

Karl Sanford Kabelac, *Book Publishing in Auburn, New York, 1851-1876, an Introduction and an Imprints Bibliography* (Aurora, N.Y., 1969);

Madeleine B. Stern, "James C. Derby of Auburn,"
    in "Books in the Wilderness: Some Upstate
    Publishers," *New York History*, 31 (July 1950):
    275-280;

Walter Sutton, "The Derby Brothers: 19th Century
    Bookmen," *University of Rochester Library Bul-
    letin*, 3 (Winter 1948): 21-29.

                                                                      —*Robert S. Becker*

Derby and Miller
(Auburn, New York: 1850-1854)
J. C. Derby and Company
(Auburn: 1840-1848)
Derby, Miller and Company
(Auburn: 1848-1850)
Miller, Orton and Mulligan
(Auburn and Buffalo, New York: 1854-1857)

James Cephas Derby began his publishing career of almost six decades as an apprentice in an Auburn, New York, bookstore in 1833. In 1840 he opened his own bookstore in that community and by the mid 1840s was publishing books under the imprint of J. C. Derby and Company; the first book to bear this imprint was *Conference Hymns, with Tunes, Adapted to Religious Meetings for Prayers* (1844) by the Reverend Josiah Hopkins, rector of an Auburn Presbyterian Church, and Henry Ivison. In 1848 Norman C. Miller, one of his clerks, became a partner, and the firm became Derby, Miller and Company. A further expansion of the firm in 1850 occasioned a change in the name to Derby and Miller. In 1853 William Orton and Eugene Mulligan became partners in the business, resulting in the firm of Derby and Miller in Auburn and Derby, Orton and Mulligan in Buffalo. Derby left in December 1853 to establish his own firm in New York, and early in 1854 the remaining partners reorganized as Miller, Orton and Mulligan of Auburn and Buffalo. The next year the Buffalo office was closed and a New York branch opened. In 1857, because of mismanagement and unfavorable economic conditions, the firm ceased operations. The New York firm of C. M. Saxton took over some of its trade list.

Derby and Miller and Miller, Orton and Mulligan (the firm's two longest-lasting imprints) published mostly popular history and biography. Only about a dozen of its 175 titles were literary, and about half of these were by three popular mid-nineteenth-century women authors, Fanny Fern (pseudonym of Sara Payson Parton), Caroline Chesebro', and Mary Jane Holmes. Literary titles included Parton's *Fern Leaves from Fanny's Port-Folio* (1853), the second series of *Fern Leaves from Fanny's Port-Folio* (1854), and *Little Ferns for Fanny's Little Friends* (1854); *The Little Cross-Bearers* (1854) and *The Beautiful Gate and Other Tales* (1855) by Chesebro'; and Holmes's *The Homestead on the Hillside, and Other Tales* (1856) and *'Lena Rivers* (1856).

References:
James C. Derby, *Fifty Years Among Authors, Books and Publishers* (New York: Carleton, 1884);

Karl Sanford Kabelac, *Book Publishing in Auburn, New York, 1851-1876, an Introduction and an Imprints Bibliography* (Aurora, N.Y., 1969);

Madeleine B. Stern, "James C. Derby of Auburn," in "Books in the Wilderness: Some Upstate Publishers," *New York History*, 31 (July 1950): 275-280;

Walter Sutton, "The Derby Brothers: 19th Century Bookmen," *University of Rochester Library Bulletin*, 3 (Winter 1948): 21-29.

                                                                      —*Karl Kabelac*

Robert M. DeWitt Publisher
(New York: 1857-1877)
DeWitt and Davenport
(New York: 1848-1856)

Robert M. DeWitt and James Davenport founded the firm of DeWitt and Davenport in August 1848 at 156 Nassau Street in New York. DeWitt had been a clerk with the publishing firm of William H. Graham, of which DeWitt and Davenport was the successor; Davenport had been a partner in the bookselling firm of Davenport and Wood. DeWitt and Davenport published popular romantic fiction, adventure stories, songbooks, and anti-Catholic pamphlets. Many of the firm's novels dealt with gambling, brothels, illicit sex, and alcoholism, while its nonfiction reported on divorce cases, murder trials, and executions.

DeWitt and Davenport advertised as widely as possible, spending over $1,500 on advertising in the *New York Tribune* alone in 1853. The public responded by buying the firm's books in large numbers. Especially successful were *New York by Gaslight* (1850) and *New York Naked* (1855) by George Foster and *Hot Corn: Life Scenes in New York Illustrated* (1854) by Solon Robinson. DeWitt and Davenport published works by well-known writers, including *The G'hals of New York* (1850) by Ned Buntline (Edward Z. C. Judson) and *Rivingstone; or, The Young Ranger Hussar* (1855) by Joseph Holt Ingraham, as well as Cornelius Mathews's *Moneypenny; or, The Heart of the World* (1849), Charles Wilkins Webber's *The Gold Mines of the Gila: A Sequel to Old Hicks the Guide* (1849), George Barrell, Jr.'s *Bubbles of Fiction* (1852), Walter Seaton's *A Man in Search of a Wife; or, The Adventures of a Bachelor in New York* (1853), and Jennie Dowling DeWitt's *Kate Weston; or, To Will and to Do* (1855). The firm moved to 160-162 Nassau Street in 1853.

DeWitt and Davenport became overextended in 1856, and the partnership was dissolved. DeWitt reorganized the firm, resumed publishing in 1857 as Robert M. DeWitt Publisher at 156 Nassau Street, and eventually paid all the creditors. DeWitt published elocution books, plays, joke books, self-help manuals, and dime novels. Each title was published as part of a numbered series: DeWitt's Ethiopian and Comic Drama series included over 100 titles, the Acting Plays series numbered over 300, and the Popular Song and Joke Books ran to 238 titles. In all, the firm published over 1,200 titles in 28 series. DeWitt's dime novels, the Ten-Cent Romances and the Twenty-Five Cent Novels, were published monthly and featured brightly colored pictorial covers. Among the titles in those series were *The Tenant-House; or, Embers from Poverty's Hearthstone* (1857) by Augustine J. H. Duganne; *The Banker's Victim; or, The Betrayed Seamstress* (1857) and *The Beautiful Half Breed; or, The Border Rovers, a Tale of 1812* (1867) by Osgood Bradbury; *Cherry Blossom; or, "Love Thy Neighbor as Thyself"* (1860) by Edward Schiller; *L'Africaine; or, The Maid of Madagascar* (1866), *Rip Van Winkle; or, The Sleep of Twenty Years. A Legend of the Kaatskills* (1866), *The Icy Deep; or, True Unto Death! A Story of Wild Adventures and Fearful Perils* (1868), and *The Serf; or, Love Levels All!* (1873) by Matt Mizen (Henry Llewellyn Williams); *Out of the Streets: A Story of New York Life* (1869) by Charles Gayler; and *Ida Goldwin; or, The Perils of Fortune* (1876) by Aleck Derby.

DeWitt reprinted many from the DeWitt and Davenport list; he also pirated works of English and American authors and engaged in disputes with Mayne Reid and Bret Harte over publication of their novels. Harte, whose *M'liss: An Idyl of Red Mountain* was published by DeWitt in an 1873 piracy, had the courts order DeWitt to cease publishing his works. The firm was located from 1860 to 1869 at 13 Frankfurt Street and from 1870 to 1877 at 33 Rose Street. DeWitt died in 1877.

References:

Edward T. LeBlanc, "A Checklist of Robert M. DeWitt Publications," *Dime Novel Round-Up*, 45 (August 1976): 97;

"Robert M. DeWitt [obituary]," *American Bookseller*, 2 (1 June 1877): 327-328.

—Edward J. Hall

DeWolfe, Fiske and Company
(Boston: 1880-1905)
DeWolfe and Fiske
(Boston; Canton, Massachusetts: 1905-   )

After the Boston publishing firm of Albert W. Lovering failed in 1879, two of its former employees, Perez Morton DeWolfe and Charles F. Fiske, established their own publishing house at 365 Washington Street in 1880. The firm expanded to 361 Washington Street in 1882. The company began by purchasing books and plates from its competitors, among them John W. Lovell, C. H. Whiting, Henry A. Young and Company, Robert Carter and Brothers, and Cupples and Hurd. DeWolfe, Fiske reprinted works published by these firms in cheap editions. In advertisements the firm always emphasized its low prices. DeWolfe, Fiske published the works of William Henry Harrison Murray, whose *John Norton's Thanksgiving Party, and Other Stories* (1886) was followed by *Mamelons, and Ungava* (1890) and *The Mystery of the Woods* [and] *The Man Who Missed It* (1891). The firm reprinted many of Susan Warner's books, originally published by Robert Carter and Brothers. DeWolfe, Fiske also published Mrs. Sarah Pratt Greene's *Leon Pontifex* (1890). In 1891 the firm established a branch at 18 Astor Place in New York.

Following the sale of some of its plates to John Lovell's United States Book Company in 1890, DeWolfe, Fiske concentrated on promoting its juvenile line, which it advertised as the finest ever published in America. These juveniles were issued in at least eight series, including the Chatter, the Fairy Land, and the Tiny Toddler. Among individual works were Johanna Spyri's *Heidi* (1884) and *Rico and Wiseli* (1885), Mary Lee Etheridge's *Dick and Joe; or, Two of a Kind* (1893), Almira George Plympton's *Gerald and Geraldine* (1898), Sarah Jones Clarke's *Boys in Clover. How the Little Dukes Found a Sister* (1898) under the pseudonym Penn Shirley, and Rebecca Sophia Clarke's *Santa Claus on Snow Shoes and Other Stories* (1898) under the pseudonym Sophie May. The firm also published a series of English classics in 110 illustrated volumes which sold for $1.25 each and included sets of works by Dickens, George Eliot, Carlyle, Thackeray, and Bulwer-Lytton. DeWolfe, Fiske also published New England regional guides, medical books, etiquette books, advice books, histories, and biographies and produced paper novelty items for children.

The company's publishing activity was declining by the turn of the century, although advertisements in 1901 featured copyright novels and a new "Board Book" line. In 1905 DeWolfe, Fiske and Company was reorganized into a corporation bearing the name DeWolfe and Fiske. The corporation ceased publishing and continued as a retail and wholesale book business. In 1907 it moved to 14-20 Franklin Street. It is now a subsidiary of Chadwick-Miller, Incorporated and is located at Pequot Industrial Park, 300 Turnpike Street, Canton, Massachusetts 02021.

Reference:
"Perez Morton DeWolfe [obituary]," *Publishers' Weekly*, 120 (18 July 1931): 249.

—*Linda Quinlan*
David Dzwonkoski

Dick and Fitzgerald
(New York: 1858-1917)
Fitzgerald Publishing Corporation
(New York: 1917-1940)

William B. Dick and Lawrence R. Fitzgerald began their careers as apprentices in the New York publishing firm of Burgess, Stringer and Company at 222 Broadway. James Stringer left in 1849 to found Stringer and Townsend, and Wesley Burgess retired in 1850. With the addition of Ransom Garrett as a partner, the firm became Garrett, Dick and Fitzgerald. In 1858 Dick and Fitzgerald took over the company and moved to 18 Ann Street.

Dick and Fitzgerald's books offered entertainment for the home. Its first publication was the *Home Circle Devoted to Literature, News, Fun, and Poetry,* a monthly journal featuring riddles, recipes, and games; it appeared from 1858 until 1863. Two of the firm's earliest book publications—George Arnold's *The Sociable; or, One Thousand and One Home Amusements* (1858) and Wiljalba Frikell's *Fireside Games; for Winter Evening Amusement* (1859)— were similar in content to the journal and very popular.

Equally successful was Dick's *Uncle Josh's Trunk-Full of Fun* (1869), written under the pseudonym Joshua Jebidiah Jinks; both Dick and his son, Harris B. Dick, were frequent contributors to the firm's list of entertainment titles. Among William Dick's other compilations were *Dick's Book of Toasts* (1883), *Dick's Comic Dialogues* (1886), and *Dick's Stump Speeches and Minstrel Jokes* (1889). His *The American Hoyle; or, Gentleman's Hand-book of Games* (1864) remained in print until at least 1928. Harris B. Dick's compilations were often intended for younger audiences and included *Dick's Little Dialogue for Little People* (1890) and *Dick's Choice Pieces for Little Children* (1892).

Dick and Fitzgerald exploited the interest in music and dance in America with *The Convivial Songster* (1862), *William H. Lingard's On the Beach at Long Branch Song Book* (1868), and *Dick's Quadrille Call-Book, and Ball-Room Prompter* (1878). Dick and Fitzgerald also published how-to books devoted to cooking, athletics, etiquette, and self-improvement, including Georgianna C. Clarke's *Dinner Napkins and How to Fold Them* (1884) and Jared Flagg, Jr.'s *How to Take Money Out of Wall Street* (1887).

During the 1860s and 1870s Dick and Fitzgerald published cheap novels, including at least four series of paperbacks priced at twenty-five cents each. Military Novels, Tales of Celebrated Highwaymen, and Sea Tales featured works by William H. Ainsworth, Joseph Holt Ingraham, Sylvanus Cobb, Frederick Marryat, and Edward Zane Carroll Judson (Ned Buntline). The firm's Series of Prize Novels, its most extensive series, comprised at least thirty titles, among them reprints of Newton Mallory Curtis's *The Matricide's Daughter; A Tale of Life in the Metropolis,* May Agnes Fleming's *The Midnight Queen, East Lynne* by Mrs. Henry Wood, and *Lady Audley's Secret* (1863) by Mary Elizabeth (Braddon) Maxwell, whose *The Outcasts; or, The Brand of Society* (1864), *Only a Clod* (1865?), and *Rupert Godwin* (1867) were first published by Dick and Fitzgerald.

Among the many plays on the firm's list were Charles Townsend's *The Woven Web* (1889), *Uncle Tom's Cabin* (1889), and *The Other One* (1901); Horace C. Dale's *Imogene; or, The Witch's Secret* (1892), *The Gypsy Queen* (1901), and *The Steel King* (1902); Gordon V. May's *John Brag, Deceased* (1902) and *The Red Rosette* (1907); C. Leona Dalrymple's *Tangles* (1907) and *Mrs. Forrester's Crusade* (1908); Eleanor Maud Crane's *A Little Savage* (1907) and *Billy's Bungalow* (1910); Anthony Wills's *Just Plain Folks* (1910) and *Never Again* (1912); Katharine Kavanaugh's *The Wayfarers* (1912) and *A Stormy Night* (1912); William and Josephine Giles's *A Bachelor's Elopement* (1913), *Bill Jones* (1914), and *Rube's Family* (1914); and Joseph H. Slater's *Peter Piper's Troubles* (1913) and *The Coon Rehearsal* (1915). In 1916 the firm issued a fifty-six-page catalogue of popular dramas, comedies, vaudeville sketches, and other theatrical material, including wigs and makeup.

Fitzgerald died in 1881. Dick continued the business until his retirement in 1898, when Harris Dick took over. The firm was reorganized as the Fitzgerald Publishing Corporation in 1917, the year after Harris's death. Its address was 18 Vesey Street and, later, East Thirty-eighth Street. The corporation was dissolved in 1940. Its assets were acquired by the Behrens Publishing Company of Danbury, Connecticut, and the Walter H. Baker Company of Boston.

Advertisement for an annual collection of vaudeville routines

References:

Nathaniel H. Puffer, "Dick & Fitzgerald, Publishers," in *This Book-Collecting Adventure Presented by the Delaware Bibliophiles* (Newark, Del.: Delaware Bibliophiles, 1978), pp. 21-25;

Madeleine B. Stern, "Dick & Fitzgerald: The Troupers of Ann Street," *Publishers' Weekly*, 150 (23 November 1946): 2919-2925.

—Linda Quinlan

Charles T. Dillingham Company
(New York: 1875-1891)
Charles T. Dillingham and Company
(New York: 1891-1896)

Part of a book-trading family from Bangor, Maine, that included the publisher George W. Dillingham, Charles Dillingham was one of the founders and a long-time president of the Stationers' Board of Trade. He also helped to organize the Booksellers' and Stationers' Provident Association. Although he published books under his own imprint, Dillingham was best known as a jobber, providing general trade in the publications of other houses, or what *Publishers' Weekly* described as "prompt dispatch . . . from a 'single pick up' to that of one hundred cases, or from one volume to the thousand."

In 1870, as the New York representative of the Boston firm Lee and Shepard, Dillingham opened Lee, Shepard and Dillingham, a branch devoted solely to the jobbing trade, at 47-49 Greene Street in New York. Shortly after moving to 678 Broadway in 1875, Dillingham purchased the business from Lee and Shepard and, as the Charles T. Dillingham Company, announced to the trade his "large and well-assorted stock" of miscellaneous, standard, and juvenile books from James R. Osgood and Company; Harper and Brothers; A. K. Loring; Little, Brown; Roberts Brothers; and Lockwood Brooks, in addition to Lee and Shepard. In the spring of 1888, still advertising himself as "Successor to Lee, Shepard and Dillingham," Dillingham moved to 718-720 Broadway.

Dillingham occasionally published books, most of them jointly with Lee and Shepard. Among these were eight novels by the popular and prolific Mary Andrews Denison. Denison's *That Husband of Mine* (1877) sold 150,000 copies in a single year and continued to sell for twenty years; *That Wife of Mine* (1877) also sold briskly. Dillingham also joined Lee and Shepard in publishing Amanda M. Douglas's popular tales of well-born young women suddenly left to support themselves, including *From Hand to Mouth* (1878), *Out of the Wreck* (1885), and *A Woman's Inheritance* (1886), as well as Virginia Townsend's *Lenox Dare* (1881) and *A Boston Girl's Ambitions* (1887). Other joint publications included *The Danbury Boom!* (1880) by James Montgomery Bailey, noted for his witty newspaper columns as the "Danbury News Man"; *Man Proposes* (1880) by Francis Underwood, one of the founders of *Atlantic Monthly; Nora's Return* (1890), a sequel to Ibsen's *The Doll's House* by abolitionist and feminist Ednah Cheney; and *The Demagogue* (1891), a political novel by David Ross Locke, better known as humorist Petroleum V. Nasby. Dillingham also published a few titles on his own, among them Frederic Pangborn's *Alice; or, the Wages of Sin* (1883), Hyland Kirk's *When Age Grows Young* (1888) and *The Revolt of the Brutes* (1893), Lida Vanamee's *An Adirondack Idyl* (1893), and Anne Reeve Aldrich's *Gabriel Lusk* (1894).

Charles T. Dillingham

George Wellington Dillingham

Moses Woodruff Dodd, founder of M. W. Dodd

Frank H. Dodd, successor to his father, Moses Dodd, and
cofounder of Dodd a.id Mead

In August 1891 Dillingham was forced to place his business under assignment—a result, he said, of "dull trade, low prices, strong competition and lack of capital." But the following month, in partnership with his nephew Edwin L. Dillingham, he resumed business as Charles T. Dillingham and Company and celebrated by offering "extraordinary bargains" for sixty days. On 24 March 1896 the company sold its stock in trade and all accounts to the Baker and Taylor Company, book jobbers specializing in miscellaneous, standard, and school stock at 5-7 East Sixteenth Street. Charles Dillingham continued to work in the trade for almost twenty years, principally as a representative of the subscription department of Little, Brown and Company. He died in 1918.

References:

"Lee and Shepard—Lee, Shepard & Dillingham," *New York Evening Post*, 9 December 1874;

"Obituary: Charles T. Dillingham," *Publishers' Weekly*, 75 (9 November 1918): 1587.

—*Susan K. Ahern*

The G. W. Dillingham Company

(New York: 1886-1916)

George Wellington Dillingham, who had earlier worked in Boston for Crosby, Nichols and for A. K. Loring, publishers of the Horatio Alger stories, joined the George W. Carleton Company in New York in 1864 as head clerk and within eight years rose to full partner. The G. W. Dillingham Company was formed in 1886 to succeed the George W. Carleton Company when Carleton retired. The new firm retained Carleton's headquarters at 33 West Twenty-third Street. Building on the reputation of its predecessor, the G. W. Dillingham Company concentrated on publishing modern American works, particularly those of women novelists and of the humorists Artemus Ward, Orpheus C. Kerr, and Josh Billings.

Several of the most important items on Dillingham's lists had first been published by Carleton. Augusta Evans Wilson's perennially popular *St. Elmo*, first published by Carleton in 1867, was still being recommended for Christmas gift-giving by the *New York Times* when Dillingham was publishing it in 1894. Dillingham also published new titles by May Agnes Fleming, who had been one of Carleton's popular authors in the 1870s, including *The Midnight Queen* (1888), *Edith Percival* (1893), *Wedded for Pique* (1897), and *The Sisters of Torwood* (1898). Like Carleton, Dillingham recognized the importance of women readers, and he encouraged and paid well the authors who attracted that audience. Their works sold rapidly, particularly those in Dillingham's 25-Cent series, which added new titles once and sometimes twice a month. Dillingham's own favorite among his authors was Mary Jane Holmes. Carleton had published her work for twenty years, and Dillingham continued to do so until her last novel in 1905. Among her many novels that Dillingham published, some of which were brought out simultaneously by S. Low in London, was her own favorite, *Gretchen* (1887), as well as *Doctor Hathern's Daughters* (1895) and *The Tracy Diamonds* (1899).

Other works published by Dillingham included Annie Lyndsay MacGregor's *"Bound, Not Blessed"* (1892) and Nevada McNeill's *A Marriage above Zero* (1894), *The Red Rose of Savannah* (1894), and *La Nouvelle Femme* (1896). In 1889 and 1900 Dillingham published twenty-two novels by Linn Boyd Porter under the pseudonym Albert Ross. One of the first, *His Private Character* (1889), was described by *Publishers' Weekly* as a "story of sin and scandal" and thus "not recommended for sale." Many of Porter's subsequent works bore such titillating titles as *Moulding a Maiden* (1891), *Thy Neighbor's Wife* (1892), *An Original Sinner* (1893), and *Out of Wedlock* (1894).

The firm added mysteries and fantasies to its list in the 1890s, including Mary E. Lane's *Mizora: A Prophecy* (1890), a "true and faithful account" of a journey to the earth's interior; Kinahan Cornwallis's *A Marvellous Coincidence; or, A Chain of Mis-*

adventures and Mysteries (1891); and Gustavus W. Pope's *Journey to Mars* (1894). The last was billed as the beginning of a series called Romances of the Planets, but Pope's *Journey to Venus* (1895), the second in the series, was published in Boston by Arena.

Dillingham ran the firm until his death at fifty-four in December 1895, the result of a fall from his horse. The following June the company was incorporated with his son Frank A. Dillingham as one of the directors, John H. Cook as president, and John W. Hesse as secretary and treasurer. In 1898 the firm moved to new quarters in the Jefferson Building at 119-121 West Twenty-third Street.

The new management continued to seek and meet popular tastes. Besides standing by its reliable authors, the firm published more humor, such as Wright Bauer's *Cinders* (1907), advertised as "a scream from cover to cover," and Hugh McHugh's *Beat It* (1907). McHugh was the pseudonym that George V. Hobart adopted for his many John Henry books, whose total sales, Dillingham claimed, reached 700,000 copies. Novelizations of

popular plays—for example, James Forbes's *The Chorus Lady* (1908) and Frederick Burton's adaptation of William De Mille's *Strongheart* (1908)—were also successful.

In January 1908, in preparation for moving its plant, the company offered for sale more than 100 sets of plates, mainly of fiction, at twenty-five dollars per set; but the move seems not to have occurred. When the G. W. Dillingham Company did move to 425 East Twenty-fourth Street in May 1915, the company's end was in sight. Bradstreet took away its credit rating that year, and the firm went bankrupt in August 1916, five weeks after Cook's death.

References:
"Contributions to Trade History: No. XXXIX, George W. Dillingham," *American Bookseller*, new series 24 (1888): 298-299;

"Jubilee of G. W. Dillingham Co.," *Publishers' Weekly*, 72 (10 August 1907): 345-347;

"Obituary. George Wellington Dillingham," *Publishers' Weekly*, 49 (4 January 1896): 10-11.

—Susan K. Ahern

Dix, Edwards and Company
(New York: 1854-1857)

In 1854 Augustus J. Dix, who had worked for the publisher George P. Putnam since 1849, and Arthur T. Edwards formed a partnership as Dix, Edwards and Company at 10 Park Place in New York. The next year the firm began publishing *Putnam's Monthly Magazine*, the periodical originated by Putnam in 1853. Dix, Edwards moved to 321 Broadway in 1856. In 1857 Dix, Edwards and Company was replaced as the publisher of the magazine but published a few more books before being dissolved that year.

In its short life the firm published about thirty books, primarily travel books and novels. Most were by American authors, some of whom had written for *Putnam's Monthly Magazine*. *Twice Married; A Story of Connecticut Life* by Calvin W. Philleo was

published in 1855. The following year the firm published *Prue and I* by George William Curtis. Two first editions of works by Herman Melville were published: *The Piazza Tales* (1856) and *The Confidence-Man* (1857). Frederick Law Olmsted's *Journey in the Seaboard Slave States* and *Journey through Texas* were published in 1856 and 1857, respectively. The Donner expedition was recounted in Eliza W. Farnham's *California, In-doors and Out* (1856). *Political Essays* by Parke Godwin, reprinted from the magazine, appeared in 1856, as did Horace Greeley's *History of the Struggle for Slavery Extension or Restriction in the U.S. from 1787 to 1856*.

—Theodora Mills

Dodd, Mead and Company
(New York: 1876-   )
Taylor and Dodd
(New York: 1839-1840)
M. W. Dodd
(New York: 1840-1870)
Dodd and Mead
(New York: 1870-1876)

In 1839 Moses Woodruff Dodd left the ministry to purchase a share in the business of John S. Taylor, a New York publisher of religious books. The firm of Taylor and Dodd had existed for barely a year before Dodd bought out his associate and set up shop as M. W. Dodd in an annex of the Brick Church Chapel on Park Row across from City Hall Park.

Dodd's first book was a volume of sermons, *Obligations of the World to the Bible, A Series of Lectures to Young Men* (1839) by Dodd's friend and landlord, the Reverend Gardiner Spring. Alexander Cruden's *Complete Concordance to the Holy Scriptures* (1847) was imported from England, as were most of the titles of Dodd's early lists. Ichabod Spencer's *Pastor's Sketches* was published in 1850. Among lighter works published by Dodd during the first decades were Charlotte Elizabeth's highly successful and morally irreproachable tales for young women, starting with *The Flower Garden* (1840) and Mrs. Andrew Charles's popular fictional history of Martin Luther, *Chronicles of the Schönberg-Cotta Family* (1863).

The Brick Church Chapel was destroyed in 1855. Dodd moved to 59 Chambers Street and then, in 1856, to 506 Broadway. The firm remained there for fourteen years before the need for expansion drew the company uptown to 762 Broadway. In 1870 a retail department was added to the business. Dodd retired that year and his son, Frank H. Dodd, and nephew, Edward S. Mead, took over the firm, which became Dodd and Mead. In 1876 the firm's name was changed to Dodd, Mead and Company when Bleecker Van Wagenen became a partner.

By 1870 Frank Dodd—who had joined the firm in 1859 at the age of fifteen—had already done much to change the company from a religious publisher to a house with a more general list. In 1867 he accepted Martha Finley's *Elsie Dinsmore*, which became one of the best-selling juvenile titles in American publishing history. That success led to twenty-seven more volumes of Elsie stories, selling about five million copies in seventy years. But it was the Reverend Edward P. Roe's *Barriers Burned Away* (1872), a novel based on the Chicago fire, that established Dodd, Mead's reputation as a publisher of popular fiction. A million copies of the book were sold—many of them in cheaper reprint editions, such as the Phoenix series, a format in which Dodd, Mead pioneered. Roe went on to write other fiction as well as nonfiction for Dodd, Mead, including *Opening a Chestnut Burr* (1874), *He Fell in Love with His Wife* (1886), *The Earth Trembled* (1887), and a popular horticultural guide, *Success with Small Fruits* (1880). Other authors of popular fiction who achieved great success in these years were Amelia Barr, who wrote the romantic novels *Jan Vedder's*

Wife (1885) and *The Bow of Orange Ribbon: A Romance of New York* (1886); and Dr. John Watson, writing under the pen name Ian Maclaren, with his picturesque tales of Scottish life, of which the most popular was *Beside the Bonnie Briar Bush* (1894).

Dodd's partner Mead wrote books for children and adults, often under the pseudonym Richard Markham. Among his works are *Colonial Days* (1881) and *A Narrative History of King Phillip's War and the Indian Troubles in New England* (1883). He also edited an illustrated edition of Robert Southey's *Chronicle of the Cid* (1883). Mead died in 1894. Frank Dodd brought back from his many trips to England a long list of authors to be published under the Dodd, Mead imprint. In the 1890s the firm began publishing the most complete collection of the work of Anthony Trollope in the United States. Works by modern British authors published by Dodd, Mead included G. K. Chesterton's *The Defendant* (1902), the first of forty-nine Chesterton titles published by Dodd, Mead; Austin Dobson's *Miscellanies* (1902); Jerome K. Jerome's *Passing of the Third Floor Back* (1904), which achieved great popularity in the United States in both book and play form; Marie Corelli's *The Master Christian* (1900); Max Beerbohm's *Zuleika Dobson* (1911); Beatrice Harden's *Ships That Pass in the Night* (1894); and S. R. Crockett's *Joan of the Sword Hand* (1900). On one trip, Dodd secured the American rights to the works of the Belgian Maurice Maeterlinck; by 1920 Maeterlinck was represented by twenty-five Dodd, Mead titles, including *Life of the Bee* (1901) and *The Blue Bird* (1908). Maeterlinck lived to see his popularity decline considerably, and in 1947, at the age of eighty-five, he brought a $250,000 suit against Dodd, Mead, claiming that the publisher had made "no reasonable effort to sell and market" his books and had published unauthorized abridgments. The suit was later dropped.

Dodd, Mead shared rights with other publishers for American editions of H. G. Wells's *The Island of Dr. Moreau* (1896), *Tono Bungay* (1908), and *The History of Mr. Polly* (1909). In 1922 Dodd, Mead strengthened its literary ties to Great Britain with the purchase of the American branch of the John Lane Company, bringing Kenneth Grahame, Richard Le Gallienne, Laurence Hope, and Agatha Christie to the Dodd, Mead list. Over seventy of Christie's works, which included plays, novels, and short stories, were published by Dodd, Mead, from *The Mysterious Affair at Styles* (1920) to *Curtain* (1975) and the posthumous *Sleeping Murder* (1976).

In 1897 Dodd, Mead published Joseph Conrad's *Children of the Sea* (which was also published

by Doubleday, Page in 1914 as *The Nigger of the Narcissus*), and in 1900 the firm published Tolstoy's *Resurrection*. By this time, the taste of the American public for a more accessible, home-bred literature was becoming increasingly apparent, and Dodd, Mead responded. The firm lured Paul Leicester Ford away from Houghton Mifflin with an offer of $6,500 and twenty percent royalty for *Janice Meredith* (1899), a sentimental novel about the American Revolution; it sold 200,000 copies in three months. The *Critic* reported that for over two weeks, Ford earned $1,000 a day in royalties. Ford's popular *Wanted—A Match Maker* followed in 1900. But it was George Barr McCutcheon who repeatedly broke all sales records, his forty-five works selling some five million copies. *Graustark*, published by Stone and Kimball in 1901, started McCutcheon's immensely popular Graustark series, which Dodd, Mead picked up. Later titles included *Beverly of Graustark* (1904) and *The Prince of Graustark* (1914). *Brewster's Millions* (1903), published by Stone in Chicago, was written by McCutcheon under the pseudonym Richard Greaves to demonstrate that his popularity was based more on the merit of his work than on a habitual following. Many of McCutcheon's works were transformed into stage productions and achieved success in that form as well.

Hamilton Wright Mabie, essayist and the "dean of literary critics of his time," had many works published by Dodd, Mead and served as literary advisor to the firm. *My Study Fire* (1890), *Essays in Literary Interpretation* (1892), and *Books and Culture* (1896) were among his collections of essays, though he is perhaps best remembered today for his translation *Norse Stories Retold from the Eddas* (1901), illustrated by George Wright. The *Bookman*, which was inspired by the British journal of the same title, was published by Dodd, Mead starting in 1895. Under the editorship of James MacArthur and Harry Thurston Peck, the *Bookman* became one of the foremost literary journals of the day, though it was never on a sound financial footing. Dodd, Mead sold it to George H. Doran in 1918.

Dodd, Mead began the twentieth century with a move to the corner of Fifth Avenue and Thirty-fifth Street. Between 1902 and 1904 the firm published the seventeen-volume *New International Encyclopedia*, edited by Peck, Daniel C. Gilman, and Frank Moore Colby. Three supplementary volumes were added in 1906, and the work was revised and republished in twenty-four volumes, edited by Talcott Williams, in 1917. More than 50,000 sets of the encyclopedia were sold before Dodd, Mead

Edward S. Mead, Frank Dodd's cousin and partner in Dodd and Mead

Edward H. Dodd became director of Dodd, Mead and Company upon its incorporation in 1917 (photograph by Robert Disraeli)

Frank C. Dodd became president of the firm in 1931 (photograph by Robert Disraeli)

sold it to Funk and Wagnalls in 1931.

In 1910 Dodd, Mead moved to 449 Fourth Avenue at Thirtieth Street and discontinued its bookstore operation. Frank Dodd died in 1916. The firm was incorporated in 1917 under the direction of Dodd's son, Edward H. Dodd. Edward's cousin, Frank C. Dodd, took over as president in 1931.

Dodd, Mead had helped to introduce several new poets around the turn of the century. Most notable among them was Paul Laurence Dunbar, America's first internationally recognized black poet, whose *Lyrics of Lowly Life* was published by Dodd, Mead in 1896. There followed *Poems of Cabin and Field* (1899), *Lyrics of the Hearthside* (1899), and a novel, *The Sport of the Gods* (1902). *The Complete Poems of Paul Laurence Dunbar* was published by Dodd, Mead in 1913. Robert Service's *Rhymes of a Rolling Stone* was published by Dodd, Mead in 1912, *Lyrics of a Lowbrow* in 1951; and though Service maintained that he wrote verse, not poetry, *The Collected Poems of Robert Service* was published in 1933. His novel *The House of Fear* appeared in 1927. The works of another Canadian poet, Bliss Carman, were acquired when Dodd, Mead bought out Small, Maynard in 1926. Carman is best known for his *Songs from Vagabondia*, written with Richard Hovey, which was published by Copeland and Day in 1894 and republished by Dodd, Mead in 1935. *Bliss Carman's Poems* was published by Dodd, Mead in 1931. The Small, Maynard acquisition also brought Dodd, Mead several works by Faith Baldwin. William Rose Benét came to Dodd, Mead in 1934 when the firm bought out Duffield and Green.

Dodd, Mead published Anatole France's *Penguin Island* (1909) and *Revolt of the Angels* (1914). The firm's most prolific novelist was the British writer Berta Ruck, who in twenty-five years had fifty-two novels published by the firm; the first was *His Official Fiancé* in 1914. The novels of Dutch writer Louis Couperus were brought to the United States by Dodd, Mead, and while they achieved some success, it was "not as much as they deserved," according to Edward H. Dodd, Jr. The novels of E. Barrington, a Canadian who also wrote under the name Louise Moresby, enjoyed great popularity during the 1920s and 1930s. The most successful was her fictionalized biography of Byron, *Glorious Apollo* (1925).

In the 1920s the firm began sponsoring literary prize competitions in the hope of discovering new talent. The first was the Dodd, Mead *Pictorial Review* (later *Redbook*) Novel Award, started in 1925. Martha Ostenso's *Wild Geese* won the prize of $13,500 that year. Her later work for the firm included *The Young May Moon* (1929) and *The Stone Field* (1937). Other winners were Margaret Flint for *The Old Ashburn Place* (1935); Elizabeth Seifert, whose popular doctor series got its start with the 1937 award for *Young Doctor Galahad;* Ellen Proctor for *Turning Leaves* (1942); Dorothea Cornwell for *They Dare Not Go A' Hunting* (1944); and Louela Grace Erdman for *Years of the Locust* (1947). The contest was discontinued after 1946.

In 1934 the firm acquired the publishing house of J. H. Sears. Two years later Dodd, Mead commenced its Red Badge Prize Competition for Mystery and Detective Novels. Christopher Morley observed in the *Saturday Review* that "the Dodd, Mead imprint has long been a pretty good hallmark in detective and mystery stories. When you see one with that publisher's name on the back you can usually depend on it." The firm's mystery editor was Raymond T. Bond, who had joined Dodd, Mead in 1919, edited *The Man Who Was Chesterton* in 1937, and later served as president of the firm. The first competition winner was Clifford Knight for *Affair of the Scarlet Crab* (1937). Other winners included Marco Page (the pseudonym of Harry Kurnitz) for *Fast Company* (1938), Hugh Pentecost (one of the most popular of the Red Badge authors) for *Cancelled in Red* (1939), Christianna Brand for *Heads You Lose* (1942), and Evelyn Berckman for *Evil of Time* (1954). While the Red Badge Prize Competition was discontinued in 1955, the Red Badge series of detective fiction continues and includes Ursula Curtis's *Letter of Intent* (1971), Michael Innes's *The Mysterious Commission* (1975), and Judson Philips's *Death Is a Dirty Trick* (1980).

For younger readers Dodd, Mead inaugurated its well-known series of Great Illustrated Classics with an edition of *Moby-Dick* illustrated by Mead Schaeffer in 1922. Other titles in the series include *Les Misérables* (1925), *The Personal History of David Copperfield* (1936), *The Scarlet Letter* (1948), and *A Journey to the Center of the Earth* (1959). A perennial children's favorite, *Honk the Moose* by Phil Strong, was published in 1935. Walter D. Edmond's *The Matchlock Gun* (1941) was awarded the Newbery Medal in 1942 as the year's most distinguished contribution to American literature for children. In cooperation with *Compact*, Dodd, Mead initiated the Seventeenth Summer Literary Competition, named for the Maureen Daly novels published by the firm in 1942. Winners of the competition included Barbara Bentley for *Hedge against the Sun* (1943), Catherine Lawrence for *The Narrowing*

Wind (1944), and Karen Kehoe for *City in the Sun* (1946). The firm started the *Boys' Life*—Dodd, Mead Prize in 1950.

Robert Burns Mantle's Best Plays series, which printed excerpts or synopses of the best plays of the New York theatrical season, was acquired from Small, Maynard in 1926. Margaret Mayorga's annual *Best One Act Plays* was published by Dodd, Mead from 1937 until 1955, when it was sold to Beacon Press. Edward J. O'Brien's *Best Short Stories* annual was taken over by Dodd, Mead in 1926, its tenth year, and sold to Houghton Mifflin in 1933.

In 1933 Dodd, Mead acquired American rights to the complete works of George Bernard Shaw when Brentano's, Shaw's former American publisher, decided to end its publishing operations and concentrate on its retail business. Sales manager Howard Lewis went to London and convinced Shaw to come to Dodd, Mead. Shaw said that he was "somewhat startled to learn that there was only one good publisher in the United States." Frank C. Dodd became chairman of the board of Dodd, Mead in 1942. Lewis served as president from 1942 until his death in 1952.

After 1950 Dodd, Mead's importance as a publisher of fiction rested primarily on its backlist, which included such sure sellers as the westerns of Max Brand (pseudonym of Frederick Faust), who also wrote mysteries, ghost stories, adventure tales, and the Dr. Kildare series. Dodd, Mead published nearly 200 of his works.

In nonfiction, Dodd, Mead developed a list of nature books, including works by Roger Tory Peterson and Edwin Way Teale, and books on travel, yachting (a Dodd family avocation), and the sea. Over the years the list also acquired strength in biography and history. Allan Nevins's important series American Political Leaders was initiated in 1930, and Nevins won a Pulitzer Prize for his *Grover Cleveland, A Study in Courage* (1932). Winston Churchill's four-volume *History of The English-Speaking Peoples* was published from 1956 to 1958. In 1957 Dodd, Mead established a college textbook division headed by William Oman. The venture was not entirely successful, and the textbook line was dropped in the late 1970s.

In 1967 Dodd, Mead moved to 79 Madison Avenue from 432 Fourth Avenue (Park Avenue South), its location since 1941. Edward H. Dodd, Jr., became president in 1952; he was succeeded by Bond in 1957. S. Phelps Platt, Jr., assumed the presidency in 1964. Late in 1981 Platt announced that the firm would be acquired by Thomas Nelson Publishers of Nashville, the largest publisher of Bibles in the country, for $1.8 million. In 1982 Lewis W. Gillenson, founder and president of Everest House, which Nelson also acquired, was installed as president. Jonathan Dodd, the most recent of five generations of Dodds to serve in the firm, is vice president for subsidiary rights and editorial. In 1983 trouble arose when the religious views of parent company Nelson conflicted with Dodd, Mead's distribution of the *Devil's Book of Verse: Masters of the Poison Pen from Ancient Times to the Present Day*. Allegedly objectionable language forced Nelson to cancel the title; the book's editor, Richard Conniff, sued Nelson and Dodd, Mead for $3.7 million.

In December 1985 Gillenson retired and was replaced as president by Lynne A. Lumsden, who had been an editorial director at Prentice-Hall. In 1986 Nelson announced that Dodd, Mead would be sold to the Gamut Publishing Company, a partnership founded in 1985 by Lumsden and Jon B. Harden. Prominent Dodd, Mead publications of 1985 included Shusako Endo's *Stained Glass Elegies*, Masako Togawa's *The Master Key*, and Penelope Gilliat's *They Sleep without Dreaming*. Dodd, Mead's address remains 79 Madison Avenue, New York 10016.

References:

"Conniff Sues Dodd, Mead, Thomas Nelson," *Publishers Weekly*, 225 (6 January 1984): 16;

David Dempsey, "Looking Backwards with Dodd, Mead," *Saturday Review*, 47 (12 December 1964): 36-37;

Edward H. Dodd, Jr., *The First Hundred Years: A History of the House of Dodd, Mead 1839-1939* (New York: Dodd, Mead, 1939);

125th Anthology, 1839-1964 (New York: Dodd, Mead, 1964);

"The Story of Dodd, Mead & Co., Inc.," *Book Production Magazine*, 81 (January 1965): 30-33.

—*Gregory Ames*

Dodge Publishing Company
(New York: 1899-1949)
Dodge Book and Stationery Company
(San Francisco: 1895-1898)
Dodge Stationery Company
(New York: 1898-1899)

The Dodge Book and Stationery Company was founded at 112 Post Street in San Francisco in 1895. In 1898 it moved to 317 Broadway, New York, as the Dodge Stationery Company. The following year it moved to 150 Fifth Avenue and became the Dodge Publishing Company.

The firm manufactured calendars, stationery, and gift books. Among its literary titles were reprint editions of *The Rubáiyát of Omar Khayyám* (1896), Emerson's *Essays*, James Allen's *As a Man Thinketh*, Francis Turner Palgrave's *The Golden Treasury*, and standard classics in series entitled Books That Inspire, the Dodge Library, the Brown Library, and the Craft Library. Original fiction included James Frederick Mason's anonymous *Cupid's Game with Hearts: A Tale as Told by Documents* (1897) and Sara Bulkley Rogers's *Ezra Hardman, M.A., of Wayback College, and Other Stories* (1900).

Dodge's People's Books was a leading nonfiction series in the early 1900s.

In 1928 the firm was purchased by Robert M. McBride and Company. With Critchell Rimington, former vice-president of the John Day Company, as editorial director, Dodge began publishing independently again in 1935. Dodge ceased operations when McBride went bankrupt in 1949.

References:

"McBride Takes Over Dodge Publishing Company," *Publishers' Weekly*, 113 (23 June 1928): 2542;

"Rimington Heads Dodge Firm," *Publishers' Weekly*, 127 (23 February 1935): 879-880.

—*Gregory M. Haynes*

Patrick Donahoe
(Boston: 1850-1876)

Patrick Donahoe, an Irish immigrant, was the owner and publisher of the *Boston Pilot* from 1836 until 1876 and from 1891 until 1901. Donahoe also published a few books appealing to Irish-Americans; one of the earliest was John T. Roddan's *John O'Brien, or, The Orphan of Boston* (1850). Donahoe published stories of the Irish in Ireland and of the difficulties and sufferings of Irish-Americans in such novels as Peter McCorry's *The Lost Rosary; or,* *Our Irish Girls, Their Trials, Temptations, and Triumphs* (1870) and *Mount Benedict; or, The Violated Tomb* (1871).

Reference:
Mary Alphonsine Frawley, *Patrick Donahoe* (Washington, D.C.: Catholic University of America Press, 1946).

—*Theodora Mills*

R. R. Donnelley and Sons Company
(Chicago: 1882-)
Church, Goodman and Donnelley
(Chicago: 1864-1870)
Lakeside Publishing and Printing Company
(Chicago: 1870-1877)
Donnelley, Gassette and Loyd
(Chicago: 1877-1882)

The printing firm of R. R. Donnelley and Sons Company traces its origin to 1864, when Richard Robert Donnelley, who had worked as a printer in New Orleans and Hamilton, Ontario, was brought in to run the printshop of the Chicago book and magazine printing firm of Church and Goodman at 51-53 La Salle Street. The new partnership was called Church, Goodman and Donnelley. In 1870 Church, Goodman and Donnelley was purchased by a group of businessmen who wanted to start a book publishing company. Donnelley was named manager of the new firm, the Lakeside Publishing and Printing Company. While still under construction, the Lakeside building was destroyed in the 1871 Chicago fire, but a new building was completed in 1873.

Donnelley's assistant manager, Alex T. Loyd, developed an idea which helped the company to succeed financially during the depression that followed the Panic of 1873. In 1875 the firm began publishing the Lakeside Library, a series of inexpensive paperback reprints. Donnelley established a subsidiary, Donnelley, Loyd and Company, to produce the library. New volumes in the series were

*Edward H. Dodd, Jr., in 1939. He became president of Dodd, Mead and Company
in 1952 (photograph by Robert Disraeli)*

Richard Robert Donnelley

*Thomas E. Donnelley succeeded his father as president of the
firm in 1899*

published every two weeks at first, then weekly at the height of the series's popularity. The books were priced at ten cents to fifty cents, depending upon the length of the work. Most of the works in the series were novels by foreign authors or Americans no longer covered by copyright. Major authors in the series included Verne, Trollope, Dickens, George Eliot, and Tennyson. The Lakeside Library was a financial success, selling thousands of copies of more than 250 titles; but by 1879 the competition of other paperback series proved to be too strong, and the series was discontinued.

In 1877 Norman T. Gassette purchased Lakeside and established the firm of Donnelley, Gassette and Loyd. Donnelley acquired controlling interest in the company and changed its name to R. R. Donnelley and Sons in 1882. The firm, then located at 140-146 Monroe Street, published novels including Gilbert A. Pierce's *Zachariah, the Congressman: A Tale of American Society* (1880) and Ray Thompson's *A Respectable Family* (1880), and travel books such as Ernest Ingersoll's *The Crest of the Continent* (1885).

After Donnelley's death in 1899, two of his sons assumed control of the business. Reuben Donnelley became head of the Chicago Directory Company, a subsidiary which had been incorporated in 1880; this firm later became the Reuben H. Donnelley Corporation. Thomas E. Donnelley succeeded his father as president of R. R. Donnelley and Sons, which had been incorporated in 1890.

During the early twentieth century, R. R. Donnelley and Sons' Lakeside Press imprint became widely respected for its fine printing. In 1903 the firm inaugurated the Lakeside Classics series of Christmas volumes. Donnelley began printing the American editions of the *Encyclopaedia Britannica* in 1910. William A. Kittredge, who joined Donnelley in 1922, was director of design and typography for twenty-three years. Under his direction, the Lakeside Press printed limited editions of literary works, exhibition catalogues, and books in education, art, history, and religion. One of Lakeside's most notable books was the three-volume *Moby-Dick* (1930) illustrated by Rockwell Kent, an outstanding example of American illustrated book production.

R. R. Donnelley and Sons is now one of America's largest printing companies. The firm is no longer active in publishing, which played a relatively minor role in the company's history. Its current address is 2223 Martin Luther King Drive, Chicago 60616.

References:

Fine Bookmaking at the Lakeside Press (Chicago, 1926);

The Lakeside Press, Chicago: A Brief Note on Its History, Aims, Purposes and Resources (Chicago: Donnelley, 192?);

"R. R. Donnelley [obituary]," *Publishers' Weekly*, 65 (15 April 1899): 654;

George H. Waltz, Jr., *The House That Quality Built* (Chicago: Donnelley, 1957).

—*Judith Bushnell*

*Reuben H. Donnelley, head of the Chicago Directory Company,
a subsidiary of R. R. Donnelley and Sons*

*The Lakeside Press building in Chicago soon after its completion in 1930. At that time it was the largest printing plant in
the United States.*

Donohue and Henneberry
(Chicago: 1871-1903)
M. A. Donohue and Company
(Chicago: 1903-   )

In 1871 two Chicago bookbinders, Michael A. Donohue—formerly of Cox and Donohue Company—and William P. Henneberry, established the firm of Donohue and Henneberry at 407-425 Dearborn Street. In its early years the firm's business was almost exclusively bookbinding. Gradually, the firm added printing to its services and by 1879 was ready to take on publishing as well. Possibly the earliest work published by Donohue and Henneberry was Walter Brown's novel *Mitylene: A Tale of New England and the Tropics,* which appeared in 1879 under the pseudonym Mi Esposa e Yo (My Wife and I). In 1890 Donohue and Henneberry launched the Dearborn series of inexpensive editions of popular novelists, including Edward Reynolds Roe's *Belteshazzar: A Romance of Babylon* (1890), Beatrice Marean's *The Tragedies of Oak Hurst: A Florida Romance* (1891), Luman Allen's *Dane Walraven (A Tale of Old Boston)* (1892), Mary Elizabeth Lamb's *The Mystery of Walderstein: A Story from the Life of Two Prussian Officers* (1894), and Harriet Osgood Bullock's *On Shifting Sands: A Sketch from Real Life* (1895).

Donohue and Henneberry concentrated its publishing almost exclusively on sets and series—or libraries, as they were then called. In addition to the Dearborn series the firm published the Optimus series, the Ideal Library, the Advance series, The Little Footprint, and the Pleasant Picture series. Donohue and Henneberry's success with such series prompted John Lovell to acquire the plates for some of them in 1890 for his short-lived United States Book Company. Prudently, Donohue and Henneberry kept the rights to the Dearborn series; and when the United States Book Company broke up in 1893, Donohue and Henneberry continued to maintain its successful business. Even more important to the firm's success during this period was job printing for other publishers, including many of its competitors in the cheap book trade, which was its main source of revenue.

Donohue and Henneberry reprinted titles by well-known English authors as well as works by such popular American authors as Mary J. Holmes and Edward Z. C. Judson (Ned Buntline). The firm's five-volume edition of Macaulay's *History of England* was especially popular, and it also reprinted the work of William Gilmore Simms in the early 1890s.

In 1903 Donohue bought out Henneberry and began publishing literature for children and young people under the M. A. Donohue and Company imprint. Donohue died in 1915. For nearly seventy years M. A. Donohue continued as a family firm at 711 South Dearborn Street, publishing juveniles, religious books, and birthday books. Among the juveniles were Harold M. Sherman's *Call of the Land* (1948), Margaret Jean Bauer's *Animal Babies* (1949), Alene Dalton's *The Story Princess Stories* (1956), and John W. Moyer's *Famous Indian Chiefs* (1957). In the early 1970s the Donohue imprint was acquired by the Hubbard Press, a division of the Hubbard Scientific Company, Northbrook, Illinois 60062.

Reference:

"Michael A. Donohue [obituary]," *Publishers' Weekly,* 88 (16 October 1915): 1185.

—Timothy D. Murray

M. Doolady
(New York: 1860?-1873?)

Although the beginning and the end of M. Doolady's career as a publisher remain obscure, his name first appears in an advertisement in the *American Literary Gazette and Publishers' Circular* in 1860, with his address listed as 49 Walker Street, New York. The firm's first advertised book was a travelogue, *Ceylon* (1860), by Sir James Emerson Tennent; its first advertised novel was *The Little Beauty* (1860) by "Mrs. Grey." In the same year Doolady published Alfred Billings Street's *Woods and Waters: or, the Saranacs and Racket*, followed by Francis Colburn Adams's abolitionist work, *An Outcast; or, Virtue and Faith* (1861); Mrs. Sarah Ann Wright's Civil War novel, *Clara Hollinbrook* (1863); and Richard Grant White's *Revelations: A Companion to the "New Gospel of Peace," According to Abraham* (1863), a satire in the style of the Bible. In September 1863 Doolady advertised himself as an agent for the Philadelphia and New York trade sales that fall. He may have ceased publishing, since he stopped advertising until 1866.

In that year, having moved to 448 Broome Street, Doolady published Mrs. Margaret Hosmer's *Ten Years of a Lifetime*, Mrs. Jane McElhinney's *Only a Woman's Heart* (under the pseudonym Ada Clare), Charles Wells Russell's *Roebuck*, a "Diamond Edition" of Thackeray's works, and a pirated translation of *Don Quixote* with illustrations by Gustave Doré. Mrs. Sarah Anne Dorsey's *Lucia Dare* was published in 1867 under the pseudonym Filia and was followed the next year by A. E. Senter's compilation, *The Diddler*, and a reprint of *Erring Yet Noble: A Tale of and for Women* by Isaac G. Reed, Jr. In 1871 Doolady published Susan Cannon's *Maidee, the Alchemist; or, Turning All to Gold*. With a new address at 98 Nassau Street, Doolady published Major Jep. Joslynn's *Tar-Heel Tales in Vernacular Verse* (1873).

—*David Dzwonkoski*

Doubleday and Company
(New York: 1946-)
Doubleday and McClure
(New York: 1897-1899)
Doubleday, Page and Company
(New York; Garden City, New York: 1900-1927)
Doubleday, Doran and Company
(Garden City; New York: 1927-1946)

1899

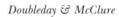

Doubleday & McClure

Doubleday Doran

Crime Club

Literary Guild

present logo

In 1897 S. S. McClure, publisher of *McClure's Magazine,* decided to branch out into book publishing by creating a subsidiary. He instructed Frank Nelson Doubleday, a vice president of the S. S. McClure Company, to form Doubleday and McClure. Doubleday was to receive fifty-one percent of the profits in the new venture. At thirty-five Doubleday had just left Charles Scribner's Sons, where he had been employed since he was fifteen. Doubleday's new partnership with McClure commenced in 1897 at McClure's headquarters in the Lexington building at 142 East Twenty-fifth Street. The firm's list for the first year included four different short story collections called *Tales from McClure's,* and the 1898 list had one more. *McClure's Magazine* attracted most of the important authors whose work was published by Doubleday and McClure. Rudyard Kipling's *Captains Courageous* (1897) was published by the firm because McClure had already won it as a serial for the magazine. Doubleday and McClure published the first novels of Frank Norris, including *McTeague* (1899), because McClure had seen Norris's sketches in San Francisco periodicals and hired him to write fiction for the magazine. Booth Tarkington sent his first novel, *The Gentleman from Indiana* (1899), to McClure, who bought it for both the magazine and the book company. Other works published by Doubleday and McClure included Stephen Crane's *The Open Boat and Other Tales of Adventure* (1898), and Edwin Markham's *The Man with the Hoe* (1899).

The partnership was a strained one, and at the end of 1899 Doubleday told McClure that he had decided to dissolve it and to take with him one of McClure's new editors, Walter Hines Page, a former editor of the *Atlantic Monthly.* Doubleday, Page and Company opened at 34 Union Square East in 1900 and moved to 133-137 East Sixteenth Street in 1904. Three new magazines were among the firm's earliest publications: *The World's Work,* a current affairs magazine; *Country Life;* and *Garden Magazine,* later *American Home.*

In its first year the firm published Theodore Dreiser's first novel, *Sister Carrie,* and kept copies off the market. The manuscript was accepted at the urging of Norris, a reader for the firm. A contract had already been signed when Mrs. Doubleday read the manuscript and was, according to Dreiser, "horrified by its frankness." The firm's lawyer advised Doubleday that the contract required him to publish the work, but he could choose not to sell it. Some review copies were smuggled out, apparently by Norris, but *Sister Carrie* did not achieve wide distribution until it was published by Heinemann in London in 1901 and by B. W. Dodge in America in 1907.

A realistic novel by Norris became the first Doubleday, Page best-seller. *The Pit* (1903) was promoted by the publisher with a $2,500 budget long before publication day. Sales of Norris's 1901 novel *The Octopus* were boosted by the success of *The Pit.* Far more popular were the cheerful, sentimental novels of Norris's sister-in-law, Kathleen Norris, who became one of the chief money-makers for Doubleday. Her *Mother* (1911) ultimately sold more than a million copies and was followed by a long list of novels that remained popular well into the 1950s.

Ellen Glasgow's realistic novels about southern life and women figured prominently in Doubleday's early lists starting with her third, *The Voice of the People* (1900). Her *The Wheel of Life* was tenth on the best-seller list in 1906. Upton Sinclair's *The Jungle* was another Doubleday best-seller in 1906 and one of the most talked-about books of the year. Two important autobiographies of the early Doubleday, Page years were Booker T. Washington's *Up From Slavery* (1901) and Helen Keller's *The Story of My Life* (1903).

The first juvenile book published by Doubleday, Page was Kipling's *Stalky & Co.* (1902). The same year saw the first edition of Kipling's *Just So Stories,* written in response to story requests from Doubleday's young son Nelson. As soon as he heard the collection was to be published, twelve-year-old Nelson went to his father and claimed a right to royalties; he received a penny on every copy of *Just So Stories* until his death in 1949. (A friend of Frank Nelson Doubleday's until the latter's death, it was Kipling who—playing on Doubleday's initials—gave him his famous nickname, "Effendi.") Another popular writer for young people was Gene Stratton-Porter, whose novels were read both by adolescents and by adults. Doubleday published her second book, *Freckles* (1904), followed by *A Girl of the Limberlost* (1909) and a long string of best-sellers about young people in rural or wilderness settings.

In 1908 Frank Nelson Doubleday, who had remained a trustee of the S. S. McClure Company, bought its book publishing division, McClure, Phillips and Company, for $118,750. The purchase included contracts with Joseph Conrad, William Sydney Porter (O. Henry), Jack London, William Allen White, Samuel Hopkins Adams, and Booth Tarkington. Among the Doubleday titles resulting from the takeover were O. Henry's *The Voice of the City* (1908); London's *A Son of the Sun* (1912); Tarkington's *Penrod* (1914), *The Magnificent Ambersons* (1918), and *Alice Adams* (1921); and Conrad's *Chance* (1915) and *Victory* (1916). Edwin Markham's *The Shoes of Happiness, and Other Poems* appeared in 1915. Kipling's *The Years Between* (1919) was Doubleday's first nonfiction best-seller.

In 1910 Doubleday, Page moved to Garden City, on Long Island, where the firm built its own printing operation, Country Life Press, as well as its publishing headquarters. Moving to the suburbs was considered a daring experiment for a New York City publisher, but the newly constructed Long Island commuter line helped make it successful. In the same year the firm opened the first Doubleday, Page bookstore in New York's Pennsylvania Station. The store was to be a "laboratory," where the books of all publishers would be sold and customers' buying habits and responses to promotion techniques would be studied. Doubleday bookstores have been part of the operation ever since. Page left the firm in 1913 to become United States ambassador to Great Britain. The company name remained Doubleday, Page and Company until 1927.

Nelson Doubleday joined the firm as a junior partner in 1918 and soon began making innovations. In 1923 he launched the first Doubleday bargain imprint, the Garden City Publishing

Frank Nelson Doubleday, who was given the nickname
"Effendi" by his friend Rudyard Kipling

Former President Theodore Roosevelt laid the cornerstone of the Country Life Press in 1910 (Underwood & Underwood)

Company, which started out by publishing paper-bound fifteen-cent pocket-size novels—reprints of books by Doubleday and other publishers. Non-fiction reprints soon followed. In 1934 Garden City added buckram-bound reprints of some scholarly books, of which the most expensive was F. W. Ruck-stull's *Great Works of Art* at $1.89, originally published by Putnam at $5.00. By 1936 Garden City Publishing Company was selling 1.3 million books a year. Another new imprint was the Crime Club, launched in 1928 with considerable fanfare and a special "selection committee" of mystery and detective writers and critics. The first monthly selection was *The Desert Moon Mystery* by Kay Cleaver Strahan. Later Crime Club offerings included titles by some top British writers, among them Edgar Wallace, Margery Allingham, and H. C. Bailey. Leslie Charteris, who moved to the United States from Britain in the 1930s, appeared in the series with his novels about "The Saint," Simon Templar. The Crime Club introduced Mignon Eberhart's first crime novel, *The Patient in Room 18* (1929). Other important American writers for the Crime Club included Carolyn Wells, with *The Doorstep Murders* (1930) and *The Skeleton at the Feast* (1931), and Doris Miles Disney, with *Who Rides a Tiger* (1946) and *Heavy, Heavy Hangs* (1952). The Crime Club remains one of the most successful Doubleday imprints.

Among the most popular Doubleday writers of the 1920s was Edna Ferber, whose *So Big* (1924) was the top seller of its year; her *Show Boat* (1926) was another big success. Christopher Morley's *Thunder on the Left* (1925), an experimental fantasy in which a character experiences his world as a child and as a man, was a departure from his earlier works of light entertainment, such as *The Haunted Bookshop* (1919). T. S. Stribling, who wrote realistic novels of small-town southern life, went to Doubleday with his fifth novel, *Teeftallow* (1926). Don Marquis's *archy and mehitabel* was published in 1927. The firm also added new magazines in the 1920s, including *Health Builder*, *Frontier*, and *Personality*.

In 1920 Doubleday formed a partnership in London with William Heinemann, Limited, a well-established firm with a strong literary emphasis. The arrangement followed the death of the British firm's founder. By the mid 1920s much of the executive control of Heinemann had passed into Doubleday hands. In 1926 Doubleday built Heinemann a printing plant in the country, the Windmill Press, along the lines of the Country Life Press.

Doubleday, Page merged with the George H. Doran Company in 1927 to form Doubleday,

Doran and Company. The following year Doubleday moved its offices to those of Doran at 244 Madison Avenue in New York; the printing operation remained in Garden City. Among the writers brought to the partnership by Doran were Arnold Bennett, W. Somerset Maugham, P. G. Wodehouse, and Mary Roberts Rinehart. The first book with the Doubleday, Doran imprint was Tarkington's *Claire Ambler* (1928), a best-seller. In the same year *John Brown's Body* by Stephen Vincent Benét won the Pulitzer Prize for poetry.

Doran resigned from the firm in 1930 and company headquarters returned to Garden City. The company name remained Doubleday, Doran and Company until 1946, when the firm became Doubleday and Company.

Frank Nelson Doubleday died in 1934. Christopher Morley, who had worked for the firm for several years in its early days, summarized Doubleday's achievements: "Effendi was really the first of a new era in book publishing—which he visualized foremost as a business, not merely as a dignified literary avocation. He realized, perhaps more clearly than any other man, that the possibilities of book distribution have hardly been scratched. He developed the mail order and subscription phases of the business to remarkable dimensions. . . . He was inexhaustible in fertile schemes for larger distribution. The idea that publishing should be essentially an intelligently conducted commerce, not a form of aesthetic bohemianism, appealed strongly to his authors. He was, I think, the first publisher anywhere to submit to his authors royalty statements backed and substantiated by outside accountants."

Nelson Doubleday, who had been president since 1928, retained the title of president and became chairman of the board on his father's death. By the mid 1930s he had withdrawn from William Heinemann, Limited and had disposed of the Doubleday magazines in order to expand the firm's reprint operations. In 1936 *Fortune* praised Nelson as a worthy successor to his father, with a whole new set of entrepreneurial ideas: "If he ever decides that there is money to be made out of selling reprints of the *Congressional Record* for seventy-nine cents a year, he will probably turn out to be right." The article attributed the firm's success—by some estimates it was already America's largest book publisher—partly to Nelson Doubleday's ability to see a potential market in "the one hundred and twenty-odd millions of Americans who never enter a bookstore."

The Literary Guild was one approach to that

market. Founded in 1926 by Harold Guinzburg, the club selected new titles by many publishers to send to members by mail. Doubleday began buying stock in the Literary Guild, and in 1934 he bought it outright. Henceforth the monthly Literary Guild selection was often but not always a Doubleday title. Specialized divisions were formed, such as the Junior Literary Guild for children and the Young People's Division for teenagers. Other Doubleday book clubs of the 1930s and 1940s, each with a specialized approach to a targeted group of readers, included the Book League of America, Family Reading Club, and Home Book Club. Today there are fifteen Doubleday book clubs. The biggest are the Literary Guild and the Doubleday Book Club, with over a million members each. Other Doubleday book clubs include the Military Book Club, the Ecstasy Romance Club, the Science Fiction Book Club, and the Doubleday Large Print Home Library.

Country Life Press printed the books of other publishers as well as Doubleday's. In the mid 1930s, about 1.5 million of its seven million annual volumes were non-Doubleday titles. New Doubleday imprints also were added in the 1930s. Three new reprint lines, Star Dollar Books, Sun Dial Library, and Lambskin Library were added under Garden City Publishing Company in the 1930s.

In 1935 Doubleday announced the formation of Doubleday, Doran of Canada, Limited at 215 Victoria Street, Toronto. Its forerunner had been Doubleday, Doran and Gundy, formed in 1928 by annexing S. B. Gundy, Limited, the Canadian representative for Doubleday, Page. The subsidiary is now Doubleday Canada, Limited at 105 Bond Street. Prominent Doubleday books of the 1930s included Sinclair Lewis's *It Can't Happen Here* (1935) and Kenneth Roberts's *Northwest Passage* (1937).

Doubleday, Page established a children's book department under May Massee in 1923. The firm's Windmill Books for children were priced at one dollar; more expensive Doubleday children's books often featured noted illustrators such as Maud and Miska Petersham, who used techniques of East European peasant art in Margery Clark's *The Poppy Seed Cakes* (1924). Later Petersham works included *Children of the Mountain Eagle* (1927) by Elizabeth Cleveland Miller and *The Christ Child* (1931) with the text from the King James Bible. Edgar and Ingri d'Aulaire wrote and illustrated *The Magic Rug* (1931) and *Ola* (1932). By the early 1950s the children's book division, under Margaret Lesser, was publishing twenty to twenty-five new titles per year,

placing Doubleday among the top five children's publishers.

In 1938 Doubleday transferred its administrative, editorial, and sales offices from Garden City to 14 West Forty-ninth Street in New York. The Country Life Press in Garden City briefly became an independent company but soon rejoined the Doubleday organization. Garden City remains the headquarters for printing and book orders. Kenneth D. McCormick, who had started with the firm as a night clerk at the Pennsylvania Station bookshop in 1930, was made editor in chief in 1942.

In the 1940s the firm started writers' contests, of which the most notable was probably the George Washington Carver Award "to encourage worthwhile books by or about American Negroes." The first winner was Fannie Cook's *Mrs. Palmer's Honey* (1946), a novel about a black maid who evolves into a labor leader. Dwight D. Eisenhower's *Crusade in Europe* was a big seller in 1948. Fulton Oursler's *The Greatest Story Ever Told* (1949), a life of Christ with fictionalized dialogue, sold three million copies in America. In 1944 Doubleday increased its wartime paper allotment by acquiring the Blakiston Company of Philadelphia, a publisher of scientific and medical books. The firm was retained as a separate division until it was sold to McGraw-Hill in 1954. Douglas M. Black became president in 1946, and Nelson Doubleday retained the title chairman of the board. Doubleday died in 1949. Like his father, Nelson Doubleday was primarily a businessman, not a literary man. He once said, "I sell books. I don't read them."

In the 1950s Doubleday published important nonfiction titles, including Anne Frank's *The Diary of a Young Girl* (1952); Bruce Catton's *A Stillness at Appomattox* (1953), winner of the Pulitzer Prize for history; and Harry S. Truman's *Memoirs* (1955-1956). Pulitzer Prizes for novels went to Herman Wouk's *The Caine Mutiny* (1951) and Allen Drury's *Advise and Consent* (1959). Other American writers whose works were published by Doubleday in the postwar decades include John A. Williams, William Goyen, Hodding Carter, and James Dickey. The firm published Nelson Algren's *The Neon Wilderness* (1947), *The Man With the Golden Arm* (1949), and *Chicago, City on the Make* (1951). Ray Bradbury's Doubleday books include *The Martian Chronicles* (1950) and *The Illustrated Man* (1951). Doubleday published *The View from Pompey's Head* (1954) by Hamilton Basso and most of the important work of Leon Uris, including *Exodus* (1958) and *Trinity* (1976). John Barth's *The Sot-Weed Factor* (1960) and *Giles Goat-Boy* (1966) were published by Doubleday.

A view of the Country Life Press in 1925

*Nelson Doubleday, head of the firm from 1928 until his death
in 1949 (painting by Sidney E. Dickinson)*

Doubleday moved to 575 Madison Avenue in 1951, and to 277 Park Avenue in 1964. The firm developed some new imprints in the 1950s and 1960s, notably Anchor Books, started in 1953 as a series of quality paperback originals and reprints with an academic cast. Anchor now includes hardcover originals. Its best-known title may be the highly respected thirty-eight-volume Anchor Bible, the first two volumes of which appeared in 1964. Image books, paperback editions of Roman Catholic works, began in 1954. Dolphin paperbacks, begun about 1959, have been joined by a Dolphin hardback line. Natural History Press was started in 1962 as a collaboration between Doubleday and the American Museum of Natural History. Zenith Books, started in 1965, deals with American minority groups.

In 1961 Doubleday acquired Aldus Books, Limited, a British firm which publishes general interest books in several languages. Two important acquisitions by Doubleday in the 1960s were J. G. Ferguson of Chicago, which publishes subscription reference books, and Laidlaw Brothers of River Forest, Illinois, one of the largest publishers of textbooks for elementary and high schools. Dell Publishing Company, acquired by Doubleday in 1976, includes the giant Dell paperback house and Delacorte Press. In 1961 John T. Sargent, son-in-law of Nelson Doubleday, became president of the firm, while Douglas M. Black moved to chairman of the board. Nelson Doubleday, Jr., who began working in the family house in 1959, was vice president until March 1978, when he became president and chief executive officer, with Sargent becoming chairman of the board. In 1985 Sargent was chairman of the executive committee; Doubleday was chairman of the board; and James R. McLaughlin was president and chief executive officer.

Despite the repeated efforts by some stockholders to make Doubleday a public corporation, the majority of its stock remains in the control of the Doubleday family. It is the only major hardcover publisher with its own presses, which produce sixty million books a year. The firm published 450 titles in 1985. Its address since 1975 has been 245 Park Avenue, New York 10167.

References:

The Country Life Press (Garden City: Doubleday, Page, 1919);

Florence Doubleday, *Episodes in the Life of a Publisher's Wife* (New York: Privately printed, 1937);

F. N. Doubleday, *The Memoirs of a Publisher* (Garden City: Doubleday, 1972);

"Doubleday, Doran and Company," *Fortune*, 13 (February 1936): 73-181;

"Doubleday Plans Fiftieth Anniversary Celebration in 1947," *Publishers' Weekly*, 150 (21 December 1946): 3284-3294;

"Frank Nelson Doubleday (1862-1934)," *Publishers' Weekly*, 125 (3 February 1934): 583-586;

"Frank Nelson Doubleday [obituary]," *New York Times*, 31 January 1934, p. 17;

Burton J. Hendrick, *The Life and Letters of Walter H. Page*, 3 volumes (Garden City: Doubleday, Page, 1922-1925);

"The House of Doubleday, Page," *Literary Digest International Book Review*, 2 (1923-1924): 620-621;

Frederick Lambeck, *Party: A Literary Nightmare* (Garden City: Doubleday, Doran, 1936);

Neil McCaffrey, "Doubleday and Company, Inc.," *Catholic Library World*, 28 (1956-1957): 215-218;

Christopher Morley, *"Effendi" (Frank Nelson Doubleday, 1862-1934)* (Garden City: Country Life Press, 1934);

"Nelson Doubleday [obituary]," *New York Times*, 12 January 1949, p. 27;

Walter Hines Page, *A Publisher's Confession* (Garden City: Doubleday, Page, 1923).

—Margaret Becket

William Doxey
(San Francisco: 1881-1901)

During the late nineteenth century, English immigrant William Doxey was perhaps the most important bookseller in San Francisco, as well as a publisher of handsomely designed and printed editions of works by local authors. Doxey's most notable publications include Flora M. Shearer's *The Legend of Aulus* (1895), with title page and cover design by Gelett Burgess; *Tales of Languedoc* (1896) by Professor Samuel J. Brun of Stanford University, for which Ernest Peixotto executed forty illustrations and the cover design; the second edition of Laura Bride Power's *Missions of California* (1897), with illustrations and cover design by Florence Lundborg; and the 1897 and 1898 editions of Edward Robeson Taylor's translation of the *Sonnets* of José-Maria de Heredia, printed by the newly formed E. D. Taylor Company. An early fantasy novel, Frona Eunice Wait's *Yermah the Dorado*, in which the present site of San Francisco is inhabited by a primitive race, was published by Doxey in 1897. That year the firm published its greatest number of books, possibly as many as sixteen.

From 1895 to 1897 Doxey published a literary magazine, the *Lark*. Supported and printed by Charles A. Murdock, the *Lark* was praised in both the United States and Europe and earned international reputations for its editors, Burgess and Bruce Porter.

Doxey went bankrupt in 1899, started his firm again in 1900, and went out of business the following year.

References:
Robert D. Harlan, " 'At the Sign of the Lark': The San Francisco Publishing Venture of William Doxey," *Kemble Occasional*, 21 (Spring 1979): 1-7;
Flodden W. Heron, "The William Doxey Book Shop: Another Chapter," *Book Club of California Quarterly News-Letter*, 15 (1949-1950): 83-85;
Wallace Kibbee, "William Doxey and 'Les Jeunes,' " *Book Club of California Quarterly News-Letter*, 6 (December 1938): 5-8;
Robert O'Brien, "The Doxey Story," *Book Club of California Quarterly News-Letter*, 15 (1949-1950): 27-31.

—*Bruce L. Johnson*

The Dramatic Publishing Company

(Chicago: 1885-   )

The Dramatic Publishing Company was founded by Charles Hubbard Sergel at 358 Dearborn Street, Chicago, in 1885. From 1887 to 1902 the firm grew by acquiring G. Pierce and Company and M. J. McGrath and Company, both of Chicago, and the De Witt Publishing House and the Roxbury Publishing Company of New York. Sergel also published under the imprint of Charles H. Sergel and Company.

In 1911 The Dramatic Publishing Company began publishing *The Drama: A Quarterly Review of Dramatic Literature*, with Sergel as editor in chief. Besides articles pertaining to the theatrical world, the magazine printed, usually for the first time, translations of short plays by foreign authors. Among these were Herman Heijermans's *The Good Hope*, Henri Becque's *The Crows*, Emile Augier's *Giboyer's Son*, and Christian Friedrich Hebbel's *Herod and Mariamne*. In 1913 the Drama League

of America took over publication of the magazine and renamed it *Drama Magazine*.

The Dramatic Publishing Company published first American editions of several early plays by W. Somerset Maugham. These editions were made up of sheets from the original London publisher, William Heinemann. The titles include *Jack Straw* (1912), *Penelope* (1912), *A Man of Honour* (1912), *Landed Gentry* (1913), and *The Tenth Man* (1913). The Dramatic Publishing Company also published Annie M. Sergel's *The Midway* (1894) and several nonfiction works by Charles Sergel. Its current list includes plays by John Osborne, Friedrich Durrenmatt, Peter Weiss, William Golding, and David Mamet. The present address of the company is 311 Washington Street, Woodstock, Illinois 60098. Its president is Christopher Sergel.

—Ruth H. Bennett

Edward Dunigan and Brother

(New York: 1840?-1868)

Beginning around 1840, Edward Dunigan and his stepbrother James P. Kirker published Bibles, almanacs, prayer books, devotional and historical works, schoolbooks, and some fiction, all concerned with Catholicism. Along with Donahoe of Boston and Sadlier of New York, Dunigan was one of the first publishers to encourage American Catholic authors. In 1844 the company was located at 151 Fulton Street, New York.

Dunigan died in 1853. Some time between 1856 and 1858 the firm moved to 371 Broadway. Kirker ran the company until his death, at forty,

in 1868. The *New York Times* obituary for Kirker commented that "the firm was long the leading publishing house, in its special line, in the city, and was noted for its enterprise and liberality." Among the firm's fiction titles were *Father Felix* (1845) by Charles James Cannon, *Shandy McGuire; or, Tricks upon Travellers. Being a Story of the North of Ireland* (1848) by John Boyce, and *The Hamiltons; or, Sunshine in Storm* (1856) by Cora Berkeley.

—Kathleen McGowan

146

William Durrell

(New York: circa 1786-circa 1802)

During the last decades of the eighteenth century, William Durrell operated a bookstore and print shop at 198 Queen Street in New York. Much of his list consisted of religious tracts and sermons, New York State government reports, histories, hymns, and almanacs; but he also published some fiction, including children's books.

In 1786 Durrell's name appeared in an imprint as the bookseller of a sermon by the Reverend Caleb Alexander. In 1790 Durrell advertised in several broadsides proposals to print by subscription the works of Flavius Josephus, with illustrations. Durrell published *The Whole Genuine and Complete Works of Flavius Josephus* in sixty numbers from 1792 to 1794. Each number contained an illustration; engravers for the work included Joel Allen,

Alexander Anderson, Amos Doolittle, William Rollinson, and Benjamin Tanner.

One of the firm's first children's offerings was *Select Verses for Little Masters and Misses* (1790), an alphabet book with woodcut illustrations. Durrell published an abridged version of *Gulliver's Travels* in 1793, as well as several books by Richard Johnson: *The Hermit of the Forest, and The Wandering Infants* (1791), *The History of Tommy Careless* (1793), *The Looking-Glass for the Mind* (1795) under the pseudonym Arnaud Berquin, and *The History of a Doll* (1800). Most of these books were illustrated with woodcut engravings. By 1800 Durrell had moved to 106 Maiden Lane. Among his last publications was a medical treatise in 1802.

—*Elizabeth Hoffman*

E. P. Dutton and Company
(Boston; New York: 1858-   )
Ide and Dutton
(Boston: 1852-1858)

Everyman's Library

1950s

1970s

In 1852 Edward Payson Dutton borrowed $3,000 from his father and invested it in a Boston schoolbook and map store recently purchased by his friend Lemuel Ide, who had a background in printing and publishing. Ide and Dutton soon found their second-floor room at 140 Washington Street too small and purchased the business on the floor below of Charles Stimpson, a seller of religious books, who was retiring. With the move came Stimpson's Boston Episcopal connections and the interest in publishing religious works which was central to the Dutton operations for many years.

Ide and Dutton's first publication was the highly successful *Lectures on Education* by Horace Mann (1855).

In 1858 Dutton bought Ide's share of the business, forming E. P. Dutton and Company. In 1864 he acquired the famous Old Corner Bookstore at 135 Washington Street from Ticknor and Fields and moved his firm there. Ticknor and Fields's head salesman, Charles Clapp, became a junior partner at Dutton; his efficient management rapidly increased the firm's retail trade. This improvement in business stimulated Dutton to enlarge the publishing department, and Sunday school books were added to a growing number of church and denominational titles, textbooks, and maps. In 1868 Dutton began to print books for the Church Book Society. The contract specified that Dutton would take over the New York business and joint premises of the Church Book Society and the General Protestant Episcopal Sunday School Union at 726 Broadway. A branch office was established in Manhattan, while the Old Corner Bookstore was maintained as E. P. Dutton's headquarters. In 1869, when the lease on the New York office expired and the rent was increased, Dutton was offered the New York branch of the Boston firm Fields, Osgood and Company on the condition that Dutton move to New York. By late 1869 E. P. Dutton and Company was settled at 713 Broadway at Washington Place. The Old Corner Bookstore was sold to A. Williams and Company. E. C. Swayne joined Dutton when the firm moved to New York, starting as an office boy and quickly rising to clerk and head salesman.

In New York, while operating what was widely considered the most handsome bookstore of its time, Dutton published some of the period's more significant religious works. By 1874 the company had a list of 700 titles in its religious and juvenile lines. Successes included the firm's first adult novel, W. M. L. Jay's *Shiloh* (1871), Dean Frederic William Farrar's *Life of Christ* (1874), and Phillips Brooks's *Sermons* (1878). Swayne's instinct for what books would sell led Dutton to send him abroad as a representative. In Germany Swayne struck a deal with the Nuremberg printer Louis Nister, whose talents enhanced the quality of color illustration in Dutton's juvenile line and helped to make the Dutton cards and calendars popular. Swayne was made a partner in 1878.

In 1882 the firm relocated at 31 West Twenty-third Street, close to the bookshops of Brentano's, Scribners, and Putnam's. Dutton continued its emphasis on theological publication with works by

Bishop Henry C. Potter, Rev. Morgan Dixon, Archdeacon Farrar, and Canon James B. Mozley. More fiction began to appear on Dutton's list, including Charlotte M. Yonge's *Langley Adventures* (1884). John Macrae, a nineteen-year-old Virginian, joined the firm as an office boy in 1884. Macrae's sales skills led Dutton to send him on the road for the house and to make him manager of the card department.

Through Swayne's efforts, E. P. Dutton and Company established relationships with the British houses of John Murray, Chapman and Hall, Smith, Elder and Company, and George Routledge and Sons. From Routledge, Dutton acquired American rights to the Universal Library and the Muses Library. When Swayne died in 1900, Dutton needed someone to carry on the firm's European publishing connections. Macrae was chosen and was made a partner.

Clapp died in 1901 and was replaced in the firm by his son-in-law, Joseph A. Smith. In 1903 Macrae arranged with J. M. Dent in London for Dutton to publish an American edition of the works of Charles Lamb in twelve volumes. In 1906 he struck one of the most important deals in the company's history: Dutton became the American publisher of Everyman's Library, a series which reached its thousandth American title in 1976 with a volume of the works of Samuel Johnson. Encouraged by the success of Everyman's Library, Dutton later brought out the Library of English Novelists, the Temple Shakespeare, the Temple Classics, and the Temple Dramatists. Smith died in 1906 and his son, Henry Clapp Smith, joined the firm.

Macrae initiated that willingness that has become characteristic of Dutton to publish the works of unknown or risky authors. He bought the rights to George Gissing's *The Private Papers of Henry Ryecroft* (1903), W. H. Hudson's *The Purple Land* (1906), Samuel Butler's *Erewhon* (1907) and *The Way of All Flesh* (1910), and Vicente Blasco Ibáñez's *The Four Horsemen of the Apocalypse* (1918). Macrae also acquired rights to works by Max Beerbohm, Hilaire Belloc, G. K. Chesterton, Leonard Merrick, Mary Webb, Anatole France, and Arthur Symons.

In April 1911 E. P. Dutton and Company moved into three floors and the basement of a building at 681 Fifth Avenue. While maintaining its solid trade title list, Dutton branched out into the educational field in 1913 by acquiring the Thompson-Brown Company, a publisher of school and college textbooks. During World War I Dutton lost the Nister business; since no more goods came

Charles Sergel founded The Dramatic Publishing Company in 1885

Edward Payson Dutton, shown in a portrait by Albert Sterner

The Old Corner Book Store, 135 Washington Street, Boston, bought from Ticknor and Fields in 1864

The building at 713 Broadway, New York, that was the home of E. P. Dutton and Company from 1869 to 1884. Dutton agreed to move his operation there when he purchased the New York branch of Boston publisher Fields, Osgood and Company.

from Germany, millions of books, calendars, and cards had to be closed out.

Dutton's encouragement of new authors was evident in 1919 when it began a long relationship with Van Wyck Brooks by publishing *The Ordeal of Mark Twain*. The publication of A. A. Milne's collection of essays and criticism, *If I May* (1921), initiated an association between Milne and Dutton which resulted in the publication of *When We Were Very Young* (1924), *Winnie-the-Pooh* (1926), *Now We Are Six* (1927), and *The House at Pooh Corner* (1928).

E. P. Dutton died in 1923, leaving the firm in the control of Macrae and Henry Clapp Smith as joint trustees. This relationship dissolved after five years, with Macrae retaining the publishing business and Smith taking the bookstore, which was renamed Dutton's, Incorporated. Soon after the split, the publishing company moved to 300 Park Avenue South. The firm published *The Story of San Michele* (1929) by Axel Munthe and *1066 and All That* (1931) by Walter C. Sellar and Robert J. Yeatman, as well as Brooks's *The Life of Emerson* (1932) and *The Flowering of New England* (1936).

The 1940s brought controversy to Dutton when the firm published several books dealing with the war, Nazism, and political subversion in America, beginning in 1940 with Donald Keyhoe's *M-Day: If War Comes, What Your Government Plans for You*. John Roy Carlson's *Under Cover* (1943), an exposé of extremist organizations, resulted in libel suits. Although many book jobbers refused to handle it, the book was a huge success, selling almost one million copies. Macrae died in 1944 and was succeeded by his son Elliott.

In 1945 Dutton won the Carey-Thomas Award for creative publishing for Brooks's *The World of Washington Irving* (1944). Gore Vidal's first book, *Williwaw*, was published in 1946; he was briefly an editor at Dutton in 1946. Elliott Macrae launched the Society in America series, to be made up of works by prominent American writers; its first volume was Cleveland Amory's *The Proper Bostonians* (1947). Dutton also published Mickey Spillane's first novel, *I, the Jury*, in 1947.

Dutton published several books on mountain climbing. While in Paris in 1952, Macrae had purchased the American rights to Maurice Herzog's *Annapurna* (1953), an account of a French climbing expedition. Macrae said that 1953 would be "The Mountain Year," and his prediction proved correct as *Annapurna* rose to the top of the best-seller list. Herzog's book was followed by John Hunt's *The Conquest of Everest* (1954), Heinrich Harrer's *Seven Years in Tibet* (1954), and Sir Edmund Hillary's *High*

Adventure (1955). While Dutton remained loyal to its older writers—publishing, for example Brooks's *The Confident Years: 1885-1915* on the hundredth anniversary of the house in 1952—it also pursued new directions. Macrae's faith in Françoise Sagan led to the publication of *Bonjour Tristesse* in 1955; the book sold 1.7 million copies in paperback. Macrae had read Lawrence Durrell's *Justine* in London; Dutton published the novel in 1957, and by the time *Clea*, the last volume of the Alexandria Quartet, came out in 1961, Durrell was being hailed as one of the century's major talents. Macrae was also responsible for building a strong bond with Soviet writers, beginning with the publication of Vladimir Dudintsev's *Not by Bread Alone* (1957). The firm later published Yevgeny Yevtushenko's *Selected Poems* (1962), *A Precocious Autobiography* (1963), and *Collected Poems* (1967), as well as Aleksandr Solzhenitsyn's *One Day in the Life of Ivan Denisovich* (1963). Dutton introduced Polish novelist Marek Hlasko to America with *The Eighth Day of the Week* (1958). In 1957 Dutton Paperbacks was created as a quality line drawn from the firm's backlist. Gavin Maxwell's *Ring of Bright Water* (1961) began a series of animal stories, and in 1962 the firm created the $7,500 Dutton Animal Book Award. The first winner was Sterling North for *Rascal* (1963).

A lawsuit, coupled with the costs of buying computers to handle orders in 1966, left the firm in financial difficulty. Macrae died in 1968 and his brother, John Macrae, Jr., became president; two years later John, Jr. became chairman of the board and his son, John Macrae III, was made president. The new president found funding and hired new editors, including Hal Scharlett from Random House and Ann Durell, who later became publisher of the juvenile division, from Holt.

Probably the most notable triumph of the late 1960s and the 1970s was the publication of work by Jorge Luis Borges: *The Book of Imaginary Beings* (1969), *Doctor Brodie's Report* (1972), *Borges on Writing* (1973), *The Book of Sand* (1977), and *The Gold of the Tigers* (1977). Popular works included Mike Royko's *Boss* (1971) and Nicholas Meyer's *The Seven-per-Cent Solution* (1974). Eliot Porter and Peter Matthiessen's *The Tree Where Man Was Born* was a Book-of-the-Month Club selection in 1972, as was Peter Farb's *Man's Rise to Civilization* in 1978. Gail Sheehy's *Passages* (1976) sold over 500,000 hardcover copies by 1977. In the juvenile list, Arlene Mosel's *The Funny Little Woman*, illustrated by Blair Lent, won the Caldecott Award in 1973.

In September 1975 Dutton was sold to the Elsevier Publishing Company, a Dutch concern. In the year of the sale, Dutton published 229 original titles through its six divisions: Dutton Adult, Saturday Review Press, Dutton Juvenile, Windmill Books, Dutton Paperbacks, and Sunrise Books. The Saturday Review Press imprint was dropped in 1976 when it was merged with the adult trade book division.

In October 1978 the company acquired the Juvenile Books Division of Thomas Nelson, Incorporated. In 1979 Hawthorn Books, Incorporated was purchased. John Macrae III served as publisher of the Adult Division, Durell as publisher of the Juvenile Division, and Ivor Whitson, a former data processing specialist with Dutton, as president of the parent company, American Elsevier. During its restructuring, Dutton retained its commitment to its established writers and adventurousness in publishing new ones, in both the juvenile and adult divisions. This commitment was reflected in some of the titles published between 1976 and 1981: Meyer's *The West End Horror* (1976); Billy Hayes's *Midnight Express* (1977); John Irving's *The World According to Garp* (1978) and *The Hotel New Hampshire* (1981); Barbara Pym's *Quartet in Autumn* and *Excellent Women* (both 1978); and Joyce Carol Oates's *Bellefleur* (1980) and *Angel of Light* (1981).

In 1981 Dutton became a subsidiary of the JSD Corporation, with Whitson as president and John S. Dyson as chairman of the board. Dutton entered into an agreement in 1982 with Seymour Lawrence to publish books under the E. P. Dutton/ Seymour Lawrence imprint; a similar arrangement was made with William Abraham in 1984. In 1985 Dutton was acquired by New American Library; Richard Marek was named president, and Joyce Engelson became editor in chief. The firm published 226 titles in 1985. Dutton moved to 201 Park Avenue South in 1962. Since 1978 its address has been 2 Park Avenue, New York 10016.

References:
"The Bookmakers . . . XIV.—E. P. Dutton & Company," *New York Evening Post*, 27 January 1875;

"Elliott B. Macrae [obituary]," *New York Times*, 14 February 1968, p. 47;

"E. P. Dutton [obituary]," *New York Times*, 7 September 1923, p. 15;

"Fifty Years with Dutton's: John Macrae Completes a Half-Century with One Publishing Firm," *Publishers' Weekly*, 128 (23 November 1935): 1891-1893;

"The House of Dutton," *Literary Digest International Book Review*, 2 (1923-1924): 68-69;

"John Macrae [obituary]," *New York Times*, 20 February 1944, p. 35;

Seventy-Five Years; or, The Joys and Sorrows of Publishing and Selling Books at Duttons from 1852 to 1927 (New York: Dutton, 1927);

"Sketches of the Publishers: E. P. Dutton & Co.," *Round Table*, 4 (11 August 1866): 26.

—Ernest Bevan, Jr.

Duyckinck and Company
(New York: 1795-1799)
Evert Duyckinck
(New York: 1799-1833)

Evert Augustus Duyckinck promoted the expanding book industry in New York and supported ι whole generation of young American writers. His ɔons Evert A. Duyckinck, Jr., and George Duyckinck became writers and editors. Evert Duyckinck, Sr., entered publishing with an edition of *Robinson Crusoe,* printed by Hurtin and Commardinger, in 1795. His firm produced mostly schoolbooks, employing the printers George Long, C. W. Bunce, and J. C. Totten. Duyckinck also reprinted works by Samuel Richardson, Thomas Campbell, and J. G. Lockhart. In 1799 the company's imprint was changed from Duyckinck and Company to Evert Duyckinck.

In 1802 Duyckinck joined nine other schoolbook publishers to found the New York Association of Book Sellers, which aimed to reduce the number of costly imported books and to provide "correct American editions" of works "interesting to the community." Because the members were unable to agree on procedure, the association was short-lived.

In 1817 the firm moved from 110 Pearl Street to 68 Water Street. Duyckinck earned a reputation for helping young men start in the publishing industry. In July 1817 he trusted the untried printing firm of J. and J. Harper to print 2,000 copies of his English version of Seneca's *Morals,* an order which started the Harpers on their publishing career. Duyckinck began the practice of furnishing customers with printed lists of the latest books. Orville A. Roorbach, compiler of the *Bibliotheca Americana* (1849), was briefly a clerk in Duyckinck's shop. When Duyckinck died in 1833, he was the oldest bookseller in New York and had been a publisher for forty years.

Reference:

William Allen Butler, *Evert A. Duyckinck: A Memorial Sketch* (New York: Trow, 1829).

—*Martha A. Bartter*

James H. Earle and Company

(Boston: 1869-1922)

James Hervey Earle went into the wholesale book business at 96 Washington Street in Boston in 1868 and began religious publishing in 1869. Earle founded the *Contributor,* a religious family periodical, in 1871. The firm published works of piety and polemic and histories of local Baptist churches. The firm's literary output included Mrs. D. S. Sherwin's anonymous *Why? or, Tried in the Crucible* (1884), Mrs. S. A. Southworth's *Gold and Dross; or, the False Life and the True* (1890), George Cook Marsh's temperance novel *Lakeside Cottage* (1894), and DeWitt Chipman's *Beyond the Verge: Home of Ten Lost Tribes of Israel* (1896). In 1891 Earle published Emma Dunham Kelley's *Megda,* one of the earliest novels by a black American woman. The firm was dissolved in 1922, having operated at 20 Hawley Street, 178 Washington Street, and 28 School Street.

—*Sharon Ann Jaeger*

The Editor Publishing Company

(Franklin, Ohio; Cincinnati: 1895-1910?)

The Editor Publishing Company was founded in 1895 in Franklin, Ohio. In 1898 the firm moved to Cincinnati. Editor's output consisted almost exclusively of romantic novels and short stories by women for female readers. The firm printed many stories of the pre- and post-Civil War South, the Southwest, and California, among them *Life at Shut-In Valley, and Other Pacific Coast Tales* (1895) by Clara Spalding Brown and *Burrill Coleman, Colored: A Tale of the Cotton Fields* (1896) by Mrs. Jeannette Downes Coltharp. Some of the more exotic romances published by Editor include *A Cuban Amazon* (1897) by Mrs. Virginia Lyndall Dunbar and *Naaman, the Leper, and Princess Sarah, the Captive Maid* (1899) by Mrs. M. I. Cash. The firm went out of business around 1910.

—*Pamela A. Graunke*

Paul Elder and Company
(San Francisco; New York: 1903-1948)
Elder and Shepard
(San Francisco: 1899-1903)

A San Francisco bookseller-publisher beginning in 1899, Paul Elder was in partnership until 1903 with Morgan Shepard, a member of San Francisco's Bohemian colony, Les Jeunes. *The Love Sonnets of a Hoodlum* by Wallace Irwin (1902), the firm's best-selling and most widely known book, probably came to Elder and Shepard through Shepard. Other books published before 1903 include William H. Hudson's *The Sphinx and Other Poems* (1900) and Gellett Burgess's *The Romance of the Commonplace* (1902). Beginning in March 1900 Elder and Shepard published *Personal Impressions*, the only publisher's magazine of personal opinion about art and books on the West Coast. Later renamed *Impressions Quarterly*, it appeared erratically until December 1905.

Shepard left the firm in May 1903. Until 1906 Paul Elder and Company published about a dozen titles annually, including David Starr Jordan's *Voice of the Scholar* (1903) and Dora Amsden's *Impressions of Ukiyo-Ye* (1905). In April 1906 Elder moved his publishing business to 43-45 East Nineteenth Street in New York, while continuing his bookselling operation in San Francisco. Elder at first contracted with New York printers to produce his books, but he soon set up his own plant, the Tomoyè Press, under the direction of the famous printer John Henry Nash. While in New York Elder published nearly seventy books, including Jennie Day Haines's *Ye Gardeyne Boke* (1906) and *Christmasse Tyde* (1907); Ambrose Bierce's *A Son of the Gods and a Horseman in the Sky* (1907); Bret Harte's *Tennessee's Partner* (1907); Robert Louis Stevenson's *The Sea Fogs* (1907); and *The Spinners' Book of Fiction* (1907). The New York operation was a financial failure, and Elder returned to San Francisco in 1909. Though Elder's publications tended to be artistic in their execution, their texts were often trite collections of quotations, essays by minor homespun philosophers, or glib humor. Exceptions included *The Rubáiyát of Omar Khayyám*, published in 1909 and again in 1911; Elizabeth Barrett Browning's *Sonnets from the Portuguese* (1910); and *Eric's Book of Beasts* (1912), a book of verse by David Starr Jordan.

Elder was never able to recover from the 1906 losses in San Francisco and the debts acquired during the three New York years. He continued to publish occasional titles into the 1940s, but after 1917 publishing was a minor sideline to his bookselling business. Elder's bookstore continued to be successful under his direction and, after his death in 1948, under that of his son. In 1968 Paul Elder, Jr., sold the remaining book stocks to various local dealers and the shop itself to Brentano's.

References:

Marion B. Allen, "The Tomoyè Press," *Book Club of California Quarterly News-Letter*, 16 (1950-1951): 84-88;

Ruth Gordon, "Paul Elder: Bookseller-Publisher (1897-1917), a Bay Area Reflection," Ph.D. dissertation, University of California, Berkeley, 1977;

"Paul Elder [obituary]," *New York Times*, 26 January 1948, p. 19;

"Specimens of the Bookmaker's Art," *Pacific Printer and Publisher*, 18 (1917): 92-95.

—*Bruce L. Johnson*

Elliott, Thomes and Talbot
(Boston: 1863-1870)
Elliott and Thomes
(Boston: 1861-1863)
Thomes and Talbot
(Boston: 1870-1885)

In 1861 James R. Elliott entered into partnership with William Henry Thomes to form Elliott and Thomes at 100 Washington Street in Boston. Elliott had previously been an editor with the Boston firm of Moulton, Elliott and Lincoln, publisher of the weekly adventure magazine *True Flag*. Thomes had been involved in journalism at an early age and had traveled extensively throughout the American West and the Orient, living the adventurous life that he and Elliott chronicled in their initial publishing venture, the *American Union*, a weekly adventure magazine.

In 1863 Elliott and Thomes added a third partner, Newton Talbot; the firm name changed to Elliott, Thomes and Talbot and moved to 118 Washington Street. Like Thomes, Talbot had spent an adventurous youth, traveling to South America and throughout the West. He had worked for Frederick Gleason's Publishing Hall, beginning in 1851 as a cashier and eventually becoming business manager after the Gleason publishing business had been taken over by Maturin Murray Ballou. When Talbot went into business with Elliott and Thomes in 1863, he brought with him three of Ballou's most successful magazines, the *Flag of Our Union, Ballou's Dollar Monthly Magazine,* and the *Novelette.* Ballou agreed to serve as an adviser to the new firm. Like the *American Union,* the new magazines featured a blend of adventure and romantic fiction, humor, travel commentary, and household advice. The Ballou magazines proved highly successful for Elliott, Thomes and Talbot.

On 10 November 1863 Elliott, Thomes and Talbot published its first book, *The Golden Eagle; or, The Privateer of 1776* by Sylvanus Cobb, Jr. The book inaugurated the Ten Cent Novelettes, launched to compete with Erastus Beadle, who had begun a dime novel series three years earlier. The monthly Ten Cent Novelette series had a yearly subscription rate of $1.00. Not wanting to duplicate the familiar orange wrappers of the Beadle dime novels, Elliott, Thomes and Talbot issued the first twenty-five Ten Cent Novelettes in pink wrappers and the other sixty-one in blue wrappers. The Ten Cent Novelettes were also physically larger than their Beadle counterparts; Elliott, Thomes and Talbot advertised their series as the "largest" of all the dime novels.

Another popular Elliott, Thomes and Talbot fiction series was the Brilliant Novelettes. These were paperbacks, better illustrated than the Ten Cent Novelettes, and sold for twenty cents apiece. In 1865 the firm moved to 63 Congress Street.

Like all of the dime novel series, Elliott, Thomes and Talbot's were composed of romances; exotic, sensational adventures; and, most frequently, stories set in the early days of American history or on the frontier. The Elliott, Thomes and Talbot series featured some of the better-known authors of the day; many of the books were reprinted from the firm's magazines or from books originally published by other firms. Edward Z. C. Judson (Ned Buntline) contributed several novels, including *The Volunteer* (1863) and *The Red Revenger* (1876). Other works reprinted by Elliott, Thomes and Talbot included Benjamin Perley Poore's *The Mameluke* (1863), *The Scout* (1863), and *The West Point Cadet* (1863); Jane G. Austin's *Kinah's Curse* (1864) and *The Novice* (1865); J. W. McCartney's *The Fenians* (1865); William Bushnell's *A Lost Life* (1865) and *Hack the Trailer* (1868); and Jane Howard's *Zelda* (1866). Ballou contributed *The Duke's Prize* (1863), *The Turkish Slave* (1863), and *The Child of the Sea* (1863), all written under the pen name "Lt. Murray." The best-known Elliott, Thomes and Talbot author was Louisa May Alcott, who contributed *The Skeleton in the Closet* (1867) and *The Mysterious Key* (1867) to the Ten Cent Novelettes series. Alcott's *V. V., or Plots and Counterplots,* number eighty in the series, was written under the pseudonym A. M. Barnard and had been printed several years earlier in the *Flag of Our Union,* in which several of her shorter pseudonymous or anonymous stories also appeared.

In 1870 Elliott, Thomes and Talbot published what Madeleine Stern has identified as the firm's "only book outside the domain of cheap literature," John B. Hill's *Proceedings of the Centennial Celebration of the One Hundredth Anniversary of the Incorporation of the Town of Mason, N.H., August 26, 1868,* in honor of Elliott, who was born in Mason and had attended the celebration. That year Elliott left the firm to become publisher of the Boston-based magazine *Western World.*

Thomes and Talbot continued to publish dime novels and magazines. In 1872 a fire at the firm's offices destroyed much of its stock, forcing a move to 36 Bromfield, the address of Elliott's *Western World.* Shortly thereafter, Thomes and Talbot moved to 23 Hawley Street. In 1885 the re-

maining partners dissolved the firm. The Thomes and Talbot publishing list was turned over to George W. Studley, an employee of the firm, who went on to reprint many of the titles in his Owl Library.

Reference:

Madeleine B. Stern, "Elliott, Thomes and Talbot and Their Blue Backs," *Publishers' Weekly,* 149 (15 June 1946): 3146-3151.

—Timothy D. Murray

The George H. Ellis Company
(Boston: 1873-1926?)

George Henry Ellis began his career as a clerk in the office of the *Christian Register* in Boston. In 1873 he started his own printing firm, located successively at 101 Milk Street, 141 Franklin Street, and 272 Congress Street. The firm was incorporated in 1902. Ellis published the *Boston Daily Advertiser* from 1883 to 1886 and was one of the founders of the *Evening Record.* For a while, the company was the American agent for the English *Modern Review* as well.

Early publications included collections of Edward Everett Hale's sermons; Ralph Waldo Emerson's *The Preacher* (1880), theological essays; and popular fiction such as James Freeman Clarke's

Deacon Herbert's Bible-Class (1890). Ellis also did a thriving commercial trade in histories of local churches, businesses, and institutions; memorial sermons; commemorative volumes of town historical celebrations; essays on temperance and civil service reform; deliberations of various official committees; and railway schedules. The firm apparently ceased operations in 1926.

Reference:

A Constructive Influence of an Inventive Age in Retrospect (Boston: Ellis, 1926).

—Sharon Ann Jaeger

Ess Ess Publishing Company
(New York: 1890-1902)
Smart Set Publishing Company
(New York: 1902-1924)

THE SMART SET PUBLISHING CO.

The Ess Ess Publishing Company was founded in 1890 at 1135 Broadway, New York, by Col. William D'Alton Mann, with Arthur Grissom as editor. The firm published books only occasionally; its main publication was *Smart Set* magazine, which was started on 10 March 1900. In 1902 the firm moved to 452 Fifth Avenue and became the Smart Set Publishing Company.

Among the firm's books was Alma Florence Porter's *Nigger Baby and Nine Beasts* (1901), a collection of animal stories printed on handmade deckle-edged paper with embossed cover and gilt top. Later volumes were often of equally fine quality. Titles included Mrs. William Allen's *The Love Letters of a Liar* (1901), G. B. Burgin's *The Shutters of Silence* (1903), Louise Winter's *Hearts Aflame* (1903), and Baroness Von Hutton's *Araby* (1904).

The books were illustrated by leading artists, including Archie Gunn, C. B. Currier, and Gustave Verbeek.

The firm was sold to John Adams Thayer in 1911. Three years later H. L. Mencken became co-owner of the firm with George Jean Nathan, coeditor of the *Smart Set*. The magazine was absorbed into the Hearst empire in 1924.

References:

Carl R. Dolmestch, *"The Smart Set": A History and Anthology* (New York: Dial, 1966);

Burton Rascoe, ed., *The Smart Set Anthology* (New York: Reynal & Hitchcock, 1934).

—David Dzwonkoski

Estes and Lauriat
(Boston: 1872-1898)
Dana Estes and Company
(Boston: 1898-1914)

Born in Gorham, Maine, on 4 March 1840, Dana Estes began his career in 1859 with the Boston bookselling firm of Henry D. Degen and Son. After serving in the Civil War, he went to work for William H. Hill, Jr., a bookseller. He then joined Henry Degen to form Degen, Estes and Company on Cornhill, specializing in the publication of children's books, but soon sold out to Degen and joined Lee and Shepard as a salesman. Charles Emelius Lauriat was born in Boston on 12 January 1842. For six years, until it closed, he worked for William Veazie's bookstore on Cornhill. During the next ten years he was with the William H. Piper and Company bookstore.

The firm of Estes and Lauriat was established in August 1872 at 143 Washington Street, Boston, as "a general bookselling, publishing, and importing business." Estes assumed responsibility for the publishing, while Lauriat managed the bookselling and importing operations.

The company's early concentration was in the publication of books about science, a reflection of Estes's personal interests. In 1872 the firm took over Half Hour Recreations in Popular Science, a pamphlet series previously published by Lee and Shepard. Edited by Estes, the series had received acclaim by the time of its completion in 1874 as one of the best digests of scientific information.

Another early speciality of Estes and Lauriat was the publication of high-quality subscription books. Many of these were histories, including F. P. G. Guizot's six-volume *A Popular History of France* (1872-1876), Alfred N. Rambaud's three-volume *History of Russia* (1879-1882), and an eight-volume *History of Rome* (1883-1886) by Victor Duruy. The firm also published books on travel and religion, biographies, and children's literature. Within the first ten years of its founding, the company began publishing deluxe editions of the works of well-known novelists, including Dickens, Thackeray, George Eliot, and Dumas. Estes's wife, Louise Reid Estes, compiled the firm's highly acclaimed *Nature and Art* (1882).

In the late 1870s the firm became involved in a much publicized legal dispute over the publication of the children's annual *Chatterbox*. Originally published in England, the book became so popular in the United States that publishers, including Estes and Lauriat, were pirating the yearly editions. In 1879 the British publishers granted Estes and Lauriat permission to continue the American editions with the British plates. For the following eight years the firm was compelled to fight pirating houses in the courts, finally emerging with the exclusive right to publish the series.

The lengthy controversy strengthened Estes's support for an international copyright law. He joined the board of the International Copyright Association of New England and was active in the American Publishers' Copyright League. When Congress held hearings on the issue, Estes was called upon to testify. Even before the international copyright issue was settled in 1891, the royalties that Estes paid European authors made him a popular publisher.

As another means to thwart pirates, Estes established a subsidiary firm, the Aldine Publishing Company, to publish inexpensive royalty editions of works by standard authors. By 1886 the Aldine Publishing Company had thirty-six titles in print; but, because the public continued to buy from pirating publishing houses, its business was undercut, and it failed.

Besides the *Chatterbox* line, the juvenile literature published by the firm included a travel series entitled Zig-Zag Journeys, which began in 1879 and

Dana Estes

John Macrae joined E. P. Dutton and Company in 1884 as an office boy. He became a partner in 1900, a joint trustee with Henry Clapp Smith in 1923, and president in 1928. He headed the company until his death in 1944.

Charles Emelius Lauriat

was edited by Hezekiah Butterworth. These books were noted for their mixture of history, folklore, and fairy tales with underlying moral lessons. In 1881 several other series were added to the list, including Young Folks' Histories—Second Series, also edited by Butterworth. From 1882 to 1892 the company published books in the Three Vassar Girls series by Elizabeth William Champney. Her husband, J. Wells Champney, illustrated these and other Estes and Lauriat publications. Laura E. Richards was a popular children's writer and later a novelist. Her most famous work, *Captain January* (1890), was well received by young and old and went through multiple printings and editions. Estes and Lauriat moved its publishing offices to 192-202 Summer Street in 1889; the firm's bookstore remained at 143 Washington Street.

During its years of operation, the firm established other subsidiaries besides Aldine, including C. J. Jewett Publishing Company, the Cassino Art Company, the Meisterschaft Publishing Company, and the Joseph Knight Company. It was also known as a good training ground for learning the book trade. Estes and Lauriat's partnership dissolved in 1898; the failure of the firm resulted from poor collections in an overexpanded subscription department. Lauriat continued to operate the firm's bookstore as the Charles E. Lauriat Company, while Estes took over the publishing business, changing its name to Dana Estes and Company.

Dana Estes and Company continued to offer the works of standard European authors in new editions, art books, popular fiction, and children's books, as Estes and Lauriat had done for the previous twenty-six years, though with a new emphasis on travel books for children and adults. Both the original and the new firm were known for the quality of their paper and printing and for the elaborate illustrations in their publications. Estes remained at the earlier business offices at 192-202 Summer Street.

In its first year the company added to its standard editions *The Waverly Novels* by Sir Walter Scott. These were offered in the Andrew Lang edition in twenty-five volumes and the Illustrated Cabinet edition in forty-eight volumes. Poetry publications that year included *Songs of Two Peoples* by James Whitcomb Riley and *The Slopes of Helicorn* by Lloyd Mifflin. In the same year the company introduced a historical series for children entitled The Privateers of 1812, beginning with James Otis Kaler's *The Cruise of the Comet*. Both *Chatterbox* and *Oliver Optics Magazine*, the firm's annuals, were continued; and Richards added *Margaret Montfort* to her Three Margarets series.

After the separation from Lauriat, Estes allowed himself more time for travel, a favorite pastime that was reflected in the travel books published by the company. In 1899 it published *Through Unexplored Asia* by William Jameson Reid and *Adventures in East Africa* by M. French Sheldon. The 1907 list offered Dr. Charles Wendell Townsend's *Along the Labrador Coast*. Travel series begun by Estes included the Great Cities series, the Beautiful England series, and the Estes' Rambles series.

Estes added new children's series to those begun by Estes and Lauriat. In 1909 the firm advertised *Chatterbox Book of Pictures*, *Chatterbox Book of Wild Animals*, and *Chatterbox Book of Birds*. The Famous Children in Literature series, edited by Frederic Lawrence Knowles, included *Story of Little David* (1903), based on Dickens's *David Copperfield*, and *Story of Little Tom and Maggie* (1904), drawn from George Eliot's *The Mill on the Floss*. In 1913 the featured series was Every Boy's Book of . . . , which offered books on woodworking, electricity, musical instruments, and sailing. Estes continued to publish Richards's novels and children's books, including *Mrs. Tree's Will* (1905) and *Miss Jimmy* (1913).

Estes died in Boston in 1909 after becoming ill while on an African safari. He left his publishing firm to his sons Frederick Reid Estes, Dana Estes, Jr., and Philip Sidney Estes, who continued the business for another five years. In 1914 Dana Estes and Company was purchased by L. C. Page and Company. Formerly known as the Joseph Knight Company, the firm was owned and operated by Estes's stepsons, Lewis and George Page, who had received their training in publishing at Estes and Lauriat.

Raymond L. Kilgour, the historian for both Estes and Lauriat and Dana Estes and Company, was convinced that Estes wanted to establish an elite publishing house for intellectuals, but found that the idea was not profitable and that he lacked the ability to accomplish it. Nevertheless, Estes did bring literature to the general reading public in attractive new editions of standard authors.

References:

"Dana Estes [obituary]," *Publishers' Weekly*, 75 (19 June 1909): 2015;

Raymond L. Kilgour, *Estes and Lauriat, A History: 1872-1898; With a brief account of Dana Estes and Company: 1898-1914* (Ann Arbor: University of Michigan Press, 1957);

"Charles E. Lauriat [obituary]," *New York Times*, 29

December 1937, p. 22;

Frederick G. Melcher, "A Boston Bookstore at the Turn of the Century," *Proceedings of the American Antiquarian Society*, new series 66 (1956): 37-50;

"Page Company Absorbs Dana Estes & Co.," *Publishers' Weekly*, 85 (28 March 1914): 1098-1100;

George H. Sargent, *Lauriat's 1872-1922: Being a Sketch of Early Boston Booksellers, with Some Account of Charles E. Lauriat Company and Its Founder, Charles E. Lauriat* (Boston: Privately printed, 1922).

—*Joan Gillen Conners*
Ronelle K. H. Thompson

R. F. Fenno and Company
(New York: 1885-1929)
Diehl, Landau and Pettit
(New York: 1929-19??)
Landau Book Company
(New York; Long Beach, New York: 19??-   )

R. F. Fenno and Company was founded in 1885 by R. F. Fenno at 112 Fifth Avenue, New York, to publish fiction. It offered editions of classics as well as new works of fiction in cloth and paper wrappers. During the 1890s Fenno published works by Doyle, Dumas, Stevenson, Barrie, and Charlotte Brontë. By the turn of the century the firm was in financial trouble and between 1903 and 1905 was managed by a committee of its creditors. In 1905 Fenno offered his creditors thirty-three percent cash on the company's outstanding debts in return for having its assets transferred back to him. His offer was accepted.

In 1906 and 1907 Fenno offered mostly holiday gift books and popular novels, among them Floyd B. Wilson's *The Human Awakening* (1906), Ambrose Pratt's *The Counterstroke* (1907), William W. Canfield's *The Spotter* (1907), and Harold Bindloss's *A Damaged Reputation* (1908). Fenno also published Howard R. Garis's Uncle Wiggily books for children. During this period the company's offices were moved to 16 East Seventeenth Street. Between 1908 and 1915 the company did little national advertising; in 1917, however, it ran an extensive advertising campaign for a love story by Gertrude Capen Whitney, *The House of Landell; or, Follow and Find*. Following this campaign there was another lapse of advertising until 1923, when Fenno bought a half-million college textbooks from the army and advertised them at bargain prices.

Fenno retired from the firm in 1929. It was continued by his associates under the name of Diehl, Landau and Pettit. This company was succeeded by the Landau Book Company, Incorporated, which is a book wholesaler specializing in technical, foreign, art, and occult books and in dictionaries. Louis Landau is president of the firm. Its address is 272 West Park Avenue, Long Beach, New York 11561.

Reference:

"Obituary Notes: Robert F. Fenno," *Publishers' Weekly*, 132 (4 September 1937): 824.

—*Ronelle K. H. Thompson*

E. Ferret and Company

(New York and Philadelphia: circa 1840-circa 1850)

E. Ferret and Company published American fiction during the 1840s out of offices in New York and Philadelphia. Most of its books were published in multiple volumes. Ferret published several books by Timothy Shay Arthur, whose works helped to arouse public support for the temperance movement. These works included *Six Nights with the Washingtonians: A Series of Original Temperance Tales* (1842) and *The Club and Other Temperance Tales* (1845). Other Ferret publications include John Beauchamp Jones's *Wild Western Scenes* (1845), Thomas Buchanan Read's *Paul Redding: A Tale of the Brandywine* (1845), and James Wilmer Dallam's *The Lone Star: A Tale of Texas* (1845).

—Ronelle K. H. Thompson

Fetridge and Company

(Boston: 1850-1855)

Publishers mostly of fiction, but also of poetry and nonfiction, sellers of books and periodicals, Fetridge and Company was founded by William P. Fetridge at 20 State Street in Boston in 1850. In 1851 William P. Fetridge was joined by T. M. Fetridge and T. Wagstaff, with the company's addresses becoming 72 Washington Street and 15 State Street. From 1852 through 1854 the company was at 72 Washington Street and 5 State Street. In 1855 and 1856 William P. Fetridge was in partnership with R. H. Rice at 100 Washington Street. The publications, however, bear only the name of Fetridge.

During its brief existence Fetridge published popular fiction and poetry by authors of no modern reputation. *New-York Aristocracy, or Gems of Japonicadom* by "Joseph" was published in 1851. The following year the firm published Marcus Lafayette Byrn's *Rattlehead's Chronicles; or, A Little Experience with Old Maids and Young Maids, Old Bachelors, Fools, and Drunkards; Quack Doctors, Men of Science, and the World at Large* and *Rattlehead's Travels; or, The Recollections of a Backwoodsman*. In 1854 Fetridge published Sarah Elizabeth Monmouth's *Eventide: A Series of Tales and Poems* under the pseudonym Effie Afton. At 431 pages, this may have been the largest of Fetridge's publications. Another 1854 title was *Home Scenes and Home Sounds; or, The World from My Window* by Harriet Marion Stephens. Her *Hagar the Martyr; or, Passion and Reality* was published in 1855, as was Fanny Cowing's *Harvestings; Sketches in Prose and Verse,* under the pseudonym Sybil Hastings. A notable nonfiction title, *The Boston Slave Riot and Trial of Anthony Burns,* was published by Fetridge in 1854. Written anonymously, it claimed to be an eyewitness account.

—Evelyn A. Walker

Fields, Osgood and Company

(Boston: 1868-1870)

On 29 October 1868 the Boston publishing firm of Ticknor and Fields was dissolved when James T. Fields, James Ripley Osgood, and John S. Clark purchased Howard Ticknor's share of the firm and formed Fields, Osgood and Company with Fields as the senior partner and Osgood and Clark as junior partners. The new firm had offices at 124 Tremont Street.

Fields, Osgood and Company continued to publish the works of many of the authors on the Ticknor and Fields list. In 1869 Osgood offered E. P. Dutton and Company the New York business of Fields, Osgood and Company in exchange for Dutton's Boston business, in order to eliminate the competition between the two firms. Among the titles published during the brief existence of the house were James Russell Lowell's *Under the Willows and Other Poems* (1869), Edward Everett Hale's *Sybaris, and Other Homes* (1869), Thomas Wentworth Higginson's *Malbone: An Oldport Romance* (1869), Harriet Beecher Stowe's *Oldtown Folks* (1869), *Passages from the English Note-books of Nathaniel Hawthorne* (1870), William Cullen Bryant's *The Iliad of Homer, Translated into English Blank Verse* (1870), and Bret Harte's *The Luck of Roaring Camp and Other Sketches* (1870). Fields, Osgood also published works by Louisa May Alcott, Richard Henry Dana, Jr., E. C. Steadman, Ralph Waldo Emerson, Oliver Wendell Holmes, Henry Wadsworth Longfellow, John Greenleaf Whittier, Robert and Elizabeth Browning, Alfred Lord Tennyson, and William Makepeace Thackeray.

In addition to its impressive list of authors, Fields, Osgood and Company also achieved a reputation for publishing editions of outstanding physical quality. Many of Ticknor and Fields's books had been bound in drab brown covers; in contrast, the Fields, Osgood volumes were distinguished by a variety of covers, bindings, and decorations designed to reflect the contents of the books. Osgood also changed the appearance of the weekly periodical *Every Saturday,* which had been established in 1866 by Ticknor and Fields under the editorship of Thomas Bailey Aldrich. *Every Saturday* had contained mostly reprints from English magazines and had no illustrations; by 1870 it had fewer reprints, the size had been changed from octavo to quarto, and woodcuts, advertisements, portraits, and cartoons had been added.

Under the ownership of Fields, Osgood, the *Atlantic Monthly,* which had been purchased by Ticknor and Fields in 1859, continued to flourish with Fields as its editor. The magazine included literary notices, poems, fiction, biography, and articles on science, politics, art, history, religion, and music. William Dean Howells served as the assistant editor, averaging twenty reviews and six other contributions a year.

On 31 December 1870 Fields retired. Osgood, Clark, and Benjamin Ticknor, who had become a partner that year, bought out his interest and formed James R. Osgood and Company on 2 January 1871.

References:

William Charvat, "James T. Fields and the Beginnings of Book Promotion, 1840-1855," *Huntington Library Quarterly,* 8 (1944-1945): 75-94;

James T. Fields, *Yesterday with Authors* (Boston: Osgood, 1872);

Warren S. Tryon, *Parnassus Corner: A Life of James T. Fields, Publisher to the Victorians* (Boston: Houghton Mifflin, 1963);

Carl J. Weber, *The Rise and Fall of James Ripley Osgood: A Biography* (Waterville, Maine: Colby College Press, 1959).

—*Lynne P. Shackelford*

John West Folsom
(Boston: 1783-1801)
Draper and Folsom
(Boston: 1778-1783)

Born in 1758, John West Folsom began his printing career in Boston in 1778, when he entered into partnership with Edward Draper "at the corner of Winter-Street." Draper and Folsom published books and a newspaper, the *Independent Ledger, and American Advertiser*. When the partnership ended in 1783, Folsom continued on his own, moving to "the corner of Ann-Street, near the Conduit" in 1785 and to 30 Union Street in 1787. He published religious pamphlets, Revolutionary War recollections, and almanacs. He continued publishing the *Independent Ledger* until 1786.

Folsom began publishing children's books in 1791. His first attempts in this area, reflecting the moralistic, didactic tone which characterized eighteenth-century children's literature, included *The Moralist: Or, Young Gentleman and Lady's Entertaining Companion* (1791) and Noah Webster's *The Prompter; or, A Commentary on Common Sayings and Subjects* (1794). Most of Folsom's books for children were printed in 1798. These titles differed from their predecessors in their emphasis on entertainment and included *Gaffer Goose's Golden Plaything* (1798), *The History of Little Goody Goosecap* (1798), and *New Holiday Present* (1798). Many were reprints of successful titles of the Newbery publishing family in England, including *Rural Felicity, or History of Tommy and Sally* (1798). Folsom had printed nearly 100 works, and had been the publisher of more than half of those, by the time he closed his business in 1801. He died in 1825.

—Linda Quinlan

Forbes and Company
(Boston; Chicago: 1864-circa 1939)

Forbes and Company had its origin in an obscure Boston imprint of the 1860s, Forbes and Russell, which published a Civil War map of Richmond in 1864. The cartographer William H. Forbes of Boston was probably the founder of the firm. Also in 1864 the anonymous *History of the Comical Cow; or, Consequences of Tale-Bearing* was published under the imprint Forbes and Company. Few of the firm's other publications before the twentieth century have survived.

Between 1898 and 1905 Forbes and Company maintained two addresses: P.O. Box 1478 in Boston and P.O. Box 464 in Chicago. Starting in 1906, the Chicago address appeared alone. The house moved to 325 South Dearborn Street in 1910, to 443 South Dearborn around 1917, and to 508 South Dearborn in 1938. A reprint of *Ben King's Verse* (1898) by the poet-humorist Benjamin Franklin King was the first big success for Forbes. Other collections by King followed, along with several books by another humorous poet, Strickland W. Gillilan, such as *Including Finnigan* (1910), *Including You and Me* (1916), and *Laugh It Off* (1924). Willis George Emerson had several of his adventure-romances published by Forbes, including *Buell Hampton* (1902), *The Builders* (1906), and *The Smoky God* (1908). In 1910 Forbes advertised *Maroon Tales*, a collection of University of Chicago stories, "cleverly told by an alumnus"; it was the first book by Will Cuppy. The firm also published *Architecture* magazine, which it sold to Scribners in 1917.

At the firm's peak around 1918, each Forbes

list contained about sixty titles. Light entertainment and self-help books were the chief categories. Besides books for the farmer and the businessman, Forbes published and heavily promoted the sex education books of Dr. Edith Belle Lowry of the United States Public Health Service. An exception to the usual Forbes categories was Floyd Dell's first book, *Women as World Builders* (1913), a serious discussion of feminism. Few new Forbes titles appeared after the mid 1920s. By the end of the 1930s the firm was no longer listed in book trade directories.

—Margaret Becket

J. B. Ford and Company
(New York: 1867-1878)

J. B. FORD AND COMPANY.

J. B. Ford and Company, a pioneering and phenomenally successful subscription house, was founded in New York in 1867 by the English immigrant John Bruce Ford, his son Edward Lloyd Ford, John R. Howard, and several other partners. The elder Ford had entered American publishing through Tallis and Company and D. Appleton. The company expanded rapidly to establish branches in Boston, Chicago, Cincinnati, St. Louis, and San Francisco, with a nationwide network of 20,000 salesmen.

The firm's first book was Horace Greeley's *Recollections of a Busy Life* (1868). *A Library of Poetry and Song* (1871), edited by William Cullen Bryant, was a big seller. Edward Eggleston's *The Circuit Rider* (1874) was the most successful title in the firm's Ford Novel series. Ford's most prominent authors were the Beechers. Henry Ward Beecher's *The Life of Jesus, the Christ* (1871), Plymouth Pulpit weekly sermon pamphlet series, and *Yale Lectures on Preaching* (1872-1874) were in high demand. The *Christian Union*, acquired by Ford in 1869 and edited by Beecher, outstripped rival papers. Harriet Beecher Stowe and Catherine F. Beecher collaborated on well-received manuals of domestic advice, and Mrs. Stowe wrote *My Wife and I* (1871), *Woman in Sacred History* (1873), and *We and Our Neighbors* (1875).

In 1878 the firm was reorganized as Fords, Howard and Hulbert, with J. B. and E. L. Ford, Howard, and George S. Hulbert as partners.

Reference:

"The Bookmakers . . . XXVI.—J. B. Ford & Company," *New York Evening Post*, 31 March 1875.

—Sharon Ann Jaeger

Fords, Howard, and Hulbert

(New York: 1877-1912?)

Fords, Howard, and Hulbert was organized in New York in 1877 by John Bruce Ford, an Englishman who had started J. B. Ford and Company in 1867; his son, Edward Lloyd Ford; John R. Howard, a journalist and editor; and George S. Hulbert.

Despite the firm's formal inception in 1878, its imprint had already appeared on an 1877 edition of William Cullen Bryant's *A New Library of Poetry and Song*, which had been published by subscription a year earlier by J. B. Ford and Company. Fords, Howard, and Hulbert continued the subscription publication of the works of the earlier firm's better-known authors, among whom were Henry Ward Beecher and Harriet Beecher Stowe. Albion Tourgée proved to be a productive source of material for Fords, Howard, and Hulbert. Of the many Tourgée titles published by the firm, *A Fool's Errand* (1879) was significant as the first novel to deal with Reconstruction. Fords, Howard, and Hulbert also published Tourgée's *Figs and Thistles* (1879), *Bricks without Straw* (1880), *A Royal Gentleman . . . and 'Zouri's Christmas* (1881), *John Eax, and Mamelon; or, The South without the Shadow* (1882), *Hot Plowshares* (1883), *Black Ice* (1888), and *The Man Who Outlived Himself* (1898).

Edward Lloyd Ford died in 1880 and John Bruce Ford in 1894. The house continued to publish Tourgée's works through 1905. The firm was out of business by 1912.

Reference:

"Obituary: John Bruce Ford," *Publishers' Weekly*, 46 (3 November 1894): 697.

—Shirley Ricker

Fowler and Wells Company

(New York: 1855-circa 1917)

L. N. and O. S. Fowler

(Philadelphia: 1838-1844)

Fowlers and Wells

(Philadelphia; New York: 1844-1855)

The brothers Lorenzo Niles Fowler and Orson Squire Fowler founded the firm of L. N. and O. S. Fowler in Philadelphia in 1838. Ardent advocates of phrenology, the Fowlers published the *American Phrenological Journal* as well as books on the subject, many of which they wrote. In 1844 Samuel Roberts Wells joined them to form Fowlers and Wells. Five years later the firm moved to New York, first to Nassau Street and then to 308 Broadway. It operated bookstores in both New York and Boston. With the departure of Orson Fowler in 1855, the firm became known as Fowler and Wells. The company is remembered because of its association with Walt Whitman at the beginning of his career as a poet. Whitman had become acquainted with the firm because of his interest in phrenology.

Although Whitman published the first edition of *Leaves of Grass* (1855) himself, he needed a distributor for his books. Fowler and Wells sold the book in its New York and Boston outlets and supported the volume through columns in *Life Illustrated*, a weekly magazine published by the firm between 1 November 1855 and 30 August 1856. After *Leaves of Grass* appeared, Whitman made frequent contributions to *Life Illustrated*. As a result of this association with Fowler and Wells, the firm agreed to finance the second edition of his work. Once again, Whitman acted as publisher, with the firm as the agent and bookseller for the volume.

The 1856 edition of *Leaves of Grass* contained twenty new poems and carried on its spine an unauthorized blurb by Ralph Waldo Emerson greeting the new poet "at the beginning of a great career," a quotation from a personal letter to Whitman after Emerson received a complimentary copy of the poet's first edition. The second edition fared even worse than the first, which probably sold not more than half of the thousand copies printed. The

Orson Squire Fowler

Lorenzo Niles Fowler

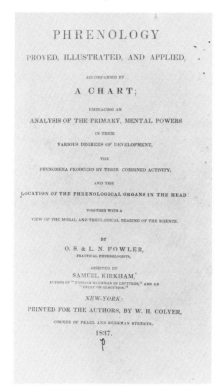

Title page for the earliest of the Fowlers' works on phrenology. Samuel Kirkham, their collaborator, was so thoroughly convinced of the value of the new "science" that he willed his skull to his wife.

Hugh Gaine (courtesy of Edward Wood, Jr.)

firm eventually returned the plates to Whitman, who subsequently went to Thayer and Eldridge of Boston to publish the third edition of *Leaves of Grass* (1860).

Lorenzo Fowler moved to England in 1860; he died in 1896. When Wells died in 1875 his widow, Charlotte Fowler Wells, took over the company. In 1880 Fowler and Wells moved to 753 Broadway and seven years later to 775 Broadway, finally settling at 27 East Twenty-first Street in 1892. The firm was incorporated in 1884 with Charlotte Wells as president. Under the leadership of this early feminist, the company published works on phrenology, the women's suffrage movement, vegetarianism, and hygiene, but little in belles lettres. The firm went out of business around 1917.

References:

Gay Wilson Allen, *The Solitary Singer* (New York: Macmillan, 1960);

"Contributions to Trade History: No. XXXVI, Fowler and Wells Co.," *American Bookseller*, new series 22 (1887): 121-122;

Madeleine Stern, *Heads and Headliners: The Phrenological Fowlers* (Norman: Oklahoma University Press, 1971).

—*David Dzwonkoski*
—*Elizabeth Hoffman*

Richard K. Fox
(New York: 1877-1919)
R. K. Fox Publishing Company
(New York: 1919-1932)

Born in Belfast, Ireland, Richard Kyle Fox immigrated to New York in 1874. Within a year after his arrival, Fox became business manager of the *National Police Gazette*. In 1877 he became the *Gazette*'s owner and founded the Richard K. Fox publishing company.

In addition to the *National Police Gazette*, Fox published a series of dime novels, at least four of which were written by Fox though published anonymously: *Devil Anse; or, The Hatfield-McCoy Outlaws* and *Trujillo; or, Bob Montclair, the Terror of Eldorado* (1889, two titles in one volume) and *Rube Burrows' Raids: Historic Highwayman* and *Night Riders of Ozark; or, The Bald Knobbers of Missouri* (1891, two titles in one volume). From 1903 to at least 1914 the firm's address was the Police Gazette Building, 340 Pearl Street, New York. In 1919 the firm, then known as the R. K. Fox Publishing Company, was located at Franklin Square. After Fox's death in 1922 his two sons inherited the business. By February 1932 the company was in bankruptcy, and in May the firm's assets were sold at auction for $545.00.

Reference:

"Mr. Richard K. Fox: Proprietor of the Richard K. Fox Publishing and Printing House," *Books and News Trade Gazette* (12 September 1896): 195.

—*David Dzwonkoski*

C. S. Francis
(New York: 1826-1860)

C. S. FRANCIS AND COMPANY.

The firm of C. S. Francis was founded as a bookstore in 1826 on Broad Street near Dey in New York by Charles Stephen Francis, who was born in Boston in 1805. His father was the publisher David Francis of the Boston firm Munroe and Francis. By 1835 Francis's bookstore had become one of the largest in the city and had moved to 252 Broadway, across from City Hall. James Miller joined the firm as a clerk in 1835 and Francis's brother David G. Francis joined in 1845.

The bookstore became a gathering place for Unitarian writers and other New England intellectuals living in New York, and Francis soon became a major publisher for the American Unitarian Association. H. W. Bellows's *A Discourse Occasioned by the Death of William Ellery Channing D.D.* (1842) and Rev. Orville Dewey's *The Appeal of Religion to Men in Power* (1844) reflect the firm's Unitarian emphasis.

Francis was in favor of an international copyright law and joined the Copyright League soon after its formation in the early 1850s. Among British works published by Francis was a two-volume edition of *The Poems of Elizabeth Barrett Browning* (1850). Francis published Mrs. Browning's *Aurora Leigh* in 1857 and her *Napoleon III in Italy* in 1860. The firm produced a library edition of Sir Walter Scott's *Waverley* novels in the 1850s.

Francis's American novelists were William Ware, who wrote *Letters of Lucius M. Piso, from Palmyra, to His Friend Marcus Curtius at Rome* (1837), republished in 1838 under the title *Zenobia; or, The Fall of Palmyra*. The book went into eight editions. Caroline Matilda Kirkland's pseudonymous *A New Home—Who'll Follow? Or, Glimpses of Western Life* was published in 1839; her *Forest Life* appeared

anonymously three years later. Anthony Ganilh's *Ambrosio de Letinez; or, the First Texian Novel* was also published in 1842. Francis also published Lydia Maria Child's *Letters from New-York* (1843) and *Fact and Fiction: A Collection of Stories* (1846), and John Codman's *Sailors' Life and Sailors' Yarns* (1847) under the pseudonym Captain Ringbolt.

For children Francis brought out Charles and Mary Lamb's *Tales from Shakespere* (1849) with forty engravings, as well as several collections of Hans Christian Andersen's fairy tales, including *Story Book* (1849)—one of the earliest works of Andersen to be published in the United States—*Wonderful Tales from Denmark* (1852), and *Hans Andersen's Story Book* (1860). *A Danish Story Book* (1851) was part of the company's Little Library series. Francis also published, under various titles, many editions of a guidebook to New York. The first was *The New Guide to the Cities of New York, and Brooklyn, and the Vicinity* (1853).

When the firm moved to 554 Broadway in 1856, Francis was the sole vendor of John James Audubon's works, including the folio edition of *The Birds of America*. Francis suffered financial losses in the Panic of 1857 but continued to manage the failing publishing house until its dissolution in 1860. Miller bought many of the plates and began business under his own name in 1860. Francis continued as a bookseller until his retirement in 1867. He died in 1887.

Reference:

"Messrs. Francis and Mrs. Browning's Poems," *Literary World*, 7 (1850): 254-255.

—Evelyn A. Walker

James French
(Boston: 1843-1860)

James French was a writing master in the arcade at 109 Washington Street, Boston, in 1841. By 1843 he was listed in the Boston city directories as a publisher, bookseller, and stationer at 78 Washington Street. In the 1850s he was joined by James Winslow, J. W. Battis, and J. L. Waterman. French published copybooks, writing books, and other stationery books, among them *French's Practical Writing-book* (1842) and *Art of Pen Drawing* (1854).

Several novels were published by French during the 1840s and 1850s. These include the anonymous *The Cooper's Son; or, The Prize of Virtue* (1846), the anonymous *The Dream Fulfilled; or, The Trials and Triumphs of the Moreland Family* (1846), Hannah Gardner Creamer's *Eleanor; or, Life without Love* (1850), Mrs. Caroline A. Hayden's *Carrie Emerson; or, Life at Cliftonville* (1855), and Mrs. Eliza Ann Hopkins's *Ella Lincoln; or, Western Prairie Life* (1857). French also published George Pickering Burnham's *The History of the Hen Fever: A Humorous Record* (1855) and Orlando Bolivar Willcox's *Faca: An Army Memoir* (1857). In 1855 the firm advertised its "New Miniature Volumes," which included *The Art of Conversing* (1854), Mrs. J. Thayer's *Floral Gems; or, The Songs of the Flowers* (1854), and several religious tracts by the Reverend Timothy Alden Taylor. The firm went out of business in 1860.

—Earl R. Taylor

Samuel French
(New York: 1846-1871; 1899-   )
Samuel French and Son
(New York: 1871-1891)
T. H. French or T. Henry French
(New York: 1891-1899)

SAMUEL FRENCH

Samuel French, Incorporated is the largest supplier of plays for amateur and stock theater in the United States and Great Britain. Born in Randolph, Massachusetts, in 1821, Samuel French moved to New York City in the 1840s and worked as a paperback distributor and seller. In 1846 he established a publishing firm bearing his name at 151 Nassau Street. During the next decade he reprinted some fifty novels from family story papers such as the *Flag of Our Union*. Among these were first editions of Maturin Murray Ballou's *The Magician of Naples; or, Love and Necromancy* (1850?) and *The Sea Witch; or, The African Quadroon* (1855?), both under the pseudonym Lieutenant Murray; John Hovey Robinson's *Angela; or, The Convent of Santa Clara* (1850?); and at least twelve first editions of Sylvanus Cobb's novels under the pseudonym Austin C. Burdick, including *Ivan the Serf; or, The Russian and the Circassian* (1853?), *The Sea Lion; or, The Privateer of the Penobscot* (1853), and *The Maniac's Secret; or, The Privateer of Massachusetts Bay. A Story of the Revolution* (1854?). Some fiction titles by Augustine Joseph Hickey Duganne, Mrs. Caroline Orne, Osgood Bradbury, Benjamin Perley Poore, and Charles F. Barrington also made their first book appearances under the French imprint.

In 1850 French became the agent for William Taylor and Company of New York, publishers of The Modern Standard Drama and The Minor Drama series. At about the same time, French himself published French's American Drama series, consisting of about 100 titles. Then he purchased Taylor's printing plates and those of Spenser's Boston Theatre and combined them and much of French's American Drama into two series: French's Standard Drama with 425 full-length plays; and French's Minor Drama, with 403 short comic works or afterpieces. The small, paperbound books were priced at twelve and a half cents until 1864, when the price was increased to fifteen cents. They contained elaborate stage directions for the benefit of amateur performers. Other series published by French included French's Amateur Operas, French's Parlor Comedies, Henry Irving's Series of Acting Plays, Booth's Series of Acting Plays, Home Plays for Ladies, The Series of Charade Plays, Shadow Pantomimes, and The Ethiopian Dramas (minstrel skits). The firm also published handbooks on acting, costume, make-up, and set design, as well as selling costumes and scenery. Also in 1850 French became the American representative of Thomas Hailes Lacy, the leading British publisher of plays. French moved to 121 Nassau Street in 1854 and to 122 Nassau in 1857.

In 1870 French's son Thomas Henry French joined the firm, which was renamed Samuel French and Son. Thomas was left in charge of the New York office in 1872 when Samuel moved to London. There he bought out Lacy for £5,000. (Lacy's firm had been established in 1830, the year the French firm now gives as its founding date.) In London French began to collect royalties from both professional and amateur performances of the firm's plays, a practice that has continued to the present. In 1878 the New York office moved to 13 East Fourteenth Street. By 1882 French had 2,500 titles in its catalogue. It moved to 19 West Twenty-

second Street and 28 West Twenty-third Street in 1887, and to 24-26 West Twenty-second Street in 1896.

Samuel French died in London in 1898, and the London and New York branches were sold separately. Thomas Henry French continued to run the New York company, first under the T. H. French or T. Henry French imprints and after 1899 as Samuel French, Incorporated. After Thomas Henry's death in 1902, Thomas R. Edwards took over. The firm moved to 28 West Thirty-eighth Street in 1910. Some notable drama titles from the early twentieth century were James M. Barrie's Walker London, A Farcical Comedy in Three Acts (1907) and The Old Lady Shows Her Medals: A Play in One Act (1918) and Edgar Lee Masters's Dramatic Dualogues (1934). The New York and London branches of the firm were merged again in 1975.

Today Samuel French, Incorporated has offices in major English-speaking cities around the world. Each year it publishes forty to fifty plays that have been produced in Broadway, Off-Broadway, or Off-Off-Broadway houses and ten to twenty plays that have not been produced. The firm continues to buy acting-edition rights to produced plays and to collect royalties on each performance. In 1980 its catalogue listed more than 3,500 titles, ranging from The Homecoming (1965) by Harold Pinter to Plaza Suite (1969) by Neil Simon. Thomas R. Edwards's grandson, M. Abbott Van Nostrand, is the present chairman. Since 1924 the firm has been located at 45 West Twenty-fifth Street, New York 10010.

References:

Leota Diesel, "Samuel French: The House that Plays Built," Theatre Arts, 39 (August 1955): 30-31, 92-94;

"Samuel French [obituary]," Publishers' Weekly, 53 (16 April 1898): 689;

"Thomas Henry French [obituary]," Publishers' Weekly, 62 (6 December 1902): 1378.

—Kathleen McGowan

Hugh Gaine
(New York: 1752-1800)

See also the Hugh Gaine entry in *DLB 43, American Newspaper Journalists, 1690-1872.*

Born in Belfast in 1726, Hugh Gaine learned the printing trade and then left for America, arriving in New York in 1745. There he found employment with the printer James Parker. In 1752 he established his own business as printer and publisher of the newspaper *New-York Mercury,* calling his shop the Bible and Crown. In 1757 Gaine moved to the prestigious Hanover Square, near the Meal Market.

In addition to publishing his newspaper and doing job printing, Gaine was a book publisher, book importer, bookseller, and stationer. In 1768 he became the public printer for the province of New York and printer for New York City. From the beginning, his book publishing emphasized standard works: almanacs, sermons, speeches, and religious and self-help books. Paul Leicester Ford's bibliography of works published by Gaine comprises eighty-eight pages, and he notes that in this mass of material there is little that is outstanding or striking. Many of Gaine's literary titles were reprints of popular English works, such as Addison's *Cato. A Tragedy* (1753), Pope's *An Essay on Man* (1786), and Sheridan's *The School for Scandal* (1786). As one of the largest importers and sellers of books in the colonies, Gaine was in a position to know what the public wanted to read.

Gaine was an important publisher of children's books, many of them reprints of works published in England by J. Newbery. Gaine was a pioneer in publishing children's books intended to entertain as well as to instruct. His list for 1762 included seven children's titles, among them *Aesop's Fables in Verse, Food for the Mind; or, a New Riddle Book* and *A Collection of Pretty Poems.* In 1774 he published the first American edition of Defoe's *The Wonderful Life and Surprizing Adventures of the Renowned Hero Robinson Crusoe,* abridged and illustrated, followed in 1775 by the first American edition of *The History of Little Goody Two-Shoes.* Gaine imported fine illustrations for inclusion in his children's books, some of which were superior in quality to those being published in England.

In 1775 Gaine published several satirical poems by the "Poet of the Revolution," Philip Freneau, including *General Gage's Confession* and *General Gage's Soliloquy,* and was himself the object of Freneau's wit in the poem "Hugh Gaine's Life" (1783), in which Freneau ridiculed Gaine for having switched the support of his newspaper from the Americans to the British during their occupation of New York. When the British evacuated New York in 1783, Gaine stopped publishing his newspaper and dropped the word *Crown* from his imprint, his place of business being known thereafter as The Bible. He apparently suffered no great loss of esteem in the community as a result of his support of the British. In 1800 Gaine sold his printing business to Alexander Ming and William Young, who advertised themselves as "successors to Hugh Gaine." He and a partner, Philip Ten Eyck, continued to operate his bookstore until his death on 25 April 1807 at the age of eighty-one.

References:

Paul Leicester Ford, ed., *The Journals of Hugh Gaine, Printer. Biography and Bibliography,* 2 volumes (New York: Dodd, Mead, 1902);

Alfred L. Lorenz, *Hugh Gaine, A Colonial Printer-Editor's Odyssey to Loyalism* (Carbondale: Southern Illinois University Press, 1972).

—*Gary R. Treadway*

Front page for Gaine's newspaper, which switched its support to the British when they occupied New York during the Revolutionary War. He was ridiculed by Philip Freneau for this in the poem "Hugh Gaine's Life."

Charles Gaylord
(Boston: circa 1830–circa 1840)

Charles Gaylord began his career in the 1820s as a partner with William Rutter and Matthew M. Teprell in the firm of Rutter, Gaylord, and Company, Boston booksellers and stationers. In about 1830 he formed his own printing and publishing business, offering reprints of works by Isaac Mitchell and Hannah Foster. His best-known publication is Henry St. Clair's anthology *Tales of Terror; or, The Mysteries of Magic. A Selection of Wonderful and Supernatural Stories, Translated from the Chinese, Turkish, and German* (1833). Gaylord apparently ceased publishing around 1840.

—David Dzwonkoski

Samuel Gerrish
(Boston: 1704–1751)

Samuel Gerrish worked as an apprentice to the Boston bookseller and publisher Richard Wilkins and took over the business when Wilkins retired in 1704. Gerrish's first place of business was "near the Old-Meeting House." The first volume bearing the Samuel Gerrish imprint was a sermon by John Williams, *God in the Camp* (1707). During his thirty-four years in business, Gerrish published more than 200 books and pamphlets, including works by William Cooper, Thomas Foxcroft, and Joseph Sewall. Gerrish moved to "the sign of the Buck over against the South Meeting-House" in Marlborough Street in 1711, and to "the North Side of the Town-House" in King Street in 1714.

Gerrish's most important author was Cotton Mather, whose works constituted nearly one quarter of all Gerrish titles. The first Mather title to appear under the firm's imprint was *The Sailours Companion* (1709); the next, and most important, was *Bonifacius* (1710). Mather's *Grace Defended* (1712) is thought to be the first Puritan Christmas sermon published in America. In 1729, the year after Mather's death, Gerrish published Samuel Mather's biography of his father.

In 1717, the year he moved "near the Brick Meeting House," Gerrish published one of the earliest catalogues in America of books to be sold at auction, a thirty-page pamphlet describing the library of Ebenezer Pemberton. John Tufts's *A Very Plain and Easy Introduction to the Art of Singing Psalm Tunes* (1721) may have been the first music book published in America, and Thomas Walter's *The Grounds and Rules of Musick Explained* (1721) is believed to be the first American publication to contain music printed in bars. Gerrish moved to "the lower end of Cornhill" in 1726 and "over against the Sun-Tavern" in 1734. He published Thomas Symmes's *Lovewell Lamented* (1725) and Thomas Prince's *A Chronological History of New-England in the Form of Annals* (1736).

Although Gerrish published and sold his books, he did not print them; most of his titles were printed by Bartholomew Green until Green's death in 1732. Gerrish died in 1741. His son Samuel Gerrish, Jr., continued the business until he died ten years later.

Reference:
"Samuel Gerrish," *Proceedings of the Massachusetts Historical Society*, 14 (March 1900): 35-43.

—Pamela A. Graunke

William F. Gill Company
(Boston: circa 1850-1900)

The William F. Gill Company was established around 1850 on Washington Street in Boston, near the publishing houses of A. K. Loring, Estes and Lauriat, and the American Tract Society. Gill published minor novels, including Linn Boyd Porter's *Caring for No Man* (1875) and Amanda M. Douglas's *There's No Place Like Home* (1875) and *Drifted Asunder; or, The Tide of Fate* (1876). The firm's most significant achievement was the publication of collected editions of shorter works. Gill edited two such volumes: *Golden Treasures of Poetry, Romance, and Art* (1876) and *Laurel Leaves: Original Poems, Stories, and Essays* (1876). *Lotus Leaves: Original Stories, Essays and Poems* (1875), edited by John Brougham and John Elderkin, included short works by Wilkie Collins, John Hay, and Mark Twain. Gill went out of business around 1900.

—*John R. Conners*

W. and J. Gilman
(Newburyport, Massachusetts: 1805-1851)

W. and J. Gilman was founded in 1805 by the brothers Whittingham and John Gilman in Newburyport, Massachusetts. Known principally as a publisher of children's literature, Gilman also published the weekly *Merrimack Magazine and Ladies' Literary Cabinet* from 17 August 1805 to 9 August 1806. The periodical was printed on Saturdays and was said to be "replete with ev'ry charm t'improve the heart, to soothe life's sorrows, and its joys impart." Another of the firm's publications was the Merrimack Circulating Library, which ran from 1815 to 1839. The firm was established at 4 Middle Street. In 1810 it moved to Federal Street after a fire destroyed the Middle Street building. Gilman's last known place of business was 9 State Street.

Gilman published more than fifty children's titles in original and reprint editions. An early example was *The Humorous Alphabet* (1814), which consisted of eight leaves with woodcuts taken from previous works. Also published in 1814 was *The Story of Quashi; or the Desperate Negro*. Besides children's books, Gilman published Pope's *An Essay on Man* (1805), George Burder's *The Power of the Gospel* (1810), and many sermons by local clergymen. After the death of Whittingham Gilman on 15 September 1849, John Gilman operated the company until his death in July 1851.

—*Karin S. Mabe*

F. Gleason's Publishing Hall
(Boston: 1844-1854)
M. M. Ballou
(Boston: 1854-1863)

Born in 1816, Frederick Gleason started a job printing firm in Boston in the early 1840s and specialized in chromolithographs. Maturin Murray Ballou, the son of a Universalist minister, was born in 1820. He worked for his cousin Hosea Ballou's religious magazines, traveled for his health, and then became deputy navy agent at the Boston custom house. In 1844 Gleason and Ballou established F. Gleason's Publishing Hall and the United States Publishing Company at 1 1/2 Tremont Row in Boston. In 1846 the partners dissolved the United States Publishing Company and started the *Flag of Our Union*, a weekly family story paper with Ballou as editor. The first issue appeared on 24 January 1846.

F. Gleason's Publishing Hall, the United States Publishing Company, and the *Flag of Our Union* all published romance and adventure stories appealing to popular tastes; sometimes the same title was published by more than one of the three enterprises. For example, F. Gleason's Publishing Hall published Osgood Bradbury's *Metallak: The Lone Indian of Megalloway* in 1844; the novel appeared the following year under the United States Publishing Company imprint. Justin Jones's *The Belle of Boston: or, The Rival Students of Cambridge* was published by F. Gleason's Publishing Hall in book form in 1844 and reprinted in the *Flag of Our Union* in 1847. Many of the firm's books were written by Ballou under the pseudonym Lieutenant Murray. His *Fanny Campbell, the Female Pirate Captain* (1845) sold over 80,000 copies in its first two months; other Ballou titles included *Red Rupert, the American Bucanier* (1845) and *The Turkish Slave; or, The Mahometan and His Harem* (1850).

The firm used contests to attract authors for its publications. On 31 July 1847 the *Flag of Our Union* announced that a prize of $100 would be awarded for each of fifty stories selected for publication: "A Grand Scheme! $5000!! To be awarded in prizes!!!" In February 1848 the paper offered $150 for a tale long enough to be published as a novelette. On 1 October 1848 the *Flag of Our Union* announced a prize of $1,000 for the best story submitted and $500 for the second best. The firm was

specific about the sort of material it desired: "We wish for such contributions as shall be strictly moral in their tone, highly interesting in their plot, replete throughout with incident, well filled with exciting yet truthful description, and, in short, highly readable and entertaining. Domestic stories, so-called, are not exactly of the class we desire; but tales—of the sea and land—of the stirring times of the revolution—or of dates still farther back, are more in accordance with our wishes." Edward Zane Carroll Judson, who wrote under the pseudonym Ned Buntline, began his long writing career in 1847 by submitting an entry for a *Flag of Our Union* contest; among his novels for the firm were *The Black Avenger of the Spanish Main; or, The Fiend of Blood* and *The King of the Sea*, both of which appeared as serials in the *Flag of Our Union* before being published in book form by F. Gleason's Publishing Hall in 1847, and *The Red Revenger; or, The Pirate King of the Floridas* (1848). Charles E. Averill also won a prize and began writing novels for the firm, among them *The Pirates of Cape Ann; or, The Freebooter's Foe* (1848). Gleason and Ballou's rivals denounced the contests as fraudulent, and the *Saturday Evening Post* published a letter satirizing the competitions. The firm denied the allegations of fraud, even though Ballou won at least three of the prizes.

F. Gleason's Publishing Hall moved to Court Street at the corner of Tremont in 1847, and to the Museum Building at 24-26 Tremont in 1850. That year the prolific Sylvanus Cobb, Jr., joined the firm. Among Cobb's many books for Gleason, written under a multitude of pseudonyms, were *The Golden Eagle; or, The Privateer of '76. A Tale of the Revolution* (1850) and *The King's Talisman; or, The Young Lion of Mount Hor* (1851). Newton Talbot joined the firm in 1850 as a cashier and later rose to business manager; another addition to the firm that year was Frank Leslie, an engraver who had been one of the founders of the *Illustrated London News* in his native England. Utilizing Leslie's skills, the firm started *Gleason's Pictorial and Drawing Room Companion*, America's first major illustrated weekly, in May 1851. The paper was an immediate success, and the three dollars yearly subscription price was raised to four dollars in 1852. That year the firm moved to 100 Tremont Row.

Gleason publications were cheap and ubiquitous. Agents in nine cities, including New York, Buffalo, Philadelphia, Baltimore, and Cincinnati, distributed the firm's books. Its papers were sold on newsstands as well as by subscription. About twenty percent of the novels published by F. Gleason's Publishing Hall had the words *love* or *romance* in their titles: for example, *The Doom of the Dolphin; or, The Sorceress of the Sea, a Tale of Love, Intrigue, and Mystery* (1848) and *The Rover of the Reef; or, The Nymph of the Nightingale. A Romance of Massachusetts Bay* (1848), both written by the pseudonymous Harry Halyard, who also contributed *The Haunted Bride; or, The Witch of Gallows Hill* (1848). About a third of the Gleason publications were sea tales, including most of Judson's novels as well as Benjamin Barker's *Francisco; or, The Pirate of the Pacific* (1845) and *The Pirate Queen; or, The Magician of the Sea* (1848) and A. G. Piper's *Conrado de Beltran; or, The Buccaneer of the Gulf* (1851), written under the pseudonym F. Clinton Barrington. Much of the rest of the firm's output concerned war, the American West, and chivalry in far-off lands. Other writers for Gleason included Joseph Holt Ingraham, who contributed *The Knights of Seven Lands* (1845) and *Scarlet Feather; or, The Young Chief of the Abenaquies* (1845); Horatio Alger, Jr.; T. S. Arthur; Mrs. Ann Stephens; and John Hovey Robinson. The *Flag of Our Union* published poetry by Edgar Allan Poe, who received five dollars for each submission and was dubbed "our regular contributor," as well as by Stephens, Mrs. Frances Sargent Osgood, Park Benjamin, and Mrs. Lydia H. Sigourney.

In 1853 Leslie went to New York to work on a rival paper, P. T. Barnum and A. E. Beach's *Illustrated News*. Within a year Gleason bought the struggling *Illustrated News* and merged it with *Gleason's Pictorial and Drawing Room Companion*, but Leslie stayed in New York and went on to establish his own magazine publishing empire. In 1854 Ballou forced Gleason to sell his share of their firm to him by threatening to start papers to compete with the *Flag of Our Union* and *Gleason's Pictorial and Drawing Room Companion*. By that time Gleason was earning $50,000 a year from the two papers. He declared that he had "realized an ample competency" and wanted to "retire from business altogether," even though he was only thirty-eight years old, and left for an extended tour of Europe. Ballou promptly changed the name of *Gleason's Pictorial and Drawing Room Companion* to *Ballou's Pictorial and Drawing Room Companion*.

By 1855 the *Flag of Our Union* was suffering from the competition of other story papers, especially that of Robert Bonner's *New York Ledger*. Ballou tried to meet the competition in January 1855 by starting *Ballou's Dollar Monthly*, a 100-page quarto devoted mainly to fiction by Cobb and Alger. The magazine was successful for a time, but in 1856 Cobb deserted Ballou and joined the *New York Ledger*. The same year Judson also stopped writing for Ballou and went to work for the *New York Weekly*, where he switched from sea stories to westerns. In April 1857 Ballou started the *Weekly Novelette*, a magazine that sold for four cents a copy and mainly reprinted stories from the *Flag of Our Union* and *Ballou's Pictorial*. The publication only lasted for thirteen weeks but is said to have given Erastus Beadle the inspiration to become the pioneer publisher of dime novels.

In 1858 Ballou lowered the price of a yearly subscription to *Ballou's Pictorial* to $2.50 to try to meet the competition from similar papers published by Leslie and by the Harpers. That year Gleason returned to Boston; Ballou turned the offices at 100 Tremont over to him and moved his firm to 22 Winter Street. In December 1859 *Ballou's Pictorial* suspended publication after 451 issues. Ballou tried to replace it with a similar but smaller publication, the *Welcome Guest*, but this paper was short-lived. Finally, in 1863, Ballou sold his firm to a new company, Elliott, Thomes and Talbot, which included Ballou's former business manager as a partner. Ballou acted as an adviser to the new firm for a time. He went on to found the *Boston Globe*, which was sold to Charles H. Taylor in 1874. Ballou also wrote travel books, reference books, and plays and built the St. James Hotel in Boston. He traveled extensively and died in Cairo in 1895.

Meanwhile, Gleason had started a series of magazines; the first was *Gleason's Line-of-Battleship*, which began in 1858 and ran for fourteen months. In 1860 he started *Gleason's Literary Companion*, which ceased publication in 1870. *Gleason's Home Circle* ran from 1871 to 1890 and *Gleason's Monthly Companion* from 1872 to 1887. Having made a fortune, Gleason died in poverty and obscurity at Boston's Home for Aged Men in 1896.

References:

Ralph Admari, "Ballou, the Father of the Dime Novel," *American Book Collector*, 4 (1933): 121-129;

George Waldo Brown, "Pioneers of Popular Literature," *Granite State Magazine*, 3 (February 1907): 51-55; (March 1907): 111-113;

"Maturin Murray Ballou [obituary]," *Publishers' Weekly*, 47 (13 April 1895): 633-634.

—*Joseph J. Hinchliffe*
Philip B. Dematteis

Godey and McMichael
(Philadelphia: 1841-1843)

Born in 1804 in New York City, Louis Antoine Godey founded *Godey's Lady's Book*, which was published from 1830 until 1898. He, Morton McMichael, and Joseph C. Neal also published a popular weekly, the *Saturday News and Literary Gazette* in Philadelphia. Born in Bordentown, New Jersey, in 1807, McMichael became editor of the *Saturday Evening Post* in 1826 and by 1836 was the editor in chief of the *Philadelphia Saturday Courier*. From 1842 to 1846 he helped to edit *Godey's Lady's Book*. In 1841 Godey and McMichael established a partnership to publish magazines and novels. The firm usually used the imprint Godey and McMichael, but it also published under the names L. A. Godey and Morton M'Michael and Godey and M'Michael.

Among titles published by Godey and McMichael were the *Young People's Book: or, Magazine of Youthful and Entertaining Knowledge* (1841) and the *Lady's Musical Library* (1842). The firm also published Timothy Shay Arthur's *Six Nights with the Washingtonians. A Series of Original Temperance Tales* (1842), *The Ladies' Fair* (1843), *Making a Sensation, and Other Tales* (1843), and *The Ruined Family and Other Tales* (1843).

After 1843 Godey and McMichael appears to have terminated its publishing activities. In 1847 McMichael became joint owner with George R. Graham of the *Philadelphia North American*. He served as mayor of Philadelphia from 1866 to 1869. Godey died in 1878; McMichael died in 1879.

References:

"Louis Antoine Godey [obituary]," *New York Times*, 30 November 1878, p. 2;

"Morton McMichael [obituary]," *New York Times*, 7 January 1879, p. 5;

Richard Fay Warner, "Godey's Lady's Book," *American Mercury*, 2 (1924): 399-405.

—*Elizabeth Hoffman*

S. G. Goodrich
(Hartford, Connecticut; Boston: 1817-1851)
Sheldon and Goodrich
(Hartford, Connecticut: 1816-1817)

See also the Samuel Griswold Goodrich entries in *DLB 1, The American Renaissance in New England*, and *DLB 42, American Writers for Children Before 1900*.

In 1816 Samuel Griswold Goodrich and George Sheldon collaborated in a publishing and bookselling venture in Hartford, Connecticut. Sheldon died in 1817. Goodrich's eight-volume edition of the novels of Sir Walter Scott (1819) was a failure; the firm then announced its intention of publishing only the works of American writers, a risky business at this early period. Goodrich's first effort in this direction, an 1820 two-volume edition of the complete poetical works of the Connecticut wit John Trumbull, was also a failure. Goodrich described the experience in his *Recollections of a Lifetime* (1856): "I quietly pocketed a loss of about a thousand dollars. This was my first serious adventure in patronizing American literature." In October 1826 Goodrich moved to Boston. He set up an office in the famous Old Corner Book Store at Washington and School Streets, run by the publisher William D. Ticknor. In the following decades, Goodrich Enterprises came to occupy the entire second floor of the building.

In Boston Goodrich published *Sketches* (1827), the first book of the young poet Nathaniel Parker Willis; Samuel Kettell's *Specimens of American Poetry* (1829), the first comprehensive anthology of American verse; and reprints of several novels by Charles Brockden Brown. Goodrich's greatest success was the publication of his own work. In 1827 he wrote and published *The Tales of Peter Parley about America*, the first of a series of books featuring the character Peter Parley, a patriotic, morally upright, and extremely opinionated old gentleman. The Parley books were read by American schoolchildren throughout the nineteenth and early twentieth centuries. In 1902 twenty-eight of the Peter Parley books were still in print, about twelve million copies having been sold. The list includes *Peter Parley's Method of Telling about Geography to Children* (1829) and *Peter Parley's Tales about the Sun, Moon, and Stars* (1831). Goodrich also wrote several popular books featuring characters other than Parley, among them *Make the Best of It; or, Cheerful Cherry* (1843) and *Inquisitive Jack and his Aunt Mary* (1852).

To modern readers Goodrich's books seem quaint, dated, and prejudiced in their presentation of alien cultures and non-Christian religions, but in the nineteenth century the Peter Parley books were revolutionary. Goodrich's books were entertaining and educational and avoided the gruesome and horrifying tales that had been typical of earlier children's literature. Goodrich was also revolutionary in his insistence on a great variety of pictures and engravings in his children's books. Goodrich published two magazines for children—*Parley's Magazine* in 1833 and *Robert Merry's Museum* from 1841 to 1850—and several textbooks besides his own: *A Grammar of Chemistry* (1825) by J. L. Comstock; a geography text by William Woodbridge; and a *History of the United States of America* (1828) by his brother, the Reverend Charles Augustus Goodrich.

Goodrich also published *The Token*, a Christmas annual intended as a gift for young men to give their sweethearts or female relatives. In his preface to the 1829 *Token*, Goodrich boasted that "the contributions are all original, and from native writers; the engravings are all by native artists." *The Token* consisted mainly of moral and sentimental poems and stories by popular minor writers of the day, including N. P. Willis, Lydia Maria Child, Mrs. Lydia Sigourney, and occasionally Goodrich himself. Goodrich also accepted for *The Token* several stories by Nathaniel Hawthorne. The young author's somber genius may have been incongruous with *The Token*'s insipid, sentimental tone, but Goodrich was one of the first to recognize Hawthorne's potential. Between 1830 and 1842 more than twenty-five of Hawthorne's sketches and stories were published in *The Token*, all anonymously.

In 1833 *The Token* was merged with a similar publication, *The Atlantic Souvenir*. Goodrich edited *The Token and The Atlantic Souvenir* until 1842. Goodrich left publishing in 1851 to serve in the Massachusetts legislature and as American consul in Paris. He died in 1860.

References:

Samuel Griswold Goodrich, *Recollections of a Life-*

time, 2 volumes (New York: Miller, Orton & Mulligan, 1856);
Peter Parley's Own Story . . . (New York: Sheldon, 1864);
Daniel Roselle, *Samuel Griswold Goodrich, Creator of*

Peter Parley (Albany: State University of New York Press, 1968).

—*David W. Raymond*

C. E. Goodspeed and Company
(Boston: 1898-1932)

Charles E. Goodspeed first opened a bookstore and publishing firm in Boston in 1898. Goodspeed's Book Store sold used and rare books, book plates, and historical prints. Among the earliest books published by the firm were Franklin Benjamin Sanborn's *The Personality of Thoreau* (1901) and *The Personality of Emerson* (1903) and Edward Carpenter's *Iolaus; An Anthology of Friendship* (1902).

Among his other publications were *Dramatic Verses* (1902) by Trumbull Stickney and *In the Dawn of the World* (1903), with illustrations of Biblical themes by Sir Edward Byrne-Jones. Goodspeed's personal favorite was a pocket-sized edition of Izaak Walton's *The Compleat Angler* (1928), a volume which he felt approached perfection in publishing form and technique. *Sidney Lawton Smith, Designer,*

Etcher, Engraver, with Extracts from His Diary appeared in 1931. Most of the Goodspeed books were printed at D. B. Updike's Merrymount Press.

Goodspeed's publishing efforts came to an end in 1932. He died in 1950. Goodspeed's Book Store is still open for business.

References:
Charles E. Goodspeed, *Yankee Bookseller* (Boston: Houghton Mifflin, 1937);
Walter Muir Whitehill, "Charles Eliot Goodspeed," *Proceedings of the Massachusetts Historical Society,* 71 (1953-1957): 362-365.

—*Mary Mahoney*

Paper cover for one of Gleason's inexpensive books

Louis A. Godey, 1850

Samuel Griswold Goodrich (Peter Parley)

Charles E. Goodspeed, 1921 (pencil drawing by E. Pollack-Ottendorf)

William H. Graham

(Philadelphia; New York: 1843-1849)

Godey's Lady's Book for September 1843 announced in its "Editors' Book Table" column that "Mr. William H. Graham . . . has commenced, in serial form, the publication of the 'Prose Romances of Edgar Allan Poe.'" This pamphlet, priced at 12 1/2¢, was *The Prose Romances . . . No. 1, Containing the Murders in the Rue Morgue, and The Man That Was Used Up;* apparently no further numbers were published. Graham's offices were at 98 Chestnut Street, Philadelphia.

Graham moved to New York in 1844, where the firm occupied an office in the Tribune buildings. It specialized in short historical romances, such as the anonymous *Legends of Lampidosa; or, The Seven Heroines* (1844), Josiah A. Fraetas's *The Master of Langford; or, The Treacherous Guest* (1845), Dennis Hannigan's *The Artisan of Lyons; or, Love's Traces* (1846), Charles Wilkins Webber's *Jack Long; or, Shot in the Eye. A True Story of Texas Border Life* (1846), Alfred W. Arrington's *The Desperadoes of the Southwest* (1847), and Charles F. Sterling's *Buff and Blue; or, The Privateers of the Revolution* (1847). In 1849 Graham published George G. Foster's *New York in Slices,* Robert F. Greeley's *The Crimes of Paris,* and a translation from the French of Achille Murat's *America and the Americans.* No Graham publications have been found beyond this date.

—Ruth H. Bennett

T. and S. Green

(New Haven, Connecticut: 1767-1825)

A great-great-grandson of the Cambridge, Massachusetts, printer Samuel Green, Thomas Green entered publishing in 1760 as an apprentice to Benjamin Mecom, the publisher of the *Connecticut Gazette* in New Haven. In 1764 he moved to Hartford to start his own printing business. There he published the *Connecticut Courant,* which, as the *Hartford Courant* of today, has been in existence longer than any other American newspaper. The firm's first book was Samuel Ellsworth's *Almanack* in 1765.

Two years later Green left his associate Ebenezer Watson in charge of the firm and joined his brother Samuel in New Haven to form the firm of T. and S. Green. Together they edited, printed, published, and sold books. They also published the *Connecticut Journal and New-Haven Post-Boy,* known today as the *New Haven Journal-Courier.* From 1767 to 1809 the firm handled most of the printing for Yale College. Other publications included Naphtali Daggett's *The Excellency of a Good Name* and Noah Hobart's *Excessive Wickedness,* both in 1768; John Trumbull's *The Progress of Dulness* (1772-1773); two books of poetry by Joel Barlow—*The Prospect of Peace* (1778) and *The Hasty-Pudding* (1796); and David Humphreys's *A Poem Addressed to the Armies of the United States of America* (1780). Upon the death of Samuel Green in 1799, Thomas Green, Jr., became a full partner, continuing the business after the elder Thomas's retirement in 1809. Thomas Green, Jr., died in 1825.

Reference:

William C. Kiessel, "The Green Family: A Dynasty of Printers," *New England Historical and Genealogical Register,* 104 (1950): 81-93.

—David Dzwonkoski

Timothy Green
(Boston: 1700-1714)

Born in 1679, Timothy Green was the son of Samuel and Sarah Clark Green. In 1700, after serving his apprenticeship at his father's press, Timothy Green opened his own printing shop on Middle Street (now Hanover) near Cross Street in the northern part of Boston.

In 1707 the Connecticut Assembly began a search for an official printer for the colony. The first to be offered the position, Green was reluctant to give up his business in Boston. Thomas Short received the appointment in October of 1708 and thus became the first printer of Connecticut. Upon Short's death in September 1712, the assembly again turned to Green, who accepted the position. He became the official printer of Connecticut in May 1713, although he continued to print in Boston until August 1714, when he moved his family to New London. He remained Connecticut's printer until his death in 1757.

While in Boston, Green reprinted, for Benjamin Eliot, James Janeway's *A Token for Children* (1700) and published Samuel Moodey's *The Vain Youth Summoned to Appear before Christ's Bar* (1707), Cotton Mather's *The Best Ornaments of Youth* (1707), and Increase Mather's *Awakening Truth's Tending to Conversion* (1710), as well as sermons and tracts by John Higginson, Thomas Bridge, and John Danforth.

References:

William C. Kiessel, "The Green Family: A Dynasty of Printers," *New England Historical and Genealogical Register,* 104 (April 1950): 81-93;
Douglas C. McMurtrie, "The Green Family of Printers," *Americana,* 26 (1932): 364-375.

—*George E. Tylutki*

Benjamin H. Greene
(Boston: circa 1830-circa 1849)

Benjamin H. Greene, a Boston publisher of the 1830s and 1840s, shared the imprint of one of his earliest books—the second edition of the anonymous novel *Isabella; or, Filial Affection* (1832)—with Leonard C. Bowles of Boston. His later publications, under his sole imprint, included the second edition of Samuel Gilman's *Memoirs of a New England Village Choir* (1834), Henry Winsor's *Pebblebrook and the Harding Family* (1839), and Harriet Vaughn Cheney's *Confessions of an Early Martyr* (1846).

—*David Dzwonkoski*

S. C. Griggs and Company

(Chicago: 1849-1896)

Griggs, Bross and Company

(Chicago: 1848-1849)

When Samuel Chapman Griggs became a partner in the Chicago bookselling and publishing firm of William Bross and Company in 1848, the firm was renamed Griggs, Bross and Company. On Bross's retirement the following year the name was changed to S. C. Griggs and Company. The firm's offices and bookstore were located on Lake Street. S. C. Griggs and Company published and sold school texts and medical, theological, and history books. The company's publications included Nathan S. Davis's *History of Medical Education and Institutions in the United States* (1851), Thomas Ford's *A History of Illinois* (1854), and John Wells Foster's *The Mississippi Valley* (1869). The firm's bookstore was known as "the Palace of Books" and "the Literary Emporium of the Prairie."

After the Chicago fire destroyed the firm's offices and stock in 1871, Griggs decided to start over as a publisher only. In 1872 he opened offices at 335 Wabash Avenue. The firm's first books at its new location were Greek and Latin texts which helped to establish Griggs as a leader in textbook publishing. One of its most important nonacademic texts was William Mathews's *Getting On in the World* (1872), which went through thirty-eight printings by 1878.

In 1875 Griggs began to publish fiction, including *Patmos; or, The Kingdom and the Patience* by Rev. J. A. Smith (1875), William Rosser Cobbe's *Doctor Judas: A Portrayal of the Opium Habit* (1895), and Mrs. A. M. Freeman's *Somebody's Ned* (1899), written in opposition to capital punishment. The firm's children's fiction included Mrs. Emily Clark Miller's *What Tommy Did* (1876). Griggs's most important publication in this period was *Pocket Manual of Rules of Order for Deliberative Assemblies* (1876) by Maj. Henry M. Robert. Griggs retired in July 1896 and sold his business to Scott, Foresman and Company.

References:

Jack C. Morris, "A Half Century of Chicago Publishing," *Publishers' Weekly*, 140 (16 August 1941): 456-458;

Morris, "The Publishing Activities of S. C. Griggs and Company, 1848-1896; Jansen, McClurg and Company, 1872-1886; and A. C. McClurg and Company, 1886-1900; with Lists of Publications," M.A. thesis, University of Illinois, 1941.

—*Louis S. Gross*

S. C. Griggs and Company's store, right, at 117-119 State Street, Chicago, before it was destroyed by fire in 1871

Alexander Grosset

George T. Dunlap

Grosset and Dunlap
(New York: 1900-   )
Dunlap and Grosset
(New York: 1898-1899)
Alexander Grosset and Company
(New York: 1899-1900)

Alexander Grosset and George T. Dunlap met when they were both working for the American Publishers Corporation; Grosset was office manager and Dunlap a traveling salesman for the firm. When the American Publishers Corporation went bankrupt in 1898 the two men formed a partnership, purchased much of the bankrupt firm's stock of books from the receiver, and went into the bookselling business as Dunlap and Grosset at 11 East Sixteenth Street in New York. Grosset served as chief executive, handling the day-to-day management of the business, while Dunlap was the firm's traveling salesman. Dunlap left the new firm briefly in 1899 to take a job with Rand McNally, and Grosset carried on as Alexander Grosset and Company. With Dunlap's return, the name was changed to Grosset and Dunlap in 1900.

Grosset and Dunlap moved from selling books to publishing them by publishing pirated editions of Rudyard Kipling's books, most of which had already been pirated by other publishers. Dunlap referred to himself and Grosset as "honorable pirates," since those were the only pirated editions their firm published. Grosset and Dunlap also brought out other reprints, but it was a variation on reprinting created by Dunlap which led to the firm's initial success.

During one of his sales trips for the American Publishers Corporation, Dunlap had noticed a large stack of paperback copies of Hall Caine's best-selling novel *The Christian*, which had been published by D. Appleton in 1897. The paperbacks were selling for thirty-nine cents a copy. Dunlap speculated that if he could rebind such a paperback title in hardcover it could be sold for fifty cents,

thus offering readers a more attractive edition for only a slightly higher price than a paperback. Grosset and Dunlap initially ran into difficulties finding a binder whose costs were low enough to permit the sale of its "rebinds" for fifty cents, so the firm gave up the idea for a while and turned instead to the Kipling piracies. When it found a binder who could do the work at the proper price, Grosset and Dunlap began its rebinding program, as originally planned, with *The Christian*. The Grosset and Dunlap rebind was a previously unknown concept of publishing, and it helped launch the young firm into the forefront of American reprint publishers. Grosset and Dunlap's rebinding efforts were enhanced greatly during its first year of operation when it acquired the book stock of the H. B. Claflin Company, a dry goods firm which was going out of the bookselling business and was liquidating its large supply of paperbacks. Many publishers were opposed to Grosset and Dunlap's rebinds of their publications, but since the firm retained the original title pages it never faced any legal challenges from the original publishers.

Shortly after it began its rebinding program Grosset and Dunlap started arranging with publishers to reprint their titles in hardcovers, another unique concept in reprint publishing. In its first such arrangement Grosset and Dunlap reprinted Harold Frederic's best-selling novel *The Damnation of Theron Ware* (1896); the title page bore the imprint of the original publisher, Herbert Stone and Company, with the addition, "The Trade supplied by Grosset & Dunlap." In 1903 the firm moved to 52 Duane Street and published the first book to bear the sole Grosset and Dunlap imprint, a reprint

Frontispiece and title page for a movie tie-in. George Dunlap pioneered the development of this marketing concept.

of Paul Leicester Ford's *Janice Meredith*. Other early Grosset and Dunlap reprints which sold well were Charles Major's *Dorothy Vernon of Haddon Hall* (1913), Winston Churchill's *Richard Carvel* (1917), and Gilbert Parker's *The Right of Way*, all of which were fiction, as were the bulk of Grosset and Dunlap's titles during this period. The firm did launch a nonfiction series, making arrangements with Macmillan to publish the Macmillan Standard Library, but this series was not nearly as successful as the reprinting of fiction.

In 1907 poor health forced Dunlap to discontinue the extensive traveling he did on behalf of the firm. His place as chief traveling salesman was taken by John May, formerly of Hurst and Company. May recommended that Grosset and Dunlap expand into children's publishing by acquiring the firm of Chatterton and Peck, a publisher with a large juvenile list. Chatterton and Peck published Edward Stratemeyer's famous Rover Boys series, to which Grosset and Dunlap obtained the rights. The Rover Boys books eventually sold more than five million copies, and Grosset and Dunlap went on to publish more than fifty of the popular Stratemeyer Syndicate series, including Tom Swift, The Bobbsey Twins, The Hardy Boys, and Nancy Drew.

Although the first decade of the twentieth century brought Grosset and Dunlap a good deal of competition, particularly from A. L. Burt and Company and the American News Company, the firm remained the leading reprint publisher. By 1910 Grosset and Dunlap had outgrown its office space, and the firm moved its offices and manufacturing operation to 518 West Twenty-Sixth Street. The retail business was moved to a separate outlet at Twenty-Sixth and Broadway; in 1916 the retail offices moved once again, to 1140 Broadway.

Grosset and Dunlap retained its leadership role largely through its inventive sales strategy. Grosset, in particular, introduced such innovative marketing techniques as in-store displays, posters, and cooperative advertising to the publishing business. He also developed new outlets for selling his firm's inexpensive books in newsstands, drugstores, and department stores. Grosset was also a pioneer in developing motion picture tie-ins between popular novels and their film versions.

In 1926 Grosset and Dunlap experimented with a new line of dollar reprints of recent trade editions. The first three titles were Louis Bromfield's *The Green Bay Tree*, E. Barrington's *The Divine Lady*, and Anne Parrish's *The Perennial Bachelor*. These reprints rivaled the original editions in qual-

ity, offering readers inexpensive yet attractive editions of recent literature. In 1931 Grosset and Dunlap introduced a highly successful edition of the Bible for one dollar, followed by a dollar *Modern Dictionary*, a dollar Shakespeare, and, in 1935, a revised edition of Roget's *Thesaurus*, also for a dollar.

In 1934 Grosset died and Dunlap succeeded him as president of the firm. Grosset's son Donald was vice-president and Frank L. Reed second vice-president and general manager. By 1939, the year the firm moved to 1107 Broadway, Grosset and Dunlap found itself faced with strong competition in the reprint market from the paperback publishing industry, which had been revolutionized by Robert de Graff's Pocket Books. The twenty-five-cent paperbacks that de Graff introduced and the innovative marketing techniques he employed to sell them brought Pocket Books a sizeable share of the reprint market, enough to make Donald Grosset believe that his firm could not compete by itself in this market. Dunlap's retirement in 1944 also influenced the firm's decision to seek outside capital. Grosset and Dunlap was thus sold in 1944 to a consortium consisting of Random House; Little, Brown; Harper and Brothers; Scribners; and the Book-of-the-Month Club. Grosset and Dunlap retained its identity as a separate business under the management of Random House, although the sale did mark the end of Grosset and Dunlap's dominance of the reprint market.

In 1945 Grosset and Dunlap, under its new president, John O'Connor, joined the large magazine publisher Curtis Circulation Company to help Ian Ballantine, formerly of Penguin, form Bantam Books, a paperback publisher which soon rivaled Pocket Books in sales. Bantam's first titles included books by Mark Twain, Zane Grey, John Steinbeck, F. Scott Fitzgerald, Booth Tarkington, and Budd Schulberg. Grosset and Dunlap now became one of the leading forces in the paperback market. Bantam Books became a wholly owned subsidiary of Grosset and Dunlap in 1964. The firm also developed several of its own paperback lines, notably the Universal Library, and acquired several additional firms, including Ace Books, one of the pioneers in the publishing of paperback originals.

Grosset and Dunlap continued to expand its strong juvenile list, complementing its Stratemeyer books with the Illustrated Treasury of Children's Literature and the We Were There series. In 1949 the firm acquired stock in Wonder Books, Incorporated, a line of low-priced children's coloring books and workbooks, which became a division of

Grosset & Dunlap presents...

Mario Puzo's LAS VEGAS

The New Nonfiction Book by the Author of THE GODFATHER

Color photographs by John Launois; black & white photographs by Michael Abramson

This book combines the special magic that made Mario Puzo's *The Godfather* a bookselling phenomenon, and the irresistible lure of Vegas, mecca of countless dreamers looking for the "big win."

A veteran of gaming tables since his youth, Puzo fills this book with provocative insights into the pitfalls and pleasures that have made a small desert town into one of the world's most exciting cities. He regales readers with personal anecdotes of Las Vegas characters, casino fact and myth, and freewheeling opinion on what makes Vegas run.

The stunning photographic collection features over 150 black & white and over 40 pages of color photographs, all taken especially for this book. It is the first time such extensive photographing has been allowed inside Las Vegas casinos and hotels, and it creates an unrivaled picture of Vegas glamour and glitter, vulgarity and pathos.

There has never been such a book on Las Vegas — or on gambling. Rich with feeling, it will touch the heart of the gambler in just about all of us.

A Book-of-the-Month Club Alternate.

$14.95 Hardcover (April)

Photos by Black Star

1977 advertisement

Grosset and Dunlap under the name of Wonder Treasure Books. In 1962 the firm introduced Tempo Books, a line of paperbacks aimed at teenage readers. Other popular Grosset and Dunlap juvenile imprints include Platt and Munk Books, Elephant Books, and Cinnamon Books.

In 1968 Grosset and Dunlap and Bantam were purchased by National General Corporation, which in 1974 sold Grosset and Dunlap to Filmways, Incorporated and Bantam to IFI International. Although the firm still emphasized its extensive reprint list, in the early 1970s it expanded into original publishing. In 1972 newly named president Harold Roth, who succeeded Manuel Siwek, felt that the firm needed to move in a new direction and launched an aggressive program of adult trade publishing. Grosset and Dunlap published trade originals of Norman Mailer's *Marilyn* (1973), Andy Warhol's *Exposures* (1979), Richard Nixon's *RN: The Memoirs of Richard Nixon* (1978), James Jones's *WW II* (1975), and Mario Puzo's *Inside Las Vegas* (1977).

During the late 1970s Grosset and Dunlap's growth began to slow. After Stanley Sills became president in 1979, the firm reduced its staff as well as its newly developed line of trade books. In 1982 Grosset and Dunlap was sold to the Putnam Publishing Group. Currently located at 200 Madison Avenue, New York 10016, Grosset and Dunlap continues to publish a varied list of trade and reprint titles.

References:

"Alexander Grosset [obituary]," *New York Times*, 28 October 1934, p. 32;

George T. Dunlap, *The Fleeting Years: A Memoir* (New York: Privately printed, 1937);

Dunlap, "Genesis of a Publishing Business," *Publishers' Weekly*, 128 (3 August 1935): 277-280; (10 August 1935): 360-363;

"George T. Dunlap [obituary]," *New York Times*, 28 June 1956, p. 29.

—*Timothy D. Murray*

E. J. Hale and Son

(Fayetteville, North Carolina; New York: 1850-1884)

On 1 January 1825 Edward Jones Hale began his publishing career by founding the *Fayetteville (North Carolina) Observer*, which became one of the leading newspapers in the South. Hale also engaged in book publishing. In 1850 his son, P. M. Hale, joined him to form the firm of E. J. Hale and Son. The company became one of the largest publishing houses in the South prior to the Civil War. The firm's buildings were burned during Sherman's march through North Carolina, and in October 1866 the Hales moved to 17 Murray Street, New York.

The firm prospered in New York, and by

1875 the Hale catalogue listed 124 titles. Its first book published in New York was the Reverend R. L. Dabney's *Defence of Virginia* (1867). Other successful books were *A Cyclopedia of the Best Thoughts of Charles Dickens* (1873) by F. D. De Fontaine, *The History of the English Language* (1874) by Henry E. Shepherd, and *A Compendium of the History of the United States* (1883) by A. H. Stephens, former vice-president of the Confederacy.

The fiction published by E. J. Hale and Son was mostly of southern interest, including Benjamin Robinson's *Dolores* (1868), set in North Carolina; Edwin Wiley Fuller's *Sea-Gift* (1873), a novel of southern life prior to and during the Civil War; and George W. Hooper's *Down the River* (1874), a fictional treatment of famous southern duels. The firm also published one of the early novels of Edgar Fawcett, *Ellen Story* (1876). Fawcett went on to write more than thirty novels of social satire of New York society.

The company ceased doing business shortly

after the elder Hale's death on 2 January 1883. At that time E. J. Hale and Son had published more than 500 titles.

Reference:

"Edward J. Hale [obituary]," *Publishers' Weekly*, 23 (6 January 1883): 15.

—*Robert McNutt*

Samuel Hall
(Salem, Massachusetts; Boston: 1768-1772, 1776-1805)
S. and E. Hall
(Salem: 1772-1776)

Born in Medford, Massachusetts, in 1740, Samuel Hall learned printing from his uncle, Daniel Fowle, publisher of the *New-Hampshire Gazette*. In 1762 Hall entered into partnership with Ann Franklin in the publication of the *Newport* (Rhode Island) *Mercury*. Franklin died in 1763 and Hall continued the business until 1768, when he moved to Salem and established the first print shop there. He was joined by his brother Ebenezer from 1772 until the latter's death in 1776. Hall then moved to State Street in Boston. He returned to Salem from 1781 until 1785. Hall then came back to Boston, where he ran a bookstore and publishing firm on State Street until 1787 and at 53 Cornhill until 1805.

Hall's early publishing efforts were journalistic. He published the *Essex Gazette*, later called the *New-England Chronicle; or Essex Gazette*, from 1768 to 1775. At the same time he wrote and published an annual, *The Essex Almanack*. For a few months in 1789 he published a French language weekly, the *Courier de Boston*, written by J. Nancrede, who taught French at Harvard. Political pamphlets and sermons bulked heavily in Hall's output but he is best remembered for his publication of children's books. In spite of the didacticism of children's books of the eighteenth century Hall published

books that were interesting and attractive to children, often with delicate covers of Dutch or gilt paper. The red and gold cover of *The Death and Burial of Cock Robin* (1798) is an example of Hall's artistry.

Children's titles included Dorothy Kilner's *Little Stories for Little Folks* (1789), *Familiar Dialogues for the Instruction and Amusement of Children of Four and Five* (1794), and *The History of a Great Many Little Boys and Girls* (1794); Isaac Watts's *Divine and Moral Songs* (1790); and *Mother Goose's Melody* (1800). Among popular favorites reprinted from England were Henry Fielding's *The Remarkable History of Tom Jones, a Foundling* (1791) and the anonymous *The Hermit of the Forest* (1795). Among the many Newbery Library books for children that Hall published was the popular *The History of Master Jackey and Miss Harriot* (1791). Textbooks included *A Short and Easy Guide to Arithmetick* (1794) and the first American edition of Alexander Adam's *The Rudiments of Latin and English Grammar* (1799). Hall sold his firm in 1805 to Thomas Edmands and Ensign Lincoln. He died two years later.

—*Linda Quinlan*
Theodora Mills

Harper and Brothers
(New York: 1833-1962)
J. and J. Harper
(New York: 1817-1833)
Harper and Row, Publishers
(New York: 1962-   )

In 1817 James and John Harper established the printing firm of J. and J. Harper at Front and Dover Streets, Manhattan; their first order, from the senior Evert Duyckinck, was a 2,000-copy run of *Seneca's Morals* in translation. The next year they published their first book, 500 copies of John Locke's *An Essay Concerning Human Understanding.* That year the firm moved to Fulton Street, and then to 230 Pearl Street. As the younger Harper brothers finished their apprenticeships, they, too, joined the firm—Joseph Wesley Harper in 1823 and Fletcher Harper in 1825. In the latter year the firm moved to 82 Cliff Street, which for the next hundred years became— according to Eugene Exman, the house historian—"the best-known publishing address in America."

Already J. and J. Harper was the largest printer in the city; by 1830 it was the largest book printing establishment in America. In 1833 the firm became Harper and Brothers. One estimate in 1850 ranked it among the three largest publishers in the world, others as the largest. By 1853 the firm was publishing annually more than 4.5 million copies of books, pamphlets, and *Harper's New Monthly Magazine.* Believed to have been the first publisher in America to use cloth for binding—the book was Charlotte A. Eaton's *Rome in the Nineteenth Century* (1827)—Harper and Brothers was also the first to adopt stereotyping as a regular procedure, and probably the first (in 1833) to use steam-powered presses. It led in the development of fine-quality, copious illustrations: *Harper's Illuminated and Pictorial Bible,* first published in 1844, was the most distinguished example of presswork and engraving in America to that time.

Part of the firm's success originated in the absolute trust and confidence of the four in each other. When asked "Who is the Mr. Harper, and who are the brothers?" they always replied, "Any one of us is Mr. Harper, and all the rest are the brothers." For years there was no accounting of money or division of income: each brother simply took from the till whatever he needed. No important decision was ever made that was not unanimous, but by tacit agreement they divided responsibilities. James was good at personal relations—he served a term as mayor of New York—and supervised the workmen. John handled finances, and Wesley handled the correspondence with booksellers and authors. To contemporaries, Fletcher seemed the most daring and innovative; he was the guiding force behind the success of Harper's magazines.

The brothers were pious Methodists, but they were also aggressive competitors whose success drew more than the usual criticism. Rivals and some authors considered them crassly commercial. They depended heavily on reprinting English works, and for a long time they opposed international copyright. Much of Harper and Brothers' early success derived from its ability to reprint new British novels more quickly than its competitors: in 1823 the firm set up, printed, and had Sir Walter Scott's *Peveril of the Peak* for sale in twenty-one hours. Its 1833 catalogue was ninety percent English reprints. Nevertheless, the firm ultimately

*Fletcher, James, John, and J. Wesley Harper, circa 1850
(photograph by Mathew Brady; courtesy of
the Library of Congress)*

Cover, engraved by Benson J. Lossing, for the first issue

*The Harper building on Franklin Square. It was among the first large commercial buildings to make skeletal use of wrought iron
columns and supporting trusses.*

paid large sums to English publishers and authors for first proof sheets, almost $250,000 by 1875. Charles Dickens had received nearly $29,000 by 1867; the fee for serial and book rights reached £1,700 for George Eliot's *Daniel Deronda* (1876). The brothers' opposition to international copyright was first of all protectionist: as printers they, like others, argued against the competition of foreigners. But the American argument for supplying cheap books to a democratic readership also had patriotic force. Among the notable English authors whose work was thus made available, usually with generous payments, were Bulwer-Lytton, Thackeray, all three Brontë sisters, Trollope, Wilkie Collins, Hardy, Macaulay, Carlyle, Darwin, and Queen Victoria.

Berated for not encouraging American authors, Harper and Brothers could nevertheless claim one or more works by Irving, Longfellow, Simms, and Bryant. Poe's anonymously published *The Narrative of Arthur Gordon Pym* (1838) carried its imprint as did R. H. Dana's *Two Years before the Mast* (1840). The firm also published John L. Stephens's pioneer accounts of Mayan ruins, *Incidents of Travel in Central America* (1841) and *Incidents of Travel in Yucatán* (1843), with Frederick Catherwood illustrations. If the brothers maintained a shrewdly commercial view, they also carried Herman Melville through almost all of his writing career. They had declined the rougher, earlier draft of *Typee*, but after that novel was published successfully in London by John Murray and in New York by Wylie and Putnam in 1846, Harper and Brothers published *Omoo* (1847), *Typee* (1849), *Mardi* (1849), *Redburn* (1849), *White-Jacket* (1850), *Moby-Dick* (1851), and *Pierre* (1852).

The Cliff Street establishment by then had spread through several adjoining buildings and through the block to Pearl Street at Franklin Square. Forty-one presses were turning out twenty-five volumes a minute, ten hours a day, six days a week, producing an income of $2 million. The great fire of 10 December 1853 destroyed everything in press or in stock, including all the unsold Melville sheets; but stereotype plates not in use, stored in underground vaults, were safe. Instead of retiring on their comfortable fortunes, the brothers immediately set about rebuilding. The two new buildings were the first of a new type of large, multi-level, nearly fireproof structure, using rolled iron beams for support of the brick and cement floors. This far-downtown area near the Fulton Fish Market was already being bypassed by new businesses, but in part for sentimental reasons the

firm remained there for another seventy years.

Among successes that helped the firm survive the recurrent financial panics and the Civil War were its school texts and, later, its magazines. When the state legislature made school libraries mandatory in New York in 1839, Fletcher Harper had secured a contract to supply the boxed Harper's School District Library. In eight years the library grew to six series of 212 titles in 295 volumes, with sales spreading far outside the state. An assessment of the moribund state of American magazines led the brothers to start *Harper's New Monthly Magazine* in June 1850 with a run of 7,500 copies; in six months the presses were printing 50,000 copies a month. The fire of 1853 fed on the January 1854 issue: 118,000 copies by one estimate, 130,000 by another. Lavish with reprinted English works and engraved illustrations, *Harper's New Monthly Magazine* was designed for the general reader. Only very slowly did American authors begin to appear, and mostly with short stories, not long-running serials. In 1885 William Dean Howells became a contributing editor to the magazine. In the *Monthly* first appeared his series of essays defending the realistic, antiromantic novel, collected as *Criticism and Fiction* (1891). Henry Mills Alden was for fifty years, until his death in 1919, the *Monthly's* principal editor, setting its respectable tone as the most widely circulated periodical in the country. It was Alden who asked Hardy to expurgate offensive passages from *Jude the Obscure* (1895) and rejected Henry James's *The Ambassadors*.

Harper's Weekly was launched during the Panic of 1857. Aimed at the audience that had responded to the news and fiction weeklies of the 1840s, the *Weekly* offered news (notably battlefield reports during the Civil War), editorials, humor, travel, biography, excellent illustrations, and the ever-popular English serials, including Dickens's *A Tale of Two Cities*, Collins's *The Woman in White*, George Eliot's *Middlemarch*, and Hardy's *The Return of the Native*. Winslow Homer was its greatest illustrator. Its political reputation was established by the eloquent editorials of George W. Curtis and the scathing cartoons of Thomas Nast. Excepting only the *New York Times*, and with the support of Fletcher Harper, Curtis and Nast were alone in their devastating attack on the corrupt Tweed Ring in New York. Later the *Weekly* used more American material: prose and pictorial sketches by Frederic Remington and serializations of James's *The Awkward Age* and Howells's *A Hazard of New Fortunes* and *The Landlord of Lion's Head*.

Fletcher Harper's third magazine, started in

IMPORTANT NEW WORKS

IN COURSE OF PUBLICATION BY

MESSRS. HARPER & BROTHERS, NEW YORK.

I.
Mr. Macaulay's New Work.

The History of England

FROM THE ACCESSION OF JAMES II.

By THOMAS BABINGTON MACAULAY.

Beautifully printed in the Octavo Library form, from New and Legible Type.

VOL. I. *Nearly Ready.*

The work of so eminent a scholar as Macaulay cannot but be a priceless treasure to posterity. We may look for a gallery of brilliant portraits from this Vandyke in literature.—*Western Continent.*

Macaulay has transmuted vast learning and varied accomplishments into one sweet and subtle thing, which really deserves the name of genius. He is the poet of facts, and the most rhetorical of writers.—GILFILLAN.

He is a master of every species of composition.—SIR JAMES MACKINTOSH.

Behind the external show and glittering vesture of his thoughts, beneath all his pomp of diction, aptness of illustration, splendor of imagery, and epigrammatic pomp and glare, a careful eye can easily discern the movement of a powerful and well cultivated intellect, as it successively appears in the well-trained logician, the acute and discriminating critic, the comprehensive philosopher, the practical and far-sighted statesman, and the student of universal knowledge.—E. P. WHIPPLE.

II.
Melville's New Work.

Mardi; and a Voyage Thither.

By HERMAN MELVILLE.

AUTHOR OF "OMOO," "TYPEE," &c.

This new book is characterized by that rare brilliancy and graphic power which have rendered the author's previous works such general favorites; it is even more stirring in its narrative, more glowing and vivid in its pictures, and will be found altogether a more unique production than either of its predecessors. Thus preserving the idiosyncrasies of his style, it cannot be doubted Mr. Melville's forthcoming work will add even to the illustrious literary reputation he has already attained in the world of letters.

III.

The Life and Letters of Thomas Campbell.

Edited by Dr. BEATTIE.

WITH AN INTRODUCTORY LETTER

By WASHINGTON IRVING.

This work presents the true character of the illustrious poet; rendering, in the words of Mr. Irving, "a great act of justice to the memory of a distinguished man, whose character has not been sufficiently known. It gives an insight into his domestic as well as his literary life, and lays open the springs of all his actions, and the causes of all his contrarieties of conduct. The biography does more: it reveals the affectionate considerateness of his conduct in all the domestic relations of life. Above all, the crowning romance of his life—his enthusiasm in the cause of suffering Poland—a devotion carried to the height of his poetic temperament, and, in fact, exhausting all that poetic vein, which, properly applied, might have produced epics; these, and many more traits set forth in his biography, bring forth his character for the first time in its true light; dispel those clouds which malice and detraction may at times have cast over it, and leave it in the full effulgence of its poetic glory."—*Extract from Mr. Irving's Introductory Letter.*

IV.
New Volumes of Mr. Jacob Abbott's Illustrated Historical Series.

1. The History of Alexander the Great.

1 volume, 12mo., with Illuminated Title and numerous Engravings.

2. The History of Hannibal.

1 volume, 12mo., with Illuminated Title and numerous Engravings.

V.
Volume V. of Chalmers's Posthumous Works.

Horæ Biblicæ Sabbaticæ;

Or, SABBATH SCRIPTURE READINGS.

By the late THOMAS CHALMERS, D.D., LL.D.

Volume Second, completing this work, forming the fifth of the series.

It is full of piety and prayer, and the fervent author earnestly extracts a moral or religious lesson from every passage or event to which he alludes. We might truly compare him to the bee gathering sweets from every object, and building up a hive of wonderful construction and everlasting richness.—*London Literary Gazette.*

The outpourings of a spirit in which simplicity and deep wisdom are beautifully combined.—*London Examiner.*

VI.
New Work on California and Oregon.

Oregon and California in 1848.

By J. QUINN THORNTON,

Late Judge of the Supreme Court of Oregon.

This work comprises some intensely thrilling incidents; a very interesting personal narrative of a journey across the Continent to Oregon, and thence by sea to the United States via California, during the years 1846, 7, 8; together with much valuable geological, statistical, and practical information, designed for the use of emigrants, &c. &c.

VII.

The Caxtons; a Family Picture.

ATTRIBUTED TO

SIR EDWARD BULWER LYTTON.

VIII.
Chapman's Illustrated Life of Franklin.

Benjamin Franklin.

HIS AUTOBIOGRAPHY, WITH A SKETCH OF HIS PUBLIC LIFE AND SERVICES.

Splendidly Embellished by numerous exquisite Designs by Chapman.

The Work, which will be elegantly printed upon fine paper, will be completed in Eight Parts, at 25 cents each, issued at brief intervals.

This pictorial Life of Franklin will, it is believed, be regarded as the *classic* edition, being in all respects worthy of the advanced state of art in this country, as well as of the fame of the distinguished "patriot, printer, and philosopher."

IX.
Lieut. Ruxton's Posthumous Work.

Life in the Far West.

By the late

GEORGE F. RUXTON, Esq.,

Author of "Adventures in Mexico and the Rocky Mountains."

WITH A BIOGRAPHICAL SKETCH OF THE AUTHOR.

This work possesses value and strong interest as a fresh, life-like picture of western life. In the opinion of *Blackwood's Magazine*, its style is as remarkable for graphic terseness and vigor, as its substance everywhere is for great novelty and originality.

MESSRS. HARPER'S LATEST PUBLICATIONS.

THE FORGERY. By G. P. R. James, Esq. 8vo. paper. 25 cts.

THE GREAT HOGGARTY DIAMOND. By W. M. Thackeray, Esq. 8vo. paper, 25 cts.

By the same Author.

VANITY FAIR; or, Pen and Pencil Sketches of English Society. With Illustrations by the Author. 8vo. muslin, $1 25; paper, $1.

This rich, racy, humorous, picturesque, inimitable book. We know not when we have been more truly grateful to an author for keeping our spirits in good humor point, and our blood to life heat, than when under Thackeray's influence.—*Union Magazine.*

COWPER'S POETICAL WORKS. Illustrated by 75 exquisite Designs. With a Biographical and Critical Introduction. By Rev. Thomas Dale. 2 vols. muslin, gilt edges, $3 75.

An edition beautifully appropriate to the purity and exceeding excellence of Cowper's writings. We have no other such elegant edition among us.—*Evangelist.*

THE ROMANCE OF YACHTING. VOYAGE THE FIRST. By Joseph C. Hart, Esq. 12mo. muslin, 60 cts.

A book of smartness and spirit; the author appears to have roamed over the seas with his eyes open.—*Tribune.*

HISTORY OF CHARLES THE FIRST. With an Illuminated Title Page and numerous Engravings. By Jacob Abbott. 12mo. muslin, 60 cts.

The subject is on many accounts one of the most interesting in all history; and the writer carries a pen so graceful and graphic, that all the scenes which he describes become to the mind of the reader undoubted and strongly felt realities. This book, by its thrilling details, will prove irresistible to the young.—*Albany Argus.*

MODEL MEN, WOMEN, AND CHILDREN. With numerous Comic Illustrations. By Horace Mayhew, Esq. 2 Parts, 18mo. paper, 25 cts. each.

Sketches of various characters smartly executed, and one of the steamboat and railway class of belles-lettres. The embellishments are very clever.—*Literary Gaz.*

THE MORAL, SOCIAL, AND PROFESSIONAL DUties of Attorneys and Solicitors. By Samuel Warren, F.R.S. Author of "Now-and-Then," &c. 12mo. muslin, 75 cents.

The author is universally known as a writer of great power; and in this little work he has set forth, strongly and impressively, in a clear and condensed form, much of interesting and valuable suggestions, useful not only for lawyers, but for all classes.—*Courier.*

MARY BARTON, A Tale of Manchester Life. 8vo. paper, 25 cents.

Gladly do we hail the advent of a true genius, who can interpret faithfully between the operatives and the masters—between the low and the high—between the starving and the well-fed.—*Jerrold's Newspaper.*

ARABIAN NIGHTS' ENTERTAINMENTS. Illustrated with Six Hundred Exquisite Engravings, &c. Newly Translated and Arranged for Family Reading, with Explanatory Notes by E. W. Lane, Esq. 2 vols. 12mo. muslin, gilt edges, $3 75.

It is a precious gallery of Oriental pictures. From the title-page to the last engraving, it is a casket of rare and beautiful gems, and from the palace to the hut, it lays bare all that is interesting to know of the followers of Mahomet.—*New York Sun.*

THE IMAGE OF HIS FATHER. A Tale of a Young Monkey. Illustrations. By the Brothers Mayhew. 12mo. muslin, 75 cents; paper, 50 cents.

A very witty production of those distinguished writers, the Brothers Mayhew, two of the most celebrated disciples of the "Punch School."—*Spirit of the Times.*

BIOGRAPHICAL HISTORY OF CONGRESS. With Portraits and Fac-simile Autographs. By Henry G. Wheeler, Esq. 8vo. muslin, $3 per volume. Vols. I., II. now ready.

Full page advertisement from the 16 December 1848 issue of Literary World

1867, was the weekly *Harper's Bazar*, modeled on a Berlin fashion publication from which at first it reprinted fashion plates. In six weeks, it boasted a circulation of 100,000. It was intended to be a companion to *Harper's Weekly*, of more general interest than merely fashions, with English serials—most notably Hardy's *Tess of the D'Urbervilles*—pictures, humor, and the like. *Harper's Young People*, also a copiously illustrated weekly, was started in 1879. Although, like the other Harper magazines, it was the most important of its kind, its life was relatively short: it became *Harper's Round Table* in 1895, a monthly in 1897, and ceased publication in 1899. When the *Bazar* also fell on hard times, it was sold to William Randolph Hearst in 1913; Hearst retained the Harper name in the title but changed *Bazar* to *Bazaar*. In the same year the *Weekly* was sold to McClure's, and it expired three years later.

By the time *Harper's Young People* was started, the original Harper brothers had all died—James in 1869, Wesley in 1870, John in 1875, and Fletcher in 1877. On Fletcher Harper's death, Philip Harper, the son of James, became head of the firm; but Joseph W. Harper, Jr.—known as Joe Brooklyn to distinguish him from other Josephs in the family—was in charge of the literary department and the dominant force in the firm.

At its high point in the 1880s Harper and Brothers had nearly 800 employees, more than 4,000 books in print, and an annual income of $4 million. Its illustrators for its books and magazines were the best—Homer, Remington, George DuMaurier, Howard Pyle, Frederick Church, and J. F. Kensett. The firm continued to add interesting or important new names to its list of authors—David Livingstone, Henry Morton Stanley, John Dewey, and H. D. Lloyd. Arthur Conan Doyle's Sherlock Holmes stories appeared alongside the novels of Howells, James, Bret Harte, Owen Wister, and Stephen Crane. The company gladly took over Mark Twain's books as he worked his way out of bankruptcy, while Lew Wallace's *Ben-Hur* (1880) produced the largest book order ever placed—a million copies for Sears, Roebuck.

Succeeding Harper sons and grandsons seemed not as able or as industriously shrewd as their fathers, and there were no proper provisions for withdrawal of capital when partners retired or died. In 1890, rather than fight the competition, the firm sold its schoolbook business to a newly formed textbook trust, the American Book Company. Philip Harper retired that year and was succeeded by John Harper's son, John W. Harper. Pressed by the financial panics of the 1890s, the partners incorporated as a stock company in 1896 and began borrowing from J. P. Morgan and Company. When the firm could not make its interest payments, the company yielded to Morgan's pressure and, at the end of 1899—after an abortive attempt at reorganization by S. S. McClure—Col. George Harvey took over as president of Harper and Brothers. Harvey sold off the college texts, fired most of the old compositors, and leased new Linotype equipment. Almost all the second and third generation cousins were retired or forced out, leaving Fletcher's grandson, J. Henry, as a vice-president. The declining *Harper's New Monthly Magazine* was revitalized with stories that had wider appeal and with improved illustrations; its name was changed in January 1900 to *Harper's Monthly Magazine* and in January 1901 to *Harper's Magazine*. By 1914 it was showing a profit of $5,000 a month, and the firm turned down an offer to buy it for $500,000. Harvey's tenure was marked by spectacular public relations and books by Zane Grey, H. G. Wells, and Theodore Dreiser were added to the firm's list, but money problems remained and Harvey was forced out in 1915.

Heavy-handed management by Harvey's successor C. T. Brainard weakened the trade list. The firm rejected, for instance, opportunities to publish works by Conrad, to keep Dreiser, and to encourage Sinclair Lewis. The printing machinery was sold off in 1922; in 1923 the Cliff Street-Franklin Square buildings were turned over to Morgan and new editorial offices were rented uptown at 49 East Thirty-third Street. The Morgan indebtedness was retired in 1923. Brainard was succeeded as president the following year by Douglas Parmentier. Cass Canfield joined the firm as an editor in 1924. Eugene Saxton, who became book editor in 1925, reduced the firm's dependence on a tired backlist of trade books. He and Canfield brought in lively new authors, including James Thurber, E. B. White, Aldous Huxley, and John Dos Passos. The firm established separate departments for college textbooks, social and economic books, children's books, and religious books. Henry Hoyns, who had been a vice-president but had exercised real editorial control over the firm, succeeded Parmentier as president in 1929. Two years later Hoyns became chairman of the board and Canfield was made president.

During the 1930s and the 1940s Harper and Brothers published Louis Bromfield's *The Farm* (1933), *The Rains Came* (1937), *Night in Bombay* (1940), and *Pleasant Valley* (1945); Thornton Wilder's *Heaven's My Destination* (1935) and *The Skin of*

Letter from Herman Melville asking Harper and Brothers for an advance on a book tentatively titled "Tortoises and Tortoise Hunting." Three days after Melville received the money, Harper's offices burned down. Assuming Harper would not be able to publish the work as agreed, Melville rewrote it as a serial titled "The Encantadas" and sold it to Putnam's Monthly. *Harper did not ask that the advance be returned, but the firm refused to publish another Melville work for twelve years (Pierpont Morgan Library).*

Our Teeth (1942); John Gunther's *Inside Europe* (1936), *Inside Asia* (1939), and *Inside Latin America* (1941); and, posthumously, Thomas Wolfe's *The Web and the Rock* (1939) and *You Can't Go Home Again* (1940). A medical book department was established in 1935. Canfield gave the presidency to Frank S. MacGregor in 1945; Canfield headed the firm as chairman of the board until 1962 and remained as director emeritus and senior editor until his death in 1986. Raymond C. Harwood became president in 1955. In the 1950s the firm published John F. Kennedy's *Profiles in Courage* (1956), Huxley's *Brave New World Revisited* (1958), and Leo Rosten's *The Return of H*Y*M*A*N K*A*P*L*A*N* (1959). Harper and Brothers also created several paperback reprint series, among them Harper Torchbooks, Perennial Classics, and Colophon Books. In 1962 Harper and Brothers merged with Row, Peterson and Company to form Harper and Row, Publishers, Incorporated.

On its 115th anniversary in 1965, *Harper's Magazine* was taken over by John Cowles, Jr., and his Minneapolis Star and Tribune Company. Concurrently with the acquisition of the magazine, Cowles was also buying up Harper and Row stock. Cowles became chairman of the board in 1968. Under the leadership of Winthrop Knowlton as president and Brooks Thomas as vice-president, Harper and Row aggressively pursued purchases of other firms, among them Basic Books in 1969, Thomas T. Crowell Company in 1977, and J. B. Lippincott in 1978. Other firms acquired by Harper and Row include Funk and Wagnalls, Gower, Hemisphere, Newbury House, Cassak, the college sociology list of Houghton Mifflin, the business management list of Pitman, and the publishing division of Barnes and Noble. Harper and Row tried to revive *Harper's Weekly* in 1975, but the magazine disappeared almost immediately.

In April 1979 Cowles stepped aside as chairman of the board, remaining chairman of the executive committee until 1981. Knowlton became chairman of the board and Thomas moved up to president and chief executive officer.

Once the largest publisher in the country, the firm is still among the half-dozen biggest in America. It published 1,200 titles in 1984. The list includes fiction, poetry, scholarly books, reference works, professional or technical texts in business and medicine, art books, and religious works. Authors include Saul Bellow, Aleksandr Solzhenitsyn, Gabriel Garcia Marquez, Milan Kundera, G. Cabrera Infante, Allen Ginsberg, and Dave Smith. The firm has published two major literary biographies: Kenneth Silverman's *The Life and Times of Cotton Mather* (1984) and Leon Edel's *Henry James: A Life* (1985). Harper and Row's school text division was acquired by Macmillan in 1984, and in that same year all Harper and Row paperbacks were consolidated under the imprint Perennial Library. Since 1972 the firm has been located at 10 East Fifty-third Street, New York 10022.

References:

Jacob Abbott, *The Harper Establishment* (New York: Harper, 1855);

Cass Canfield, *Up and Down and Around* (New York: Harper's Magazine Press, 1971);

Eugene Exman, *The Brothers Harper* (New York: Harper & Row, 1965);

Exman, *The House of Harper* (New York: Harper & Row, 1967);

J. Henry Harper, *The House of Harper* (New York: Harper, 1912).

—*Howard C. Horsford*

James P. Harrison Company
(Atlanta: 1873-1907)
Harrison Company
(Atlanta; Norcross, Georgia: 1907-   )

In 1873 James P. Harrison bought the Franklin Steam Printing House, established in Atlanta in 1859, and formed the James P. Harrison Company with the Franklin Printing and Publishing Company as a subsidiary. The primary business of both firms was printing for the state government, but they also published trade books and a small amount of fiction. Harrison's literary publications were limited mostly to Civil War romances and sentimental novels of regional interest, including *The Waif; or, The Web of Life* (1883) by Emma Erichsen, *Saved by a Woman; or, the Hidden Romance. A Story of the Late War* (1884) by Whitemarsh B. Seabrook, and *Amanda, The Octoroon* (1891) by Francis Fontaine. Harrison also published *Bill Arp's Scrap Book* (1884), a popular collection of sayings, sketches, and anecdotes by the backwoods philosopher whose real name was Charles Henry Smith. The Franklin company was sold in 1906, and in 1907 the James P. Harrison Company was reorganized as the Harrison Company by George W. Harrison, George W. Harrison, Jr., and J. T. Doonan. The Harrisons died in 1936. When Doonan died in 1951 the firm was acquired by John M. Elliott and other long-time employees. It was reorganized in 1970 with Elliott as president and chairman of the board and Henry H. Blake as editor in chief. In 1975 Elliott retired and Blake became president and chairman of the board. The firm specializes in law books. Its address is 3110 Crossing Park, Norcross, Georgia 30071.

—Robert McNutt

Willis P. Hazard
(Philadelphia: circa 1851-1864)

Founded about 1851, the Philadelphia firm of Willis P. Hazard published an edition of Oliver Goldsmith's *The Vicar of Wakefield* (1852) and Leigh Hunt's *Imagination and Fancy* (1854). Works by contemporary women authors included Catharine M. Sedgwick's *The City Clerk and His Sister, and Other Stories* (1851), Lydia Maria Child's *The Power of Kindness and Other Stories* (1853), and Harriet Beecher Stowe's *Uncle Sam's Emancipation* (1853). Children's books published by Hazard included *Story Book of Animals* (1851), David W. Belisle's *The American Family Robinson; or, the Adventures of a Family Lost in the Great Desert of the West* (1854), and *Katy's Story, and Other Poems and Tales* (1855) by Edith May (pseudonym of Anne Drinker).

The last known Hazard publication was *The Wind Harp and Other Poems* by Ellen C. Howarth in 1864. After the Civil War Porter and Coates acquired Hazard's assets.

—Elizabeth Hoffman

B. Herder Book Company
(St. Louis: 1873-1967; 1969-1972)
Herder of St. Louis
(St. Louis: 1967-1969)

In 1873 Joseph Gummersbach founded the B. Herder Book Company at 17 South Broadway, St. Louis, as a branch of Herder Verlag of Freiburg, Baden, the largest Catholic publisher in Germany at the time. Herder offered German Catholic immigrants religious textbooks and catechisms, along with popular novels such as Lelia Hardin Bugg's *Orchids* (1894) and Mary F. Roulet's *Lasca, and Other Stories* (1898) and *A Harp of Many Chords* (1899). Herder also published *Westchester: A Tale of the Revolution* (1899) by Henry Austin Adams; *Guy's Fortune* (1900) by M. B. Eagan, the pseudonym of Mary Pauline Smith; and *The Little Maid of Israel* (1900) by Emma Howard Wight. In the twentieth century, Herder's output consisted almost exclusively of theological works.

In 1917 Herder severed its ties with Herder Verlag. In 1963 it moved to 314 North Jefferson. Four years later its name was changed to Herder of St. Louis, but in 1969 it reverted to the B. Herder Book Company. The firm came to an end in 1972. In 1957 Herder Verlag established a new branch in New York, Herder and Herder, which was later bought by The Seabury Press, Incorporated.

References:

Jordan Aumann, "Herder of St. Louis," *Catholic Library World*, 30 (1958-1959): 219-222;

Justus George Lawler, "Herder and Herder," *Catholic Library World*, 31 (1959-1960): 409-412, 458.

—*David Dzwonkoski*

E. R. Herrick and Company

(New York: 1897-1900)

E. R. Herrick and Company was founded by Edward R. Herrick in 1897 at 70 Fifth Avenue in New York. Primarily a religious publishing house, the firm also published novels intended mostly for female readers. Among these works were Virginia Boyle's *Brockenburne: A Southern Auntie's War Tale* (1897) and Thomas Winthrop Hall's *An Experimental Wooing* (1898) and *The Little Lady, Some Other People, and Myself* (1898). *The Fight for Dominion: A Romance of Our First War With Spain* by Gay Parker (the pseudonym of M. P. Green) appeared in 1899, as did *And Then Came Spring; A Story of Moods* by Edward Payson Buffet under the pseudonym Garret Van Arkel. Herrick also published Grace Boylan's books of verse *If Tam O'Shanter'd Had a Wheel* (1898) and *The Old House* (1897). Herrick went out of business in 1900. He worked for several other publishing houses until his death in 1917.

Reference:
"Edward R. Herrick [obituary]," *Publishers' Weekly,* 91 (3 March 1917): 677.

—*David Dzwonkoski*

George M. Hill Company

(Chicago: circa 1896-1902)

The George M. Hill Company was founded at 166-174 South Clinton Street, Chicago, around 1896. L. Frank Baum's *Father Goose: His Book* (1899) sold about 75,000 copies in its first year, due largely to the inspired packaging of the firm's general manager, Frank Kennicott Reilly, and its head of sales, Sumner C. Britton. *Father Goose* was illustrated by W. W. Denslow, whose unique interpretations of Baum's bizarre characters also graced the pictorial cloth covers and pages of *The Wonderful Wizard of Oz* (1900) and caught the imagination of thousands of children; Baum's book sold 25,000 copies in its first two months.

A New York office was opened in 1900 to handle the increase in sales, but Baum was not enough to carry the firm. After publishing Baum's *The Songs of Father Goose* (1900) and *Santa Claus: His Life and Adventures* (1902), the Hill Company was placed in receivership and its stock and plates of Bibles, reference works, and a set of Dickens were auctioned off. Reilly and Britton retained Baum's contract and had continued success with his Oz books under their own imprint.

References:
David L. Greene and Dick Martin, *The Oz Scrapbook* (New York: Random House, 1977);
Douglas G. Greene and Peter E. Hanff, *Bibliographia Oziana* (N.p.: International Wizard of Oz Club, 1976).

—*David Dzwonkoski*

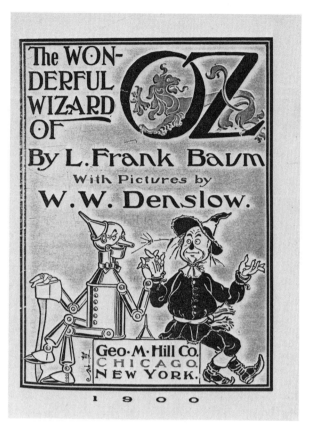

Title page for the second of Baum's books to be published by George M. Hill Company. It sold 25,000 copies in two months.

Henry Holt in 1866, the year he invested $6,000 to form the partnership Leypoldt and Holt

Hilliard, Gray and Company
(Boston: 1827-1843)

Hilliard, Gray and Company of 134 Washington Street, Boston, succeeded Cummings and Hilliard in 1827 when Timothy H. Carter left the latter company. The new firm was headed by William Hilliard, a founder of Cummings and Hilliard. The other three principals had all worked in the original house. Harrison Gray had been a bookseller and bookbinder before coming to the firm; John Hubbard Wilkins, a Swedenborgian minister, had written one of Cummings and Hilliard's textbooks, *Elements of Astronomy* (1823); Charles C. Little, Hilliard's son-in-law, had been in charge of the legal books department and was also connected with the Boston Type and Stereotype Foundry, started by Carter and used by both the former publishing house and the new one. Besides its offices and bookstore in Boston, Hilliard, Gray maintained a bookstore in Cambridge that catered to the Harvard University trade.

Wilkins left the firm in 1833 to become a paper dealer; he was replaced by Charles Brown. At the same time James Brown joined the firm. Hilliard, Gray and Company carried on the tradition of its predecessor as a major publisher-bookseller in Boston, publishing scholarly textbooks by Harvard professors, classics, and legal books and importing foreign books. Early biographies of Americans, written or edited by Jared Sparks, were published by the company. The first volume of Longfellow's *Outre-Mer* (1833) also bore the firm's imprint.

A year after Hilliard's death in 1836 Little and James Brown started the firm of Little, Brown, taking with them Hilliard, Gray's law books, foreign books, and Spark's Library of American Biography and moving into Hilliard, Gray's offices at 112 Washington Street. Gray and Charles Brown carried on the business at 10 Water Street and finally at 107 Washington Street, where they published textbooks, classics, and a book apiece by three American women writers of romantic fiction, Eliza Lee Follen, Louisa Jane Hall, and Eliza Lee.

By 1843 Brown had left and Gray joined the bookselling business of T. H. Webb and Company. Most of the Hilliard, Gray stock, including James Ripley's outstanding series, Specimens of Foreign Literature, was taken over by James Munroe.

References:

George Stillman Hilliard, *Memoir of James Brown* (Boston: Privately printed, 1856);

Madeleine B. Stern, "Hilliard, Gray & Company: Booksellers to the University," *Publishers' Weekly*, 150 (19 October 1946): 2380-2388.

—Theodora Mills

Hilton and Company
(New York: 1865-1869; 1871-circa 1873)
Hilton and Syme
(New York: 1870)

Hilton and Company was established in New York in 1865 by Winthrop E. Hilton, a printer, bookseller, and stationer, primarily to compete with Beadle and Adams in the publication of dime novels. Hilton called his books Hilton's Dime Books. The firm was located initially at 11 Spruce Street, but soon moved to 128 Nassau Street. It remained there until it went out of business around 1873, with the exception of 1868, when it was located briefly at 19 Beekman Street. During 1870 the firm was known as Hilton and Syme.

Hilton's most popular author, and the one the firm most frequently published, was Edward Zane Carroll Judson, who wrote under the pseudonym Ned Buntline. At least sixteen of his dime novels were published by Hilton in 1865 and 1866. Judson's story about the assassination of Lincoln, *The Parricides; or, The Doom of the Assassins, the Authors of a Nation's Loss* (1865), was the first novel in the Ned Buntline's Own series. Hilton also published Henry Edwards's *The Poor of New York* (1865), based on a play of the same title; several songbooks, some of which contained songs of the Fenian Society; W. B. Phillips's *The Diamond Cross* (1867); and T. O. English's *Ambrose Fecot; or, The Peer and the Painter* (1867).

—*Philip A. Metzger*

Hogan and Thompson
(Philadelphia: 1832-1852)

Two Philadelphia printer-publishers, David Hogan and John Thompson, formed the partnership of Hogan and Thompson in 1832. The firm published books on manners, drawing, and public speaking; American politics and history also received attention in James Bayard's *A Brief Exposition of the Constitution of the United States* (1833) and John Lewis Thomson's *History of the Second War between the United States and Great Britain* (1848). Literary titles for children included *The Good Child's Library* . . . *in Easy Verse* (1850-1851) and *The Youth's Historical Cabinet, a Series of Narratives* (1850). Adult literary titles were mostly new editions of European works, including Samuel Johnson's *The History of Rasselas* (1850), with color illustrations, and a translation of Bernardin de Saint-Pierre's *Paul and Virginia* (1852). The Hogan and Thompson partnership ended in 1852.

—*Margaret Becket*

Henry Holt and Company
(New York: 1873-1960)
Leypoldt and Holt
(New York: 1866-1870)
Leypoldt, Holt and Williams
(New York: 1870-1871)
Holt and Williams
(New York: 1871-1873)

Leypoldt & Holt (1868)   *Henry Holt & Co. (1880s)*   *ca. 1900*   *1920s*

1940s   *1950s*

See also the Holt, Rinehart and Winston entry in *DLB 46, American Literary Publishing Houses, 1900-1980: Trade and Paperback.*

Culminating a long-term trend toward specialization and division of labor in the publishing business, Henry Holt was one of the first Americans to become a publisher without first owning a printing shop or bookstore. Born in Baltimore in 1840, Holt graduated from Yale in 1862 and from Columbia Law School in 1864. He collaborated with George Palmer Putnam in publishing the Artists' Edition of Washington Irving's *The Sketch Book* in 1863 and *The Rebellion Record*, a chronicle of the Civil War, until David Van Nostrand purchased the project in 1864.

In 1865 Holt offered his translation of Edmond About's *The Man with the Broken Ear* to pub-

lisher Frederick Leypoldt, who offered to publish the book at Holt's expense. Holt declined that offer but accepted a clerkship in Leypoldt's firm. Five years older than Holt, Leypoldt had immigrated from Stuttgart, Germany, to America in 1854. After five years with the firm of F. W. Christern, Leypoldt had opened his own bookstore in Philadelphia where, in 1863, he began publishing European titles, a few in his own translations. In 1864 he opened a New York branch at 644-646 Broadway and soon closed his Philadelphia store. When the twenty-five-year-old Holt agreed to invest $6,000—all that was left of an inheritance—the firm of Leypoldt and Holt was formed in January 1866. The partnership soon offered its first publication, Joseph von Eichendorff's *Memoirs of a Good-for-Nothing* (1866), translated by Charles Godfrey Leland. Like most major publishers of the

205

time, the new firm published mainly translations and reprints of European works. In 1867 Holt took advantage of his position to publish his translation of *The Man with the Broken Ear*. Holt and Leypoldt also introduced the Russian novelist Ivan Turgenev to American readers by publishing his *Fathers and Sons* (1867).

In 1870 the firm took on a former Yale classmate of Holt's, Ralph C. Williams, and, rechristened Leypoldt, Holt and Williams, moved to 25 Bond Street. By this time Leypoldt was devoting most of his energies to his *Literary Bulletin and Trade Circular,* which he had developed out of the firm's house bulletin in 1868. In 1870 he compiled the publishers' lists that had appeared in the *Bulletin* the previous year and published them in the first issue of what eventually became the *Publishers' Trade List Annual.* The following year, Leypoldt left the firm, which then became Holt and Williams, to pursue his own projects. In 1872 Leypoldt purchased George F. Childs's *American Literary Gazette and Publishers' Circular* which, combined with Leypoldt's own bulletin, was in 1873 renamed *Publishers' Weekly.*

Between 1869 and 1873 the firm published four books by the French critic and essayist Hippolyte Adolph Taine. Taine's *History of English Literature* (1871), considered a gamble by Holt, proved to be the firm's first financial success. The firm also published John Stuart Mill's *Autobiography* (1873).

Holt and Williams continued until 1873 when, upon Williams's departure, the firm became Henry Holt and Company. Five years later, Holt's brother Charles joined the firm. Holt also hired E. L. Godkin, editor of the *Nation,* as his chief literary adviser. In 1879 the company moved to 12 East Street, and in 1882 to 29 West Street. These moves were due to the expansion of the firm, which as early as 1872 had claimed a publishing output more than double that of any other American firm.

One of the earliest publishers of Thomas Hardy, Holt paid him full ten percent royalties even in the absence of an international copyright law. Holt was able to do so because of a "courtesy" principle among major American publishers: the first house to announce its intention of publishing a foreign work and to obtain a copy of it could claim exclusive rights to the title and, to a certain extent, to future works by that author. This arrangement was an informal, not a legal, one. On this basis Holt published Hardy's *Under the Greenwood Tree* (1873), *The Return of the Native* (1878), and *The Mayor of Casterbridge* (1882). These books were included in the Leisure Hour series, an in-

expensive line of fiction Holt and Williams had inaugurated in 1872 with Turgenev's *Smoke* and reprints of *Fathers and Sons* and E. F. Poynter's *My Little Lady.* In 1880 Hardy signed with Harper and Brothers to publish *A Pair of Blue Eyes,* a title first published in America by Holt in 1873. Holt, a staunch defender of the courtesy principle, persuaded Harper to release one of his English authors, William Edward Norris, in exchange. Though Holt published Norris's *Matrimony* in 1881 and five other Norris titles during the 1880s, he also continued to publish Hardy's works in competition with Harper.

Holt increasingly found himself competing with piratical publishers, most notably John W. Lovell, who ignored the courtesy principle and flooded the market with cheap reprints. No fewer than thirty-four publishers pirated Hardy's works. Holt responded with the paperback Leisure Moment series, which grew by 1888 to about 100 titles drawn mostly from the hardcover Leisure Hour series. But his prices—twenty to thirty-five cents— were still twice as high as those of the pirates. Consequently, his profits on European titles plummeted, and he was forced to sell both series in 1890. In its final year, the Leisure Hour series exceeded 200 volumes, including works by Hardy, Goethe, Heine, Norris, Dostoyevski, Gustave Freitag, Frances Anne Kemble, and Octave Feuillet. The first American writer in the series was Theodore Winthrop, followed by Henry Adams, whose anonymous *Democracy, An American Novel* appeared in 1880. Adams's *Esther* (1884) was the third number in Holt's American Novel series. This series marked the beginning of Holt's trend away from European and toward American literature.

This trend was slowed by the passage of the International Copyright Act in 1891. A leading advocate of the act before Congressional committees and in articles in the *Forum,* Holt was quick to return to publishing works by European authors upon its passage. These authors included Jerome K. Jerome, Ethel Lillian Voynich, George Gissing, Charles N. and Alice M. Williamson, and May Sinclair. Significant Holt titles of this period were H. G. Wells's *The Time Machine* (1895), Anthony Hope's *The Prisoner of Zenda* (1894), and William de Morgan's first novel, *Joseph Vance* (1906). Holt published many other titles by Hope and de Morgan.

In 1903 the firm was incorporated with Holt as president, his son Roland—who had been with the firm since 1882—as vice-president, Edward N. Bristol—who had supervised the textbook division since 1882—as secretary, and Joseph Vogelius as treasurer. The firm moved to 34 West Thirty-third Street in 1908.

One of Holt's major achievements in the nineteenth century was the publication of the works of the most prominent American scientists and social scientists. The firm's American Science series consisted of textbooks in fourteen branches of science, including Ira Remsen's *The Elements of Chemistry* (1887) and William James's *The Principles of Psychology* (1890). Other significant nonfiction titles of this period were Mill's five-volume *Dissertations and Discussions* (1873-1875) and James's *Talks to Teachers on Psychology* (1899). Several works published after the turn of the century reflected Holt's belief in evolution: Vernon Kellogg's *Darwinism Today* (1908), John Dewey's *The Influence of Darwin on Philosophy* (1910), and Henri Bergson's *Creative Evolution* (1911).

Textbooks provided Holt's major source of profit. Though a novelist himself—his *Calmire* (1892) and *Sturmsee, Man and Man* (1905) had both been published anonymously by Macmillan—Holt wrote in the *New York Times* in 1909 that "it is only the publication of . . . books related to the utilities . . . that will justify any house in keeping in business, as some people holding different opinions have learned to their loss." He concluded that fiction and poetry were "not worth doing" by themselves.

By the turn of the century, Holt was a firm fiscal conservative, but the times were changing. Though he had once called royalties of more than ten percent "immoral," Holt was persuaded to pay de Morgan twenty percent, and up to twenty-five percent if sales exceeded a certain level. By 1905 Holt was opposed to the International Copyright Act he had fought for because it disrupted the courtesy principle and increased competition in the trade. Later, Holt helped form the Publishers' Lunch Club, which took the place of the American Publishers Association. The latter, with Holt as president, had been ruled an illegal restraint of trade.

In 1910 when Alfred Harcourt took over the trade department and Holt retired to Fairholt, his estate in Burlington, Vermont, the firm entered a renewed phase of literary importance. Harcourt had come to Holt in 1904 as an editor and salesman, bringing with him his Columbia University classmate Donald Brace, who entered the production side of the business. Though retired, Holt kept a close watch over the firm, especially the trade department. Initially mistrusting Harcourt's un-

proven judgment, Holt rejected several books suggested by Harcourt—among them Arnold Bennett's *The Old Wives' Tale*—which later sold well for other firms or became classics. Harcourt finally convinced Holt to publish the Home University Library, originally published in England by Williams and Norgate. In 1911, its first year, 300,000 volumes in the series were sold.

During Harcourt's term as editor the firm published Romain Rolland's *Jean-Christophe* (1910); Algernon Blackwood's *The Education of Uncle Paul* (1910); Dorothy Canfield's *The Squirrel Cage* (1912), *Hillsboro People* (1915), and *The Bent Twig* (1915); and Martin Anderson Nëxo's four-volume *Pelle the Conqueror* (1915-1917). Other novelists brought in by Harcourt were Rose Macauley, Romeo Wilson, Julien Binda, C. E. Montague, and Henry Handel Richardson. Harcourt was also responsible for the firm's decision to publish Carl Sandburg's second book, *Chicago Poems* (1916), at Marianne Moore's suggestion. It was followed in 1918 by Sandburg's *Cornhuskers*.

Holt's family also made significant contributions to the firm's trade list. Roland Holt selected work by the poets Louis Untermeyer and Padraic Colum, and he was also responsible for the publication of John Crowe Ransom's first book, *Poems About God* (1919), and Walter de la Mare's *The Listeners* (1916). Florence Talen Holt—Henry Holt's second wife—came across a copy of Robert Frost's first book, *North of Boston*, which had been published in 1914 by the London firm of David Nutt. In 1915 Holt published the book, which had been rejected by Houghton Mifflin and Macmillan. Due to a contractual problem with Nutt, Harcourt made Frost a literary adviser, rather than pay him royalties. Nutt soon went bankrupt and Frost began receiving royalties but remained an adviser for the rest of his life. Holt became Frost's main American publisher.

Under Harcourt, Holt published nonfiction by H. L. Mencken, Simeon Strunsky, Henri Bergson, J. Arthur Thomson, Leon Trotsky, and Bertrand Russell. Disagreements with the conservative Holt over Russell's socialistic *Proposed Roads to Freedom* in 1919 led to Harcourt's departure in that year, although the book was published. In addition to Brace, with whom he founded Harcourt, Brace and Company, Harcourt took with him sales manager August H. Gehrs and his secretary Ellen K. Ayers. Further losses among Holt's personnel by 1920 were Vogelius, who retired; promotion manager Maxwell Aley, who joined another firm; and Ambrose Dearborn, who died.

After these departures, Lincoln MacVeagh became head of trade, while Robert Cortes Holliday was added as an editor. Under MacVeagh, Holt published Stephen Vincent Benét's *Heavens and Earth* (1920), *The Beginnings of Wisdom* (1921), and *Jean Huguenot* (1923); Marcel Proust's *Swann's Way* (1922); A. E. Housman's *Last Poems* (1922); and Thomas Mann's *Bashan and I* (1923). Nonfiction works by Albert Einstein, Robert Benchley, Francesco Nitti, Frederick Jackson Turner, and Benedetto Croce also appeared. With MacVeagh's departure to found the Dial Press in 1923, the trade department was controlled by Holt's son Elliot. Misjudgments by Elliot Holt resulted in the loss of Proust and Mann. Meanwhile, the firm moved to 1 Park Avenue. Henry Holt died in 1926. The corporation went public two years later with Edward N. Bristol as president and majority stockholder and Herschel Brickell as head of trade, and Holt's sons Elliot and Henry, Jr., left the firm. Few new authors were added, though Hermann Hesse's *Steppenwolf* appeared in 1929. During the Depression, the firm fared poorly, distinguishing itself mainly with the works of Frost and nonfiction by Paul Tillich, Albert Schweitzer, and Karl Jaspers.

R. H. Thornton succeeded Bristol in 1932. The firm moved to 257 Fourth Avenue in 1937. Bristol's son Herbert took over as president in 1939. A year earlier, William Sloane had become trade editor; under Sloane, Holt published Marion Hargrove's *See Here, Private Hargrove*—the bestselling book of 1942—Ernie Pyle's *Here Is Your War* (1943), and Bill Mauldin's *Up Front* (1945). With the assistance of Frost, Sloane produced poetry volumes that included Stanley Kunitz's *Passport to the War* (1944), Mark Van Doren's *The Seven Sleepers* (1944), E. E. Cummings's *I x I* (1944) and *Santa Claus: A Morality* (1946), and collected poems of Housman (1940), de la Mare (1941), and Lew Sar-

rett (1941). Sloane left in 1946 to start his own firm, William Sloane Associates.

During the late 1940s Joseph A. Brandt served as president, with Denver Lindley as trade editor. Texas oilman Clint Murchison and other financiers, having gained majority control of the firm's stock, replaced Brandt with Edward T. Rigg in 1948. Through Murchinson, Holt acquired *Field and Stream* magazine in 1951. In 1953 the firm moved to 383 Madison Avenue. *Popular Gardening* magazine was purchased in 1955. Glen Gosling, Theodore Amussen, William Raney, William E. Buckley, Howard S. Cady, and Harry Shaw served in the trade department under Rigg. In addition to textbooks—which remained the firm's biggest money-makers—and nonfiction by Daniel Boorstin, Omar Bradley, Martin Buber, Bernard Baruch, Karl Barth, and David Ben-Gurion, the firm published François Mauriac's *The Unknown Sea* (1948), Hesse's *Demian* (1948), and Babette Deutsch's *Poetry in Our Time* (1955). The Dryden Press was acquired in 1958, as were *New Homes Guide* and *Home Modernizing Guide* magazines. In 1960 Henry Holt and Company merged with Rinehart and Company and the John C. Winston Company to form Holt, Rinehart and Winston.

References:

Alfred Harcourt, *Some Experiences* (Riverside, Conn.: Quinn & Boden, 1951);

"Henry Holt, 1840-1926," *Publishers' Weekly*, 109 (20 February 1926): 601-604;

Henry Holt, *Garrulities of an Octogenarian Editor* (Boston & New York: Houghton Mifflin, 1923);

Charles A. Madison, *The Owl Among Colophons: Henry Holt as Publisher and Editor* (New York: Holt, Rinehart & Winston, 1966).

—*David Dzwonkoski*

Home Publishing Company
(New York: 1887-1908)

Born in Liverpool, Archibald Clavering Gunter had been successful as a civil engineer, a chemist, and a broker before he moved in 1879 from San Francisco to New York to fulfill his lifelong ambition of writing a play. The success of the play, *Prince Karl,* encouraged Gunter to try his hand at a novel, and, though he finally had to pay the firm of Deshler, Welch and Company to publish the book, *Mr. Barnes of New York* (1887) was successful. Gunter apparently resented the publisher's cutting into the author's profits, and later that year he founded the Home Publishing Company, with himself as president and his wife as manager, at 7 East Fourteenth Street. He was at first the firm's sole author, imitating the format of his first triumph in thirty-eight other novels, including *Mr. Potter of Texas* (1888), *The Frenchman* (1889), *Miss Nobody of Nowhere* (1890), *Baron Montez of Panama and Paris* (1893), *Don Balasco of Key West* (1896), and *The Power of Woman* (1897).

The Home Publishing Company eventually published titles by other authors, including Col. Richard Henry Savage's *My Official Wife* (1891), *His Cuban Sweetheart* (1895), *Her Foreign Conquest* (1896), and *The Shield of His Honor* (1900) and Clarice Clingham's *Girl from Bogota* (1896).

A typical Home list included fifty to sixty titles, half of them by Gunter, another quarter by Savage, and the rest by other authors. The books were published in hardcover for $1.25 or $1.50 and in paperback for 50¢. The Home Publishing Company advertised its books as "the most successful novels ever published in America." Several of them were reprinted by Hurst and Company and published in London by G. Routledge or Ward and Lock.

In December 1904 Gunter reorganized the firm as the A. C. Gunter Publishing Company, with himself as president and his wife as secretary-treasurer, but continued to use the Home Publishing Company imprint. This reorganization coincided with the establishment of *Gunter's Magazine,* which was to be a medium for publishing Gunter's books in serial form. After Gunter's death in February 1907, his wife unsuccessfully attempted to maintain the business; it was put into receivership in January 1908, and Mrs. Gunter declared bankruptcy in February of that year.

References:

"Archibald Clavering Gunter [obituary]," *Publishers' Weekly,* 71 (2 March 1907): 856;

"Former Manager of the Home Publishing Company Arrested," *Publishers' Weekly,* 105 (21 March 1908): 1243;

"*Gunter's Magazine* Announced by Home Publishing Company," *Publishers' Weekly,* 66 (24 December 1904): 1704-1705;

"Mrs. Archibald Gunter Files for Bankruptcy," *Publishers' Weekly,* 73 (29 February 1908): 970.

—*Jane I. Thesing*

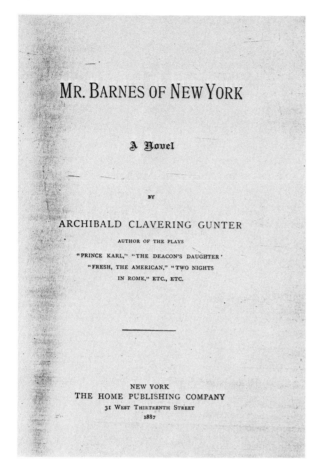

Title page for the novel that formed the base of Home Publishing Company's first list. Gunter had originally paid Deshler, Welch and Company to publish this successful novel.

Henry Oscar Houghton in 1864, the year he formed the publishing firm Hurd and Houghton with Melancthon M. Hurd

E. and E. Hosford

(Albany, New York: 1806-1828)

Born in Hebron, Connecticut, in 1779, Elijah Hosford entered publishing, bookselling, and bookbinding in Albany, New York, on 1 May 1802. On 1 May 1806 his twin brother, Elisha, joined him, forming the company of E. and E. Hosford. The firm published mainly children's literature. It also printed a periodical, the *New York Statesman*. In 1820 the brothers made an unsuccessful bid to become the state printers of New York. The firm continued to do a solid business in juveniles and primers.

A popular Hosford reprint was *Cinderella; or, The Little Glass Slipper* (1810) by Charles Perrault. Copied from the original, the woodcut illustrations for *Cinderella* were of poor quality. Hosford included six riddles in its edition, some of which had appeared in previous publications. Hosford also reprinted *The Death and Burial of Cock Robin* and *The Wonderful History of an Enchanted Castle*, both in 1813. An original Hosford publication was *The Life, Travels, Voyages and Daring Engagements of Paul Jones* by John Paul Jones. Published in 1809, the book includes *The Life and Adventures of Peter Williamson*. The firm also published *A New History of Blue Beard* (1816) by Perrault, *The Pleasures of Poverty* (1823) by Solomon Southwick, and technical journals for medical and historical societies.

E. and E. Hosford continued in business until 1828, when Elijah Hosford died in Albany. Elisha Hosford died two years later in Hartford, Connecticut.

—*Karin S. Mabe*

Hotchkiss and Company

(Boston: circa 1845-circa 1853)

The first known publication of Hotchkiss and Company, Boston publishers of the mid nineteenth century, was a reprint of Joseph Holt Ingraham's *Morris Graeme; or, The Cruise of the Sea-Slipper* in 1845. It was published at the "Yankee" Office at 22 Congress Street by Hotchkiss and Company and Haliburton and Dudley. In 1850 the firm published *The Banker's Clerk* by George Pickering Burnham and *Mary Bean, the Factory Girl: A Domestic Story, Illustrative of the Trials and Temptations of Factory Life* by "Miss J. A. B. of Manchester." Three years later Hotchkiss and Company copublished the anonymous *Turnover: A Tale of New Hampshire* with Redding and Company and James French.

—*David Dzwonkoski*

211

Houghton Mifflin Company
(Boston: 1908-   )
Houghton, Mifflin and Company
(Boston: 1880-1908)

used until 1885

1950s to date

Born in 1823 in Sutton, Vermont, Henry Oscar Houghton endured a poverty-stricken childhood which forced him at the age of thirteen to become a printer's apprentice for the *Burlington (Vermont) Free Press*. After attending the University of Vermont he returned to Boston, where he held several newspaper and printing jobs; one of these jobs was with the printing firm of Freeman and Bolles. In 1849 the firm became Bolles and

Houghton. The partners decided to move the printing plant from Boston to land by the Charles River owned by Little, Brown in Cambridge. In 1852, a year after Bolles retired, this establishment became the Riverside Press. In 1864 Houghton and Melancthon M. Hurd formed the publishing firm of Hurd and Houghton.

In contrast to Houghton's background, George Harrison Mifflin was born into a distin-

The Riverside Press, built on land beside the Charles River

Albert F. Houghton, James Murray Kay, Henry O. Houghton, Jr., George Harrison Mifflin, and Oscar R. Houghton, partners of the firm in the early 1900s (courtesy of Virginia Houghton Dole)

guished and wealthy Boston family. He went to the Boston Latin School, then attended Harvard, and after graduation took an extensive tour abroad. In 1868, due to Mifflin's persistence, Houghton hired him to work in the Riverside Press counting room, where he learned about the financial side of printing. Mifflin later was placed in charge of the bindery and in 1872 was made a partner in Hurd and Houghton.

When Hurd retired in 1878, Houghton joined with James R. Osgood, a former partner in Ticknor and Fields, to form Houghton, Osgood and Company. A third partner, Lawson Valentine, provided the firm with $200,000 in capital. Osgood brought to the partnership the impressive Ticknor and Fields list, which included Hawthorne, Emerson, Holmes, Howells, Longfellow, Lowell, Dickens, and Tennyson. Houghton, Osgood seemed to face brilliant prospects, but, from its outset, the company was plagued by heavy financial obligations, mostly personal debts incurred by Osgood. In 1880 the partnership was dissolved, and Houghton and Mifflin formed Houghton, Mifflin and Company at 47 Franklin Street. The firm soon moved to 4 Park Street; it also moved the Houghton, Osgood New York branch from Astor Place to 11 East Seventeenth Street.

Although with the dissolution of Houghton, Osgood and Company all copyrights published by that firm were to be transferred to Houghton, Mifflin, disagreement arose with Osgood as to whether Houghton, Mifflin had first rights to new works by the authors whose works Houghton, Osgood had published. Longfellow, Lowell, Holmes, Whittier, and Emerson, however, all agreed to transfer their contracts to Houghton, Mifflin.

In 1882 the firm established an Educational Department headed by Henry Wheeler, a Harvard mathematics professor, and began the Riverside Literature series. Masterpieces of prose and poetry in English were made available to schools and colleges at the lowest possible cost. The series started with Longfellow's *Evangeline* in the author's approved text. Subsequent volumes included works by Whittier, Hawthorne, Lowell, Tennyson, Keats, Byron, Browning, Wordsworth, Emerson, and Poe. By 1900 the series numbered more than 140 volumes, with annual sales in the hundreds of thousands. The firm also published the American Commonwealths series, studies of individual states edited by Horace Scudder; the American Men of Letters series, edited by James T. Fields until his death in 1881 and then by Charles Dudley Warner; and the American Statesmen series, edited by John

T. Morse. Perhaps the best-known author writing for the American Statesmen series was Henry Adams, who wrote a biography of John Randolph and then became embroiled in an argument with Houghton over whether Aaron Burr should be included in the series. Houghton won, and Adams's biography of Burr remained unpublished. New biographies were added yearly until the American Statesmen reached thirty-one volumes. Houghton, Mifflin published revisions of three venerable textbooks to which the firm had obtained the rights: Warren Colburn's *First Lessons: Intellectual Arithmetic upon the Inductive Method of Instruction* (1821), revised by Wheeler; Ethan A. Andrews and Solomon Stoddard's *Grammar of the Latin Language* (1836), revised by Henry Preble; and Anne Charlotte Lynch Botta's *Hand-book of Universal Literature* (1860), revised by the author.

The firm published several successful limited and subscription editions, including Francis James Child's *English and Scottish Popular Ballads* (1882) and Edward FitzGerald's translation of *The Rubáiyát of Omar Khayyám*, illustrated by Elihu Vedder and bound in Levant morocco lined with silk. Vedder's frontispiece for the *Rubáiyát*, showing a naked boy on a riverbank watching paper boats, was adapted by Sidney L. Smith at Houghton's suggestion to form the Houghton, Mifflin logo of a man in a loincloth piping paper boats toward a tiny handpress. Houghton, Mifflin also published editions of the complete works of Longfellow, Emerson, and Hawthorne in the 1880s. The Riverside Paper series, begun in 1885, included reprints of novels by Holmes, Howells, and Thomas Bailey Aldrich bound in olive grey paper covers and sold for fifty cents apiece. Periodicals published by Houghton, Mifflin during the 1880s included the *Atlantic Monthly*, edited by Aldrich, as well as *Dwight's Journal of Music*, the *Boston Medical and Surgical Journal*, the *Reporter*, the *Andover Review*, the *Journal of American Folk-Lore*, and the *United States Official Postal Guide*.

In an effort to reduce the debts left over from the Houghton, Osgood days, four partners were added to the firm: James D. Hurd, the son of Melancthon Hurd, in 1884; and James Murray Kay, Thurlow Weed Barnes, and Henry Oscar Houghton, Jr., all in 1888.

The 1890s were a critical period for Houghton, Mifflin as more than twenty of its authors died, including Lowell, Whittier, Holmes, and Harriet Beecher Stowe. Moreover, its copyrights were running out. The firm responded by publishing new illustrated editions of its standard authors. The

PARK STREET. *21 August* 1888

MS. No. *2104*   Received *20 August* 1888
By *W. Coolidge*
Title: *The Birds' Christmas Carol*

Author: *Kate Douglas Wiggin*

Author's instructions:
Receipt of MS. acknowledged:
Submitted to *H. E. S.*
Reported by reader *20 Aug.*
Character: *A striking, well-written little
story, with elements of popularity in
it. I would recommend a few pictures, + board covers with lithographic design, so as to make it
50¢ worth.*

Recommendation: *To publish.*
Report   approved   *Aug. 23* 188 *8*
Author advised
MS.   *HOH*

Horace E. Scudder, Houghton Mifflin's editor in chief for general publications from 1864 to 1902, prepared this reader's report on Wiggin's book, which had originally been privately printed in 1887. Henry Houghton approved his recommendation and published the work in November 1888. By year's end it had sold 4,000 copies.

house followed a conservative policy which allowed it to survive the Panic of 1893. On 25 August 1895 Houghton died and Mifflin assumed leadership of the firm. Henry Houghton, Jr., was placed in charge of the Riverside Press. In 1896 the firm announced 130 titles, including juveniles, poems, biographies, histories, and novels. Among the publications of that year were Lafcadio Hearn's *Kokoro: Hints and Echoes of Japanese Inner Life,* Sarah Orne Jewett's *The Country of the Pointed Firs,* John Burroughs's *Whitman: A Study,* and Woodrow Wilson's *Mere Literature.* Henry James's *The Spoils of Poynton* appeared in 1897. Elizabeth Stuart Phelps's *A Singular Life* (1895), Kate Douglas Wiggin's *Marm Lisa* (1896), Paul Leicester Ford's *The Story of an Untold Love* (1897), and F. Hopkinson Smith's *Caleb West, Master Driver* (1898) each sold more than 10,000 copies.

Two successful publications in the early twentieth century were Jack London's first book, *The Son of the Wolf* (1900), and Wiggin's *Rebecca of Sunnybrook Farm* (1903). Less commercially successful was Edwin Arlington Robinson's *Captain Craig* (1902). Between 1900 and 1909 the *Atlantic Monthly*'s fiftieth anniversary and the centenaries of Emerson, Hawthorne, Longfellow, Whittier, and Holmes led to memorials, new editions, and the publication of literary remains. In 1908 Houghton, Mifflin and Company changed from a partnership to a corporation as the Houghton Mifflin Company, with Mifflin as president, Albert F. Houghton as vice-president, and Kay as treasurer. At the same time, the *Atlantic Monthly* was sold to Ellery Sedgwick.

During the first two decades of the twentieth century, the firm's educational sales increased enormously, exceeding those of the subscription and trade divisions combined. The increase can be attributed to the leadership of James Duncan Phillips and Stephen B. Davol, joint directors of the Educational Department, and Franklin Sherman Hoyt, their editor. The enormous success of Frank M. McMurry's *How to Study* and *Teaching How to Study* (1909) led to two new series: Riverside Educational Monographs and Riverside Textbooks in Education; the most significant title was Lewis Madison Terman's *The Measurement of Intelligence* (1916) in the Textbooks in Education series. In 1911 the firm began the Riverside Readers series, which offered selections from American authors for students from the first to the eighth grades. Also in that year the firm published Lucy Fitch Perkins's *The Dutch Twins,* which inaugurated a series designed to teach American children about foreign

lands. In 1919 Hoyt introduced a new series of readers by Emma Miller Bolenius which were widely accepted. During the first two decades of the new century the Riverside Literature series added titles by Jewett, Aldrich, and Howells. By 1922 the series had over 300 titles with sales of over a million per year.

In 1910 Ferris Greenslet became editor in chief of the trade department. Important publications between 1910 and 1920 included Willa Cather's *Alexander's Bridge* (1912), *O Pioneers!* (1913), and *My Ántonia* (1918); Amy Lowell's *A Dome of Many-Colored Glass* (1912); Adams's *Mont Saint Michel and Chartres* (1913) and *The Education of Henry Adams: An Autobiography* (1918); and the New Poetry series, with works by Conrad Aiken, Hilda Doolittle, and John Gould Fletcher.

Mifflin died in 1921. In 1923 the firm moved to 2 Park Street. The textbook department brought in the major portion of profits with its Riverside Literature series, which was selling over a million copies per year. Houghton Mifflin's trade list consisted mostly of biography and personal narratives. Among its authors were Adams, Wiggin, the British historian George M. Trevelyan, and John Buchan. The company published Amy Lowell's *Legends* (1921), *A Critical Fable* (1922), and *John Keats* (1925). It also published beautifully illustrated editions of the works of Emerson, Hawthorne, James Russell Lowell, and Holmes. By the 1920s Houghton Mifflin, which had rejected the work of Vachel Lindsay, H. L. Mencken, William Rose Benét, and James Branch Cabell, had acquired a conservative reputation which made the young writers of the decade seek other publishers.

In the 1930s the firm was run by an executive committee which included Edward R. Houghton, James Duncan Phillips, Greenslet, Franklin S. Hoyt, and Henry A. Laughlin. Greenslet was the dominant figure. In the mid 1930s the firm established a separate children's department. Perhaps the major publication of the 1930s was Adolf Hitler's *Mein Kampf* (1939). Laughlin became president of the firm in 1939.

During the 1940s Houghton Mifflin published *Let Us Now Praise Famous Men* (1941) by James Agee; *Number One* (1943), *State of the Nation* (1944), *Tour of Duty* (1946), and *The Grand Design* (1949) by John Dos Passos; and *The Heart Is a Lonely Hunter* (1940), *Reflections in a Golden Eye* (1941), and *The Member of the Wedding* (1946) by Carson McCullers. It also published Winston Churchill's *The Second World War* (1948-1953) in six volumes.

William E. Spaulding, head of the Educational Department, succeeded Laughlin as president in 1957. A new logo, showing a piper riding a dolphin, was designed by Ismar David in 1958. In the 1950s and 1960s Houghton Mifflin published Agee's *The Morning Watch* (1951); Louis Auchincloss's *Sybil* (1952) and *A Law for the Lion* (1953); reprints of several Raymond Chandler novels, including *The Long Good-bye* (1954); Rachel Carson's *The Edge of the Sea* (1955) and *Silent Spring* (1962); and McCullers's *Clock without Hands* (1961). Popular children's books included H. A. Rey's stories about Curious George, Michael Bond's Paddington Bear series, and Bernard Waber's *Lyle, Lyle Crocodile* (1965). Stephen W. Grant succeeded Spaulding as president in 1963. Houghton Mifflin became a publicly owned corporation in 1967. The Riverside Press was sold in 1971.

During the 1970s Houghton Mifflin published works by Isaac Asimov, A. B. Guthrie, Jr., Roger Tory Peterson, and Agnes Sligh Turnbull. Two notable works of this period were a reprint of J. R. R. Tolkien's *The Lord of the Rings* (1974) and the first American edition of his *The Silmarillion* (1977). In 1976 Houghton Mifflin acquired Time Share Corporation, a firm in Hanover, New Hampshire, which develops computer-based educational programs and career educational materials. Three additions in 1979 were the revival of Ticknor and Fields as a subsidiary in New Haven and New York under Chester Kerr, the former director of Yale University Press; the creation of a school publishing subsidiary, The Riverside Publishing Company, in Chicago; and the acquisition of J. P. Tarcher, Incorporated, a Los Angeles trade publishing company, as a subsidiary.

Houghton Mifflin designated 1980 as the "Year of the Bird." The fourth edition of Roger Tory Peterson's *A Field Guide to the Birds* made publishing history by appearing on both the hardcover and paperback best-seller lists in the *New York Times Book Review* at the same time. Howard Fast's *The Establishment* and Tolkien's *Unfinished Tales* also made the 1980 list of best-sellers.

Houghton Mifflin's major operating segments are General Publishing and Educational Publishing. Within General Publishing, the Trade and Reference Division and Ticknor and Fields publish books for a general readership including dictionaries and reference works; and the International Division markets Houghton Mifflin publications outside the United States. Ed-

ucational Publishing includes the Houghton Mifflin School Division which publishes texts and programs for elementary and high schools; The Riverside Publishing Company in Chicago, which produces textbook programs and test materials for schools; and the College Division which publishes texts and materials for colleges and graduate schools. Educational materials accounted for more than eighty percent of the firm's sales in 1985.

Harold T. Miller is chairman, president, and chief executive officer of Houghton Mifflin. The firm's headquarters are at 1 Beacon Street, Boston 02108, with additional editorial offices at 2 Park Street in Boston and in New York and Chicago. The firm also has a Toronto branch, Houghton Mifflin Canada Limited.

References:

Ellen B. Ballou, *The Building of the House: Houghton Mifflin's Formative Years* (Boston: Houghton Mifflin, 1970);

A Catalogue of Authors Whose Works Are Published by Houghton, Mifflin and Company, Prefaced by a Sketch of the Firm, and Followed by Lists of the Several Libraries, Series, and Periodicals, with Some Account of the Origin and Character of These Literary Enterprises (Boston: Riverside Press, 1899; reprinted with supplement, 1901);

A Complete Catalogue of the Books of Houghton Mifflin Company, 1864-1922 (Cambridge: Riverside Press, 1922);

Fifty Years of Publishing: A History of the Educational Department of Houghton Mifflin Company (Boston: Houghton Mifflin, 1930);

"George Harrison Mifflin [obituary]," *New York Times*, 6 April 1921, p. 15;

Ferris Greenslet, *Under the Bridge: An Autobiography* (Boston: Houghton Mifflin, 1943);

"Henry Oscar Houghton [obituary]," *Publishers' Weekly*, 48 (7 September 1895): 307-309;

Henry A. Laughlin, *An Informal Sketch of the History of Houghton Mifflin Company* (Cambridge: Riverside Press, 1957);

Mercedes Rehm Lewis, *Houghton Mifflin Company, Past and Present* (Geneva, Ill.: Midwestern Division, 1962);

James Duncan Phillips, "Recollections of Houghton Mifflin Company Fifty Years Ago," *Publishers' Weekly*, 152 (1 November 1947): 2165-2167.

—Lynne P. Shackelford

Henry Hoyt

(Boston: circa 1858-circa 1878)

The earliest known publication of the Boston firm of Henry Hoyt was Miss O. A. Johnstone's anti-Catholic novel *Sophie de Brentz; or, the Sword of Truth* (1859). Although Hoyt was better known for its religious publications, the firm published at least twenty-five works of fiction in its roughly twenty-year history. *The Old Distillery* (1865) by Jane Greenough Avery and *The Family Doctor; or, Mrs. Barry and Her Bourbon* (1868) by Mrs. Mary (Spring) Walker reflect the firm's support of the temperance movement. Mrs. Mary Denison's *Lieutenant Messinger* (1863), M. H. Whiting's *Faith White's Letter Book, 1620-1623, Plymouth, New England* (1866), and Mrs. Caroline E. K. Davis's *Heart's Delight* (1873) were written by and for Christian women. Hoyt also published at least four novels by Mrs. Julia McNair White, two by Anna Shipton, and two by Mrs. Lydia Ann Porter. The firm's address was 9 Cornhill. During the 1870s Hoyt had an arrangement, perhaps for distribution purposes, with the Willard Tract Depository. Hoyt went out of business around 1878.

—*David Dzwonkoski*

Hudson and Goodwin

(Hartford, Connecticut: 1779-1815)

Founded in Hartford, Connecticut, in 1779 by Barzillai Hudson and George Goodwin, the printing firm of Hudson and Goodwin mainly offered reprints but occasionally published its own first editions. Among the latter were the first complete edition of John Trumbull's *M'Fingal! A Modern Epic Poem in Four Cantos* (1782), Amelia Simmons's *American Cookery* (1796), *Memoirs of Miss Elvira Van Wyck* (1813), and several works by Noah Webster. The firm printed and sold the *Children's Magazine* in 1789; it also published the *Connecticut Courant*. Many of the firm's publications were children's books. Among Hudson and Goodwin's many reprints were *The New-England Primer Improved* (1781), Webster's *The American Spelling-Book* (1787), and works by Isaac Watts.

In 1815 the partners separated to found their own firms. Hudson and Company reprinted works by Hannah More and Lucy Lyttelton Cameron for the Hartford Evangelical Tract Society and published the second American edition of Mrs. Mary Martha Sherwood's *The History of Little Henry and His Bearer* (1817). George Goodwin and Sons published reprints as well as Barbara Hoole Hofland's *The Sisters* (1815).

—*David Dzwonkoski*

Hurd and Houghton
(New York: 1864-1878)
Houghton, Osgood and Company
(New York: 1878-1880)

The New York firm of Hurd and Houghton was founded on 1 March 1864 by Melancthon Montgomery Hurd and Henry Oscar Houghton. Hurd put $50,000 into the new company; his father, a wealthy real estate speculator and railroad man, granted the firm a $20,000 loan at six percent interest. Houghton put up no cash, using his Riverside Press in Cambridge, Massachusetts, as an investment, with Hurd acquiring a half interest in the plant.

The firm was housed temporarily at 46 Walker Street; in May 1865 it moved to 401 Broadway.

Primarily a reprinter, Hurd and Houghton often published books in sets from stereotype plates acquired from other publishers. In 1865 Hurd and Houghton acquired most of the stock of the New York publisher James G. Gregory, including Nathaniel Hawthorne's *The Snow-Image* (1864), which Hurd and Houghton republished in 1868. Gregory also held the publishing rights to James Fenimore Cooper's works but retained ownership of the plates and charged Hurd and Houghton a sixteen percent royalty to use them.

In 1866 the firm took Albert G. Houghton as a partner and moved to 459 Broome Street. That year, Hurd and Houghton started two magazines, *London Society* and the *Riverside Magazine for Young People*. The latter was edited by Horace Elisha Scudder, who considered the magazine an instrument for moral instruction by example rather than by preaching. Its high-quality illustrations were contributed by Winslow Homer, Thomas Nast, F. O. C. Darley, S. G. W. Benjamin, and John La Farge. Among the writers published by the magazine were Jacob Abbott, Rose Terry, Edward Ev-

erett Hale, and Hans Christian Andersen. The magazine was a financial failure, and Hurd and Houghton transferred its subscription lists to *Scribner's Monthly* in 1870. The magazine did, however, bring to the firm books by Andersen, Helen Campbell Weeks, and Frank Stockton. Hurd and Houghton next took over the *Journal of the American Social Sciences* from Leypoldt, Holt and Williams and started a four-page monthly, the *Riverside Bulletin*, with a circulation of about 4,000. The latter publication was edited by Scudder, who filled it with critical commentary and statements of publishing philosophy. It ceased publication in December 1873.

Scudder became a partner in 1872; that same year George Harrison Mifflin and Edmund Hatch Bennett joined the firm as partners. Hurd, Henry Oscar Houghton, and Albert Houghton each had twenty-five percent shares, Scudder and Mifflin each had ten percent, and Bennett had five percent. In the 1870s Hurd and Houghton's catalogue included works by Dickens, Bacon, Macaulay, and Andersen, as well as dictionaries and books on arithmetic, medicine, Bible history, and law. Of its approximately 600 titles, the best known were its Riverside Classics—editions in which special care was given to the beauty of the volumes. The company emphasized the publication of standard works rather than the discovery of new talent; but it did publish Algernon Swinburne's play *Chastelard* (1866) and William Dean Howells's *Venetian Life* (1866), *Italian Journeys* (1867), and *Suburban Sketches* (1871). Less successful were Sidney Lanier's novel *Tiger-Lilies* (1867) and the books of Alice and Phoebe Cary.

In December 1873 Hurd and Houghton purchased from James R. Osgood and Company the *Atlantic Monthly* and *Every Saturday*. The *Atlantic Monthly* published in serial form *Roderick Hudson* (1875) and *The American* (1876) by Henry James, "A True Story" by Samuel Langhorne Clemens, and poems by Bret Harte. Although the *Atlantic Monthly* was of small commercial value, it brought prestige to the firm. In early 1878 Hurd and Albert Houghton retired for health reasons, and on 4 February of that year James R. Osgood Company and Hurd and Houghton merged to become Houghton, Osgood and Company.

Beset by disagreements among the partners, financial difficulties, and a devastating fire in December 1879, Houghton, Osgood and Company remained in business for only two years. Its sole successful publication was Howells's *The Lady of the Aroostook* (1879). In 1880 Osgood went back into business for himself, while Henry Houghton and Mifflin joined to form Houghton, Mifflin and Company.

References:

Ellen B. Ballou, *The Building of the House: Houghton Mifflin's Formative Years* (Boston: Houghton Mifflin, 1970);

"Melancthon M. Hurd [obituary]," *Publishers' Weekly*, 82 (7 December 1912): 2011-2012.

—*Lynne P. Shackelford*

Hurst and Company
(New York: 1871-1919)

Hurst and Company was founded in 1871 by the English immigrant Thomas D. Hurst at 122 Nassau Street in New York. A former electrotyper, Hurst pioneered in the production of cheap, small-format, clothbound reprints, known as "twelvemos," and other standard works unprotected by copyright. Most Hurst publications, like those of other firms specializing in cheap books, were badly printed on paper of the lowest quality.

Three of Hurst's best-known series were the Cameo Editions of the Poets, priced at thirty cents each; the Nassau Editions of classics such as *Robinson Crusoe* and *Pilgrim's Progress*, also selling for thirty cents a volume; and the Arlington Editions of popular and standard works, which were priced at one dollar and were physically somewhat superior to the usual Hurst publications. The firm published paperback dime novels in its Library of Choice Romance, Fiction and Adventure and its Popular Series of Fiction, Fancy and Face, as well as dictionaries, self-help books, etiquette guides, and medical books for laymen. Hurst also published cheap editions of juveniles, including the Young America Library for Boys and the Horatio Alger stories. Along with works bearing the Hurst imprint, Hurst's Argyle Press also printed the pirated edition of the *Encyclopaedia Britannica* published in 1890 by the Henry G. Allen Company.

In 1890 John W. Lovell leased Hurst and Company's plates for his United States Book Company, but they were returned to Hurst when Lovell's company failed in 1893. In that year Hurst sold the Argyle Press to Harris Wolff but continued to publish long after the popularity of the cheap twelvemo had passed its peak. In 1900 the firm was located at 135 Grand Street. After its founding in 1902, the Chicago firm of Reilly and Britton distributed Hurst's books in the Midwest and Far West. Hurst acquired the stock of the A. C. Gunter Publishing Company of New York when Gunter went bankrupt in 1908. In 1919, the last year the Hurst catalogue was carried by *Publishers' Trade List Annual,* the firm's address was 354 Fourth Avenue. Some of Hurst and Company's plates were bought by Platt and Munk, a firm formed in 1920 and specializing in juveniles.

Reference:

"Obituary Notes: Thomas D. Hurst," *Publishers' Weekly,* 105 (9 February 1924): 432.

—Christy L. Brown

M. J. Ivers and Company
(New York: circa 1882-circa 1905)

M. J. Ivers and Company was founded around 1882; its only known address was 379 Pearl Street, New York. Among Ivers's first publications were two books by George G. Small under the pseudonym Bricktop, *The Quiet Youth; or, Just Like His Uncle* (1882) and *The Trip of the Sardine Club; or, Tacking Up the Hudson* (1882). These, along with Henry Guy Carleton's *The South Fifth Avenue Poker Club* (1888) and Marie Corelli's *My Wonderful Wife* (1890), were among the few fiction titles published by Ivers that were not reprints.

In 1886 the firm began its American series, which, though it emphasized romances by Mrs. Humphry Ward, Ada Ellen Bayly, and Charlotte Brame, also reprinted works by H. Rider Haggard, Thomas Hardy, Jules Verne, and R. L. Stevenson. This series was followed in 1896 and 1897 by the Union series, which featured reprints of novels by Mrs. E. D. E. N. Southworth. The firm also published joke books, a self-instruction book for learning German (1886), and a parliamentary practice manual (1887).

As its business succeeded, Ivers had to face the threat of John W. Lovell, who in 1890 tried to corner the market for cheap books through his trust, the United States Book Company. Ivers, then owned by James Sullivan, was one of several publishers that successfully opposed Lovell's attempt. In 1898 Ivers purchased the plates and stock of Beadle and Adams and continued that firm's dime novel series. Ivers went out of business around 1905; its assets were acquired by the Arthur Westbrook Company of Cincinnati.

Reference:

Denis R. Rogers, *Bibliographic Listing of "Beadle's Frontier Series"* (Fall River, Mass.: Edward T. LeBlanc, 1962).

—John R. Conners

George W. Jacobs and Company
(Philadelphia: 1892-1925)

See also the Macrae Smith Company entry in *DLB 46, American Literary Publishing Houses, 1900-1980: Trade and Paperback.*

George W. Jacobs and Company was founded in Philadelphia in 1892. The firm specialized in juvenile literature and genre fiction. The former appeared in the series: The Washington Square Classics; The Children's Favorites; the Dear Little Girl series; the Four Corner series; Classics Retold to Children; the Green Acre series; the Polly Page Books; and Caroline E. Jacobs's Joan Books, including *Joan of Juniper Inn* (1907) and *Joan's Jolly Vacation* (1909). The firm's genre fiction consisted of westerns, including Ridgwell Cullum's *Night-Riders* (1913) and Edwin L. Sabin's *The Rose of Santa Fé* (1923); stories for young women, such as Amanda B. Hall's *The Little Red House in the Hollow* (1918), Doris Egerton Jones's *The Year Between* (1919), Katherine H. Taylor's *Natalie Page* (1921)

and *Cross Currents* (1922), and Shirley Watkins's *Georgina Finds Herself* (1922) and *Jane Lends a Hand* (1923); and mysteries, especially the popular works of Rupert Sargent Holland, such as *Refugee Rock* (1920), *The Panelled Room* (1921), and *The Mystery of the "Opal"* (1924). In 1925 the firm was purchased by two of its employees, Durant L. Macrae and Allan M. Smith, who renamed it the Macrae Smith Company and continued to publish many of the firm's popular authors and series. Jacobs concentrated on bookselling until his death in 1936.

References:
"George W. Jacobs [obituary]," *Publishers' Weekly*, 130 (29 August 1936): 734;

"The Macrae Smith Company: Jacobs Sells Publishing Business," *Publishers' Weekly*, 107 (3 January 1925): 38.

—David Dzwonkoski

Ferris Greenslet became editor in chief of Houghton Mifflin Company's trade department in 1910

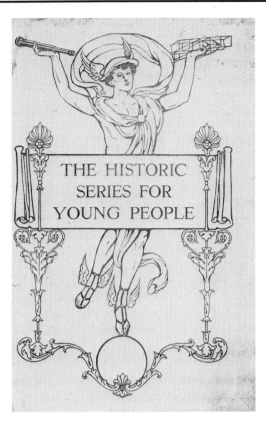

Endsheet for one of the many George W. Jacobs & Company series

Uriah Pierson James

U. P. James
(Cincinnati: 1831-1835; 1837-1847; 1854-1880)
J. A. James and Company
(Cincinnati: 1835-1837)
J. A. and U. P. James
(Cincinnati: 1847-1854)

Joseph A. and Uriah Pierson James of Goshen, New York, founded a series of publishing, bookselling, printing, and stereotyping businesses in Cincinnati, Ohio. The brothers were in business alternately as partners or separately; in each case, U. P. James was the publisher and bookseller, while J. A. James engaged in printing and stereotyping. From 6 August 1831, when they arrived in Cincinnati, until 1835, they conducted business separately under their own names; from 1833 they were located at 1 Baker Street. In 1835 they merged to form J. A. James and Company. On 1 July 1837 the partnership was dissolved and U. P. James carried on as a publisher and bookseller, moving in 1838 to 26 Pearl Street. In 1847 they formed a partnership under the imprint J. A. and U. P. James, which continued until 1 April 1854. Then the partnership was dissolved for the last time, although U. P. James maintained the firm name until 1 July of that year. At that time the business was located at 167 Walnut Street. U. P. James continued in business until the late 1870s.

U. P. James published textbooks, popular fiction, history, science, music, religion, and biography in both regular trade format and cheap (unbound or paperbound) editions. When he began his activities, Cincinnati was a center of printing and publishing, and James became the most important publisher in the region; at its peak, the firm was known as "the Harpers of the West." As railroad transportation improved in the 1850s, however, allowing more competition from East Coast firms, James was forced to rely more and more on the sale of cheap reprints, to the exclusion of trade editions.

The first work published by James was *The Eolian Songster* (1832), a copyrighted work which remained on the firm's backlist for many years. James also published such popular titles as *The Story of Sinbad the Sailor* (1833) and *The Life of Dr. Ben-jamin Franklin, Written By Himself* (1833). By the late 1830s an increasing number of the firm's novels appeared in paper covers and sold for about fifty cents. Among these editions were Edward Bulwer's *Calderon, the Courtier* and *Leila; or, The Siege of Granada,* both in 1838. Scott's Waverly novels were published in this format in the mid 1840s.

James's most popular author was Emerson Bennett, whose *The Prairie Flower* and *Leni-Leoti* the firm reprinted in 1850. Eventually James had stereotype plates for thirteen of Bennett's approximately fifty novels. James occasionally bought plates from other publishers, as in 1860, when he acquired seven novels by G. P. R. James, three by Bulwer, and two by Eugène Sue. In addition to selling his publications in his own shop and exchanging copies of his books for those of other firms, James employed canvassers. For this market he created several special volumes, among them *The Library of General Knowledge; Embracing History, Biography, Astronomy, Architecture, Natural History, Poetry, Tales, Etc. Etc.* (1850) and *The Universal Pictorial Library* (1851).

After 1860 James's cheap publications began to face increased competition from dime novels, a format in which James never published. Currency difficulties in the United States compelled him to conduct his business strictly on a cash basis, further limiting his activity. In 1880, after several years of inactivity as a publisher, he sold the stereotype plates of 137 works. At that time the firm's address was 177 Race Street. When James died in 1889 at the age of seventy-eight, his son inherited the firm as a bookstore with no associated publishing business.

Reference:
"Uriah Pierson James," *American Geologist*, 3 (May 1889): 281-285.

—Philip A. Metzger

*Agreement between Albert and John W. Picket, authors of a series of schoolbooks, and U. P. James and Cyrus Cropper,
their publishers*

John P. Jewett and Company

(*Boston: 1847-1857*)

Born in 1814, John P. Jewett began his career in a bookstore and bindery in Salem, Massachusetts. In 1847 he started his own book and music store in Boston at 20 Washington Street, where he began publishing. The early publications of John P. Jewett and Company were primarily textbooks and readers. The firm's first novel was Elizabeth Stuart Phelp's *The Sunny Side; or, The Country Minister's Wife* (1851), followed a year later by her *The Angel over the Right Shoulder; or, The Beginning of a New Year.* Though both of these books were brief—135 and 29 pages, respectively—Jewett rapidly took on longer novels and expanded into other fields, gaining a reputation as a publisher of religious, temperance, and abolitionist titles. The firm set up a branch in Cleveland known as Jewett, Proctor and Worthington.

Today the firm is remembered for its grand coup in securing the publishing rights to Harriet Beecher Stowe's *Uncle Tom's Cabin* (1852). The abolitionist novel was first published as a serial in the *National Era.* While it was running there, Mrs. Stowe offered the novel to Phillips, Sampson and Company for book publication, but the house turned her down in fear of offending its southern customers. Jewett, who had been reading the serial, sought out the author and offered her a choice of an equal share in the costs and profits or a ten percent royalty; Stowe chose the royalty and thus lost out on a fortune. In March 1852, two months before the conclusion of the serial, the book was published in two volumes at $2.50. Within a few days the first printing of 10,000 copies was sold out; by the end of the year 305,000 copies had been sold, including a one-volume edition priced at 37 1/2¢. Jewett ran advertisements recording the phenomenal sales; he also took copies of the book to Washington and encouraged important political figures to read it. When national interest in the book rose he published Mrs. Stowe's *A Key to Uncle Tom's Cabin* (1853).

Most of the fiction Jewett published reflected his interest in religious topics and New England history: Jane Chaplin's *The Convent and the Manse* (1853); Martha Hubbell's *The Shady Side; or, Life in a Country Parsonage* (1853); Cora Lynn's *Durham Village: A Temperance Tale* (1854); Charles P. Ilsley's *Forest and Shore, or, Legends of the Pine-Tree State* (1856), a collection of short stories; Joseph Reynolds's *Peter Gott, the Cape Ann Fisherman* (1856); and Martha Russell's *Leaves from the Tree Igdrasyl* (1854), another short story collection. The firm also published theological works, a history of California, a music encyclopedia, and a reprint of Margaret Fuller's *Woman in the Nineteenth Century* (1855). Lucy Larcom's first book, *Similitudes,* was published by Jewett in 1854. In the same year, the firm published another best-seller—*The Lamplighter* by Maria Susanna Cummins, a sentimental novel of the adventures of a young girl. The novel sold 40,000 copies in the first eight weeks. Jewett went out of business in the Panic of 1857, selling his stock to the firm of Crosby and Nichols. He later resumed bookselling but never returned to publishing. He died in 1884.

—*Lynne P. Shackelford*
Everett C. Wilkie, Jr.

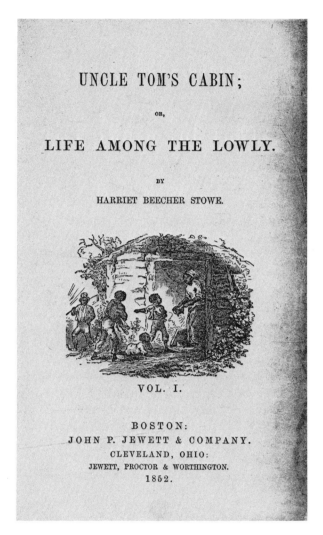

Title page for Stowe's most famous novel. Offered a choice between an equal share in printing costs and profits or a ten percent royalty, Stowe chose the royalty. John P. Jewett and Company made a fortune on the book's sales.

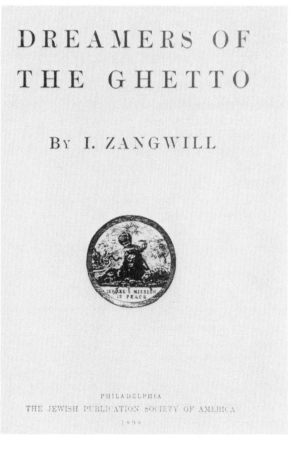

Title page for the second of Zangwill's books to be published by the Society

The Jewish Publication Society
(Philadelphia: 1985-   )
The Jewish Publication Society of America
(Philadelphia: 1888-1985)

THE JEWISH PUBLICATION SOCIETY OF AMERICA

The Jewish Publication Society is the successor to two earlier organizations. The American Jewish Publication Society was founded in Philadelphia in 1845 by Rabbi Isaak Leeser to provide inexpensive scholarly and religious works to the growing number of Jewish immigrants to America. The society had published only fourteen books when a fire in 1851 destroyed its plates and stock and thus ended its brief existence. Twenty years later, a second American Jewish Publication Society was founded in Philadelphia by Leopold Bamberger, B. J. Hart, Myer Stern, and Simon Wolf. This society published five volumes before it went out of business in 1875.

The Jewish Publication Society of America was established in Philadelphia in 1888 by a group of Jewish leaders who elected Morris Newburger as president and Rabbi Joseph Krauskopf as secretary. The firm's first publication was Lady Katie Magnus's *Outlines of Jewish History* (1890). From 1891 to 1898 it published Heinrich Graetz's six-volume *History of the Jews*. While the society stresses works relating to Jewish history, culture, and religion, a small percentage of its more than 700 publications have been literary. Its first novel was Israel Zangwill's *The Children of the Ghetto* (1892), followed by Louis Schnable's *Vögele's Marriage* (1892), Zangwill's *Dreamers of the Ghetto* (1898), and Samuel Gordon's *Sons of the Covenant* (1900). Later fiction included Ludwig Lewisohn's *Renegade* (1942) and Charles Reznikoff's *The Lionhearted* (1944). The society also published fiction by Selma Stern, Richard Beer-Hoffman, and Soma Morgenstern during the 1940s.

Among the society's translations from the Yiddish were I. L. Peretz's *Stories and Pictures* (1906) and *Yiddish Tales* (1912), Sholem Asch's *Kiddush Ha-Shem* (1926) and *Sabbatai Zevi* (1930), and Joseph Opatoshu's *In Polish Woods* (1938) and *The Last Revolt* (1952). Translations from the Hebrew include Judah Steinberg's *In Those Days* (1915), H. N. Bialik's collection of poetry *Aftergrowth* (1939), and A. M. Klein's *Poems* (1944). Since 1920 the Jewish Publication Society has published books in Hebrew, Slavic, and Oriental languages under the imprint of The Hebrew Press.

With Charles R. Weiner as president, the society continues its contribution to literature mainly through its Jewish Poetry series. Edited by Yehuda Amichai and Allen Mandelbaum, the series includes *In Light of Genesis* (1980), by Pamela White Hadas; *The Syrian-African Rift and Other Poems* (1980), translated from the Hebrew of Avoth Yeshurun; and *Hebrew Ballads and Other Poems* (1981), a translation from the German of Else Lasker-Schüler. The society has also published Haim Hazaz's novel *Gates of Bronze* (1975), as well as several anthologies. Although the society offers discounts to members, it is not a book club. Sales are by mail and through book dealers. From 1958 to 1975 the society was located at 22 North Fifteenth Street; from 1975 to 1977 at 1528 Walnut Street; and from 1975 to 1983 at 117 South Seventeenth Street. Its current address is 1930 Chestnut Street, Philadelphia 19103. The society dropped *of America* from its name in 1985.

References:

Joshua Bloch, *Of Making Many Books: An Annotated List of the Books Issued By the Jewish Publication Society of America* (Philadelphia: Jewish Publication Society of America, 1953);

Maurice Jacobs, "Two Generations of Jewish Literary Labor: Sixty Years of the Jewish Publication Society of America," *Jewish Book Annual*, 7 (1948-1949): 89-100;

"Jewish Society Celebrates Anniversary," *Publishers'*

Weekly, 133 (21 May 1938): 2002;

Charles A. Madison, *Jewish Publishing in America 1890-1952* (New York: Sanhedrin Press, 1976), pp. 25-42.

—David Dzwonkoski

Benjamin Johnson
(Philadelphia: 1792-circa 1810)

Benjamin Johnson's printing and publishing business was located at 147 Market Street, Philadelphia. As early as 1790 he is known to have worked at this location with a man named James. Johnson's name appears alone in his imprints from 1792 until 1796, when it frequently appears with that of Jacob Johnson. Another Johnson—Robert—sometimes jointly published with them in 1804 and 1805. The relationship of the three men is unknown, but because they all published during the same time period, and frequently from the same location, it is assumed that they were members of the same family.

Benjamin Johnson published Vicesimus

Knox's *Essays Moral and Literary* (1792), the second and third American editions of *The Christian, a Poem; in Six Books* (1794) by Charles Crawford, a reprint of *Captain Cook's Third and Last Voyage to the Pacific Ocean in the Years 1776-1780* (1796), reprints of Hannah More's *Tawney Rachel; or The Fortune Teller* (1798) and *The History of Tom White, the Postillon* (1798), and William Collins's *The Poetical Works* (1805). Johnson also published almanacs, textbooks, technical works, and religious tracts. His business apparently terminated around 1810.

—Elizabeth Hoffman

Benjamin, Jacob, and Robert Johnson
(Philadelphia: 1796-1805)

From 1796 to 1805 the names of two Philadelphia publishers, Benjamin and Jacob Johnson, appear alone or jointly on title pages; in 1804 and 1805 Robert Johnson's name sometimes appears with theirs. Because the three men published from the same location, it has been assumed that they were members of the same family.

Dealing mainly in reprints, the Johnsons published almanacs, juveniles, textbooks, and the works of European authors. In 1799 Benjamin and Jacob Johnson published *Christmas Tales, for the Amusement and Instruction of Young Ladies and Gentlemen in Winter Evenings* by "Solomon Sobersides" and *The Life and Adventures of Baron Friedrich Trenck* by Trenck. In 1800 Benjamin and Jacob published several dozen religious pamphlets, most of them

by the British author Hannah More, as well as an abridgment of *Murray's English Grammar* by Lindley Murray. The following year they published Edward A. Kendall's *The Canary Bird: A Moral Story*.

In 1804 Robert Johnson's name appears with Benjamin's in the publication of Robert Burns's *The Poetical Works*. That year Benjamin, Jacob, and Robert Johnson published Mark Akenside's *The Pleasures of Imagination*, Thomas Gray's *The Poetical Works*, and Milton's *The Poetical Works*, while Benjamin and Jacob published *Paradise Lost*. In 1805 all three published William Hayley's *The Life and Posthumous Writings of William Cowper* and *The Poetical Works of Joseph Addison with the Life of the Author*.

—Elizabeth Hoffman

Jacob Johnson and Company
(Philadelphia: 1792-1808)
Johnson and Warner
(Philadelphia: 1808-1833)
Grigg, Elliot and Company
(Philadelphia: 1833-1850)

Starting in 1792, Jacob Johnson, a printer, publisher, and bookseller, maintained a bookstore at 147 Market Street in Philadelphia; apparently he operated his printshop at the same location. Johnson's name frequently appears on imprints with that of Benjamin Johnson, who was located at the same address. Some publishing historians have speculated that Benjamin and Jacob Johnson may have been the same person, but imprints showing Jacob's and Benjamin's names together as well as separately suggest that they were two different men. In 1804 and 1805 a third Johnson occasionally joined them at the same address under the imprint Benjamin, Jacob, and Robert Johnson. The relationship of these three men is unknown, but they were probably members of the same family.

Reprints and children's books constituted most of Jacob Johnson's literary publications. The firm published Henry Fielding's *The History of Tom Jones, a Foundling* (1794); *The Death of Cain, in Five Books; after the Manner of the Death of Abel* (1796) by "a Lady"; and *Footsteps to the Natural History of Birds* (1803), illustrated by the renowned engraver Dr. Alexander Anderson. Johnson's children's titles included William Darton's *First Chapter of Accidents, and Remarkable Events* (1802) and *A Present for a Little Boy* (1802); Clara English's *The Children in the Wood* (1803); *The Prize for Youthful Obedience* (1803), another volume with illustrations by Anderson; Maria Edgeworth's *Idleness and Industry Exemplified* (1803) and the first American editions of her *The Bracelets* (1804) and *The Barring Out; or, Party Spirit* (1804); and *The Peasant's Repast; or, The Benevolent Physician* (1808) by Arnaud Berquin.

In 1808 Johnson formed a partnership with Benjamin Warner. Johnson and Warner maintained a bookselling and publishing business, primarily in children's literature, until around 1815, when Johnson sold his share of the partnership to Warner. Among the firm's children's titles were *Remarks on a Set of Cuts for Children* (1809) by Lady Eleanor Fenn, *Juvenile Anecdotes* (1809) by Priscilla Wakefield, and *The Cowslip, Or More Cautionary Stories, in Verse* (1813) by Mrs. Elizabeth Turner.

In 1816 Warner and John Grigg became partners. Warner died in 1823; in 1833 Hugh Elliot became a partner with Grigg, and the firm's name was changed to Grigg, Elliot and Company. Joshua Ballinger Lippincott bought the business in 1850.

—*Elizabeth Hoffman*

Jones's Publishing House

(Boston: circa 1844-circa 1894)

Justin Jones, an aspiring author of adventure tales, founded Jones's Publishing House around 1844 at 82 Washington Street, Boston, with the intention of doing book and job printing. Around this time Jones began to sell his adventure stories, most of which were written under the pseudonym Harry Hazel, to magazine and cheap book publishers. In 1846 Jones, seeing the success of other publishers in bringing out his Harry Hazel stories, began to publish his own work under the imprint of Jones's Publishing House, although just as often the imprint was "Published by the author."

In 1847 Jones founded the *Star Spangled Banner*, a weekly story paper patterned after Maturin M. Ballou and Frederick Gleason's *Flag of Our Union*, which had been started in January 1846 and to which Jones had contributed. The *Star Spangled Banner* offered adventure stories, romances, advice columns, and general interest items. Jones's Harry Hazel stories were the predominant feature of the magazine, but he also published work by J. H. Robinson, Joseph Holt Ingraham, and Edward Z. C. Judson, who, under the pen name Ned Buntline, was one of the most successful writers of his day.

Jones next started the *Union Jack*, a story paper concentrating on tales of piracy and nautical adventure, and followed it with another nautical magazine, the *Yankee Privateer*, around 1850. In 1856 Jones launched yet another story weekly, the *Parlour Casket;* this effort only lasted two years. Around this time Jones moved his offices to 2 Water Street. Jones had also begun to publish novels and novelettes by writers other than himself, using the imprints Jones's Publishing House and "At the offices of The Star Spangled Banner." Among the few literary titles published under the Jones's Publishing House imprint were Mrs. Eliza Sheridan's *Ellen Fenton; or, The Miser of the North End* (1847) and John Townsend Trowbridge's *Kate the Accomplice; or, The Preacher and the Burglar* (1849) under the pseudonym Paul Creyton. Jones achieved his greatest success publishing his own Harry Hazel books, including *Fourpe Tap; or, The Middy of the Macedonian* (1847) and *Hasserac, the Thief-Taker; or, The Rival Sisters of Trimount* (1849).

By the late 1850s Jones had apparently concluded that selling his Harry Hazel stories to other publishers would be more profitable than publishing them himself. In 1859 he sold the subscription list of his remaining magazine, the *Yankee Privateer,* to Street and Smith and became a regular contributor to that publisher's *New York Weekly*. In 1864 he bought the *Yankee Blade*, a literary weekly, converted it to a story weekly, and published it until 1894. Although the date of Jones's death is unknown, it appears that his publishing career ended with the *Yankee Blade*.

—Timothy D. Murray

Orange Judd, who bought Charles M. Saxton's publishing company when Saxton died in 1864. Judd had been editor of Saxton's American Agriculturist *magazine.*

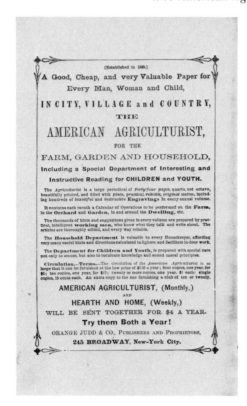
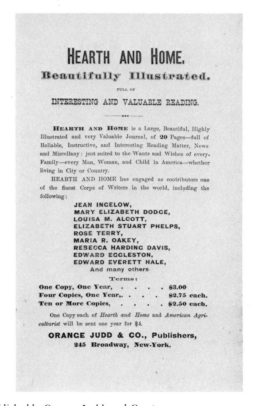

Advertisements for the two magazines published by Orange Judd and Company

Orange Judd Publishing Company
(New York: 1864-1972)
Charles M. Saxton
(New York: 1836-1843; 1845-1864)
Miles and Saxton
(New York: 1843-1845)

In 1836 Charles M. Saxton founded a firm at 191 Nassau Street in New York to sell and publish books on agriculture and gardening. In 1843 Early E. Miles became a partner in the firm, which moved to 205 Broadway. Miles sold his interest to Saxton in 1845. Around the early 1850s Saxton moved to 152 Fulton Street. In 1853 Orange Judd was hired as an assistant on the staff of Saxton's magazine, the *American Agriculturist;* by 1864 Judd was editor of the magazine and had also published a few agriculture books. When Saxton died that year, Judd bought the company and renamed it the Orange Judd Publishing Company. The firm's address was 245 Broadway, New York.

Judd published *Hearth and Home,* a weekly whose contributors included Louisa May Alcott. The firm also published Edward Eggleston's *The Hoosier School-Master* (1871), *The End of the World* (1872), and *The Mystery of Metropolisville* (1873); John Esten Cooke's *Pretty Mrs. Gaston and Other Sto-* ries (1874); and Rebecca Harding Davis's *John Andross* (1874).

Orange Judd Publishing Company failed in 1883 but was reorganized under the presidency of Judd's brother, David Judd. Orange Judd died in 1892. In 1921 the book division was purchased by George E. Eiermann, who was succeeded by his son George in 1951. The firm of Orange Judd was acquired in 1963 by Howell Book House of New York. The Orange Judd imprint disappeared in 1972.

References:

"Obituary: Orange Judd," *Publishers' Weekly,* 42 (31 December 1892): 1158;
"Orange Judd—100 Years Old," *Publishers' Weekly,* 129 (15 February 1936): 800-803.

—John H. Laflin

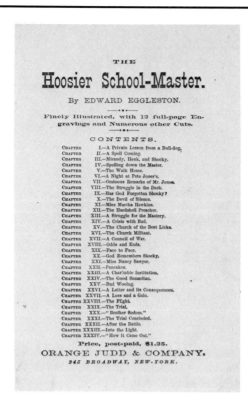

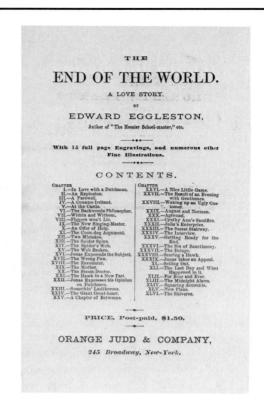

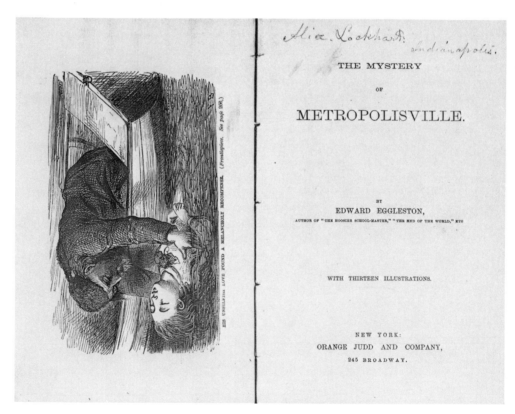

Advertisements and frontispiece and title page for the three Edward Eggleston works published by Orange Judd and Company. The
Hoosier School-Master *was a popular success for the firm.*

W. B. Keen, Cooke and Company

(Chicago: 1869-1877)

In 1850 William Brantley Keen joined his brother Joseph Keen, Jr., a retail bookseller and stationer on State Street in Chicago. In 1852 D. B. Cooke, having served an apprenticeship with H. W. Derby and Company in Cincinnati, established his own store at 135 Lake Street in Chicago. In 1869 William Keen and Cooke formed the partnership of W. B. Keen, Cooke and Company at 113-115 State Street. The firm sold books and stationery.

The company's store was destroyed in the great Chicago fire of 1871. After a time in temporary quarters near the lakeshore, the firm moved to the elegantly appointed William and Ferry Building, which it shared with A. S. Barnes and Company. Keen, Cooke and Company embarked on a publishing schedule that included *The Expressman and the Detective* by Allan Pinkerton, the famous Chicago detective. With *The Expressman and the Detective* an immediate best-seller, Keen, Cooke and Company rapidly published more books by Pinkerton. The publishers assured readers that the "thrilling and beautifully written Detective Stories, all true to life," were based on Pinkerton's actual ex-

periences. Another popular book published by Keen, Cooke and Company was J. Stanley Grimes's *Mysteries of the Head and the Heart Explained* (1875), a work on phrenology, hypnotism, and spiritualism. From 1874 to 1876 the firm published a monthly literary magazine, the *Owl*, which sold for twenty-five cents a year but was distributed to libraries.

Weakened by the hard times brought on by the panic of 1873, Keen, Cooke and Company declared bankruptcy in 1877 and the partners went separate ways. W. B. Keen and Company became a wholesale jobber in books and stationery, and D. B. Cooke and Company returned to the retail book business.

Reference:

Madeleine B. Stern, "Keen and Cooke: Prairie Publishers," *Journal of the Illinois State Historical Society*, 42 (1949): 424-445.

—*Linda DeLowry-Fryman*

Kelly, Piet and Company
(Baltimore: 1869-1879)
Kelly, Hedian and Piet
(Baltimore: 1859-1863)
Kelly and Piet
(Baltimore: circa 1863-1869)
John B. Piet
(Baltimore: 1879-1882)
John B. Piet and Company
(Baltimore: 1882-1884)
Baltimore Publishing Company
(Baltimore: 1884-1894)

Michael J. Kelly, John B. Piet, and P. J. Hedian founded Kelly, Hedian and Piet at 174 West Baltimore Street, Baltimore, in 1859. Kelly, Hedian and Piet published Catholic novels, including Thomas Low Nichols's *Father Larkin's Mission in Jonesville* (1860) and John Boyce's *Mary Lee; or, The Yankee in Ireland* (1860). After Hedian's departure in the early 1860s, the firm became Kelly and Piet. When Theophilus J. Kelly joined his brother Michael and Piet in 1869, the name was changed to Kelly, Piet and Company. By 1874 the firm offered a catalogue of over fifty textbooks, catechisms, and liturgical works, including the Virginia Military Institute series of textbooks. The firm also published the *Maryland School Journal* and the *Catholic Mirror*.

In addition to volumes of Molière, Racine, de Staël, and de Sévigné in French and Aesop and Ovid in Latin, Kelly, Piet and Company published several novels by contemporary American writers, including Lady Georgiana Fullerton's *The Gold-digger and Other Verses* (1872); Cardinal Wiseman's *Dramas* (1872); Mrs. Charles Snell's *Isabelle de Verneuil; or The Convent of St. Mary's* (1873); and Julia Amanda Wood's *Hubert's Wife* (1875), *The Brown House at Duffield* (1876), and *Strayed from the Fold* (1878), all under the pseudonym of Minnie Mary Lee. Soon after the death of Michael Kelly in 1879, the firm became John B. Piet. It was renamed John B. Piet and Company in 1882 when John B. Piet, Jr., and Stephen Tongue joined the firm. It went through bankruptcy proceedings in July 1884 and was reorganized as the Baltimore Publishing Company. In 1894 its plates and stock were purchased by P. J. Kenedy.

—David Dzwonkoski

P. J. Kenedy and Sons
(New York: 1904-1982)
John Kenedy
(Baltimore; New York: 1826-1865)
John Kenedy and Son
(New York: 1865-1866)
P. J. Kenedy
(New York: 1866-1904)

John Kenedy, after immigrating to America from Ireland, supported himself as a schoolmaster trader, and bookseller before branching out into publishing. Starting out in 1826 on Franklin Street in Baltimore, the firm soon moved to the Maryland Arcade at Center Market Place. Kenedy started his publishing endeavors with short-lived general humor weeklies, *The Budget of Blunders* in 1830 and *The Budget of Fun* in 1833. His earliest recorded Catholic publication, the Reverend Edward Damphoux's *The Practice of Christian Perfection*, appeared in 1834. The following year Kenedy published *The American Songster,* and also moved to 17 Harrison Street. In 1838 the business was relocated to New York, where it specialized in Catholic and Irish publications. Operations were conducted successively at 39 Elm Street, 180 1/2 Division Street, 47 Centre Street, and by 1847 at 47 Mott Street.

After Kenedy's death in 1866, his son Patrick John stabilized and built up the business, supporting expansion through a prosperous real estate empire. P. J. Kenedy expanded the prayerbook offerings, beginning with *The Key of Heaven* (1867) and continuing with such religious classics as *Gems of Prayer*. The firm moved to 5 Barclay Street in 1873.

Irish books were important Kenedy staples from the start. John Kenedy had published Edward Hay's *History of the Irish Insurrection of 1798* in 1846, and at 5 Barclay Street, P. J. Kenedy sublet space for a while—with good results for business—to the editorial offices of the politically active paper *Irish World*. Kenedy published the Irish Fireside Library and such titles as *Turf-Fire Stories and Fairy Tales of Ireland* (1890). Under the pseudonym Christine Faber, Mary E. Smith wrote *Carroll O'Donoghue: A Tale of the Irish Struggles of 1866, and of Recent Times* (1881), *A Mother's Sacrifice; or, Who Was Guilty* (1885), *The Guardian's Mystery; or, Rejected for Consciences' Sake* (1888), and *Ambition's Contest; or, Faith and Intellect* (1896).

Kenedy expanded for the most part by acquiring the plates and stock of failing publishing firms. In 1877, through the purchase of the stock and plates of T. W. Strong's Excelsior Catholic Publishing House, Canon Schmid's children's stories came to Kenedy. In 1894 Kenedy acquired the poems of Father Abram Ryan, "Poet Priest of the South," and the writings of Bishop John England from the Baltimore Publishing Company. Plates and titles were also purchased from Sheehy, Haverty, McGee, Collier, and Sadlier. Kenedy was named publisher to the Holy Apostolic See in 1895.

Kenedy's sons Arthur and Louis Kenedy officially joined the enterprise in 1904, when it was incorporated as P. J. Kenedy and Sons. At P. J. Kenedy's death in 1906, Arthur Kenedy succeeded to the presidency. The firm moved to 44 Barclay Street in 1911. Also in 1911 Kenedy and Sons acquired *The Official Catholic Directory,* a record of

Patrick John Kenedy, who took over the company after his father's death in 1866 and supported it with money earned from his real estate dealings

Engraved title page for a bound edition of the firm's German-language humor magazine, started in 1876. One year later the company began publishing an English edition.

Catholic activities in America, from Wiltzius and Company of Milwaukee. Under Arthur Kenedy, the firm acquired American rights to works by St. Thérèse of Lisieux, Archbishop Goodier, and Monsignor Robert Hugh Benson's *By What Authority?* (1925) and *The King's Achievement* (1925). Louis Kenedy became president in 1927. The firm moved to 12 Barclay Street in 1932. In 1943, with the acquisition of the lists of the John Murphy Company of Baltimore, Kenedy gained Cardinal James Gibbons's *The Faith of Our Fathers*, first published in 1876.

The Kenedy backlists were reduced from more than 500 titles in 1904 to fewer than 300 in 1926 and fewer than 150 in 1951. When Louis Kenedy retired as president in 1953, retaining his position as chairman of the board, Arthur Reid Kenedy, great-grandson of the founder and a member of the board since 1938, became president. In 1955 a selection of the writings of Orestes Augustus Brownson came out. Father Martin Scott and Bishop Fulton J. Sheen were also represented on the list.

In 1969 the house became a subsidiary of the Macmillan Publishing Company at 866 Third Avenue. By the late 1970s Kenedy and Sons was publishing only *The Official Catholic Directory*. The Kenedy logo, designed by William Dana Orcutt, represents, according to Robert C. Healey, the firm's official chronicler, "a tree planted in 1826, bearing fruit in books, illumined by the light of faith."

References:
Lisa Fay, "P. J. Kenedy & Sons," *Catholic Library World*, 28 (1956-1957): 67-70;
Robert C. Healey, *A Catholic Book Chronicle: The Story of P. J. Kenedy & Sons, 1826-1951* (New York: Kenedy, 1951);
"Patrick John Kenedy [obituary]," *Publishers' Weekly*, 69 (13 January 1906): 48;
Philip N. Schuyler, ed., "P. J. Kenedy," in *The Hundred Year Book* (New York: Barnes, 1942), pp. 97-98.

—Sharon Ann Jaeger

Keppler and Schwarzmann
(New York: 1876-1913)

After Joseph Keppler, a Viennese immigrant, failed in attempts to start German comic periodicals in St. Louis, he moved to New York. There he formed a partnership at 23 Warren Street with A. Schwarzmann, a printer, to publish *Puck*, a weekly magazine of humor and satire in German. Publication of the magazine began in September 1876, and by the following year, with the encouragement of the playwright Sidney Rosenfeld, who served as editor in 1877 and 1878, the firm began publishing an English edition. Within five years circulation had soared to 80,000. *Puck* thrived because of the sharp political satire in Keppler's lithograph cartoons; the literary talent of H. C. Bunner, who edited the journal from 1878 until his death in 1896; and Schwarzmann's technical and business ability.

During the 1890s the firm published several collections of material from *Puck*. Though he wrote poetry and novels (most published by Scribner), Bunner was best known for his short stories and sketches, published by Keppler and Schwarzmann as "*Short Sixes*" (1891), *The Runaway Browns* (1892), *More "Short Sixes"* (1894), and *The Suburban Sage* (1896). "*Made in France*" (1893) contained Bunner's adaptations of Maupassant stories, and one of his own which so closely matched Maupassant's style that no one noticed the difference. Keppler and Schwarzmann also published collections by other contributors to *Puck*, including James Lauren Ford's *Hypnotic Tales and Other Tales* (1891), Richard Munkittrick's *Some New Jersey Arabian Nights* (1892), and *Zigzag Tales from the East to the West* (1894) by

Harry Leon Wilson, who succeeded Bunner as editor from 1896 to 1902. *Mavericks* (1892) and *Hanks* (1893) were other collections from *Puck*. The volumes were illustrated with lithographs by C. J. Taylor and other artists, and were advertised only in the pages of the journal.

When Keppler died in 1894, his son carried on his work and *Puck* continued until 1918, though its most successful period was over. The firm of Keppler and Schwarzmann published the magazine until December 1913, when the company was disbanded and *Puck* was sold to a company headed by Nathan Straus, Jr.

Reference:

"Joseph Keppler [obituary]," *Publishers' Weekly*, 45 (24 February 1894): 356.

—*Jane I. Thesing*

Charles H. Kerr and Company
(Chicago: 1886-   )

Charles H. Kerr and Company, the major socialist publisher of the late nineteenth and early twentieth centuries in the United States, was established in Chicago in 1886 by Charles Hope Kerr, the son of abolitionists. The company was incorporated as a cooperative enterprise in 1893. A 1900 catalogue advertised "books on socialism, free thought, economics, history, hypnotism, hygiene, American fiction, etc." According to Walter B. Rideout, the cooperative published, for the most part, "subliterary material—theoretical writing, editorial comment, exposé story, personal narrative, polemic, and the like," dealing with international socialism.

Among the firm's socialist novels and story collections were *Beyond the Black Ocean* (1901) by Thomas McGrady, *Rebels of the New South* (1905) by Walter Marion Raymond, *The Recording Angel* (1905) by Edwin Arnold Brenholtz, *When Things Were Doing* (1908) by C. A. Steere, and *Stories of the Struggle* (1908) by Morris Winchevsky. The firm's most notable publications of literary interest were an early Carl Sandburg pamphlet, *You and Your Job* (1905); Ernest Poole's first book, *Katharine Breshkovsky: For Russia's Freedom* (1905); and Jack London's *The Apostate* (1906?).

Kerr was the first publisher of the complete English text of Karl Marx's *Capital* (1906-1909), translated by Ernest Untermann. The company also published the first extended piece of Marxist literary criticism by an American to be published in the United States—*Goethe's Faust: A Fragment of Socialist Criticism* (1908) by Marcus Hitch. The firm's ten-volume Library of Science for the Workers included Wilhelm Boelsche's *The Evolution of Man* (1905), translated by Untermann, and *The Triumph of Life* (1906), translated by May Wood; M. Wilhelm Meyer's *The End of the World* (1905) and *The Making of the World* (1906); R. H. France's *Germs of Mind in Plants* (1905); Dr. E. Teichmann's *Life and Death: A Study in Biology* (1906); and Friedrich Nietzsche's *Human, All Too Human* (1908), translated by Alexander Harvey. The Nietzsche volume was one of the earliest translations of the philosopher's works into English.

The firm began publishing the monthly *International Socialist Review* in July 1900. The *Review* began as a scholarly journal edited by Algie M. Simons. It contained theoretical articles by European and American socialists, book reviews, and an occasional short story, including a few by London. Simons resigned in 1908 and Kerr briefly took over as editor before Mary Marcy assumed the position. Under her editorship the *Review* shifted its orientation to a popular and more radical format, to coincide with the rapid growth of the Socialist party and the Industrial Workers of the World. Publishing graphic accounts of worldwide labor and industrial conflicts, as well as poems by Sandburg, Joe Hill, and Charles Ashleigh, the *Review* had a circulation of 50,000 in 1912. Increasingly harassed by the federal government for its antiwar views and alleged violations of the Espionage Act, the *Review* ceased publication in February 1918.

After the First World War, Kerr experienced financial difficulties and began to retrench, confining itself mostly to republishing Marxist classics. It currently publishes about eight titles a year on American labor history, including *The Pullman Strike* (1973) by William H. Carwardine, *Lucy Parsons, American Revolutionary* (1976) by Carolyn Ashbaugh, and *Haymarket Scrapbook: A Centennial Anthology* (1986), edited by Dave Roediger and

Franklin Rosemont. Joseph Giganti is president. Fred Thomspon is vice-president, and Penelope Rosemont is secretary-treasurer. The company has had several addresses since its founding, including 56 Fifth Avenue, 175 Monroe Street, 264 East Kinzie Street, 118 West Kinzie, 153 East Kinzie, 341-349 East Ohio Street, 500-510 North Dearborn Street, and 600 West Jackson. Its current address is 1740 West Greenleaf, Chicago 60626. Kerr died in 1944.

References:

Herbert G. Gutman, "The International Socialist Review," in *The American Radical Press: 1880-1960*, edited by Joseph R. Conlin, 2 volumes (Westport, Conn.: Greenwood Press, 1974), I: 82-86;

Allen M. Ruff, "Socialist Publishing in Illinois: Charles H. Kerr & Company of Chicago, 1886-1928," *Illinois Historical Journal*, 79 (Spring 1986).

—Kathleen McGowan

Key and Biddle
(Philadelphia: 1833-1836)

From 1833 to 1836 Key and Biddle of Philadelphia published works of contemporary popular writers, including James Hall's *Legends of the West* (1832), *The Harpe's Head; A Legend of Kentucky* (1833), and *The Soldier's Bride and Other Tales* (1833); William Gilmore Simms's *The Book of My Lady: A Melange* (1833); the first edition of Lydia H. Sigourney's *Sketches* (1834), which was reprinted at least five times by other publishers; and two editions of Sigourney's *Poems* in 1834 and 1836. Several works of the Scottish scientific writer Thomas Dick, including three editions of *The Philosophy of Religion*, were published by Key and Biddle between 1833 and 1836; *The Works of Thomas Dick*, in three volumes, appeared in 1836. Key and Biddle also published the *American Quarterly Review* during 1834. The firm's address was 23 Minor Street, Philadelphia.

—Elizabeth Hoffman

Kiggins and Kellogg
(New York: 1830?-1866)
Kiggins and Tooker
(New York: 1866-1882)
Henry Kiggins and Company
(New York: 1882-1885)

Kiggins and Kellogg was operated by Henry Kiggins and A. W. Kellogg during the early to mid nineteenth century in New York. Although the firm published children's literature and schoolbooks, its major business was the manufacture of account books and the sale of stationery.

Located first at 10 John Street and later at 88 John Street, Kiggins and Kellogg moved in 1856 to 123-125 William Street, where it began publishing rather flimsy children's books. Referred to as "Toy Books" due to their size, about 3 1/8 x 2 inches, they were published in four twelve-book series. Titles included *Tom Thumb's Alphabet in Rhyme, The Little Sketch Book; or, Useful Objects Illustrated,* and *The Book of the Sea; for the Instruction of Little Sailors,* all illustrated with woodcuts. Other Kiggins and Kellogg publications of the 1850s were

The Book of Fables, in Prose & Verse; Child's Book of Waterbirds; Little George; or, Temptation Revisited; and *The Young Sailor; or, The Sea Life of Tom Bowline.*

Kellogg retired in 1866. Kiggins then took Charles P. Tooker into partnership, forming the company of Kiggins and Tooker. Later Isaac Kiggins was admitted to the firm. In 1882 the Kiggins and Tooker partnership was dissolved, and a stock company was formed with Henry Kiggins as president until he retired in 1885. Henry Kiggins died on 3 February 1905.

Reference:

"Henry Kiggins [obituary]," *New York Times,* 4 February 1905, p. 9.

—*Karin S. Mabe*

Solomon King
(New York: 1821-1832)

Solomon King founded his firm in 1821 at 386 Broadway, New York. The firm moved to 136 William Street in 1823, to 81 Fulton Street in 1826, to 150 William Street in 1827, to 148 Fulton Street in 1829, and to 147 Fulton Street in 1832. King is remembered chiefly as a publisher of children's books. The firm's children's titles numbered 39 in 1824 and increased to 105 by 1828. These titles included *Jack and His Rocking Horse* (1821), *Adventures of Little Red Riding Hood* (1824), and *The Story of Aladdin; or, The Wonderful Lamp* (1828). A King specialty was children's books illustrated with color engravings. Many plates illustrating King books represent the early work of the notable American engraver John Francis Eugene Prud'homme. Other engravings were contributed by O. H. Throop.

For adults, King published religious and biographical works, fiction, joke books, songbooks, and books about dreams and fortune-telling. The first books published by King were *The Art of Making Fire-Works* and *Old Mother Shipton's Universal Dream Book,* both in 1821. King died on 15 September 1832.

Reference:

Harry B. Weiss, "Solomon King, Early New York Bookseller and Publisher of Children's Books and Chapbooks," *Bulletin of the New York Public Library,* 51 (September 1947): 531-544.

—*Kathleen R. Davis*

Laird and Lee
(Chicago: 1883-1974)

A publisher of reference books, fiction, children's literature, and dime novels, Laird and Lee was founded at Lake and South Water streets in Chicago in 1883 by Frederick C. Laird and William H. Lee. The firm became a successful publishing house, offering such strong sellers as a World's Fair viewbook (1893); William T. Stead's *If Christ Came to Chicago* (1894); and George W. Conklin's *Conklin's Handy Manual of Useful Information and World's Atlas* (1899), of which two million copies were sold. Authors whose work was published by the firm included B. Freeman Ashley, H. A. Stanley, and Edmondo de Amici. Laird and Lee also published a series of detective dime novels by A. Frank Pinkerton, including *Dyke Darrel the Railroad Detective* (1886), *Saved at the Scaffold* (1888), and *The Whitechapel Murders* (1889).

The firm's most important author was perhaps the regional humorist Opie Read, many of whose novels first appeared in the Opie Read's Select Works series. Novels in the series included *The Jucklins* (1896), *My Young Master* (1896), and *Old Ebenezer* (1897). Other Read titles, including *A Tear in the Cup* (1894), were also published by Laird and Lee but not in the Select Works series.

Laird withdrew from the firm in 1894, although the imprint remained the same. By 1899, when the firm moved to 263-265 Wabash Avenue, Laird and Lee had become the third largest publisher in Chicago. The firm moved to 1732 Michigan Avenue in 1910 and later to 2001 Calumet Avenue. Laidlaw Brothers, Incorporated purchased Laird and Lee after Lee's death in 1913 and continued to use the imprint as late as 1974.

Reference:

"Mystery Surrounding William Henry Lee, the Chicago Publisher," *Publishers' Weekly*, 84 (2 August 1913): 341-342.

—*David Dzwonkoski*

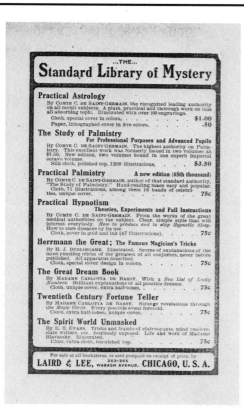

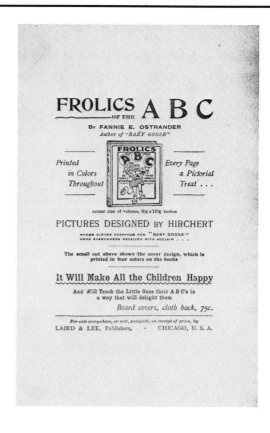

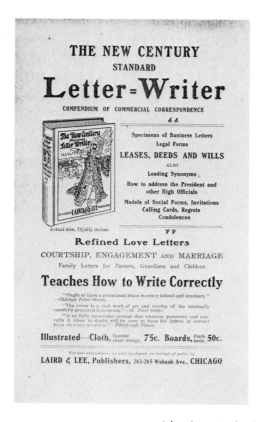

Advertisements showing the range of Laird and Lee books

Lamson, Wolffe and Company

(Boston: 1895-1899)

Lamson, Wolffe and Company was formed in Boston in 1895 while W. B. Wolffe was a Harvard undergraduate. When he learned that Harvard rules prohibited him from running a business between classes, Wolffe withdrew. E. R. Lamson was unable to run the firm by himself, and it failed in the spring of 1899.

Lamson and Wolffe were book lovers who strove to produce volumes of high technical quality. Their publications were distinguished by their attractive and sturdy bindings, the excellence of the printing, and the care with which they were manufactured. In its short existence Lamson, Wolffe and Company published the work of several well-known writers, including Henry Clews and Julia Ward Howe. Among the firm's titles were Constance Harrison's *A Virginia Cousin & Bar Harbor Tales* (1895), a reprint of Edward Everett Hale's *My Double & How He Undid Me* (1895), Charles G. D. Roberts's *The Forge in the Forest* (1896) and *A Sister to Evangeline* (1898), William Eleazar Barton's *A Hero in Homespun: A Tale of the Loyal South* (1897), and Pauline Bradford Hopkins's *Ye Lyttle Salem Maide: A Story of Witchcraft* (1898). The firm's most popular author was the Canadian poet Bliss Carman, three volumes of whose verse were printed by Lamson, Wolffe and Company.

When the firm ceased operations, the rights to several of the more than seventy books it had published were acquired by other publishers. The most important of these transactions was the acquisition by Small, Maynard and Company of the rights to the Carman volumes.

—John R. Conners

The John Lane Company
(New York: 1896-1922)

The John Lane Company originated in 1896 when the English publisher John Lane sent Mitchell Kennerley to New York to open a branch of John Lane The Bodley Head at 140 Fifth Avenue. Previously, books published by Lane in England had been placed with American publishers for distribution in an American edition. The firm later moved to 4 West Thirty-second Street.

The John Lane Company introduced several young British and American authors to American audiences, including Max Beerbohm, Arnold Bennett, H. G. Wells, Kenneth Grahame, and W. J. Locke. Lane was the first to publish works by Agatha Christie, beginning with *The Mysterious Affair at Stiles; A Detective Story* in 1920. The firm also published works by Stephen Leacock, Muriel Hines Coxon, John Ferguson, Compton Leith, Ernest Boyd, G. L. Hunter, and Edith Wherry and poetry by Laurence Hope, Rupert Brooke, Lascelles Abercrombie, Hazell Hull, Amory Hare, Eleanor Cox, Benjamin R. C. Low, Thomas Walsh, Danford Barney, and Angela Morgan.

The John Lane Company published Sherwood Anderson's *Windy McPherson's Son* (1916) and *Marching Men* (1917). An edition of Theodore Dreiser's *The Titan* (1914) was followed by Dreiser's *A Hoosier Holiday* (1916). A 1916 edition of Dreiser's *The "Genius"* provoked a court battle when John Sumner, the secretary of the New York Society for the Suppression of Vice, attempted to force Lane to remove the book from circulation. The Appellate Division of the New York State Supreme Court dismissed the charges. Also in 1916, the firm published H. L. Mencken's *A Little Book in C Major* and *A Book of Burlesque*.

Although The John Lane Company did not depend completely on imports of British titles—the American branch produced its own list—much revenue came from sales of London editions. Fluctuations in tariff regulations made it increasingly difficult for the American branch to operate profitably, and Lane finally found himself unable to maintain the two offices. In 1922 the company's holdings were transferred to Dodd, Mead and Company.

Reference:

J. Lewis May, *John Lane and the Nineties* (London: John Lane The Bodley Head, 1936), pp. 158-162.

—Arlene Shaner

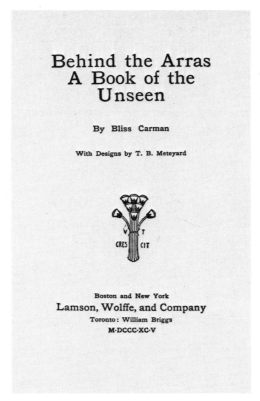

Title page for the first of Carman's books to be published by Lamson, Wolffe and Company. The Canadian poet was the firm's most popular author.

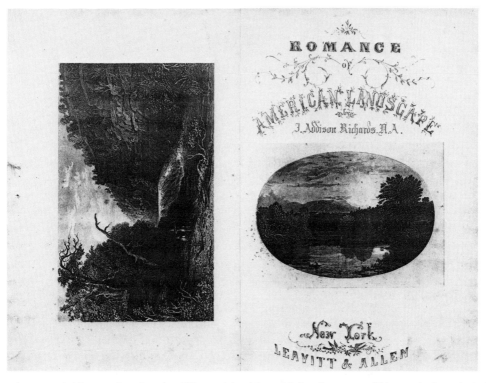

Frontispiece and engraved title page for Thomas Addison Richards's semifictional account of his travels through the United States. Richards made sixteen steel engravings of selected landscapes for the book.

W. A. Leary and Company
(Philadelphia: 1836-circa 1866)

In 1836 W. A. Leary established a bookstore in Philadelphia and began publishing books under such imprints as W. A. Leary and Company, Leary and Company, and Leary and Getz. Reprints of British and American authors comprised Leary's literary publications. In 1844 Leary published John Bunyan's minor works, including *Grace Abounding*, *Heart's Ease*, and *The World to Come*. Leary published one of the many editions of R. Maria Roche's *Children of the Abbey* in 1847. The following year the firm published Timothy Shay Arthur's *The Lady at Home; or, Leaves from the Every-day Book of an American Woman*. In 1850 Leary published *The Arabian Nights' Entertainments* and Richard Baxter's *The Saints' Everlasting Rest*. The firm published Charles Rotteck's *History of the World* in 1851 and reprinted Goldsmith's *The Vicar of Wakefield* in 1852. Leary's Book Store remained in business until 1968, more than 100 years after the firm discontinued its publishing activities.

Reference:
Joseph Jackson, *An Old Landmark, A Famous Book Store* (Philadelphia: Leary's Book Store, 1920).

—*Elizabeth Hoffman*

Leavitt and Allen
(New York: 1851-1870)
Jonathan Leavitt
(New York: 1830-1840)
Leavitt and Trow
(New York: 1840-1851)
Leavitt and Allen Brothers
(New York: 1870-1876)
World Publishing Company
(New York: 1876-1878)

Jonathan Leavitt, the proprietor of a successful bookbindery in Andover, Massachusetts, came to New York in 1825 as a partner in the bookstore of his brother-in-law, Daniel Appleton, located in Exchange Place. In 1830 Leavitt withdrew from the partnership and established a bookselling and publishing business under his own name at the corner of Broadway and John Street. In 1840 the printer John F. Trow associated himself with Leavitt and the firm took the name Leavitt and Trow. George A. Leavitt, a recent graduate of Phillips Academy and an apprentice at the bookstore of Robinson and Franklin in New York, joined his father's business as a partner in 1842.

At the death of Jonathan Leavitt in 1851 the partnership with Trow was dissolved, and George Leavitt took as his partner John K. Allen, who had learned the trade at Mark H. Newman and Company in New York. The company name was changed to Leavitt and Allen, and the firm was relocated at Vesey Street, near Broadway. Leavitt and Allen later moved to 27 Dey Street and in January 1856 settled at 379 Broadway at White Street. Sometime previous to the Second Regular Trade Sale on 20 March 1856 Leavitt formed a partnership with Richard L. Delisser, establishing the book auction house of Leavitt, Delisser and Company. In 1857 Delisser withdrew and J. M. Alden joined the company; the name of the auction business was changed to George A. Leavitt and Company. The publishing and bookselling business continued through all these changes as Leavitt and Allen. Following the movement of the book trade uptown, both businesses moved to 24 Walker Street in May 1860 and to 21-23 Mercer Street in February 1861.

William Lee

Charles A. B. Shepard

The activities of the Leavitt auction house overshadowed the publishing and bookselling business, but Leavitt and Allen was a successful publishing house. From his father's business Leavitt inherited a good stock of educational books, to which he added the work of Rev. Albert Barnes, Prof. John J. Owen, Jonathan Edwards, and Samuel N. Sweet. Leavitt and Allen also published gift books and annuals with titles such as *Forget Me Not, Memory's Gift,* and *Friendship's Offer.* Annual sales of these volumes often reached 50,000. Leavitt and Allen also published standard authors, English poets, juvenile literature, and writing and photograph albums. Thomas Addison Richards's *The Romance of American Landscape* (1854) was illustrated with steel engravings by the author.

In 1862 the publishing and bookselling business was sold to meet the obligations of the auction firm. Allen's brother Henry S. Allen managed the firm on behalf of the creditors until 1866, when Leavitt regained control. In 1870 Leavitt formed a partnership with the Allens to carry on a publishing and bookselling business at 8 Howard Street under the name Leavitt and Allen Brothers. The partnership expired by limitation in 1876, and John K. Allen retired from the business. Henry S. Allen became manager of the publishing firm, which was renamed the World Publishing House and moved to 139 Eighth Street. In 1878 Leavitt retired from publishing and bookselling to devote the remainder of his career to the auction business. He retired in 1885 and died in 1888.

References:

"Contributions to Trade History: No. XL, George A. Leavitt," *American Bookseller,* new series 25 (1889): 9-10;

"George A. Leavitt—In Memoriam," *Publishers' Weekly,* 34 (29 December 1888): 1023-1024.

—*Harry F. Thompson*

Lee and Shepard
(Boston: 1862-1904)
Lothrop, Lee and Shepard
(Boston; New York: 1904-   )

1932

William Lee and Charles A. B. Shepard joined in 1862 to form Lee and Shepard at 149 Washington Street in Boston. Lee brought to the new firm several key contacts which he had established during his employment at Phillips, Sampson and Company. He had also been a partner at Crosby, Nichols and Company, a short-lived relationship which he had left a year before meeting Shepard, whose firm—Shepard, Clark and Brown—had failed in 1859. Lee and Shepard's first book was a reprint of John Ruskin's *The King of the Golden River* (1863).

Lee's purchase from his old firm Phillips, Sampson of the plates for two Oliver Optic series— the Boat Club series and the Riverdale Story

THE MORNING RIDE. — Page 167.

GOODY SLOPER'S PROPHECY. — Page 37.

MY FIRST SUITOR. — Page 62.

IN THE STUDIO. — Page 153.

CRAZY TURNER. — Page 169.

REVERSES. — Page 189.

Lizzie B. Humphrey's illustrations for Sarah A. Emery's Three Generations, *published by Lee and Shepard in 1872. Humphrey illustrated many books for the firm.*

Books—formed the basis for a long line of juvenile publications by Lee and Shepard. These reprints were followed by many original titles by William Taylor Adams under the Oliver Optic pseudonym, including *Palace and Cottage; or, Young America in France and Switzerland* (1868) in the Young America Abroad series, *On Time; or, The Young Captain of the Ucayga Steamer* (1869) in the Lake Shore series, and *Going West; or, The Perils of a Poor Boy* (1875) in the Great Western series, as well as titles in the Blue and the Gray, the Old Glory, and the All-Over-the-World series. Each Optic series consisted of six titles, as did those by Rebecca Sophia Clarke under the pseudonym, Sophie May. Among these were the Little Prudy, Dotty Dimple, and Flaxie Frizzle series. Lee and Shepard was also notable as the publisher of an early American edition of Lewis Carroll's *Alice's Adventures in Wonderland* (1869). Other fiction titles of this period included William Henry Thomas's *The Gold Hunter's Adventures; or, Life in Australia* (1864), which was followed by six more novels by Thomas; Sara Hammond Palfrey's *Herman; or, Young Knighthood* (1866); John Townsend Trowbridge's *Neighbor's Wives* (1867); and Mrs. Harriette Newall Baker's *Juliette; or, Now or Never* (1869).

Most of Lee and Shepard's output was non-literary. Brisk sales in photographic albums accounted for much of the firm's early profits. Lee and Shepard also developed a nonfiction list which was considered radical at the time. Specializing in politics and the occult, the firm published works by Charles Sumner, Horace Mann, Wendell Phillips, and the Reverend Charles Beecher.

In addition to publishing, Lee and Shepard was among the largest book jobbers in the United States. In 1870 the firm opened a New York branch with Charles T. Dillingham at 47-49 Green Street under the name Lee, Shepard and Dillingham. While jobbing accounted for most of the branch's business, several works of fiction were published in New York, including Francis Henry Underwood's *Cloud-Pictures* (1872), Mrs. Adeline Knox's *Katherine Earle* (1874), and Mrs. Caroline Elizabeth Corbin's *His Marriage Vow* (1874). These titles were also published in Boston under the Lee and Shepard imprint in the same years. This joint publishing arrangement continued even after Dillingham formed his own imprint in New York in 1875.

The great Boston fire of 1872 forced the firm to move to 41-45 Franklin Street. Another fire and the Panic of 1873, together with aggressive price-cutting by department stores and other new competitors and overexpansion by Lee and Shepard, led to a declaration of bankruptcy in 1875.

Within months, however, the firm's finances were returned to order and Lee and Shepard reopened. The firm had a best-seller in Mary A. Denison's *That Husband of Mine* (1877). The company's output remained below its previous level but included James Montgomery Bailey's *England from a Back-Window, with Views of Scotland and Ireland* (1879), Fanny D. Bates's *My Sister Kitty: A Story of Election Day* (1881), and John Martin Luther Babcock's *The Dawning* (1886).

In 1885 Lee and Shepard moved to 10 Milk Street. In 1886 the firm's drama-publishing subsidiary, George M. Baker and Company, split off as Walter H. Baker and Company. Shepard died in 1889. The firm moved to 202 Devonshire Street in 1895. In 1898 Lee retired and formed the American Lineage Publishing Company with Shepard's son Charles to research genealogies; Lee and Shepard was purchased by E. Fleming and Company, a Boston bookbinding firm. Approximately 2,000 titles had been published under the Lee and Shepard imprint prior to Lee's retirement, but the output declined under the new ownership. About twenty titles were published in 1904. In that year, Lee and Shepard purchased the bankrupt Lothrop Publishing and became Lothrop, Lee and Shepard at 93 Federal Street.

The firm moved to 419 Fourth Avenue, New York, in 1942. A year later, Lothrop, Lee and Shepard was purchased by Crown Publishers. The firm was acquired by Scott, Foresman and Company in 1966; in 1968 it became a division of William Morrow, which was then a subsidiary of Scott, Foresman. Morrow later became a subsidiary of the Hearst Corporation. Juveniles have remained Lothrop, Lee and Shepard's specialty, with works by authors including Shirley Hughes, Jamie Gilson, Helen Roney Sattler, and Vera Cleaver. In 1984 sixty titles, all juveniles, were published under the imprint Lothrop, Lee and Shepard Books. Dorothy Briley heads the division as vice-president and editor in chief. The firm's address is 105 Madison Avenue, New York 10016.

References:

Richard G. Badger, "An Interview with Mr. William Lee," *Literary Review*, 1 (February 1897): 20-21;

"Charles A. B. Shepard [obituary]," *Publishers' Weekly*, 35 (2 February 1889): 98-99;

Raymond L. Kilgour, *Lee and Shepard: Publishers for the People* (Hamden, Conn.: Shoe String Press, 1965);

The bankrupt Lothrop Publishing Company was purchased in 1904 to form Lothrop, Lee and Shepard Company

Charles A. B. Shepard, "Memories of the Boston Book Trade," *Publishers' Weekly*, 29 (23 January 1886): 105;

"William Lee [obituary]," *Publishers' Weekly*, 70 (8 December 1906): 1772-1773.

—*David Dzwonkoski*

The Frank Leslie Publishing House
(New York: 1854-1905)

See also the Frank Leslie entry in *DLB 43, American Newspaper Journalists, 1690-1872.*

Although the primary business of The Frank Leslie Publishing House was the production of approximately thirty periodicals during its fifty-one years of operation, the firm also published eighty-six books. Founded in 1854 at 10 John Street, New York, by Frank Leslie and continued by his widow, Miriam Florence Follin Leslie, the firm's major innovation lay in developing as a market the growing number of railway passengers who purchased Leslie's books and periodicals from the aggressive salesboys of the American News Company.

Henry Carter was born in Ipswich, England, in 1821. He used the name Frank Leslie as a pseudonym so that he could keep his work as an illustrator for the *Illustrated London News* and, later, the *Pictorial Times* a secret from his father, who opposed the idea of an art career for his son. After moving to America in 1848, Carter legally changed his name to Frank Leslie. In 1850 he began work as an engraver at *Gleason's Pictorial and Drawing Room Companion* in Boston. From 1852 to 1853 he served as managing foreman for P. T. Barnum and A. E. Beach's *Illustrated News* in New York.

In January 1854 Leslie began to publish *Frank Leslie's Lady's Gazette of Fashion*, with the novelist Ann S. Stephens as editor. Emphasizing crime and other sensational stories, *Frank Leslie's Illustrated Newspaper*—the most famous and successful venture of his career—was launched on 15 December 1855, continued under the Leslies until 1889, and survived in other hands until 1922. The firm moved to 19 City Hall Square in 1860. Leslie established twenty-six more periodicals, including *Frank Leslie's Ten Cent Monthly* (1863-1896), *Frank Leslie's Chimney Corner* (1865-1885), *Once a Week* (1871-1881), and *Frank Leslie's Popular Monthly* (1876-1905).

Leslie's earliest book publications were paperbound collections of illustrations from the firm's periodicals. These books included *Frank Leslie's Christmas Pictorial* (1856); *Frank Leslie's Great Eastern Steamship Pictorial* (1858); and *Frank Leslie's Pictorial History of the War of 1861* (1862), published in thirty-three numbers. The firm's first fiction in book form appeared in Frank Leslie's Series of New Novels, which consisted of *Annette; or, The Lady of Pearls* (1863) by Alexandre Dumas fils; piracies of Mary Elizabeth Braddon's *Aurora Floyd* (1863), *Lady Audley's Secret* (1863), and *Eleanor's Victory* (1864); Frederick John Fargus's *Living or Dead* (1864); and Isa Craig Knox's *Half Sisters* (1864).

Several more pictorials, almanacs, travel books, cookbooks, and children's books were published before Leslie issued four new fictional series in 1876 and 1877. Distributed by the American News Company to railway passengers, these cheap reprints often consisted of serialized fiction collected into book form from Leslie's periodicals. The Chimney Corner series (1876-1877) included Charlotte Mary Brame's *Wife in Name Only* (1877) among its five titles, while Frank Leslie's Popular Library consisted of Jules Verne's *Michael Strogoff* (1876-1877), Charles Gayler's *Fritz, the Emigrant* (1876) and *Montague; or, The Belle of the Matinee* (1877), and Mary Cecil Hay's *Reaping the Whirlwind* (1876). The Boys Library Series of Stories included Samuel Bracebridge Hemyng's *Jack Harkaway out West among the Indians* and W. O. Stoddard's *Lone Wolf, the Apache Chief.* Leslie's best-known series, Frank Leslie's Home Library of Standard Works by the Most Celebrated Authors, published in 1877, consisted of paperbound reprints of standard works by Daniel Defoe, Victor Hugo, George Eliot, Wilkie Collins, Edward Bulwer-Lytton, and Charles Reade, as well as Rhoda Broughton's *Goodby Sweetheart!*, Dinah Craik's *Hannah*, Mrs. Annie

Frank Leslie was the name assumed by Henry Carter to keep secret from his father his job as an illustrator for the Illustrated London News *and the* Pictorial Times *(courtesy of the New York Public Library, Astor, Lenox and Tilden Foundations)*

Miriam Florence Follin Leslie, who legally changed her name to "Frank Leslie" soon after her husband died (courtesy of Mr. Hiram Todd)

Edwards's *A Vagabond Heroine,* and James Payn's *Murphy's Master.* There were seventeen titles in the series.

Although Leslie's business tripled between 1876 and 1877, he found himself overextended during the panic of 1877. His property was assigned to Isaac W. England, publisher of the *New York Sun,* in September 1877, although Leslie continued as general manager. Leslie had made significant progress in paying off his debts when he died on 10 January 1880. His widow borrowed to pay off the remainder of his creditors and regained ownership of the firm. Legally changing her name to Frank Leslie, she had the good fortune and good news sense to beat other periodicals to the story of the assassination of President Garfield; the quick sales of the assassination issue of *Frank Leslie's Illustrated Newspaper* enabled Mrs. Leslie to pay back the money she had borrowed.

This remarkable woman had been married twice before her marriage to Leslie. In 1863, two years after her second husband, the archaeologist Ephraim George Squier, had become editor of *Frank Leslie's Illustrated Newspaper,* the then Mrs. Squier had become editor of *Frank Leslie's Lady's Magazine.* She had later edited *Frank Leslie's Chimney Corner* and *Frank Leslie's Lady's Journal.* A year after her divorce from Squier in 1873, she had married Leslie.

Mrs. Leslie quickly reorganized the business, shifting from railroad to mail-order sales. While she eventually sold or eliminated all but two weekly periodicals and four monthlies, she added *U.S. Mail* (1888) and *Frank Leslie's Afloat and Ashore* (1888-1890). Much of her energy was focused on *Frank Leslie's Popular Monthly,* which was distributed to every railroad in the United States. Books published under her direction included *Frank Leslie's Bubbles and Butterflies* (1881) and *Queen Titania's Book of Fairy Tales* (1883), as well as the firm's last fiction title, Etta W. Pierce's *Prince Lucifer* (1890).

The firm was incorporated in 1889. Two years later Mrs. Leslie married William Charles Wilde; by 1893 she was filing for divorce. Facing the testimony of Leslie's detectives and a London madam, Wilde had no more luck in court than had his famous brother Oscar. Mrs. Leslie leased the business in 1895 for a term of five years to a syndicate run by Frederic L. Colver. In 1898 she became president of the stock company the syndicate had formed but was forced to retire two years later due to financial problems and personality conflicts. The stock company had purchased the remainder of her holdings by 1903 and within two years The Frank Leslie Publishing House was dissolved.

Mrs. Leslie spent her last years presiding over her famous salon as the Baroness de Bazus, a title she derived from creatively interpreting her genealogy. Upon her death in 1914, her $2 million estate was bequeathed to the woman suffrage movement.

References:

A Brief History of Frank Leslie's Publishing House (New York: Leslie, 1887);

Madeleine B. Stern, "The Frank Leslie Publishing House," *Antiquarian Bookman,* 7 (June 1951): 1973-1975;

Stern, *Purple Passage: The Life of Mrs. Frank Leslie* (Norman: University of Oklahoma Press, 1953).

—*David Dzwonkoski*

Frank Leslie's Publishing House in 1882, at the corner of Park Place and College Place, New York City

Cover of an issue depicting the murder of financier James Fisk by his former business associate Edward S. Stokes. The men were rivals for the attentions of actress Josie Mansfield.

Lilly, Wait and Company

(Boston: circa 1810-1814; circa 1833-1834)

From 1810 to 1835 a group of Bostonians, including Robert Lilly and Thomas B. Wait, who were printers, and William Wells, a Court Street bookseller and stationer, published a variety of books under several imprints. Wait's press was first located at 10 1/2 Court Street. Lilly and Wait were partners in 1810, when Wait published Lucy Aikin's *Epistles on Women* under a joint imprint with Wells. The Lilly and Wait partnership had dissolved by 1814 when Lilly joined Wells in a printing, publishing, and bookselling business at 97 Court Street. Wait continued with his sons as Thomas B. Wait and Company, publishers of such children's books as the anonymous *Felix, the Woodcutter; or, Good and Evil. A Moral Tale For Youth* (1812) and *Isabel and Louisa. Some Account of Two Little Girls Who Lived in Boston* (1813). Wait died in 1830.

The Wells and Lilly imprint first appeared on William Hull's *Defence of Brigadier General W. Hull* (1814). Although travel books and histories predominated, the firm published some literary titles, among them the anonymous *History of Samuel Bonner; or, Cruelty to Animals. By the Author of "The Prodigal"* (1820); Henry Cogswell Knight's *Poems* (1821); Sarah Wentworth Morton's *My Mind and Its Thoughts, in Sketches, Fragments, and Essays* (1823), Eliza Lanesford Cushing's second book, *Yorktown:*

An Historical Romance (1826); and two titles by Harriet Vaughn Cheney. Perhaps the firm's best-known author was William Ellery Channing, whose sermons and incidental writings were published in 1815 and 1816.

From at least 1833 to 1834, Lilly and probably one of Thomas Wait's sons, either Silas or William, were publishers under the imprint of Lilly, Wait and Company—or, with the inclusion of two other partners, as Lilly, Wait, Colman and Holden. The firm's publications included Oliver Wendell Holmes's *The Mariner's Library or Voyager's Companion* (1833), Seba Smith's *Life and Writings of Major Jack Downing of Downingville* (1833), and Catherine Read Williams's anonymous *Fall River: An Authentic Narrative* (1833). After Lilly's death in 1834, only Colman's name remained on the imprint.

References:
Rollo G. Silver, *The Boston Book Trade: 1800-1825* (New York: New York Library, 1949);

Roger E. Stoddard, "Notes on American Play Publishing, 1765-1865," *Proceedings of the American Antiquarian Society*, 81 (1971): 161-191.

—David Dzwonkoski
Theodora Mills

Lincoln and Edmands
(Boston: 1805-1833)

Ensign Lincoln, an apprentice with Manning and Loring, in Boston, decided in 1800 to enter publishing and printing for himself. His first book was the first complete edition of William Cowper's poems in America, with engravings by Samuel Hill. For six months in 1803 he printed Phineas Adams's *Monthly Anthology,* the forerunner of the *North American Review.*

In 1805 Lincoln was joined by Thomas Edmands, who had advanced from apprentice to foreman at Manning and Loring. The firm of Lincoln and Edmands had offices at 53 Cornhill. Edmands ran the press while Lincoln edited the firm's books. During its first year, Lincoln and Edmands bought the stock and equipment of Samuel Hall.

Among the firm's earliest titles was a work of verse and prose, *Compositions, Original and Selected* (1805?) by Mrs. Jane Ames. Most of the firm's output seems to have been nonfiction, especially religious tracts, and material for children. Typical of the former were John Lauris Blake's *The Biblical Reader* (1826) and George Campbell's *Lectures on Systematic Theology and Pulpit Eloquence* (1832), while the latter included Isaac Watts's *Divine and Moral Songs for Children* (1808); the first American editions of John Campbell's *Alfred and Galba; or, The History of Two Brothers, Supposed to Be Written by Themselves. For the Use of Young People* and *Walks of Usefulness in London and its Environs,* both in 1812; and two collections of verse, *Poems for Little Children* and *A Poetic Selection,* both in 1819. Some of the material in Lincoln and Edmands's Series of Evangelical Tracts could be considered juvenile fiction; among these titles were the anonymously published *The Dairyman's Daughter* (1812) and *Dialogue between Two Seamen after a Storm* (1813).

Lincoln died in December 1832; Edmands retired the following year. Edmands's son B. F. Edmands, James Waitt, and Robert S. Davis purchased the stock and business under the name Lincoln, Edmands and Company, but the new firm soon went bankrupt.

—*Martha A. Bartter*

Joshua Ballinger Lippincott

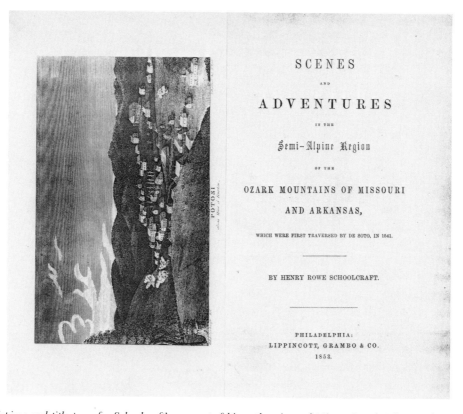

Frontispiece and title page for Schoolcraft's account of his explorations of Missouri and Arkansas during 1818

J. B. Lippincott Company
(Philadelphia: 1885-1978; 1981-   )
J. B. Lippincott
(Philadelphia: 1836-1849)
Lippincott, Grambo and Company
(Philadelphia: 1850-1855)
J. B. Lippincott and Company
(Philadelphia: 1855-1885)
Lippincott and Crowell, Publishers
(New York: 1978-1981)

1902

1970s

The J. B. Lippincott Company dates its origin to the establishment of a bookstore and printing firm, Jacob Johnson and Company, at 147 Market Street in Philadelphia in 1792. This firm was known successively as Johnson and Warner, Benjamin Warner, Warner and Grigg, John Grigg, Grigg and Elliot, and Grigg, Elliot and Company. By 1849 the firm was a leading book jobber and stationer, as well as the nation's chief medical publisher. That year John Grigg and Hugh Elliot sold the business to Joshua Ballinger Lippincott.

Lippincott had started his career in the late 1820s working in a bookshop owned by a man named Clarke at Fourth and Race Streets in Philadelphia. About 1831 Clarke's creditors took over the business and put Lippincott in charge. By 1836 Lippincott had bought the business and was ready to expand into publishing. He concentrated on Bibles and other religious titles, with some general literature as well, and rapidly achieved local prominence. When Lippincott bought Grigg, Elliot and Company, he took on Henry Grambo, a partner in the purchased firm, as his own partner. The business opened on 1 January 1850 as Lippincott, Grambo and Company and soon acquired new of-

fices at 20 North Fourth Street. Also taken on as partners from Grigg, Elliot were Edmund Claxton and George Remsen. When Grambo retired in 1855, Lippincott resumed his former imprint, J. B. Lippincott and Company. Charles C. Haffelfinger, a long-time employee of Grigg, Elliot, was made a partner in 1858. In 1868 Claxton, Remsen, and Haffelfinger withdrew to start their own publishing firm.

One early title quickly established the company name in schools and libraries around the country: *Lippincott's Pronouncing Gazetteer*, first published in 1855, with new editions for nearly a century afterward. A companion volume, the *Universal Pronouncing Dictionary of Biography and Mythology* by Joseph Thomas, was published in 1870. Another important early title was Henry Schoolcraft's six-volume *History of the Indian Tribes of the United States* (1851-1857). The firm took over Samuel Austin Allibone's *A Critical Dictionary of English Literature* (1858) from Childs and Peterson and added seven volumes to the work in 1870-1871. Lippincott also published such specialty items as gift books, photograph albums, and fine editions of British authors. Published in the late 1860s, Lippincott's

A page of testimonials published in the 1866 revised and expanded edition

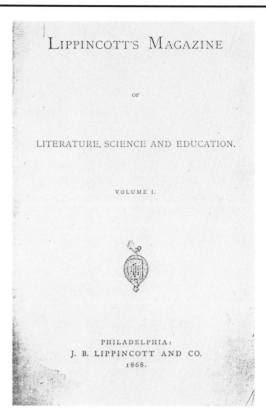

Title page for the bound edition of the magazine that featured a complete novel or novelette in each issue

J. B. Lippincott Company's main office at 227 East Washington Square, Philadelphia, built in 1901, two years after fire destroyed the firm's office and manufacturing plant at 715 Market Street

Pocket Classics, also featuring British authors, offered traditional poetry and prose in boxed collections of convenient size.

Three important fields in Lippincott publishing have been medicine, religion, and textbooks. The firm has been the publisher of medical journals, including *The North American Medico-Chirurgical Review*, the *Annals of Surgery*, the *American Journal of Nursing*, and *Medical Science*. In 1878 Lippincott published *A Hand-book of Nursing*, the first nursing textbook in America. Other milestone medical books include *Human Anatomy* (1907) by Dr. George A. Piersol, *Essentials of Medicine* (1908) by Dr. C. P. Emerson, and *Histology* (1950) by Dr. Arthur W. Ham.

The important Lippincott religious titles in the nineteenth century were *The Comprehensive Commentary on the Holy Bible* (1846), edited by William Jenks, and John Newton Brown's *Encyclopedia of Religious Knowledge* (1846). Both were continued in later editions through the 1870s. Religious books played a smaller role at Lippincott in the first half of the twentieth century, but returned to prominence in the 1960s. In 1961 Lippincott reestablished a religious book department in its Trade Division. In its first few years, the new department's most successful publication was *The Comfortable Pew* (1965) by Pierre Berton.

Lippincott has published a long line of textbooks from elementary school to college. The firm was one of many publishers of Noah Webster's *American Dictionary of the English Language* (1859), but switched to Joseph E. Worcester's competing *Academic Dictionary* (1888). In 1918 Lippincott established a branch office in Chicago to handle textbook publishing; it was transferred to Philadelphia in 1961. Widely recognized twentieth-century textbooks include the Horn-Ashbaugh Spellers, launched in 1921; Sidney Harcave's *Russia, A History* (1952); the Preceptor series of college paperbacks, established in 1961; and *Basic Reading* (1963) by Glenn McCracken and Charles C. Walcutt.

Literary publishing at Lippincott received an important boost in 1868 with the first issue of *Lippincott's Magazine*. It became one of the leading publishing-house flagship magazines of the day, along with *Scribner's*, *Century*, *Appleton's* and *Harper's*. Lippincott's special feature was a complete novel or novelette in each issue; among the early ones were Rudyard Kipling's first version of *The Light That Failed* (1890) and Oscar Wilde's *The Picture of Dorian Gray* (1890). Other contributors to the magazine were Jack London, A. C. Swinburne, Bret Harte,

Maurice Hewlett, Owen Wister, Arthur Conan Doyle, and Sir Gilbert Parker. Lippincott continued to publish the magazine until 1914, when it was sold to McBride, Nast and Company. It was renamed *McBride's Magazine* in September 1915 and merged with *Scribner's Magazine* in April 1916. In 1871 the firm increased its literary prestige when it published the first volume, *Romeo and Juliet*, of the New Variorum Edition of Shakespeare, edited by Dr. Horace Howard Furness.

Importing of British books had become an important part of Lippincott's business by the 1870s, and in 1875 the firm opened an agency in London to handle this operation. The office continued to operate until 1955. In 1879 Lippincott published Henry Adams's *The Life of Albert Gallatin*, along with the three-volume *The Writings of Albert Gallatin* edited by Adams.

In 1885 the firm was reorganized as a stock company, the J. B. Lippincott Company. When Joshua Ballinger Lippincott died the following year, ownership passed to his sons Craige, Walter, and J. Bertram. Craige, the eldest, was elected president and served until his death in 1911.

Occasionally Lippincott published a novel that provoked intense controversy by challenging a current cultural norm. The first such novel for the firm was *The Quick or the Dead?* by Amélie Rives, published in *Lippincott's Magazine* in April 1888 and in book form the following year. Sometimes called the first "love problem" novel, its "problem" is that a widow falls in love. Many critics denounced her tempestuous romance as overstepping the bounds of good taste, but the book helped to dispel the sentimental myth of the ever-faithful widow permanently purified from all sexual attraction. In 1913 Lippincott published Hall Caine's *The Woman Thou Gavest Me*, an indictment of the Roman Catholic church for its refusal to recognize divorce. Caine's sympathetic treatment of the plight of an unhappily married woman offended some readers, while others thought that the message was long overdue.

By the end of the nineteenth century, Lippincott's headquarters at 715 Market Street, where it had moved in 1861, had become a Philadelphia tourist attraction. The firm's twenty-nine presses were printing about 2,000 titles a year. A Canadian branch office was opened in Montreal in 1897; it moved to Toronto in 1966. In 1898 Lippincott sold its bookstore and stationery departments and became exclusively a publisher and manufacturer of books and magazines. A fire in 1899 destroyed the

J. Bertram Lippincott, president of the firm from 1911 until 1926, when he was named chairman of the board. Under his direction the house experienced one of its most prosperous periods.

Christopher Morley (left) and Joseph Wharton Lippincott, president of J. B. Lippincott Company, March 1940. Morley's novel Kitty Foyle *was a controversial best-seller for the company (photograph by Harry West).*

firm's offices and manufacturing plant; only the printing plates and the contracts survived. The house set up temporary offices in a hotel and hired presses and binderies until it could rebuild. By 1901 the new building at East Washington Square was ready for occupancy.

About the same time, Lippincott modified its publisher's device. The original designer of the Lippincott tree of knowledge is unknown; it had been in use for many years by 1900. Lippincott art director Edward S. Holloway's new design included the lamp of enlightenment burning under the tree, cornucopias, a rising sun, and the motto "Droit et Avant," a rough Latin equivalent for J. B. Lippincott's personal motto, "Be sure you are right, and go ahead." The modern version of the device is simpler: the tree of knowledge in a circle, with the firm's founding date—1792—at its base.

In 1902 Lippincott published London's *A Daughter of the Snows*. Typical Lippincott fare in this period was purely popular, with few literary pretensions. In 1908 the firm published *Marcia Schuyler*, a first novel by Grace Livingston Hill. She became a Lippincott mainstay, turning out more than eighty sentimental romances over the next forty years, sometimes at the rate of three a year. Paperback reprints of her novels are still on sale. Another best-seller was *Bella Donna* (1909) by the popular English novelist Robert Hichens.

Craige Lippincott died in 1911. J. Bertram Lippincott became president and directed the house through one of its most prosperous periods. In 1926 he was made chairman of the board and his son, Joseph Wharton Lippincott, became president.

Among the most successful trade titles for Lippincott in the 1920s was *Anatole France Himself* (1925), a "Boswellian record" by J. J. Brousson. Textbooks and medical works were still bringing in a large share of the house's profits, but the trade operation was growing. In 1928 the manufacturing plant was sold to permit concentration on publishing. By 1936 trade publishing had expanded to such an extent that a New York editorial office was opened at 250 Park Avenue; it later moved to 521 Fifth Avenue.

In 1934 Lippincott published a first novel, *Jonah's Gourd Vine*, by a black writer, Zora Neale Hurston. Her studies in anthropology made her work an unusual fusion of literature and ethnology. Most of her important work was published by Lippincott, including a folklore collection, *Mules and Men* (1935); her best-known novel, *Their Eyes Were Watching God* (1937); a book about the myths and magic of Jamaica and Haiti, *Tell My Horse* (1938); and her autobiography, *Dust Tracks on a Road* (1942).

In 1939 Lippincott was once again the publisher of a controversial best-seller, Christopher Morley's *Kitty Foyle*. Morley later described the novel: "*Kitty Foyle*, which caused indignation in many readers, was an unexpected revelation, told in the person of an Irish-American 'white collar girl,' of the mind and heart and biology of a young woman of the 1930s." *Stars on the Sea* (1940) was one of F. van Wyck Mason's most popular historical novels. Others included *Three Harbours* (1938), *Rivers of Glory* (1942), *Eagle in the Sky* (1948), *Proud New Flags* (1951), and *Blue Hurricane* (1954). Osa Johnson's *I Married Adventure*, number one on the list of nonfiction best-sellers for 1940, told of her adventures with her explorer husband Martin.

In 1940 Lippincott bought the firm of Carrick and Evans of New York, which had published some well-received titles in its three years, including *Two Wars and More to Come* (1938) by Herbert L. Matthews. Carrick and Evans contracts produced several successful Lippincott titles for 1941, including Frank O. Hough's *The Neutral Ground* and Charles de Gaulle's *The Army of the Future*.

In 1941 Lippincott acquired Frederick A. Stokes Company of New York, a sixty-year-old firm with a trade list of 1,000 titles. About 400 of these were children's books, including Hugh Lofting's Dr. Dolittle books and the stories of Munro Leaf. Children's writers who came to Lippincott with Stokes included Mabel Leigh Hunt, best known for her stories of Colonial Quaker children, such as *Little Grey Gown* (1939). Her Lippincott titles included *Matilda's Buttons* (1948) and *Better Known as Johnny Appleseed* (1950). Even before the Stokes purchase, Lippincott had published a small list of children's books. The firm's most notable children's illustrator had been Arthur Rackham, whose Lippincott titles included Charles Dickens's *A Christmas Carol* (1915), Clement Moore's *The Night before Christmas* (1930), and *The Arthur Rackham Fairy Book* (1933).

Forrest Wilson's biography of Harriet Beecher Stowe, *Crusader in Crinoline* (1941), won a Pulitzer Prize in 1942. Wyoming ranch owner Mary O'Hara Alsop's *My Friend Flicka* (1941) was originally a short story; Lippincott editors persuaded the author to develop it into a novel. Ultimately her horse story sold more than a million copies. Two best-selling novels of World War II were

Gwethalyn Graham's *Earth and High Heaven* (1944) and James Ramsey Ullman's *The White Tower* (1945).

With the war over, readers wanted to escape from serious issues and to be amused. Lippincott met that mood with a book which became the firm's all-time best-seller: Betty MacDonald's *The Egg and I* (1945) remained on the best-seller list from 1945 through 1947, sold 1.5 million copies, and created a vogue for what the trade called "funny women" books. Another popular Lippincott book took a serious issue and gave it a light, satiric treatment. In *Mr. Adam* (1946), a novel by Pat Frank (pseudonym of Harry Hart), a nuclear accident leaves all males on earth sterile except one.

Joseph Wharton Lippincott became chairman of the board in 1949. The presidency went outside the family for the first time when Howard K. Bauernfeind was elected the fifth president of Lippincott. In 1958 Bauernfeind became chairman of the board and Joseph Wharton Lippincott, Jr., became the firm's sixth president.

Lippincott authors of the 1950s and 1960s included Marya Mannes, whose biting comments appeared in the essay collections *More in Anger* (1958), *The New York I Know* (1961), and *But Will It Sell?* (1964). Probably the most distinguished biography ever published by Lippincott was Leon Edel's five-volume *Henry James*, published between 1953 and 1972. The second and third volumes, *The Conquest of London* and *The Middle Years*, appeared in 1962 and won the 1963 Pulitzer Prize for biography as well as the National Book Award. In fiction, Harper Lee's *To Kill a Mockingbird* (1960) won the 1961 Pulitzer Prize for fiction and ranked high on the year's best-seller list. Muriel Spark's *The Prime of Miss Jean Brodie* was published in 1962. Thomas Pynchon's first book, *V* (1963), was followed by *The Crying of Lot 49* (1966). In 1971 the Lippincott list included two works by Gordon Parks: *In Love*, a book of his poetry with color photographs by the author, and *Born Black*, a collection of his articles about black Americans.

By the 1970s Joseph W. Lippincott, Jr., was both president and chairman of the board. He retired in 1978 and was succeeded by Barton H. Lippincott, a cousin. In the same year the J. B. Lippincott Company, which had seen a decline in its trade and general textbook operations throughout the decade and had lost more than a million dollars in 1977, was bought by Harper and Row. The adult trade division was combined with its counterpart at Thomas Y. Crowell, another Harper and Row subsidiary, as Lippincott and Crowell, Publishers. This name was dropped in 1981; Harper and Row now lists Thomas Y. Crowell as an imprint and J. B. Lippincott as a subsidiary specializing in medical books. Another imprint, Crowell/Lippincott Junior books, formed from the children's divisions of the merged subsidiaries, appeared between 1979 and 1983. Barton H. Lippincott is chairman and chief executive officer of the J. B. Lippincott Company, which is located at East Washington Square, Philadelphia, Pennsylvania 19105.

References:

The Author and His Audience, with a Chronology of Major Events in the Publishing History of J. B. Lippincott Company (Philadelphia: Lippincott, 1967);

"Harper & Row in an Agreement to Acquire Lippincott," *Publishers Weekly*, 213 (2 January 1978): 12;

"J. B. Lippincott [obituary]," *Publishers' Weekly*, 29 (9 January 1886): 49-50;

"J. B. Lippincott Company, 1792-1936," *Publishers' Weekly*, 130 (7 November 1936): 1840-1843;

"Joseph Wharton Lippincott," *Publishers' Weekly*, 124 (25 November 1933): 1857-1858;

"The Lippincotts of Philadelphia," *Bulletin of the American Library Association*, 51 (June 1957): 428-431;

Edith M. Stern, "J. B. Lippincott Company," *Saturday Review of Literature*, 24 (14 June 1941): 11-12.

—Margaret Becket

Charles C. Little and James Brown, who formed their publishing company in 1837

Little, Brown and Company
(Boston: 1847-   )
Charles C. Little and James Brown
(Boston: 1837-1847)

1923   *1937*

Little, Brown and Company had its beginnings in a bookstore opened by Ebenezer Battelle in 1784 on Marlborough Street (now part of Washington Street) in Boston. The bookstore changed ownership several times, being purchased by Benjamin Guild in 1787, by Samuel Cabot in 1792, by William T. and Samuel Blake in 1797, by William Andrews in 1806, and by Jacob A. Cummings and William Hilliard in 1813. The firm of Cummings, Hilliard and Company became Carter, Hilliard and Company when Timothy Carter became a partner in 1821. Carter was replaced by Harrison Gray in 1827, and the firm's name was changed to Hilliard, Gray and Company. Charles C. Little and James Brown, both former clerks, had become partners in the bookstore in 1826. In 1837 they bought the firm and formed their publishing company at 112 (now 254) Washington Street. They were joined a year later by Augustus Flagg.

One of the house's first titles was William H. Prescott's *Ferdinand and Isabella* (1838). In 1839 the firm, then known as Charles C. Little and James Brown, published the first book of the mystic poet Jones Very, edited by Emerson. Little, Brown grew largely because the interests and talents of its partners complemented each other. Brown focused on importing foreign books, while Little managed an increasingly impressive list of legal publications, and Flagg managed the bookstore.

Although the house published James Russell Lowell's first book, *A Year's Life* (1841), *Letters of John Adams* (1841), and several works by Francis Parkman, it was generally reluctant to advertise native titles, usually consigning American books to the back of its yearly catalogue. Legal publications, on the other hand, were given special prominence. In 1847 the firm's name was changed to Little, Brown and Company. The company's most ambitious early project was the publication, beginning in 1853, of the works of British poets from Chaucer to Wordsworth. Harvard professor Francis J. Child edited the series, which in five years comprised ninety-six volumes. Brown died in 1855. In 1859 John Bartlett became a partner in the firm, bringing with him the rights to his *Familiar Quotations* (1855). Although in a preface to the ninth edition (1891) Bartlett predicted the end of the volume's "tentative life," Little, Brown went on to publish the fifteenth edition in 1980, 125 years after its first appearance.

John Bartlett brought the rights to his Familiar Quotations *with him when he became a partner in Little, Brown and Company in 1859*

Augustus Flagg, managing partner of the firm following the death of Charles C. Little in 1869

Flagg became managing partner of the firm on Little's death in 1869. The company had two young men on its staff who would eventually broaden the character of its list. They were James Brown's son, John Murray Brown, who became head of the firm when Flagg retired in 1884, and James W. McIntyre, who had started with the company in 1865. At the urging of McIntyre in particular, the company began in the 1890s to expand into general publishing, including fiction. In 1896 it published Henryk Sienkiewicz's *Quo Vadis*, a best-seller. In 1898, again at McIntyre's instigation, the company purchased the general list of the Boston house of Roberts Brothers. This acquisition brought a successful group of fiction writers under the Little, Brown imprint, including Edward Everett Hale, Helen Hunt Jackson, and Louisa May Alcott. McIntyre became head of the firm on Brown's death in 1908. In 1909 the company purchased the Cabot family residence at 34 Beacon Street, on the corner of Joy Street, overlooking the Boston Common. The early-nineteenth-century brownstone still houses the company's offices.

Upon McIntyre's death in 1913, the company was incorporated and its eldest partner, Charles W. Allen, became the first president. Allen's role was primarily financial; editorial chores fell to Herbert F. Jenkins and Alfred R. McIntyre, son of James McIntyre. Jenkins was the first to recognize the work of Thornton W. Burgess, and he also acquired Erich Maria Remarque's *All Quiet on the Western Front* (1929) and A. J. Cronin's first novel, *Hatter's Castle* (1931). McIntyre became the company's driving force after World War I and was named its second president in 1926.

In 1925 Little, Brown signed an agreement with The Atlantic Monthly Press to publish all Atlantic Monthly books. Notable books published under the Atlantic Monthly Press/Little, Brown imprint include James Truslow Adams's history *The Adams Family* (1930), Charles Nordhoff and James Norman Hall's *Bounty* trilogy (1932-1934), James Hilton's *Good-bye, Mr. Chips* (1934), and Walter D. Edmonds's *Drums along the Mohawk* (1936). The joint imprint was discontinued in 1985, but Little, Brown continues to act as distributor for Atlantic Monthly Press books.

The company flourished in the 1930s and 1940s, focusing on trade and law publishing. Some of the most noteworthy Little, Brown literary titles of this period were imports from England. The firm was the chief American publisher of works by Cronin, of whose many books the best known are *The Citadel* (1937), *The Keys of the Kingdom* (1941), and *The Green Years* (1944). Little, Brown published C. S. Forester's *The African Queen* (1935), followed by *Captain Horatio Hornblower* (1939). Little, Brown was also the chief American publisher of works by Evelyn Waugh, including *Scoop* (1938), *Brideshead Revisited* (1946), and *The Loved One* (1948). Two important and prolific American authors came to Little, Brown during this period. After having some of his early books published elsewhere, John P. Marquand turned *Warning Hill* over to the firm in 1930 and began a relationship which resulted in the publication of twenty-two volumes, including the Mr. Moto books and *The Late George Apley* (1937). Ogden Nash, after a few early books with Simon and Schuster, went on to have more than twenty-five volumes of his humorous verse—and some other writings—published by Little, Brown. Little, Brown had published the first edition of Oliver Wendell Holmes's classic study *The Common Law* (1881). By 1940 the law book department had an active list of over 100 titles.

In the early 1950s Arthur H. Thornhill, who had become the company's third president in 1948, undertook to expand nonfiction publishing, strengthen the firm's list of children's books, and modernize the law book department. In addition, he decided in 1952 to enter medical book publishing and Little, Brown is now one of the largest publishers in the field. In 1958 the company established a college textbook department, which has become prominent in English, political science, and history.

One of the most widely read novels of the 1950s was J. D. Salinger's *The Catcher in the Rye*, which Little, Brown published in 1951, followed by the rest of Salinger's scant literary output: *Nine Stories* (1953); *Raise High the Roof Beam, Carpenters, and Seymour* (1959); and *Franny and Zooey* (1961). Norman Mailer's *Of a Fire on the Moon* (1970) was followed by *The Prisoner of Sex* (1971), *Existential Errands* (1972), and *The Fight* (1975). Though most of Bruce Catton's Civil War books were published by other firms, Little, Brown published his *Grant Moves South* in 1960 and *Grant Takes Command* in 1969. Among Edwin O'Connor's novels published by the firm were *The Last Hurrah* (1956) and *The Edge of Sadness* (1961). Catherine Drinker Bowen had biographies of Oliver Wendell Holmes (1944), John Adams (1950), and Francis Bacon (1963) published by the firm. Most of J. Frank Dobie's novels, including *Apache Gold & Yaqui Silver* (1939), *The Mustangs* (1952), and *Cow People* (1964), were published by Little, Brown.

John Murray Brown, youngest son of James Brown, became head of the firm upon Augustus Flagg's retirement in 1884

Henryk Sienkiewicz (right) with Jeremiah Curtin. Curtin's translation of Quo Vadis, *published by the firm in 1896, gained Sienkiewicz a large audience for his earlier romances of Poland.*

In 1962 Arthur H. Thornhill, Jr., was named president and chief executive officer. He continued the policy set by his father of balancing general publishing with textbook, law, and medical publishing. During his tenure, titles on the company's list included John Fowles's *The Magus* (1965) and *The French Lieutenant's Woman* (1969); Lillian Hellman's *An Unfinished Woman* (1969), *Pentimento* (1973), and *Scoundrel Time* (1976); Herman Wouk's *The Winds of War* (1971) and *War and Remembrance* (1978); and Henry Kissinger's *White House Years* (1979). Donald Barthelme's first book, *Come Back, Dr. Caligari,* appeared in 1964. The firm published the first eight books of Hortense Calisher, beginning with *In the Absence of Angels* (1951) and concluding with *The New Yorkers* (1969). Since *No, But I Saw the Movie* (1952), his fourth book, all of humorist Peter De Vries's major works have been published by the firm. Gore Vidal's Little, Brown titles include *Visit to a Small Planet* (1956), *Washington, D.C.* (1967), *Myra Breckinridge* (1968), and *Burr* (1973). Books by William Manchester, the works in sexology by William H. Masters and Virginia Johnson, James Crockett's gardening books, and the photography of Ansel Adams have also been featured on Little, Brown's lists.

In 1968 Time, Incorporated, purchased Little, Brown, which operates as a wholly owned subsidiary. In January 1985 Kevin L. Dolan, former controller of Time Incorporated, was appointed president and chief operating officer; Thornhill remains as chairman and chief executive officer of Little, Brown. The company publishes more than 300 titles each year; its backlist contains over 3,000 titles. The firm's address is 34 Beacon Street, Boston 02106.

References:

Books from Beacon Hill: The Story of the Boston Publishing House of Little, Brown and Company, 1837-1926 (Boston: Little, Brown, 1926);

George Stillman Hillard, *A Memoir of James Brown* (Boston: Privately printed, 1856);

"Little, Brown & Company, 1837-1937," *Publishers' Weekly*, 131 (13 March 1937): 1233-1237;

"Little, Brown's 125 Years of Publishing," *Publishers' Weekly*, 181 (19 March 1962): 22-27;

One Hundred Years of Publishing, 1837-1937 (Boston: Little, Brown, 1937);

"The Story of Little, Brown and Company," *Book Production Magazine*, 77 (June 1963): 50-54.

—*Bill Oliver*

*James W. McIntyre succeeded John Murray Brown as head of
the firm in 1908*

*34 Beacon Street, Boston, purchased in 1909 to house the offices
of Little, Brown and Company*

Thornton W. Burgess. Little, Brown and Company published his first collection of animal stories, Old Mother West Wind, *in 1910 at the urging of Herbert F. Jenkins.*

Charles W. Allen became the first president of the firm following its incorporation in 1913

H. Long and Brother
(New York: 1847?-1860)

H. Long and Brother was founded by H. Long and E. D. Long at 43 Ann Street, New York, around 1847, relocating at 121 Nassau Street in 1855. The firm published popular fiction. Some of its titles included H. R. Howard's *The Life and Adventures of John A. Murrell, the Great Western Land Pirate* and *The Life and Adventures of Joseph T. Hare, the Bold Robber and Highwayman*, both published anonymously in 1847; M. M. Huet's *Silver and Pewter: A Tale of High Life and Low Life in New York* (1852) and *Morgan, the Buccaneer; or, The True History of the Freebooters of the Antilles* (1853); and James A. Maitland's *The Lawyer's Story; or, The Orphan's Wrongs* (1853), *The Old Doctor; or, Stray Leaves from My Journal* (1853), and *The Watchman* (1855). Novels by Justin Jones, written under the pseudonym Harry Hazel, included *Red King, the Corsair Chieftain, A Romance of the Ocean* (1850), *Sylvia Seabury; or, Yankees in Japan. The Romantic Adventures of a Sailor Boy* (1850), *The Flying Artillerist; or, The Child of the Battle-Field. A Tale of Mexican Treachery* (1853), and *Ralph Runnion; or, The Outlaw's Doom* (1858).

E. D. Long published titles under his own imprint from the Nassau Street address, including Louise Reeder's *Currer Lyle; or, The Stage in Romance and the Stage in Reality* (1856) and Maitland's *The Wanderer: A Tale of Life's Vicissitudes* (1856). The publishing firm of Frederick A. Brady of 24 Ann Street may have succeeded H. Long and Brother and E. D. Long after 1860.

—Kathleen R. Davis

Longmans, Green and Company
(New York: 1887-1961)

Longmans, Green and Company was established at 15 East Sixteenth Street in New York in 1887 to distribute the titles of its London parent firm, founded by Thomas Longman in 1724. Charles J. Mills came from England in 1889 to manage the New York branch and was succeeded by his sons and grandsons until the firm was dissolved in 1961. Expanding beyond its original function as a distributor, the company published its own books in education, religion, and history. In 1895 Longmans, Green moved to 91-93 Fifth Avenue. In 1896 the firm published *The Will to Believe* by William James, who had sold it to Longmans in 1895 after a disagreement with his usual publisher, Henry Holt. Among Longmans, Green's literary publications were Brander Matthews's *A Family Tree, and Other Stories* (1889), J. W. DeForest's *A Lover's Revolt; A Romance of the American Revolution* (1898), and *Parson Kelly* (1899) by A. E. W. Mason and Andrew Lang. The firm published Thomas W. Higginson's *Afternoon Landscape* in 1889 and a reprint of his *Atlantic Essays* (1894), followed by Matthews's *Notes on Speech-Making* (1901) and *The Philosophy of the Short Story* (1901).

Primarily education-oriented like its parent firm, Longmans, Green published notable historical series, including the eleven-volume Historic Towns (1891-1897), edited by E. A. Freeman. Henry Cabot Lodge wrote the Boston volume and Theodore Roosevelt contributed the volume on

New York. Woodrow Wilson wrote *Division and Reunion 1829-1889* (1893), the third book in the Epoch of American History series (1891-1893), edited by A. B. Hart of Harvard. College Histories of Art (1894), edited by John C. Van Dyke of Rutgers, was another important Longmans, Green series, along with the American Citizen series, Living Thoughts Library, Our Debt to Greece and Rome, and the American Teachers series. The firm also published textbooks for elementary and high schools, and the New York branch carried on the parent firm's tradition of publishing theological works.

In 1903 Walter Jefferay arrived from England and joined Mills in managing Longmans, Green for many years. In 1910 the firm became a tenant of the new Dodd, Mead Building at 443-444 Fourth Avenue at Thirtieth Street. In 1921 Longmans, Green moved to 55 Fifth Avenue. In January 1932 Coward-McCann made an operating arrangement to share shipping and billing with Longmans, Green; after a year, however, the arrangement dissolved by mutual consent. An arrangement with the Oxford University Press, similar to the one with Coward-McCann, necessitated a move to 114 Fifth Avenue in 1934. Six years later the firm returned to its former address at 55 Fifth Avenue.

During its last forty years, the firm published a great deal of fiction, especially juveniles and adventures, but few of its titles were of literary significance. Some of Longmans, Green's better fiction publications during this period were Owen Francis Dudley's *The Shadow on the Earth* (1926) and *The Masterful Monk* (1929), Henry Clune's *The Good Die Poor* (1937), and Isobel Field's *This Life I've Loved* (1937). Laura Adams Armer's novel about the Navaho Indians, *Waterless Mountain* (1931), was illustrated by the author and her husband, Sidney Armer. *The Gospel According to St. Luke's* (1931), an example of the proletarian fiction of the 1930s, was the second novel of Philip Stevenson, who later wrote under the pseudonym Lars Lawrence. Longmans, Green gave Irving Stone his first major break by publishing his fictionalized biography of Van Gogh, *Lust for Life* (1934). The book had been rejected eighteen times before Stone's future wife, Jean Factor, edited it. By 1936 Longmans, Green was the seventh largest publisher in the United States.

On 1 June 1953 Longmans, Green once again entered into an arrangement with another company, this time sharing billing, warehouses, sales, shipping, publicity, and manufacturing with the David McKay Company. The latter firm moved to Longmans, Green's offices at 55 Fifth Avenue. Five years later, both firms moved to 119 West Fortieth Street. On 1 August 1961 the two companies merged, the Longmans, Green titles were integrated into the McKay list, and the American Longmans, Green imprint disappeared. The London Longmans, Green had no financial involvement in the new firm; the McKay Company continued to distribute its books in America, but even this arrangement lasted only until August 1962, when the London firm found other distributors. Later, the London Longmans, Green appointed Lothar Simon to form a new company in the United States; in 1973 Longman Incorporated was established at 19 West Fortieth Street, New York, with Simon as president. Currently, Longman Incorporated is located at 1560 Broadway, New York 10036; the president is Robert C. Kyle.

Reference:

"Longmans, New York, to Merge with McKay," *Publishers' Weekly*, 180 (7 August 1961): 35.

—*Jutta Willmann*

D. Longworth

(New York: 1796-1821)

David Longworth started business as a seller of maps and prints at 11 Park Street in New York in 1796. The following year he edited and published the first of his many New York city directories. In 1802 he moved to the Dramatic Repository, Shakespeare Gallery, and began publishing plays. Actors, theatergoers, and others bought these small books with so much interest that he sold them both separately and bound together in series. In 1807 he began to publish Washington Irving's *Salmagundi* (1807-1808) in twenty serial numbers and also started a new drama series, The English and American Stage, which ran to forty volumes. After his son Thomas joined him in 1811, they published under the imprints The Longworths, D. Longworth, or T. Longworth. Thomas Longworth continued to publish plays after his father retired in 1820; after his father's death in 1821 he ceased publishing drama, though he continued to publish directories and occasional other works for many years. He died in 1855. From 1802 through 1821 the Longworth firm published 429 editions of 347 plays, of which 37 were American. Longworth was the first American publisher to specialize in drama, and most of the plays published during this period came from the Longworth firm.

References:

Jacob Blanck, "*Salmagundi* and Its Publisher," *Papers of the Bibliographical Society of America*, 41 (1947): 1-32;

Roger E. Stoddard, "A Catalogue of the Dramatic Imprints of David and Thomas Longworth, 1802-1821," *Proceedings of the American Antiquarian Society*, 84 (1974): 317-398;

Stoddard, "Notes on American Play Publishing, 1765-1865," *Proceedings of the American Antiquarian Society*, 81 (1971): 161-187.

—Theodora Mills

A. K. Loring

(Boston: 1859-1881)

Born in Sterling, Massachusetts, in 1826, Aaron K. Loring began his career in the book trade as an apprentice with Phillips, Sampson and Company in Boston. In 1859 he opened the Up-town Bookstore, Periodical Counter, Fashionable Stationery Store, and Select Circulating Library at 319 Washington Street, where he loaned books for two cents per volume per day. Loring advertised his books in catalogues and provided home delivery service. A few years after opening his bookstore, Loring began publishing cheap books, thus becoming one of the more than thirty publishers operating on Boston's Washington Street during the second half of the nineteenth century. Loring's first book was *Faith Gartney's Girlhood* (1863), a book for girls by Mrs. A. D. T. Whitney.

From 1864 to 1867 Loring published five novels by Horatio Alger, Jr.: *Frank's Campaign* (1864), *Paul Prescott's Charge* (1865), *Charlie Codman's Cruise* (1866)—these became known as the Campaign series—followed by *Helen Ford* and *Timothy Crump's Ward*, both in 1866. Soon Loring began publishing Alger books in series, most notably the Ragged Dick series, which came out between 1868 and 1870 in six volumes at $1.25 per volume. Other Alger series published by Loring were Luck and Pluck (1869-1875), the Tattered Tom series (1871-1879), Brave and Bold (1874-1877), and the Pacific series (1878-1880). Loring published, in all, thirty-six Alger books. For girls, Loring published Louisa May Alcott's *Kitty's Class Day*, *Aunt Kipp*, *Psyche's Art*, and *Louisa M. Alcott's Proverb Stories*, all in 1868. That year, Alcott's most popular book, *Little Women*, was published by Roberts Brothers. Loring also published Virginia F. Townsend's Breakwater series, including *Joanna Darling; or, The Home at Breakwater* (1868) and *Hope Darrow: A Little Girl's Story* (1869); Mrs. Adeline Dutton Train Whitney's *Patience*

Alfred R. McIntyre succeeded Allen as president of Little, Brown and Company, Incorporated in 1926 (photograph by Bachrach)

Front cover for a book by Henry Johnson Brent

Strong's Outings (1869) and *Mother Goose for Grown Folks* (1870); and *Marion Berkley: A Story for Girls* (1870) and *The Hartwell Farm* (1871) by Laura Caxton (Elizabeth Barker Comins). One of Loring's most popular novels was John Habberton's *Helen's Babies, with Some Account of Their Ways, ... Also a Partial Record of Their Actions During Ten Days of Their Existence by Their Latest Victim* (1876).

For adults, the firm published Alcott's *Moods* (1865), as well as series and libraries of cheap books. Included in this group were Select Novels (thirty paperbacks at fifty cents each), Railway Library, Standard English Novels, and Popular Books. Although Loring mainly published fiction, it did not neglect the popular do-it-yourself or how-to manuals of the time. One of the firm's more notable series of manuals was Mrs. Warren's Stories by Eliza Warren, which included *How I Managed My Children from Infancy to Marriage* (1866) and *How to Furnish and Adorn a Home with Small Means* (1868).

In 1870, after operating out of temporary quarters at 35 School Street and 205 Washington Street, Loring moved to the corner of Washington and Bromfield Streets. In 1876 he scandalized the Boston publishing community by opening a coffee shop in his bookstore. Probably because the coffee shop distracted him from his book business and because the market had become flooded with cheap books, Loring went bankrupt on 15 June 1881. At that time the firm had published approximately 200 titles. Various firms bought the Loring plates; Porter and Coates obtained those for the Alger books. Loring subsequently worked as a stationer, bookseller, and librarian. He died in poverty on 26 September 1911.

References:
"Obituary Notes: Aaron K. Loring," *Publishers' Weekly,* 80 (30 September 1911): 1284;
Madeleine B. Stern, "The Rise and Fall of A. K. Loring," *Publishers' Weekly,* 149 (16 March 1946): 1654-1658.

—*Mary Mahoney*

D. Lothrop and Company
(Boston: 1868-1895)
Lothrop Publishing Company
(Boston: 1895-1904)

In 1868 Daniel Lothrop and N. P. Kemp formed D. Lothrop and Company at 38-40 Cornhill in Boston. Lothrop's brothers John C. and James E. Lothrop joined the firm in 1870. In 1875 the firm moved to Franklin and Hawley Streets.

Lothrop's first important book was Mrs. Mary Andrews Denison's *Andy Luttrell*, written under the pseudonym Clara Vance and published simultaneously in Boston and in Dover, New Hampshire, by G. T. Day and Company in 1869. The Dover connection lasted at least through the 1870s when Mrs. Denison's books continued to appear with dual imprints, as did her *Silent Tom* (1872) and *Barbara* (1876). In 1872 Lothrop published *From Night to Light* by Emma Elizabeth Brown and the anonymous *Ivy Fennhaven; or, Womanhood in Christ.* Novels published by the firm included Theodosia Foster's *Echoing and Re-Echoing* (1878), written under the pseudonym Faye Huntington; *Five Little Peppers and How They Grew* (1881) by Margaret Sidney, the pseudonym of Harriet Mulford Stone, Daniel Lothrop's second wife; Alphonso Alva Hopkins's *Sinner and Saint: A Story of the Woman's Crusade* (1881); Thomas Loyd Baily's *Possibilities* (1887); Abel B. Berry's *The Last Penacock: A Tale of Provincial Times* (1887); Emma Connelly's *Tilting at Wind-*

Daniel Lothrop, cofounder with N. P. Kemp of D. Lothrop and Company

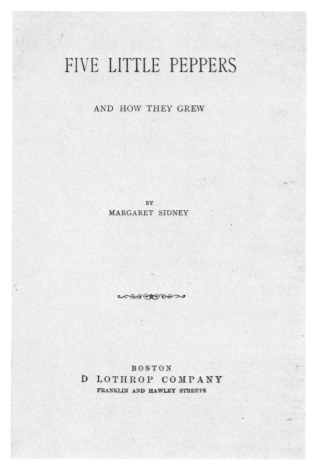

Title page for the pseudonymous novel written by Harriet Mulford Stone, Daniel Lothrop's second wife. It was published in 1881, one year after their marriage.

Harriet Mulford Stone Lothrop, Elizabeth Palmer Peabody, Daniel Lothrop, and Margaret Lothrop at Wayside, the Lothrop home in Concord Massachusetts, circa 1887 (Concord Free Public Library)

mills (1888); and Isabella Alden's *Aunt Hannah and Martha and John* (1890), which appeared under the pseudonym Pansy. Lothrop himself compiled several books, including *Ideal Poems* (1883), *Household Primer* (1885), *Pictures for Our Darlings* (1887), *Separate Lists of Religious and Secular Books for Sunday Schools* (1890), and *The Best Two Hundred and Sixty-seven Books for Libraries* (1890).

Lothrop also published Edward Everett Hale's *Boys' Heroes* (1885) and *A Family Flight through Mexico* (1886), Elbridge Streeter Brooks's *The Story of the American Indian* (1887) and *The Story of the United States of America* (1891), and H. H. Boyesen's *Vagabond Tales* (1889). Lothrop was among the largest publishers of American writers, with 2,000 titles by 1892.

Lothrop founded two literary magazines for children. *Pansy*, started in 1874, was followed by *Wide Awake* in 1875. The latter was designed for older children, and Lothrop hoped readers would graduate to it from *Pansy*. The early issues were called the *Wide Awake Pleasure Book*. Among the authors whose work appeared in *Wide Awake* were Hale, Sara Orne Jewett, and Mary Mapes Dodge. The magazine was merged with *St. Nicholas* magazine in 1893; *Pansy* ceased publication in 1896. Lothrop's other periodicals included *Babyland*, started in 1877, and *Little Men and Little Women*, started in 1894, which were combined in 1898. Lothrop also published the *Boston Book Bulletin: A Quarterly Eclectic Record of American and Foreign Books* from 1877 to 1886.

In 1887 the Lothrops accepted three more partners—W. H. Arnold, E. S. Brooks, and E. H. Pennell—and the firm moved to 364-366 Washington Street. After Daniel Lothrop died in 1892, Harriet Lothrop managed the firm for three years. In 1895 the firm was renamed Lothrop Publishing Company, with E. H. Pennell as president. The firm published Harold Frederic's *The Deserter, and Other Stories* (1898) and Irving Bacheller's *Eben Holden: A Tale of the North Country* (1900). In 1904 the firm went bankrupt and its assets were purchased by Lee and Shepard, which then became Lothrop, Lee and Shepard.

References:

"Contributions to Trade History: No. XXX, D. Lothrop & Co.," *American Bookseller*, new series 19 (1886): 281-283;

"Daniel Lothrop," *Publishers' Weekly*, 41 (26 March 1892): 494-495;

John N. McClintock, "Daniel Lothrop," *Bay State Monthly*, no. 2 (1883-1884): 121-131.

—*Neal L. Edgar*

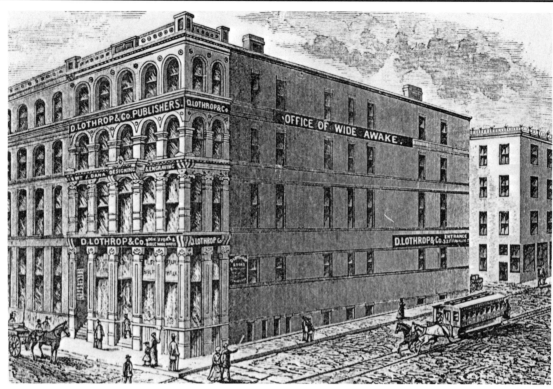

The building at Franklin and Hawley Streets, Boston, that was the firm's home from 1875 until 1887, when it moved to 364-366 Washington Street

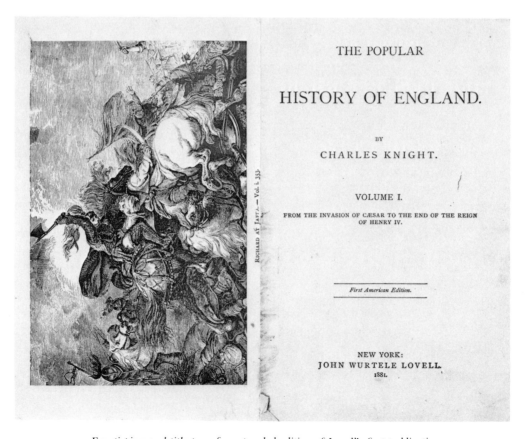

Frontispiece and title page for expanded edition of Lovell's first publication

John W. Lovell Company
(New York: 1882-1891)
John W. Lovell
(New York: 1878-1881)

The career of John Wurtele Lovell represents a paradoxical blend of piracy, monopoly, occultism, and socialist publishing. A sincere advocate of the working man, Lovell could nevertheless be called the John D. Rockefeller of the book industry. Lovell started out in 1864 as an apprentice printer in Montreal at his father's Lovell Printing and Publishing Company. By 1873 he was managing his father's Lake Champlain Press at Rouse's Point, New York. The firm distributed British literature to Canada. In 1876 Lovell joined his father and G. Mercer Adam to form Lovell, Adam and Company, specializing in cheap reprints of British copyright books, in New York City. With the addition of Francis L. Wesson, the partnership soon became Lovell, Adam, Wesson and Company at 764 Broadway. This firm published the Lake Champlain Press series as well as foreign reprints. The company was dissolved in 1877. Lovell started his own firm at 24 Bond Street in New York in 1878, moving later to 16 Astor Place.

Although there was as yet no international copyright law, publishers maintained inflated prices through an informal arrangement, known as "courtesy of the trade," by which only one firm would reprint a given foreign book. Lovell planned to upset this de facto cartel by selling his pirated reprints at the lowest possible cost and thus opening up a completely new market among the masses.

Lovell's first book was *The Popular History of England* (1878) by Charles Knight. Later, works by Dickens, Milton, Coleridge, Kipling, and Thackeray were included in several series of inexpensive reprints—Lovell's Editions of the Poets, Caxton Classics, Standard Histories, and Popular Twelve-mos—all printed from new electrotype plates at Lovell's father's plant in Rouse's Point. Although Lovell promised authors a ten percent royalty for reprint rights, this promise was evidently not always kept. Perhaps because of such lapses, Lovell's reputation suffered. His business failed in 1881 but was reorganized at 14 Vesey Street as the John W. Lovell Company a year later.

Starting with Lovell's Library—a series of paperbacks—in 1882, the John W. Lovell Company soon emerged as one of the largest publishers of inexpensive popular and literary books in America. Lovell's Library offered not only popular titles such as *Her Mother's Sin* (1883) and *Love Works Wonders* (1884) by Charlotte Mary Brame (under the pseudonym Bertha M. Clay), *Dick's Sweetheart* (1885) by Mrs. Margaret Wolfe Hungerford, and *A False Scent* (1889) by Mrs. Annie Hector but also such literary reprints as Bunyan's *The Pilgrim's Progress* (1883), Thackeray's *Vanity Fair* (1883), and Longfellow's *Voices of the Night* (1885). The series, published at the rate of one—later three—titles a week, also included histories, biographies, and travel books. After Lovell obtained a second-class postal rate for these books, his sales exceeded seven million volumes a year, with over four million in stock. By 1890 the firm had published nearly 1,500 titles. At one point, a new title was published each day, earning Lovell the nickname of "Book-a-Day Lovell."

In spite of the aggressive capitalism of his own ventures, Lovell championed the causes of organized labor, socialism, feminism, and radical politics with Edward Kellogg's *Labor and Capital* (1883), S. Robert Wilson and A. J. Starkweather's *Socialism* (1884), and Albert K. Owen's *Integral Co-Operation* (1885). Jean Baptiste André Godin's *Social Solutions* (1886) criticized the wage system and offered a plan for organizing unions. Translated from the French by Marie Howland and edited by Edward Howland, this work appeared in twelve semimonthly parts. A year earlier, Lovell had reprinted Marie Howland's *Papa's Own Girl*, a socialistic novel set in France. Lillie Devereux Blake's *Woman's Place To-Day* (1883), Margaret Lee's novel *Divorce* (1889), and August Bebel's *Woman in the Past, Present, and Future* (1891) reflected the firm's dedication to women's rights.

One of the firm's best-selling political volumes was Henry George's *Progress and Poverty* (1883), which inaugurated Lovell's Political and Scientific series. (The book also appeared as number 52 in Lovell's Library.) A later series, Lovell's Occult series, reflected Lovell's membership in Madame Blavatsky's American Theosophical Society. In 1892 he formed with Ursula Gestefeld, another theosophist, the firm of Lovell, Gestefeld and Company, which specialized in occult, feminist, and labor tracts. Lovell also helped found and served as the

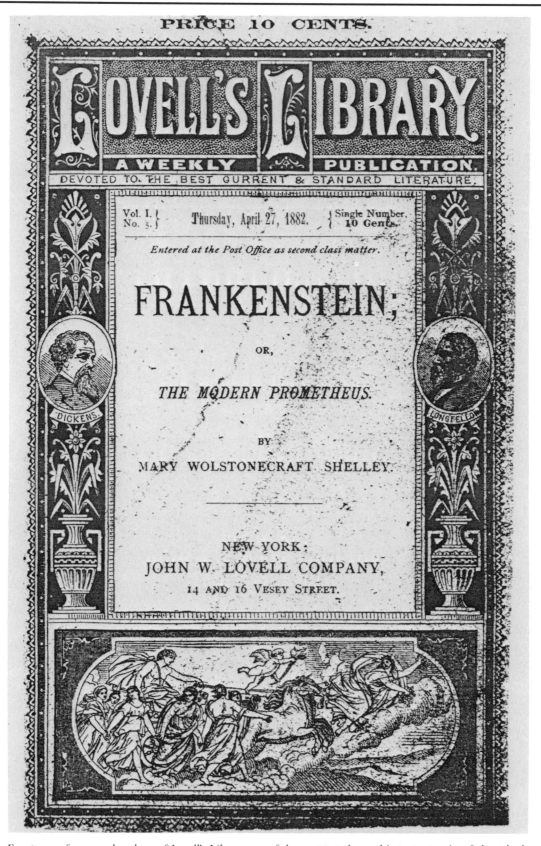

Front cover for an early volume of Lovell's Library, one of the most popular and important series of cheap books

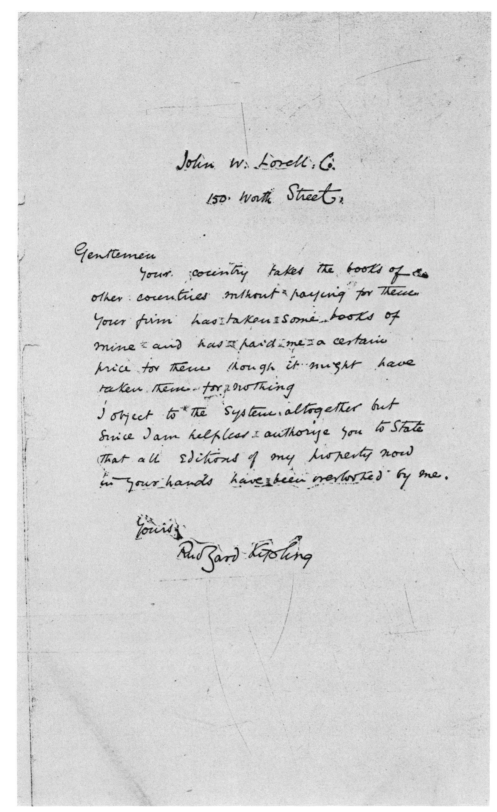

John W. Lovell. C.
150. Worth Street.

Gentlemen
    Your country takes the books of
other countries without paying for them.
Your firm has taken some books of
mine and has paid me a certain
price for them though it might have
taken them for nothing
    I object to the system altogether but
since I am helpless I authorize you to state
that all editions of my property now
in your hands have been overlooked by me.

        Yours
            Rudyard Kipling

In the absence of international copyright, Rudyard Kipling's works were pirated by American publishers. This letter appeared as the frontispiece in the 1890 Lovell "Authorized Edition" of Kipling's Soldiers Three.

treasurer of a Utopian cooperative community called Pacific City in Sinaloa, Mexico.

Lovell's publishing empire continued to expand. In 1888 the firm acquired the plates and stock of the Munro Library. Many new series appeared, including Lovell's American Novelists series, the Foreign Literature series, Lovell's American Authors series, the Universal series, and the Franklin series. This expansion in output was facilitated by the development of several subsidiary firms: in Boston and New York, Lovell's brother Frank controlled Frank F. Lovell and Company; his brother Charles presided over the Lovell Manufacturing Company, a bookbinding operation. A Chicago branch was also added.

In 1888 Lovell sent Wolcott Balestier to London to acquire works by British writers, resulting in the publication of Mrs. Humphrey Ward's *Robert Elsmere* (1888), Rudyard Kipling's *Soldiers Three* (1890), and James M. Barrie's *The Little Minister*

(1891). Lovell's International series, with a new title published each week, provided a vehicle for many British novels, including Hungerford's *April's Lady* and *A Born Coquette*, both published in 1890 under the pen name The Duchess. These editions were authorized, not pirated, and occasionally represented first American printings. By 1891 the firm had published 147 titles in Lovell's International series and 149 titles in Lovell's Literature series, which featured works by Ruskin, Carlyle, Plutarch, Whittier, and Longfellow. By this time the company was located at 142-150 Worth Street.

In an attempt to gain a monopoly of cheap book production in the United States, Lovell founded the United States Book Company. The new firm, incorporated under New Jersey law in July 1890, absorbed the John W. Lovell Company a year later.

—*David Dzwonkoski*

Lovell, Coryell and Company
(New York: 1892-1897)
Coryell and Company
(New York: 1897-1904)

Lovell, Coryell and Company was founded at 43-47 East Tenth Street, New York, in 1892 by John Wurtele Lovell and Vincent M. Coryell, with the latter serving as president. The firm was a subsidiary of Lovell's cheap book conglomerate, the United States Book Company, which specialized in piracies of European books. When the passage of the International Copyright Act of 1891 threatened to ruin Lovell's business, he quickly organized Lovell, Coryell and Company as a producer of reprints of better quality.

The new firm republished many of the United States Book Company's series, including the Standard Twelvemos, the Universal series, and the Illustrated Series of American Novels, in still inexpensive but better-made volumes. Limited Deluxe Editions on fine paper with gilt tops, occasionally signed, featured works by James N. Barrie, Henrik Ibsen, and James Whistler.

Having moved in May 1893 to the offices of the United States Book Company at 5-7 East Six-

teenth Street, Lovell, Coryell and Company was forced to move again in February 1894 upon the bankruptcy of the parent company to the Cammeyer Building at the corner of Sixth Avenue and Twentieth Street. Here were stocked about one and a half million volumes on one floor, including the New Oxford series of gilt-topped two-volume sets bound in silk vellum, with works by George Eliot and Charles Dickens; the Century series of two-volume sets of essays by Darwin, Spencer, and Ruskin; and sets offering well-made volumes of the works of the Brontës, Sir Walter Scott, Washington Irving, and William Makepeace Thackeray. In spite of the new copyright act, the firm continued to pirate many of its titles.

In 1897 Lovell, Coryell and Company was renamed Coryell and Company and taken over by the American Publishers Corporation, which had been organized by Lovell's creditors to recoup their losses. The American Publishers Corporation soon went into receivership and was reorganized as the

Publishers Plate Renting Company. The company went through years of litigation before the final settlement of its complex affairs. In 1904 Coryell and Company sold the last of the Lovell printing plates at auction and liquidated itself.

Reference:

John T. Winterich, "Good Second-Hand Condition," *Publishers' Weekly*, 123 (21 January 1933): 248-249.

—*David Dzwonkoski*

Fielding Lucas, Jr.
(Baltimore: 1810-1854)

The firm of Fielding Lucas, Jr., was established in 1810 at 170 Market Street, Baltimore, when Lucas purchased the remaining stock of books and stationery from Conrad, Lucas and Company, which had been formed in 1807 by Lucas and the Conrads, a Philadelphia publishing family. In its first decades, the Lucas firm maintained a close relationship with Mathew Carey, the prominent Philadelphia publisher. Between 1810 and 1820, Lucas relied heavily on Carey for financial support. Carey and Lucas also exchanged stereotyped plates.

Lucas became one of the major Catholic publishers in America with the acquisition in 1830 of plates for the Catholic Family Library and Catholic Tracts, series begun by another publisher, Eugene Cummisky. Between 1838 and 1841 Lucas published 154 Catholic titles; the biggest seller was the *Catholic Catechism*, of which 3,800 copies were sold in 1838. Lucas also published the *Metropolitan Catholic Calendar* and *Laity's Directory* annually. The firm published some fiction, including Tobias Watkins's *Tales of the Tripod; or, A Delphian Evening. By Pertinax Particular* (1821) and Charles Constantine Pise's *Father Rowland: A North American Tale* (1829) and *The Indian Cottage: A Unitarian Story* (1831). A dis-

tinguished mapmaker, Lucas included twenty maps of his own design in the seven atlases published by his firm, starting with *A New and Elegant General Atlas Containing Maps of Each of the United States* (1814). Although Lucas also published standard works, some schoolbooks, drawing books, and children's books, religious works were the firm's main source of income.

When Lucas died in 1854, the business was turned over to his three sons, Edward, William, and Henry. William F. Lucas, Jr., was the last of the Lucas family to be an active head of the business, which continued as a stationery and business supply house called Lucas Brothers.

References:

James W. Foster, "Fielding Lucas, Jr., Early 19th Century Publisher of Fine Books and Maps," *Proceedings of the American Antiquarian Society*, 65 (20 April 1955-19 October 1955): 161-212;

Richard J. Tommey, "Fielding Lucas, Jr., First Major Catholic Publisher and Bookseller in Baltimore, Maryland, 1804-1854," M.A. thesis, Catholic University of America, 1952.

—*Elizabeth Scott Pryor*

The F. M. Lupton Publishing Company
(New York: 1892-1902)
F. M. Lupton
(New York: circa 1882-1892)
Federal Book Company
(New York: 1902-1904?)

Frank Moore Lupton began publishing domestic and agricultural reference works in New York under the imprint F. M. Lupton around 1882. By 1888 his firm was located at 63 Murray Street. Later it moved to 106-108 Reade Street, where it was incorporated in 1892 with Walter S. Trigg, Thomas H. Marshall, Stuart H. Moore, Albert B. Beers, and August Schlegel as directors. Shortly after its incorporation the firm moved to 65 Duane Street and began publishing sets and series of literary works on a massive scale. The Standard Sets included octavo editions of the complete works of Dickens, Thackeray, George Eliot, and Shakespeare. The Bijou, Souvenir, and Elite series of paperback books were priced at six to seven cents each in lots of 100, while the clothbound Stratford, Avon, and Lenox twelvemo series were priced at eleven to fourteen cents in lots of 1,000. Most of these books were cheaply bound, crudely typeset, and printed on paper of the lowest quality, although the Cambridge series was advertised as having "silk cloth covers, gold tops, and fine book paper." The firm moved to 72-76 Walker Street in 1894.

Passage of the International Copyright Act of 1891, the panic and subsequent depression of 1893, and intense competition had so altered the publishing business that by 1896 Lupton was trying to dump its entire line on the market, offering it to the trade "regardless of value or cost." Finding few takers, Lupton continued its series and added the National series of copyrighted works by authors including Mrs. E. D. E. N. Southworth, Frances Hodgson Burnett, and Caroline Lee Hentz.

In 1897 J. M. Ruston, formerly of Hurst and Company, became manager of The F. M. Lupton Publishing Company and introduced the Goldenrod series, reprinting works by Arthur Conan Doyle and Rudyard Kipling; the Violet series, with reprints of Alexandre Dumas's *Camille*, Charlotte M. Brame's *My Sister Kate*, and Susannah Rowson's *Charlotte Temple;* the Windsor twelvemos; and the Colonial twelvemos, a deluxe series with deckle-edged antique laid paper, gold tops and stampings, and satin cloth covers.

The firm moved in 1899 to 52-58 Duane Street. That year it published a series of 124 titles by Mrs. Southworth, as well as other series which offered the works of Balzac, W. E. Norris, Mrs. Alexander (pseudonym of Annie Hector), and Henryk Sienkiewicz. Soon the firm was publishing such original titles as Anna Katherine Green's *A Difficult Problem* (1900), Florence Hull Winterburn's *Southern Hearts* (1900), and Frederick W. Hayes's *Kent Squire* (1900) and *Gwynett of Thornhaugh* (1900).

In 1902 the firm moved to the Lupton Building at 23-27 City Hall Place and changed its name to the Federal Book Company. The firm seems to have gone out of business in 1904. Until his death in 1910, Lupton concentrated on magazine publishing—not a new occupation, since he had earlier published *Ladies World, Fireside and Home,* the *People's Home Journal,* and *Good Literature,* though not in connection with The F. M. Lupton Publishing Company.

Reference:
"Frank Moore Lupton [obituary]," *Publishers' Weekly,* 78 (8 October 1910): 1398.

—*David Dzwonkoski*

The Macmillan Company
(New York: 1896-1973)
Macmillan and Company
(New York: 1869-1896)
Macmillan Publishing Company
(New York: 1973-   )

In 1843 the brothers Alexander and Daniel Macmillan founded Macmillan and Company in London. Macmillan books were distributed in America by Scribner and Welford until 1869, when George Edward Brett, a London bookseller, sailed to New York to establish an American office at 63 Bleecker Street. It was only the second establishment of an American branch of an English publishing house—Thomas Nelson was first. Originally planned merely as a distribution agency, the American Macmillan began publishing its own books in 1886.

In 1874 George Platt Brett, at sixteen, joined his father on the Macmillan staff as a traveling salesman. After high school the son's poor health sent him out West. When his father became ill he returned to assume the management of the branch, rigorously training himself in publishing while attending New York University in the evenings. In 1890, the year of the elder Brett's death, the New York office was made a semi-independent operation with the young Brett as a partner along with some of the London partners. Six years later the American firm was incorporated as The Macmillan Company with Brett as president, while the London parent firm reorganized as Macmillan and Company, Limited; members of the British Macmillan were appointed to the American Macmillan's board of directors. From his ascent to the presidency to his death in 1936, Brett shaped a remarkable publishing success story, with annual revenues rising from $50,000 in 1890 to well over $10 million in 1935.

During the early years Macmillan's strength lay in its British list, which included Thomas Hardy, John Masefield, May Sinclair, Rudyard Kipling, H. G. Wells, Sir James Frazer, C. S. Lewis, William Butler Yeats, A. E. (George William Russell), Sean O'Casey, and James Stephens. Among Macmillan's first important American authors were Francis Marion Crawford, Henry James, Winston Churchill, and Hamlin Garland. Crawford's first book, the highly successful *Mr. Isaacs: A Tale of Modern India* (1882), was published by Macmillan in London first. Then, in what remained standard procedure for some years, the English second printing was distributed in America by the New York Macmillan. *Doctor Claudius: A True Story* (1883), Crawford's second novel, was followed by *Zoroaster* (1885), *Casa Braccio* (1895), and *The White Sister* (1909). James's books for Macmillan included *Partial Portraits* (1888), *The Aspern Papers/Louisa Pallant/The Modern Warning* (1888), and *The Two Magics/The Turn of the Screw/Covering End* (1898). After *The Soft Side* (1900), James moved to Scribner. Brett had his first best-seller in Churchill's *Richard Carvel* in 1899, with sales of over a half-million copies. In the same year Macmillan published its first title by Garland, *The Trail of the Goldseekers: A Record of Travel in Prose and Verse.* Although Garland was not a regular author at Macmillan, the firm published his *A Daughter of the Middle Border* (1921) and *Back-trailers from the Middle Border* (1928).

In 1902 Macmillan had best-sellers in Gertrude Atherton's *The Conqueror* and Owen Wister's *The Virginian.* Brett, who combed magazines in search of new writers, started a correspondence with Jack London that resulted in Macmillan's publication of London's fourth book, *Children of the Frost* (1902). The promise Brett had seen in London was fulfilled the following year with *The Call of the Wild,* followed by *The Sea-Wolf* (1904), *White Fang* (1906), *Martin Eden* (1909), *South Sea Tales* (1911), and *The Star Rover* (1915).

One of Macmillan's most distinguished poets, Edwin Arlington Robinson, began at the firm with a play, *Van Zorn,* in 1914 and went on to produce a long line of works that included *The Man against the Sky* (1916), *Collected Poems* (1921), *The Man Who Died Twice* (1924), *Tristram* (1927), and *Cavender's House* (1929). Also in 1914 Macmillan published Conrad Aiken's first book, *Earth Triumphant and*

Fielding Lucas, Jr., (Collection Maryland Historical Society)

George Platt Brett joined Macmillan and Company in 1874 as a traveling salesman. He became president of the American branch when it was incorporated as the semi-independent Macmillan Company in 1896.

Other Tales in Verse, and in 1915 its first titles by two other poets, Sara Teasdale and Edgar Lee Masters. The latter's *Spoon River Anthology,* published in that year, remains his best-known work. Teasdale's works include *Rivers to the Sea* (1915), *Dark of the Moon* (1926), and *Collected Poems* (1937). Macmillan also published works by Ida Tarbell, Walter Lippmann, James Lane Allen, Alice Brown, Zona Gale, and DuBose Heyward.

Macmillan established an education department in 1894. In 1906 a college division, the first in the nation, was formed. The medical department was established in 1913, the juvenile department in 1919, and the outdoor-household arts department in 1927. Publications in these fields, along with encyclopedias and reference works—including the *Cyclopedia of American Agriculture* (1907) and *A Cyclopedia of Education* (1911)—were the basis of Macmillan's enormous prosperity. Textbooks provided half the house's income by 1920. Macmillan was notable for publishing significant scholarship, in accordance with Brett's belief that the public was becoming increasingly well educated and would welcome works of scholarly merit. Macmillan's important nonfiction books include *The Development of English Thought* (1899) by Simon Patten, *The Shifting and Incidence of Taxation* (1899) by Edwin R. Seligman, *Main Currents in 19th Century Literature* (1901) by George Brandes, *A History of Political Theories* (1902) by W. A. Dunning, *Elementary Principles of Economics* (1904) by Richard T. Ely, *The Supreme Court and the Constitution* (1912) by Charles A. Beard, *The Outline of History* (1920) by H. G. Wells, and *The Rise of American Civilization* (1927) by Charles A. and Mary Beard. Macmillan also published the journal *Physical Review* for Cornell University. Like other major houses, Macmillan produced books in series: Macmillan Standard Library, Modern Readers, European Statesmen, Macmillan's Novelists Library, English Men of Letters, Illustrated Standard Novels, National Studies in American Letters, and The Temple Shakespeare.

In 1919 Macmillan became the first American publishing house to set up a separate children's department under the editorship of Louise Seaman, who developed the Children's Classics and the Little Library series. In 1927 Macmillan entered the market in color picture books, previously supplied mostly by European publishers, with its forty-eight-page, fifty-cent Happy Hour Books.

In 1923 Macmillan moved to 60 Fifth Avenue, on the corner of Twelfth Street. A dynamic, outspoken man, Brett was a leader in publishing and

a spokesman for the industry. His genius for wholesale distribution led him to set up branch offices in Atlanta, Boston, Chicago, Dallas, and San Francisco, as well as in England, Canada, Australia, India, Japan, China, and the Philippines. George H. Doran described Brett as "an emperor among publishers," who built for himself "a miniature empire, commanding the greatest volume of business in American publishing history." He was probably the anonymous author of the publishers' and booksellers' creeds printed in the *Atlantic Monthly* in January 1925. He pronounced and predicted frequently, but not all his predictions proved accurate. He had forecast a new era of public appreciation of poetry around World War I and had declared the best-seller dead. In the year of his death, 1936, Macmillan published Margaret Mitchell's giant among best-sellers, *Gone with the Wind.*

George Brett, Jr., had begun working for the company in 1913, unpacking crates. After a further apprenticeship at Doubleday he returned as a salesman, traveling throughout the East. In 1921 he was appointed sales manager, and in 1928 he was made general manager. He succeeded his father as president when the elder Brett moved up to chairman of the board in 1931. With him worked editor in chief Harold S. Latham, Latham's assistant James Putnam, sales manager Alexander J. Blanton, and children's books director Doris Patee.

Other best-sellers followed *Gone with the Wind*: Rachel Field's *All This and Heaven Too* (1938), Richard Llewellyn's *How Green Was My Valley* (1940), and Kathleen Winsor's *Forever Amber* (1944). Two major reference works were B. E. Stevenson's *The Home Book of Proverbs* (1948) and Robert Spiller, T. H. Johnson, and H. S. Canby's *Literary History of the United States* (1948). But World War II marked the end of Macmillan's status as the largest publishing house in the United States: the firm's conservative financial policies allowed it to be overtaken by more energetic companies, including Doubleday, McGraw-Hill, and Prentice-Hall. Immanuel Velikovsky's *Worlds in Collision* (1950), which theorized that ancient myths and religions recorded actual catastrophes produced by the near approach to the earth of a comet, brought outraged attacks from much of the scientific community. Even though the book had been published by the trade division and the firm had made no scientific claims for it, Macmillan's textbook sales—a major source of the firm's profits—were jeopardized by the controversy. Therefore, in spite of the fact that *Worlds in Collision* was a popular best-seller, the book was turned over to Doubleday, which had no textbook department. (One of the key points which had drawn ridicule from the scientific establishment was Velikovsky's deduction, on the basis of his theory, that the surface of Venus is extremely hot—around 800 degrees Fahrenheit—and that its atmosphere contains hydrocarbons. The Mariner II space probe in 1963 confirmed both of those predictions.) In 1951 Brett forced the English publishing house to relinquish its hold on the American Macmillan, and the house entered into full independence. Brett retired in 1958, leaving the presidency to his son Bruce Y. Brett.

Under Bruce Brett, Macmillan initiated several new series, among them the Macmillan Paperback Poets, Macmillan Paperbacks, and *The Macmillan Everyman's Encyclopedia* (1959). In December 1960 Macmillan was acquired by the Crowell-Collier Publishing Company, Incorporated. The next year Crowell-Collier merged with Macmillan the social science publishing company, The Free Press of Glencoe, Illinois. Jeremiah Kaplan, the founder of The Free Press, became president of the Macmillan publishing subsidiary, while the president of Crowell-Collier, Raymond C. Hagel, became head of the parent company.

The takeover by Crowell-Collier inaugurated a period of tremendous expansion. The corporation acquired P. J. Kenedy; Benziger; Bruce; Science Materials Incorporated, which was renamed Professional and Technical Programs and developed into Macmillan Book Clubs; Brentano's; Berlitz Schools of Languages; Stechert-Hafner, Incorporated; Hafner Publishing Company; Hagstrom Company; LaSalle Extension University; Katherine Gibbs School; G. Schirmer; C. G. Conn; Turtox; Standard Rate and Data Service; Ferdinand Roten Galleries; Gump's; Uniforms by Ostwald; C. E. Ward; Collier-Macmillan Schools, Limited; and the English publishing companies Cassell's, Studio Vista, and Geoffrey Chapman. In 1965 the parent firm was renamed Crowell-Collier and Macmillan, Incorporated. In 1966 the company moved to 866 Third Avenue. In 1973 the parent company changed its name to Macmillan, Incorporated, and the publishing subsidiary became the Macmillan Publishing Company.

Macmillan has published the *Encyclopedia of Philosophy* (1967), the *International Encyclopedia of the Social Sciences* (1968), and the *Encyclopedia of Educational Research* (1969). In 1973 a new line of school dictionaries was established. Macmillan's psychological works are especially distinguished, with titles by B. F. Skinner, Bruno Bettelheim, and Gordon

W. Allport. Other authors of nonfiction have included Émile Durkheim, Herbert Hoover, Mortimer J. Adler, A. J. Ayer, and Franz Boas. While maintaining its strength in educational and reference publications, Macmillan has continued to be a force in the trade area with best-sellers including Barbara Tuchman's *The Guns of August* (1962), Albert Speer's *Inside the Third Reich* (1970), Richard Bach's *Jonathan Livingston Seagull* (1970), and Richard Adams's *Watership Down* (1974). From 1979 through 1982 Macmillan, Incorporated divested itself of thirty-five of its subsidiaries; then it began to acquire properties again, including Bradbury Press, Maclean Hunter Learning Resources, and the McKnight and Bennett publishing companies. In April 1984 the company took over Scribner Book Companies, making Scribner a subsidiary of Macmillan while allowing it to maintain its editorial independence. At the time of the agreement Scribner included Charles Scribner's Sons, Atheneum, and Rawson Associates. In 1984 Macmillan also acquired the School Division of Harper and Row, renaming it Scribner Educational Publishers; Dellen Publishing was added to Macmillan's college division the same year. In 1985 Bobbs-Merrill and G. K. Hall were acquired from ITT and added to Macmillan's publishing group as part of a continuing program of acquisition and development. Edward P. Evans is chairman of Macmillan, Incorporated; Kaplan is chairman and president of Macmillan Publishing Company. The firm's address is 866 Third Avenue, New York 10022.

References:

George Brett, Jr., "Activities of a Publishing House," *Texas Library Journal*, 27 (1951): 134-144;

"Crowell-Collier, Macmillan Agree on Merger Terms," *Publishers' Weekly*, 178 (24 October 1960): 28-29;

John P. Dessauer, "Coming Full Circle at Macmillan: A Publishing Merger in Economic Perspective," *Book Research Quarterly*, 1 (Winter 1985-1986): 60-72;

"George Platt Brett [obituary]," *Publishers' Weekly*, 130 (July-December 1936): 1331-1332;

Harold S. Latham, *My Life in Publishing* (New York: Dutton, 1965);

"Macmillan Acquires Scribner," *New York Times*, 26 April 1984, p. C17;

The Macmillan Company (New York: Macmillan, 1954);

"The Macmillan Company and Its Departments,"

The Macmillan Company building at the corner of Fifth Avenue and Twelfth Street, New York, was headquarters for the firm from 1923 until 1966 (Underwood & Underwood)

Louise Seaman, editor of the first separate children's books department in the United States, set up by The Macmillan Company in 1919

in *The Author's Book* (New York: Macmillan, 1944), pp. 1-23;

Charles Morgan, *The House of Macmillan (1843-1943)* (New York: Macmillan, 1944);

"The Story of The Macmillan Company," *Book Production Magazine* (December 1963): 26-29.

—*Ada M. Fan*

Manning and Loring
(Boston: 1793-1815)

The firm of William Manning and James Loring was a major Boston book printer, bookseller, and publisher at the end of the eighteenth century. The business was established on Quaker Lane in 1793. It moved to Spring Lane two years later and to 2 Cornhill in 1798. From 1793 to 1800 Manning and Loring printed more than 200 publications, about half of them for other Boston booksellers who took their business to Manning and Loring because the firm's printing was generally of fine quality and often innovative. Most books which bore only the Manning and Loring imprint were either religious or educational.

Notable among the books Manning and Loring printed for others were Samuel Rogers's *The Pleasures of Memory* (1795), printed for David West, and Duncan Mackintosh's *Essai Raisonné sur la Grammaire et la Prononciation Angloise* (1797), printed for the author. The latter was only one of many French works printed by the firm, often for the Franco-American firm of Joseph Nancrede. Manning and Loring also frequently printed for the Baptists of New England, as well as for Thomas and Andrews—a firm which Manning managed from 1795 to 1804 while also running his own business—William Spotswood, Samuel Hall, John West, James White, and many others.

Of the firm's literary titles, the most important

works were Sarah Wentworth Morton's *Beacon Hill: A Local Poem, Historic and Descriptive* (1797) and *The Virtues of Society: A Tale Founded on Fact* (1799), both printed for the author. Manning and Loring also printed *The Ruling Passion* (1797) for the poet Robert Treat Paine, Jr.

The firm's output declined during its last fifteen years, although in 1805 Manning and Loring purchased the business of Hall and Hiller. For a year after Manning moved to Worcester in 1814 to publish the *Massachusetts Spy*, some books still bore the Manning and Loring imprint. From 1815 to about 1837, Loring published, under the imprint of James Loring, works for children including Andrew Fuller's *New Year's Gift for Youth* (1802) and the first American edition of Mallès de Beaulieu's *The Modern Crusoe. A Narrative of the Life and Adventures of a French Cabin Boy, Who Was Shipwrecked on an Uninhabited Island* (1827).

Reference:

Jane Isley Thesing, "William Manning and James Loring," in *Boston Printers, Publishers, and Booksellers: 1640-1800*, edited by Benjamin Franklin V (Boston: G. K. Hall, 1980), pp. 347-354.

—*Mary Mahoney*

Marsh, Capen, Lyon and Webb
(Boston: 1838-1842)
Marsh and Company
(Boston: 1823-1828)
Marsh and Capen
(Boston: 1828-1830)
Marsh, Capen and Lyon
(Boston: 1830-1838)

Marsh, Capen, Lyon, and Webb began in 1823 as Marsh and Company. In 1828 Nahum Capen, an early advocate of American adoption of an international copyright convention, joined Robert A. Marsh as a partner. Lyon became a partner in 1830 and Webb after 1838; their first names are unknown. The firm was located at 362 Washington Street in Boston. Its most famous publication was Nathaniel Hawthorne's first book, *Fanshawe* (1828). The partners also published *Flora's Interpreter* (1832) and *The Ladies' Wreath* (1837), both edited by Sarah J. Hale, the literary editor of *Godey's Lady's Book*. These anthologies went into several editions. The firm published several histories; books on phrenology, including the American editions of those by J. G. Spurzheim; and Francis Joseph Grund's *The Americans* (1837), which answered Frances Trollope's criticism of American manners. Marsh, Capen, Lyon and Webb went out of business in 1842.

—*Joseph J. Hinchliffe*

William S. Martien
(Philadelphia: circa 1836-1856)
W. S. and A. Martien
(Philadelphia: 1856-1864)
Alfred Martien
(Philadelphia: 1864-circa 1876)

For approximately forty years the Philadelphia firm originally known as William S. Martien, from 1856 to 1864 as W. S. and A. Martien, and finally as Alfred Martien, published religious books. The firm's first known publication was Cornelius C. Cuyler's sermon *Believers, Sojourners on Earth, and Expectants of Heaven* (1836), which was followed by his *The Signs of the Times* (1839). Later books included the Reverend George Burrowes's *A Commentary on the Song of Solomon* (1853) and *Octorara, a Poem and Occasional Pieces* (1856). F. R. Goulding's *Robert and Harold; or, the Young Marooners on the Florida Coast* was published by William S. Martien in 1852, by W. S. and A. Martien in 1864, and by Alfred Martien in 1873 under the subtitle only. The Martien firm often published for a juvenile audience, offering *Children in Paradise* (1865) by the Reverend F. H. Wines, *A Mended Life; or, The Carpenter's Family* (1870) by Ruth Buck Lamb, and *Charity Helstone, a Tale* (1872) by Mrs. Carey Brock.

By 1876 Alfred Martien appears to have ceased publishing in order to concentrate on operating a bookstore at 21 South Seventh Street. For several years after 1876 he advertised "A New Cheap Sunday School Library" in *Publishers' Weekly*.

—*Elizabeth Hoffman*

Mason Brothers
(New York: 1855-1869)

Daniel Gregory Mason and Lowell Mason, Jr., established the firm of Mason Brothers at 23 Park Row, New York, in 1855 to publish music and music-related books, especially the musical texts of their father, Lowell Mason, one of the most famous and prolific musicians of nineteenth-century America. The firm published the elder Mason's *Mammoth Musical Exercises* (1856), *The People's Tune Book* (1860), and *Asaph; or, The Choir Book* (1861). Mason Brothers also published fiction and non-fiction, including Samuel Hayes Elliot's *The Parish-Side* (1854), Henry William Herbert's *Wager of Battle: A Tale of Saxon Slavery in Sherwood Forest* (1855), and George Pickering Burnham's temperance novel, *The Rag-Picker; or, Bound and Free* (1855). Other temperance novels included *Cone Cut Corners* (1855) and *Matthew Caraby* (1859), written jointly by Austin, Benjamin, and Lyman Abbott and published under the pseudonym Benauly. Mrs. Frances Irene Smith Griswold's *Elm Tree Tales* (1856), Caleb Starbuck's *Hampton Heights; or, The Spinster's Ward* (1856), and Thomas Butler Gunn's *The Physiology of New York Boarding-Houses* (1857) all displayed the moralistic tone typical of Mason Brothers books.

In 1855 Mason Brothers began publishing some of the work of James Parton. *Life of Horace Greeley* (1855) was followed by *The Humorous Poetry of the English Language, from Chaucer to Saxe* (1856), *Life of Andrew Jackson* (1860), *General Butler in New Orleans* (1863), and *Life and Times of Benjamin Franklin* (1864). Also in 1855 Mason Brothers published *Ruth Hall* by Fanny Fern, the pseudonym of Mrs. Sara Payson Willis, who became Sara Payson Willis Parton when she married Parton in 1856. The firm also published her *Rose Clark* (1856) and *Fresh Leaves* (1857).

In 1855 Mason Brothers joined the Copyright League, which had been formed in 1853 by a group of publishers, including Appleton, Carter and Brothers, Putnam, Scribner, and Stafford and Swords. An international copyright act, however, was not passed until 1891. In 1857 Mason Brothers took over the remaining assets of the temporarily defunct George P. Putnam and Company. Although Putnam eventually revived and flourished, this acquisition established the Mason Brothers as an important firm. In 1867 the firm decided to concentrate on music and sold its literary output to Smith Sheldon, a publisher who had absorbed Blanchard and Lea and Pratt, Oakley and Company at the outbreak of the Civil War. When Daniel Gregory Mason died in 1869, Mason Brothers was dissolved.

—*Neal L. Edgar*

H. Maxwell
(Philadelphia: 1798-1808)
Smith and Maxwell
(Philadelphia: 1808-circa 1810)

Primarily a printing house, H. Maxwell of 3 Letitia Court, Philadelphia, printed and published some works by America's earliest important novelist, Charles Brockden Brown. Maxwell was the printer for the *Weekly Magazine,* a Philadelphia journal, from 5 May to 25 August 1798. It was probably at this time that the firm became associated with Brown, who had contributed to the magazine a series of articles entitled "The Man at Home," as well as part of his novel *Arthur Mervyn.* Maxwell published the first volume of the novel in 1799; the second volume was published by George F. Hopkins in New York, where Brown completed it in 1800. Maxwell also published Brown's three-volume *Edgar Huntly; or, Memoirs of a Sleep-walker* (1799-1800). Maxwell published no other significant books. About 1808 the firm's name changed to Smith and Maxwell, and by 1810 the company had apparently ceased operations.

—Elizabeth Hoffman

A. C. McClurg and Company
(Chicago: 1886-1931)
W. W. Barlow and Company
(Chicago: 1844-1848)
Griggs, Bross and Company
(Chicago: 1848-1849)
S. C. Griggs and Company
(Chicago: 1849-1872)
Jansen, McClurg and Company
(Chicago: 1872-1886)

In 1844 W. W. Barlow and Mark H. Newman established a book and stationery store at 147 Lake Street, Chicago. The firm also published books under the imprint W. W. Barlow and Company, including the *Prairie Farmer Almanac* (1846). Samuel Chapman Griggs and William Bross took over the operation in 1848 and established a wholesale and retail book business known as Griggs, Bross and Company at 111 Lake Street. When Bross withdrew in 1849, the firm became S. C. Griggs and Company. The Chicago fire of 1871 destroyed the building and all of Griggs's stock. A new building was erected at 117-119 State Street, but Griggs withdrew in 1872 to pursue publishing independently.

E. L. Jansen, Alexander C. McClurg, and Frederick B. Smith, junior partners in the firm, took over the bookselling end of the business. The partners soon began publishing. The first book published under the Jansen, McClurg and Company imprint was H. W. S. Cleveland's *Landscape Architecture* (1873). The firm also published Friedrich Max Müller's *Memories: A Story of German Love* (1875), Joaquin Miller's *First Fam'lies in the Sierras* (1876) and *Shadows of Shasta* (1881), Mary Murdoch Mason's *Mae Madden* (1876), John Habberton's *The Jericho Road* (1876), and Stephen T. Robinson's *The Shadow of the War* (1884). In 1880 Jansen, McClurg and Company started publishing the *Dial,* "a monthly review and index of current literature." The firm moved to the corner of Wabash Avenue and Madison Street in 1883.

In 1886 Jansen resigned because of ill health, and the firm became A. C. McClurg and Company. McClurg was in charge of the publishing department, while Smith took care of the retail operations. The first title published under the new imprint was a second edition of George Putnam Upton's *Woman in Music* (1886), which had originally been published in 1880 by James R. Osgood of Boston. McClurg's first originally published work was Thorold King's *Haschisch* (1886).

McClurg supervised purchases for the company's secondhand and rare book department, which Eugene Field named the "Saints' and Sinners' Corner." The store became a gathering place for literary figures of the Midwest, including Field, James Whitcomb Riley, Bill Nye, Emerson Hough, and Henry B. Fuller. The only work of Field published by McClurg was a limited edition of *Echoes from the Sabine Farm* (1893), rhymed translations of Horace by Field and his brother Roswell. Until 1900 two-thirds of McClurg's titles were American editions of English authors and translations. The firm published Mary Hartwell Catherwood's *The Story of Tonty* (1890), Thomas Jay Hudson's *The Law of Psychic Phenomena* (1893), and Elizabeth Wormeley Latimer's popular histories of nineteenth-century Europe, including *Italy in the Nineteenth Century* (1897).

In 1899, after fire destroyed the firm's stock, the store was moved to 215-221 Wabash Avenue. McClurg died in 1901. Twentieth-century publications included W. E. B. Du Bois's *The Souls of Black Folk* (1903), William Dana Orcutt's *The Flower of Destiny* (1905), Gelett Burgess's *The Cat's Elegy* (1913), and twelve titles by Randall Parrish. Edith Granger's *An Index to Poetry and Recitations* (1904)

and Clarence Mulford's Hopalong Cassidy books were also published by the firm. McClurg and Company achieved its greatest success with the publication of ten of the nineteen Tarzan books by Edgar Rice Burroughs, including *Tarzan of the Apes* (1914), *The Return of Tarzan* (1915), and *The Son of Tarzan* (1917).

In 1923 the retail store was sold to Brentano's. Although now primarily a wholesale distributor of books—one of the largest in the United States— A. C. McClurg and Company continued to publish until 1931. Among its last publications were Otis Adelbert Kline's *Maza of the Moon* (1930), Frederick J. MacIsaac's *The Mental Marvel* (1930), and Dan Steele's *Snow Trenches* (1931).

References:
"A. C. McClurg & Company Chicago's Largest Booksellers," *Publishers' Weekly*, 93 (29 June 1918): 1970;

"General Alexander Caldwell McClurg," *Publishers' Weekly*, 59 (20 April 1901): 1022-1023;

"McClurg Has Completed Its First Hundred Years," *Publishers' Weekly*, 146 (2 September 1944): 814-819;

Frederick B. Smith, *A Sketch of the Origin and History of the House of A. C. McClurg & Co.* (Chicago, 1900?);

"The Story of A. C. McClurg and Company," *Mountain-Plains Library Quarterly*, 11 (Winter 1967): 19-20.

—*Kathleen R. Davis*

The David McKay Company

(Philadelphia; New York: 1882-)

Having moved from his native Scotland to Philadelphia, David McKay was hired by J. B. Lippincott and Company in 1860 at the age of thirteen. He became manager of the used book division of Rees Welsh and Company at 23 South Ninth Street in 1881. The following year, while still employed by Welsh, McKay published his first book: the ninth edition of Walt Whitman's *Leaves of Grass* (1882). McKay purchased the plates from James R. Osgood, the Boston publisher, who had been forced to drop the work because the attorney general of Massachusetts regarded it as immoral. The work still bore the Osgood imprint. McKay later published Whitman's *Specimen Days & Collect* (1882) under Rees Welsh's imprint.

McKay's primary business for several years after he purchased Welsh's bookstore and founded The David McKay Company in September 1882 remained bookselling, with publishing as a sideline. In 1885 he published a collection of Shakespeare's works, and in 1891 he published *Leaves of Grass* under his own imprint. Having purchased H. C. Watts and Company, publishers of classics, in 1888, in 1896 McKay added the publishing plant and line of interlinear translations of Charles De Silver and Sons and the engineering and technical books of E. E. Claxton and Company. The same year McKay sold the bookstore and moved to 1022 Market Street.

During the 1890s the firm began one of its better-known juvenile series, the clothbound Boys of Liberty Library, which included Harrie Irving Hancock's *Captain of the Minute Men; or, The Concord Boys of 1775* (1890) and Capt. Ralph Frank's *The King's Messenger; or, The Fall of Ticonderoga* (1904). With the acquisition of the American branch of George Routledge and Sons in 1903 and the impressive juvenile list of Street and Smith in 1905, McKay's list reached 700 titles, including 160 juveniles. Among the juveniles were The Newbery Classics and The Golden Books for Children, illustrated by N. C. Wyeth and John Cameron. In subsequent years the list included children's books by Beatrix Potter and Lois Lenski.

McKay moved to larger quarters at 610 South Washington Square in 1904. After McKay's death in 1918, his sons Alexander and James took over the company. They established the firm's famous series of chess books and published Christopher

Morley's *Travels in Philadelphia* (1920); the first American edition of A. A. Milne's *A Gallery of Children* (1925); Sir James and Lady Frazer's book of juvenile poetry, *Pasha the Pom* (1937); and Walt Disney's Mickey Mouse books.

In 1950 McKay was bought by a small group of investors led by Kennett Rawson, who assumed the presidency and moved the firm's headquarters to 225 Park Avenue, New York. Weldon Hill's *Onionhead,* a 1957 best-selling novel, was followed by successful nonfiction by Vance Packard, the Duchess of Windsor, Euell Gibbons, LeComte Du Noüy, and Ladislas Farago. Under Rawson, McKay acquired Fodor's Modern Guides, Weybright and Talley, Peter H. Weyden, Charterhouse, and the American branch of Longmans, Green. In 1968 Rawson sold the firm to Maxwell Geffen but remained as president. Dr. David Reuben's *Everything You Always Wanted to Know about Sex* (1970) was a number one best-seller for the firm. Literary titles included Harry Mark Petrakis's *Odyssey of Kostas Volakis* (1963) and *A Dream of Kings* (1966); John Nichols's *The Sterile Cuckoo* (1965); Dotson Rader's first book, *I Ain't Marchin' Anymore!* (1969); and eleven science fiction novels by A. E. Nourse, including *The Bladerunner* (1974).

In 1973 the firm merged with the Henry Z. Walck Company. The same year Geffen sold McKay to Morgan-Grampion, Incorporated, a subsidiary of a British firm. Rawson and his wife, Eleanor, a vice-president, left in 1974 to start their own firm, Rawson Associates, and James R. Louttit became president. McKay has deemphasized adult fiction: it now publishes general nonfiction, cookbooks, dictionaries and language guides, chess books, and juveniles. Since 1979 the firm has been located at 2 Park Avenue, New York 10016.

References:

"David McKay [obituary]," *Publishers' Weekly*, 94 (30 November 1918): 1799;

"David McKay's Silver Anniversary," *Publishers' Weekly*, 72 (5 October 1907): 1009-1011;

"Henry Z. Walck Merges with David McKay," *Publishers Weekly*, 203 (23 April 1973): 49-50;

"Rawson and Bossi Purchase David McKay Company," *Publishers' Weekly*, 157 (11 March 1950): 1345-1346.

—*Deborah G. Gorman*

Harold Strong Latham joined The Macmillan Company advertising department in 1909 and became head of general publications

David McKay

The first home of The David McKay Company at 23 South Ninth Street, Philadelphia. McKay purchased the store from Rees Welsh and Company in 1882.

McLoughlin Brothers
(New York and Springfield, Massachusetts: 1850-1969)
John McLoughlin
(New York: 1828-1840)
John Elton and Company
(New York: 1840-1848)
John McLoughlin, Jr.
(New York: 1848-1850)

Much of the history of children's books in America can be traced in imprints of the McLoughlin Brothers, from *Moral Stories* (1834) to *Jolly-Jump-Ups, Journey through Space* (1938). For many years this firm was the most important American supplier of children's literature. It pioneered in color illustrations and led in the employment of up-to-date technology and outstanding illustrators.

In 1819 John McLoughlin, a Scottish apprentice coachmaker, obtained a job with the Sterling Iron Company in New York. He met Robert Hoe, a fellow Scotsman who was working on the use of iron for printing presses, married Hoe's sister, and learned the printing trade. In 1827 he worked for the *New York Times,* and a year later he set up his own printing shop on Tryon Row. For the entertainment of his children McLoughlin wrote and illustrated moral tales, which in time he collected, printed, and bound in colored wrappers. In 1840 he merged his shop with John Elton's under the name John Elton and Company at 24 Beekman Street. The firm published joke books and children's books. John McLoughlin, Jr., began work at the shop in 1841. In 1848, when both Elton and McLoughlin retired, John, Jr. took over the firm. His brother Edmund became a partner in 1850, and the firm was renamed McLoughlin Brothers.

John and Edmund McLoughlin developed the market for children's books, using stencils to hand-produce multicolored illustrations and soon employing the etched zinc plate process. In 1861 the firm moved to 30 Beekman Street; by 1869 it was necessary to build a separate plant in Brooklyn for the production of illustrated books, valentines, and toys. At the same time the business office was moved to 111 Green Street, and early the following year to 71-73 Duane Street. The Brooklyn building was enlarged, and in 1894 a complete lithographic plant was installed. Seventy-five artists were employed, including Thomas Nast, G. A. Davis, Helena Maguire, Josephine Pollard, Palmer Cox, and Howard Pyle. Mother Goose books, Santa Claus books, alphabet books, painting books, and stories for the very young, sometimes in German, were among the firm's publications.

Edmund McLoughlin retired in 1885. The following year the Manhattan office was moved to 632 Broadway, and in 1888, the year of Edmund's death, James and Charles McLoughlin, sons of John, Jr., joined the firm. The firm moved to 874 Broadway in 1892 and to 890 Broadway six years later. When John McLoughlin, Jr., died in 1905, James and Charles McLoughlin took over the business. Charles died on 8 November 1913, and James continued to run the firm until 1920, when he sold it to the large toy and game manufacturer Milton Bradley Company of Springfield, Massachusetts. McLoughlin Brothers, Incorporated remained an auxiliary of the Milton Bradley Company, publishing under its own imprint at a separate address in Springfield. Edward O. Clark, Sr., was the president, and Edward, Jr. was literary and art editor. *Jolly-Jump-Ups,* with three-dimensional illustrations created by Geraldine Clyne, was published in 1938; the firm sold about 500,000 items that year. During World War II, however, the business declined. By 1951 the firm was bankrupt.

That year the company was sold to Julius Kushner, a New York toy manufacturer. He attempted to revitalize the firm by lowering prices and enlarging the print runs. In spite of his efforts, McLoughlin Brothers was taken over by Grosset and Dunlap in June 1954. The McLoughlin imprint continued to appear on the line of toy books and some new titles introduced after the takeover, but by 1970 the name had disappeared.

References:
"John McLoughlin [obituary]," *Publishers' Weekly,* 67 (6 May 1905): 1286-1287;
"McLoughlin Brothers Complete a Century of Pub-

lishing," *Publishers' Weekly,* 113 (25 February 1928): 779-780;

"McLoughlin's 125 Years," *Publishers' Weekly,* 163 (14 March 1953): 1290-1292;

P. K. Thomajan, "Children's Books with a Purpose," *Direct Advertising,* 48, no. 4 (1963): 4-10.

—*Theodora Mills*

The Merriam Company
(St. Paul, Minnesota; New York: 1893-1897)

In 1893 The Merriam Company of St. Paul, Minnesota, succeeded the Price-McGill Company, which had been formed in 1891. The firm moved to New York early in 1894 when it acquired the jobbing business of Saalfield and Fitch, 12 Bible House, Astor Place. Merriam soon moved to 67 Fifth Avenue and was incorporated there in February 1895.

During its brief existence the company advertised a variety of titles, many of them juveniles. Among its early publications Merriam listed two titles by Edward S. Ellis, taken over from Price-McGill: *The River Fugitives* (1893) and *Through Apache Land* (1893), published under the pseudonym Lt. R. H. Jayne. The company published titles in several series: Ellis's works appeared in the River and Wilderness series, while books by Helen M. Bowen and Mary Kyle Dallas were part of the Waldorf series. Merriam published the first books of Edward Stratemeyer: *The Last Cruise of the Spitfire* (1894) in the Ship and Shore series, *Richard Dare's*

Venture (1894) in the Bound to Win series, and *Reuben Stone's Discovery* (1895) in the Ship and Shore series. Books by Lydia Hoyt Farmer and Constance Goddard Du Bois were also published by Merriam.

In the fall of 1897 Merriam went into receivership upon the application of Robert H. Merriam, president, and Arthur James Saalfield, a director. Merriam blamed the company's losses on Edward R. Gilman, in whose hands management had been left when Merriam became ill in June 1895. Merriam claimed that the company sustained a substantial loss by the exchange of notes with the Great Western Manufacturing Company of Chicago, of which Gilman was president.

Reference:

"The Merriam Company Fails," *Publishers' Weekly,* 52 (2 October 1897): 583.

—*Earl R. Taylor*

Merrill and Baker
(New York: 1893-1904)

Daniel David Merrill began his career publishing schoolbooks with his father in St. Paul, Minnesota. When his father's business failed in 1893, Merrill formed a partnership with his brother L. K. Merrill and Francis E. Baker to found Merrill and Baker, which became one of the largest subscription book businesses in the United States.

The firm specialized in sets by standard authors. For example, The Ruby Poets consisted of fifteen volumes by Burns, Gray, Hood, Keats, Scott, and Shelley, along with a selection of songs from the dramatists. In addition to English authors, the firm sold sets of works by Irving and Cooper and occasional single volumes, such as Albion Tourgée's *Out of the Sunset Sea* (1893) and *An Outing with the Queen of Hearts* (1894) and Edgar Fawcett's *Her Fair Fame* (1894). In December 1904 the firm went bankrupt.

Reference:
"Obituary Notes: Daniel David Merrill," *Publishers' Weekly*, 69 (12 May 1906): 1373.

—*Elizabeth Scott Pryor*

The Mershon Company
(New York: 1897-circa 1904)

In March 1897 The Mershon Company, printers and bookbinders in Rahway, New Jersey, announced the opening of a publishing house at 156 Fifth Avenue in New York City. For a dozen years, Mershon had been preparing sets of standard authors for other publishers, but, after increasing its manufacturing facilities and adding new titles, it decided to sell directly to the trade. Mershon's multivolume Queen Edition Sets, Golden Gem series, Favorite Library, and the Standard and Sterling series comprised, as the firm advertised, works by the "best authors in the world," including Dickens, the Brontës, Hugo, George Eliot, and Thackeray. Quality of paper and bindings varied from series to series. The Premium Library, used by schools and colleges for supplementary reading, offered classic titles bound in paper at ten cents a copy. Other series included G. A. Henty's books and the New Holly Library, 150 novels priced at twenty-five cents. Mershon also published Arthur W. Winfield's Rover Boys series and the "authorized and copyright" edition of Mrs. L. T. Meade's stories for girls, as well as "attractive love stories" by Edna Winfield that had been serialized in newspapers. By 1905 Mershon was out of business, its stock sold to the Stitt Publishing Company.

—*Susan K. Ahern*

J. Metcalf
(Northampton, Massachusetts: 1832-1846)
Metcalf and Company
(Northampton: 1846-1916)

John Metcalf established his printing firm at 2 Crafts Avenue, Northampton, Massachusetts, in 1832, after conducting business for twenty years in nearby Wendell. He printed books for Northampton publisher Simeon Butler and is believed to have printed the first Northampton Bible, which was published by J. H. Butler in 1834. Metcalf was known for the thousands of children's toy books he turned out between about 1835 and 1845, including *A Little Present for a Good Child* (1835) and *Duties of Children* (1836). Barbara Gilmore describes them as charming little lectures to children, with woodcut illustrations. The books were "really an innovation and, in their way, a step in the slow secularization of a Puritan town." The name of the company was changed to Metcalf and Company in 1846 when Metcalf's sons Lyman and William joined the firm. After the death of John Metcalf in 1864, his family carried on the job printing business, finally selling out in 1916.

References:

Barbara Gilmore, *A Puritan Town and Its Imprints: Northampton 1786-1845* (Northampton: Hampshire Bookstore, 1942);

Clifford H. Lyman, "Reminiscences of John Metcalf," *Daily Hampshire Gazette*, 2 May 1933;

Newton F. McKeon, *Metcalf Imprints at Wendell, Mass. (1814-1832)* (Amherst, Mass., 1950).

—Deborah L. Brandt

The Methodist Book Concern
(New York and Cincinnati: 1819-1939)
Methodist Book Company
(Philadelphia; New York: 1789-1819)
The Methodist Publishing House
(Nashville, Tennessee: 1939-1968)
The United Methodist Publishing House
(Nashville: 1968-   )

Methodism and book publishing have gone hand in hand since John Wesley, the founder of the religion, became—according to *Publishers' Weekly*—"the earliest devisor in England of cheap publications for the common people." Wesley marketed the books of his religion through itinerant preachers. Since the preachers depended on the sales of these books for much of their income, this strategy proved successful and was later used in America.

Originally called the Methodist Book Company, The Methodist Book Concern is the oldest religious publishing house in America. Representatives of the Methodist Episcopal Church in America founded the company in the rear of Old St. George's Church in Philadelphia in 1789 with $600 contributed by its first book steward, John Dickins. The company's first publications were Wesley's *An Extract of the Christian's Pattern* (1789), his abridged translation of Thomas à Kempis's *Imitation of Christ*, followed by Richard Baxter's *The Saints' Everlasting Rest* (1791). As did other early stewards, Dickins carried out almost all aspects of the business himself—editing, clerking, packing, and shipping—except printing and binding, which were contracted out. He remained steward until 1798, when Ezekial Cooper assumed the post. The stewards were later called agents.

In 1804 the company moved to a one-room shop on Fulton Street in New York. The name of

304

John Dickins, first steward of the Methodist Book Company. He served from 1789 until 1798 (painting by Charles Hargens, courtesy of The Methodist Publishing House).

Title page of the Methodist Book Company's first publication (University of Maine Library)

the firm was changed to The Methodist Book Concern in 1819. Three years later, a bindery was established on Crosby Street, and in 1825 a printing plant was set up at the same address. In 1826 the *Christian Advocate*, the first weekly newspaper of the American church, was founded. At about the same time, an assistant agent, John Emory, suggested that the firm change its business format from commissions to cash sales. This change—instituted while Nathan Bangs was principal agent from 1824 to 1828 and continued under Emory, who was principal agent from 1828 to 1832—greatly expanded the operations of the firm. The firm moved to 206 Mulberry Street in 1833. When fire destroyed this building in 1836, a new one was erected at 200 Mulberry Street in 1839.

The beneficiaries of this expansion were charitable causes. Early proceeds were contributed to Cokesbury College, missions, schools, and a pension fund for preachers and their survivors. The expansion of the church in America brought new customers to The Methodist Book Concern, while the growth of The Methodist Book Concern aided the expansion of the church.

Agents were selected for renewable four-year terms by the General Conference of the Methodist Episcopal Church in America. Usually, the assistant agent would assume the office of principal agent upon the latter's retirement. The firm's books were usually published under an imprint consisting of the names of the principal agent and his assistant, in that order. Imprints of the firm after 1856, when it began printing more literary titles, included Carlton and Porter (1856-1868), Carlton and Lanahan (1868-1872), Nelson and Phillips (1872-1878), Phillips and Hunt (1879-1889), Hunt and Eaton (1889-1896), and Eaton and Mains (1896-1913).

The Western Methodist Book Concern was founded in Cincinnati in 1820 by Martin Ruter to serve the growing frontier population. Early agents for the western firm were Ruter (1820-1828), Charles Holliday (1828-1836), and John F. Wright (1832-1836). For its first twelve years the Cincinnati branch served only as a distributor for books published in the East. Around 1833 the western branch obtained a printing press and began publishing hymnbooks and, in 1834, the *Western Christian Advocate*, a weekly newspaper. The western agents were granted equal status with the New York agents by the General Conference in 1836. They were also permitted to reprint any book in the Methodist General Catalogue, excepting those which had been stereotyped by the eastern branch. Thus, while still excluded from publishing most of

the eastern branch's more profitable books, the Cincinnati branch began to publish original titles, including William Phillips's *Campbellism Exposed* (1837) and James B. Finley's *History of the Wyandotte Mission at Upper Sandusky, Ohio* (1840). The firm's more than twenty-five publications over the next ten years were all religious in nature. Imprints of The Western Methodist Book Concern after 1836 included J. F. Wright and L. Swormstedt (1836-1844), Swormstedt and Mitchell (1844-1848), Swormstedt and Power (1848-1852), Swormstedt and Poe (1852-1860), Poe and Hitchcock (1860-1868), Hitchcock and Walden (1868-1880), Walden and Stowe (1880-1884), Stowe and Cranston (1884-1892), Cranston and Curts (1892-1896), Curts and Jennings (1896-1900), and Jennings and Pye (1900-1913).

The Cincinnati branch was incorporated in 1839. Its growth remained slow until 1840, when it was finally allowed to purchase stereotyped plates from the eastern branch at cost, while being released from all debts to the New Yorkers. The revitalized Western Methodist Book Concern soon began publication of the *Ladies' Repository and Gatherings of the West,* a monthly magazine of literary, as well as religious, significance. Edited by L. L. Hamline, the journal featured Alice and Phoebe Cary, Metta Victoria Fuller, and Mrs. Lydia Sigourney.

As early as 1828, the Methodists had begun to divide into factions with the founding of The Methodist Protestant Church, which established the Methodist Protestant Book Concern at Baltimore. Disputes over the slavery issue led to the formation in the mid 1840s of the Methodist Episcopal Church, South, which removed its assets from The Methodist Book Concern to form the Southern Methodist Publishing House at Nashville, Tennessee. The New York and Cincinnati branches continued their relationship, and business continued to expand. A San Francisco branch was opened in 1852.

The earliest fiction by the eastern and western branches usually described the lives of the itinerant preachers and their flocks. This emphasis is reflected in Carlton and Porter's publication of Sarah Babcock's *The Itinerant Side; or, Pictures of Life in the Itinerancy* (1857), Lucius Daniel Davis's *Life in the Laity; or, The History of a Station* (1858), and Mrs. H. C. Gardner's *The Power of Kindness* (1865). Carlton and Porter also published Julia Gill's *Legends of New England* (1864) and Frances Lee's *False Shame* (1866), while Poe and Hitchcock published Virginia Townsend's *Temptation and Triumph* (1863), Mrs.

Martin Ruter founded The Western Methodist Book Concern in Cincinnati in 1820

Nathaniel Bangs, under whose tenure as principal book agent (1824-1828) The Methodist Book Concern experienced its most vigorous growth. Bangs acquired property, a bindery, and a print shop and began three new periodicals.

H. C. Gardner's *Rosedale: A Story of Self-Denial* (1863), and David W. Clark's *Home Views of the Picturesque and Beautiful* (1863). The Clark title was one of The Methodist Book Concern's illustrated gift books, which were praised for their typography and bindings.

In 1868 the New York editorial offices moved to 805 Broadway. The manufacturing plant remained on Mulberry until 1890, when the departments were reunited at 150 Fifth Avenue. By 1872 there were depositories for the sale of books in Boston, Buffalo, Auburn, Pittsburgh, Chicago, St. Louis, Atlanta, and San Francisco, in addition to several bookstores across the nation.

Throughout the last quarter of the nineteenth century, polite literature for ladies—temperance novels, historical romances, and stories about young Christian women—became extremely popular. The eastern and western branches gradually adapted to this mild secularization, both in their catalogues and in their organization. In New York in 1872 John M. Phillips became the first layman elected book agent. He and the principal New York agent, the Reverend Reuben Nelson, published three books of poems by Mrs. J. P. Newman, M. M. Pollard's *The Brother's Legacy; or, Better than Gold* (1873) and *The Miner's Son and Margaret Vernon* (1873), and five novels by Emma Leslie, including *Leofwine the Saxon* (1875), as well as hymnbooks and other religious works.

The Cincinnati branch expanded its printing plant in 1870 and changed to electrotype printing in 1883. The growth of the railroads, telegraphy, and other technologies made cooperation between east and west quicker and easier. Titles published in New York by Phillips and Hunt between 1879 and 1889 were usually published in the same year by Hitchcock and Walden, Walden and Stowe, or Stowe and Cranston. Temperance novels included Mrs. C. E. Wilbur's *The Thread of Gold* (1885) and John W. Spear's *Out of the Toils* (1887), while historical romances included Enoch Fitch Burr's *Dio, the Athenian; or, From Olympus to Calvary* (1880), Frederic Myron Colby's *The Daughter of the Pharoah: A Tale of the Exodus* (1886), and Mary Harriott Norris's *Dorothy Delafield* (1886) and *A Damsel of the Eighteenth Century; or, Cicely's Choice* (1889). Perhaps the best remembered of Phillips and Hunt's authors was Amelia Edith Barr. While Dodd, Mead and Company published most of her approximately sixty historical romances, The Methodist Book Concern published *The Hallam Succession: A Tale of Methodist Life in Two Countries* (1885), *The*

Lost Silver of Briffault (1885), and *Christopher, and Other Stories* (1888).

In the 1860s the sales of the New York branch were more than twice those of the Cincinnati branch, but from the 1890s on, the western branch's sales surpassed those of the eastern firm. Also during the 1890s, fiction titles copublished by the two branches reached their peak. Together, the branches published N. D. Bagnell's *Carl and Violet* (1890) and *Poky Clark: A Story of Virginia* (1890), Edwin McMinn's *Nemorama the Nautchnee: A Story of India* (1890), Minnie Baines Miller's *His Cousin, the Doctor* (1891), and Ellen Maxwell's *The Bishop's Conversion* (1892). Among The Methodist Book Concern's biggest sellers were Samuel W. Odell's *Samson: An Historical Romance* and *Delilah: A Sequel to "Samson,"* both in 1891. Other authors included R. F. Bishop, Mrs. Belle V. Chisholm, Julia A. Woodhall DeWitt, Erasmus W. Jones, Ellen A. Lutz, W. A. Robinson, and Mrs. Emma Lefferts Super.

Under Eaton and Mains in New York and Curts and Jennings and Jennings and Pye in Cincinnati, the two branches shared the same manufacturing plant. Sales continued to expand, but fiction declined. *Taught by Experience* (1900) by Mrs. Sarah Cannon Leamon was one of the last of the relatively few fiction titles published solely by the western branch (Curts and Jennings). The two branches jointly published Albion Tourgée's *The Mortgage on the Hip-Roof House* (1896), *Dwellers in Gotham: A Romance of New York* (1898) by Annan Dale (the pseudonym of James Wesley Johnston), L. K. Parks's *With British and Braves: Story of the War of 1812* (1898), Alden W. Quimby's *Valley Forge* (1906), W. Arthur Noble's *Ewa: A Tale of Korea* (1906), and Frank Bullen's *The Seed of the Righteous* (1908).

A year after Homer Eaton's death in 1913, the two branches united under the imprint of Abingdon Press, with offices at the eastern branch's New York address. The name of the firm as a whole remained The Methodist Book Concern, and occasionally books were published under that imprint as well. In 1913 the Methodist Protestant Book Concern had established the Stockton imprint; in 1923 the Southern Methodists' publishing arm, The Methodist Publishing House, created the Cokesbury Press imprint. In 1939 the two branches of Methodism which had split off in the early nineteenth century—The Methodist Protestant Church and the Methodist Episcopal Church, South—reunited with the Methodist Church. After the

John Berry McFerrin, founder of the Southern Methodist Publishing House at Nashville, Tennessee, in 1844. The firm was begun after a dispute over the slavery issue split the Methodist congregation.

201 Eighth Avenue South, Nashville, headquarters of The United Methodist Publishing House since 1957

merger, the combined book concerns were renamed The Methodist Publishing House and the imprint became the Abingdon-Cokesbury Press. Main offices were at 810 Broadway in Nashville, Tennessee, while the New York office continued at 150 Fifth Avenue. In 1954 the imprint became simply Abingdon Press again; after the Evangelical United Brethren merged with the Methodist Church in 1968, the name of the firm as a whole became The United Methodist Publishing House. The firm's address since 1957 has been 201 Eighth Avenue South, Nashville, Tennessee 37202. Gary H. Vincent is general manager of the house. The book editor and editor of general publications is Ronald P. Patterson.

References:

H. C. Jennings, *The Methodist Book Concern: A Romance of History* (New York: Methodist Book Concern, 1924);

John Lanahan, *The Era of Frauds in the Methodist Book Concern at New York* (Baltimore: Methodist Book Depository, 1896);

"Methodist Book Concern: The Oldest Publishing House in Continuous Operation in America Today," *Publishers' Weekly*, 129 (29 February 1936): 981-983;

W. G. Roberts, "The Methodist Book Concern in the West, 1820-1870," Ph.D. dissertation, University of Chicago, 1947;

Walter Sutton, *The Western Book Trade: Cincinnati as a Nineteenth-Century Publishing and Book Trade Center* (Columbus: Ohio State University Press, 1961), pp. 150-165;

William F. Whitlock, *The Story of the Book Concerns* (Cincinnati: Jennings & Pye/New York: Eaton & Mains, 1903).

—David Dzwonkoski

James Miller
(New York: 1860-1883)

The firm of James Miller was formed in 1860 when Miller assumed the proprietorship of the C. S. Francis firm following Francis's retirement. Miller had joined Francis as an errand boy in 1835 when the business, a fashionable gathering place for book lovers, was located at 252 Broadway, opposite City Hall. Francis had moved to 554 Broadway in 1856, and in 1861 Miller moved to 522 Broadway. Described by *Publishers' Weekly* as a "shrewd-faced energetic little man . . . one of the pillars of the tradesale," Miller is credited with beginning the practice of publishing works in boxed sets.

His most active years as a publisher were 1866, when he brought out seventy-five books; 1867, when he published thirty-five; and 1868, when he produced twenty-one books. During these years Miller owned a large and popular list of juvenile publications, including Hans Christian Andersen's stories, but he sold the line of well over a 100 plates to Allen Brothers in what was then the largest sale of stereotype plates ever transacted in New York. Following the sale, Miller concentrated on publishing illustrated gift books and finely bound poetical works, which he also offered in popularly priced editions. In 1868 he moved to 647 Broadway.

Miller's "chief singer," in the words of a contemporary, was Elizabeth Barrett Browning. As her sole publisher in the United States, Miller brought out ten different editions of Browning's works, with and without illustrations, with total sales of over 100,000 copies. Francis had published *Aurora Leigh* simultaneously with its London publication in 1857, and Miller published nine editions of *Aurora Leigh and Other Poems* between 1861 and 1875. Among the firm's elegant gift books were a two-volume quarto of Hogarth's works and Rufus W. Griswold's *The Poets and Poetry of America* (1872), *The Female Poets of America* (1873), and *The Poets and Poetry of England* (1874), the last three revised and updated by Richard Henry Stoddard. In the 1870s Miller reprinted illustrated quarto editions—including James Thomson's *The Seasons* and Thomas Babington Macaulay's *Lays of Ancient Rome and Other Poems*—the plates of which he had purchased from E. H. Butler in Philadelphia. Miller also returned to reprinting juvenile titles, acquiring plates from other publishers, including the popular Aimwell Stories from Gould and Lincoln in Boston. The

Elizabeth Barrett Browning. James Miller was the exclusive American publisher of her works (National Portrait Gallery, London).

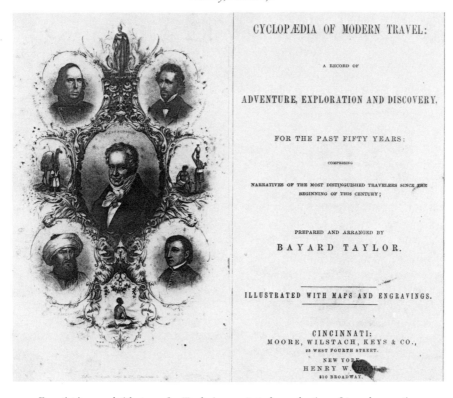

Frontispiece and title page for Taylor's very popular redaction of travel narratives

company was known for its "useful" titles, such as Ebenezer Cobham Brewer's *A Guide to the Scientific Knowledge of Things Familiar* (1872), which sold over 100,000 copies, as well as guidebooks to Central Park, the Hudson River and New York City.

In the late 1870s Miller, then located at 779 Broadway, was more active as a bookseller than as a publisher, dealing largely in fine editions of British and American poets and in expensive foreign books. According to *Publishers' Weekly*, the store became "a favorite headquarters for literary men and scholars, and . . . some of the distinguished people

of the time." Miller's business declined in the 1880s, hastened by his own faltering health. He died on 7 March 1883, shortly after a court official broke into his bedchamber, where he lay ill, to serve him with bankruptcy papers.

References:

"The Bookmakers . . . XXXV—James Miller," *New York Evening Post,* 23 June 1875;

"James Miller [obituary]," *Publishers' Weekly,* 23 (24 March 1883): 344-345.

—*Susan K. Ahern*

Moore, Wilstach, Keys and Company
(Cincinnati: 1854-1864)
Moore and Anderson
(Cincinnati: 1851-1852)
Moore, Anderson, Wilstach and Keys
(Cincinnati: 1852-1854)
Moore, Wilstach and Baldwin
(Cincinnati: 1864-1869)
Moore, Wilstach and Moore
(Cincinnati: 1869-1870)

William H. Moore kept a stock of miscellaneous books for sale in his Cincinnati store in the early 1840s; in 1843 he began publishing schoolbooks. In 1851 he formed a partnership with D. Anderson, a bookseller, and they published *Service Afloat and Ashore during the Mexican War* (1851) by Raphael Semmes. In October 1852 Moore and Anderson were joined by Charles P. Wilstach, who since the mid 1840s had been running a bindery, and Samuel B. Keys. In the summer of 1854 Anderson withdrew from the firm, and William Overend, a printer, was taken on. Moore, Wilstach, Keys and Company moved into a new building at 25 West Fourth Street. This partnership remained unchanged for a decade, and during the late 1850s it was the largest publishing house in Cincinnati. In 1859 the firm employed 135 workers and stocked blankbooks and stationery as well as its own publications. The binding department, run by Wilstach, occupied three large rooms with sixty to seventy-five employees.

In the mid 1850s the firm was known for its travel literature, including the Reverend C. B. Boynton and T. B. Mason's *A Journey through Kansas* (1854), John Ballou's *The Lady of the West; or, The Gold Seekers* (1855), and Bayard Taylor's celebrated *Cyclopaedia of Modern Travel* (1856). David Christy's influential *Cotton Is King* (1855) was a treatise on the economics of slavery and "the culture of cotton" in the South. Fiction published by the firm during this time included works by Charles Barnard, Isaac Kelso, and Mrs. Angelina Collins.

The firm's publishing program was disrupted by the Civil War, and after the war it did not regain its former stature. Other partnership arrangements were tried—Moore, Wilstach and Baldwin (1864-1869); Moore, Wilstach and Moore (1869-1870)—but by the 1870s the principals had gone their own ways, and Cincinnati's "frontier" market had changed. Moore auctioned off his stock and worked with subscription books for a time in Chicago.

Reference:

Walter Sutton, *The Western Book Trade: Cincinnati as a Nineteenth-Century Book Trade Center* (Columbus: Ohio State University Press, 1961), pp. 75, 81, 108, 118-125, 291.

—*Alan J. Filreis*

John P. Morton and Company
(Louisville: 1864-1942)
Morton and Smith
(Louisville: 1825-1858)
Morton and Griswold
(Louisville: 1858-1864)

John P. Morton and Company, with offices at 440-446 Main Street, Louisville, was one of the largest publishing houses in Kentucky during the nineteenth century. Begun as Morton and Smith in 1825, the company soon began to publish schoolbooks and was the foremost textbook firm in the South by 1850. The firm became Morton and Griswold in 1858 and John P. Morton and Company in 1864.

In the 1870s Morton began publishing literature by southern writers, including *The Confederate Spy* (1871) by R. H. Crozier and *Blooms of the Berry* (1887) by Madison Cawein. Morton eventually published eleven of Cawein's thirty-six volumes of verse. Other books of poetry with the Morton imprint were *The Blood of Rachel* (1916), *The Legend of the Silver Band* (1932), and *The Valleys of Parnassus* (1935), all by Cotton Noe, Poet Laureate of Kentucky; *The Path of Dreams* (1916) by the black poet George Marion McClellan; and *Blades o' Bluegrass* (1892) and *All That's Kentucky* (1915), anthologies of Kentucky verse. Besides textbooks and literary works the firm published *The Western Farmer's Almanac* (1825-1940) and publications of the Filson Club dealing with Kentucky history. Morton died on 19 July 1889. In 1942 the company was acquired by the Standard Printing Company of Louisville.

—*Dorsey Kleitz*

440-446 Main Street, Louisville, Kentucky, in 1920. This building was headquarters of the firm from its founding in 1825.

George Munro established his company in 1864

Cover for a volume in George Munro's biweekly dime novel series. After number 345, the series was issued monthly.

George Munro
(New York: 1868-1893)
George Munro and Company
(New York: 1864-1868)
George Munro's Sons
(New York: 1893-1906)
George Munro Publishing House
(New York: 1906-1908)

In 1856 George Munro came to New York from Nova Scotia, where he had been a theology student and mathematics instructor. In 1863 he was working in the stockroom of Beadle and Adams; within a year he formed a partnership with Irwin Beadle at 137 William Street and began publishing dime novels. In 1864 Munro took over the business and renamed it George Munro and Company. In 1867 Munro established the *New York Fireside Companion*, a family newspaper which reached a peak circulation of 275,000 copies. Its popularity bolstered Munro's publishing reputation. In 1868 the firm became George Munro and moved to 118 William Street; two years later it moved to 84 Beekman Street and in 1883 to 17-27 Vandewater Street.

By far the most popular of Munro's dime novelists was Harlan P. Halsey, whose stories, written under the pseudonym Old Sleuth, saved the *Fireside Companion* from financial ruin in the early 1870s. These stories later appeared in book form in the Old Sleuth Library and included *Black Raven, the Georgia Detective; or, The Terror of the "Mountain Mooners"* (1885), *The Yankee Detective; or, Shadowed to Doom* (1885), and *The American Detective in Russia; or, "Piping a Conspiracy"* (1892). Halsey's *The Shadow Detective; or, The Mysteries of a Night* and *Old Sleuth the Detective; or, The Bay Ridge Mystery* inaugurated the Calumet series in 1891.

Prior to the discovery of Halsey, the firm's most popular dime novelist had been Edward S. Ellis, whose *The Hunters; or, Life on Mountain and Prairie* (1864) had been the first number in Irwin P. Beadle's Ten Cent Novels series. After five more numbers the name of the series had been changed to Munro's Ten Cent Novels when Beadle retired from the firm. Works by Ellis in Munro's Ten Cent Novels series include *Brette: the Death Shot; or, Adventures in the Far South-west* (1870) and *The Irish Hunter; or, Pat O'Dougherty's Adventures among the Red Skins* (1872). Also appearing in Munro's Ten Cent Novels series were L. Augustus Jones's *The Bold Scalp-Hunter; or, The Mysterious Being of the Cave*

(1865) and *The Black Prophet; or, The Spirit of the Sioux* (1866), George G. Small's *The Silent Trapper; or, Lank Josh, Backwoodsman: A Tale of the Wilds of Arizona* (1869) and *Old Timberlick; or, The Girl Hunters of Utah* (1873), and John Milton Hoffman's *Calamity Joe, the Ranger; or, The Spectre Horseman* (1873) and *Slashaway, the Fearless; or, The Hermit of Spectre Island* (1875).

The 1870s saw a rapid expansion of cheap book publishing. The lack of an international copyright agreement made it easy to reprint popular English fiction, and by holding costs to a minimum the reprint house was able to turn a quick profit. Such a venture was the Seaside Library, which Munro began in May 1877 with the publication of Mrs. Henry Wood's *East Lynne*. The Seaside Library was a series of cheap quartos, often printed two or three columns to a page. Single volumes sold for ten cents, two-volume sets for twenty. Despite strong competition, the Seaside Library quickly dominated the market. Among Munro's first titles were *Jane Eyre*, *Adam Bede*, and *The Last Days of Pompeii*; new titles were published almost daily. With sales of 5.5 million volumes in its first two years, the Seaside Library had eliminated most competing sets of reprints except Harper's Franklin Square Library by 1880. An average of 10,000 copies of each Seaside title were sold. The Seaside Library included first American editions of Charles James Lever's *Kate O'Donoghue* (1877) and *Paul Gosslett's Confessions* (1881) and Mary Elizabeth (Braddon) Maxwell's *The Mystery of Leighton Grange* (1878), *Asphodel* (1881), and *Married in Haste* (1883), while Charlotte Mary Yonge's works, among them *The Two Sides of the Shield* (1885), *Under the Storm; or, Steadfast's Charge* (1887), and *Our New Mistress; or, Changes at Brookfield Earl* (1888), appeared in the Seaside Library's Pocket Edition. Another major contributor to the Pocket Edition was Mrs. Charlotte Mary Brame, whose works, published under the pseudonym Bertha M. Clay, included *At War with Herself* (1884) and *A Gilded Sin* bound with *A*

Bridge of Love (1884). Other women who contributed to the Seaside Library's Pocket Edition similarly followed the fashion of the day and chose such pen names as Mrs. Alexander (Mrs. Annie Hector), Mrs. Humphry Ward (Mary Augusta Ward), Edna Lyall (Ada Ellen Bayly), and The Duchess (Mrs. Margaret Wolfe Hungerford). The Pocket Edition also included H. Rider Haggard's *Allan's Wife* (1887) and *Beatrice* (1888), while Haggard's *He, A Companion to She* (1887) and *"It." A Wild, Weird History of Marvelous, Miraculous, Phantasmagorial Adventures in Search of He, She, and Jess, and Leading to the Finding of "It"* (1887) appeared in Munro's Library. In the late 1880s Munro began the Deutsche Library, a series of German works, as well as translations into German from English and French. This series became so popular in cities with large German populations that by 1890 the Deutsche Library had published more than 200 titles.

Although the Seaside Library dominated its market for seven years, increased competition forced Munro to cut his prices in 1887. As a means of regulating competition, Munro had proposed a royalty payment system as early as 1879; by 1888 he was demanding a copyright law. Munro became one of several cheap book publishers who joined John Lovell in his massive trust, the United States Book Company, in 1890. Like Lovell, Munro hoped that by eliminating competition prices could be stabilized and duplication eliminated. In 1890 Munro "leased" the Seaside Library to Lovell for three years; it was returned to him in two. Poor management and the passage of the international copyright act had forced Lovell into receivership.

Munro's business suffered during the panic and subsequent depression of 1893. After his retirement that year the firm continued for ten years under his sons George and John as George Munro's Sons but dissolved in 1906. Its successor, the George Munro Publishing House, lasted only two years.

References:

"Obituary Notes: George Munro," *Publishers' Weekly*, 49 (2 May 1896): 769;

Denis R. Rogers, *Munro's Ten Cent Novels* (Fall River, Mass.: LeBlanc, 1958).

—*David Dzwonkoski*

Norman L. Munro
(New York: 1873-1921)

In 1869, at the age of twenty-five, Norman L. Munro moved from his native Nova Scotia to New York, where he worked in the publishing business of his brother, George Munro. In 1873 Norman Munro joined Frank Tousey at 163 William Street to begin the weekly *New York Family Story Paper*. It was not an auspicious beginning: Munro and Tousey had chosen the first day of the panic of 1873 to launch their paper, at a time when the cheap book business was already overcrowded and fiercely competitive. One of their strongest competitors was George Munro, and the brothers were never on speaking terms again. George Munro was particularly annoyed by Norman's practice of copying his innovations. For instance, it was George's *Fireside Companion* that first ran adaptations of popular plays in the form of serialized novels, but Norman's *Family Story Paper* quickly followed suit.

In 1875, moving to 28-30 Beekman Street, Munro and Tousey followed the success of the *Family Story Paper* with the *Boys Own Story Teller*, a ten-cent, sixty-four-page biweekly magazine offering short fiction—in both complete and serialized form—and novelettes. Soon, it was renamed *Our Boys of New York* with each eight-page issue selling for five cents. At about the same time, Munro and Tousey established the New York Boy's Library, which eventually ran to 138 titles.

In 1876 Tousey left to start his own firm, taking both his investment and one of Munro's dime novel writers, George G. Small, with him as a partner. Then, just as Munro was launching Munro's Library and *Munro's Pocket Magazine*, a fire destroyed most of his stock and equipment. Each issue of the 350-page monthly magazine, which Munro managed to publish in spite of the fire, offered a complete novel, short stories, serialized fiction, and poetry. In Munro's Library, Munro reprinted works by Dickens, George Eliot, and other European authors in ten- and twenty-cent books of reasonable quality. The setbacks of 1876, combined with the incessant competition, drove Munro into bankruptcy. Though forced to sell *Our Boys of New York* and the New York Boy's Library to Tousey and Small, Munro did keep the *Family Story Paper* and thereby resurrected his firm.

The following year Munro established the Riverside Library, a name that both echoed Houghton's prestigious Riverside Press and fit in with such other cheap book libraries as Donnelly, Lloyd and Company's Lakeside Library, Beadle and Adams's Fireside Library, and George Munro's Seaside Library. In its two-year existence, the Riverside Library totaled 143 titles, each twenty to seventy-five pages long, printed with three columns on each page, and priced at ten to twenty cents. Although the practice of choosing similar titles and series in order to obscure the difference between one product and another was widespread, George Munro was so incensed at his brother's competition that he unsuccessfully sued to prevent Norman from using the name Munro in his Munro's Library.

In 1883 Norman Munro moved to 24-26 Vandewater Street and began the Old Cap. Collier detective stories, which were a competitive response to George Munro's detective, Old Sleuth. These stories published in the Old Cap. Collier Library, were written by several authors, usually under pseudonyms. The first of over 700 titles was *Old Cap. Collier; or, "Piping" the New Haven Mystery* by W. I. James. In addition, Munro published several novels written by women and generally for women, including Mrs. Lenox Bell's *Not to Be Won* (1883), Mary Dallas's *Adrietta; or, Her Grandfather's Heiress* (1888), Florence Blackburn Schoeffel's *Miss Davis*

of Brooklyn (1888) under the pseudonym Wenona Gilman, and Mrs. Mary Jane Hoffman's *The King's Daughters; or, The Heiress and the Outcast* (1889). Laura Jean Libbey contributed at least thirteen titles to the firm's list, beginning with *Pretty Freda's Lovers; or, Married by Mistake. A Thrilling Romance of a Beautiful Young School Girl* (1889) and including *Lyndall's Temptation; or, Blinded by Love. A Story of Fashionable Life of Lenox* (1892).

The Munro Library, which Munro established in 1884, was similar to the earlier Munro's Library, although it was pocket-sized. It, too, consisted largely of European fiction which was not covered by copyright, but, as this field was now overexploited, Munro began to add histories, biographies, verse, and other nonfiction to his list. This plan failed to boost Munro's sagging profits, and in 1888 Munro joined the cheap book publishers who were selling their plates to the would-be monopolist, John W. Lovell. Only The Munro Library was sold, however; Munro's dime novels, series, and papers continued. After his death in 1894, his wife Henrietta managed the business until its demise in 1921.

References:

I. S. Cobb, *A Plea for Old Cap Collier* (New York: Doran, 1921);

"Contribution to Trade History: No. XXIV, Norman L. Munro," *American Bookseller*, new series 19 (1886): 103-104;

Ross Craufurd, *Bibliographic Listing. OUR BOYS and NEW YORK BOYS WEEKLY: The Great Tousey-Munro Rivalry* (Fall River, Mass.: Edward T. LeBlanc, 1979);

"Norman L. Munro [obituary]," *Publishers' Weekly*, 45 (3 March 1894): 389.

—*David Dzwonkoski*

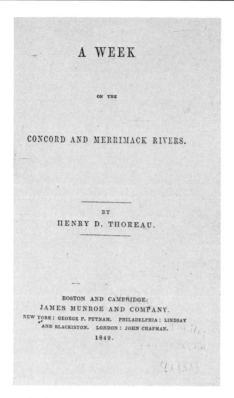

Title page of Thoreau's first book. Thoreau paid Munroe to publish 1,000 copies of the work, of which only 286 were sold.

Cover for a late number of the Norman L. Munro weekly series. It eventually included over 700 titles.

Frank A. Munsey (© Burr McIntosh)

James Munroe and Company

(Boston and Cambridge: 1835-1862)

James Munroe founded Munroe and Nichols, a bookselling and publishing firm in Boston and Cambridge, Massachusetts, with George Nichols in the early 1830s. John Owen became a partner in 1835, but this arrangement lasted for less than a year, after which Owen became the owner of the Cambridge branch of James Munroe and Company, which was located in the Lyceum Building. Munroe continued to publish under the imprint of James Munroe and Company at 134 Washington Street, Boston, until 1841 with Nichols as a partner, and from 1842 to 1860 with William H. Dennett. The firm is listed in the Cambridge city directories through 1861 and in the Boston directories through 1862, although Munroe had died the year before.

Among the firm's publications were three periodicals: volumes fifty-two through fifty-five of the *North American Review* for 1841 and 1842; volumes twenty-two through thirty-five of the *Christian Examiner* for 1837 to 1844; and the last four issues of the *Dial.* James Munroe and Company also published Eliza Lee Follen's *The Skeptic,* Catharine Maria Sedgwick's *Home,* and Hannah Farnham Lee's *The Backslider,* all in 1835. Four years later it published Robert Cassie Waterston's *Arthur Lee and Tom Palmer; or, The Sailor Reclaimed.* The second edition of Hawthorne's *Twice-Told Tales,* with twenty-one additional stories, was published by Munroe in 1842. After poor sales, the company republished the work in 1845 with a new title page, but apparently with no more success.

James Munroe was the first publisher of Emerson's essays, starting with *Nature* in 1836 and followed by *Essays* in 1841, *Essays; Second Series* in 1844, and *Poems* in 1847. *Nature: Addresses and Lectures* (1849) was the first collection of Emerson's earlier prose. Emerson's interest in the writings of Carlyle led to the first American edition of *Sartor Resartus* (1836). The first edition of Carlyle's *Critical and Miscellaneous Essays,* edited by Emerson, was also published by Munroe in four volumes in 1838 and 1839. Munroe is also noted as the publisher of Henry David Thoreau's first book, *A Week on the Concord and Merrimack Rivers* (1849). Thoreau paid Munroe to publish the first edition of 1,000 copies, of which Munroe was able to sell only 286. The rest he returned to Thoreau, who wrote, "I now have a library of nearly nine hundred volumes, over seven hundred of which I wrote myself."

Munroe also published William Ellery Channing's *Poems: Second Series* (1847), *The Woodman, and Other Poems* (1849), and *Near Home: A Poem* (1858). John Lothrop Motley's *Merrymount: A Romance of Massachusetts* appeared in 1849. Other authors of the firm's fiction included Louisa Jane Hall, Richard Hildreth, Eliza Lee, Sarah Savage, James Jackson Jarves, Mrs. Frances West Pike, and James Robinson Newhall. The company also published books on education and religion, such as Elizabeth Palmer Peabody's *Record of a School, Exemplifying the General Principles of Spiritual Culture* (1835) and A. Bronson Alcott's *Conversations with Children on the Gospels* (1836-1837). James Munroe also acted as an agent for the Massachusetts Peace Society.

—*Earl R. Taylor*

Munroe and Francis
(Boston: 1802-1853)

Edmund Munroe, born in Lexington, Massachusetts, in 1775, and David Francis, born in Boston in 1779, formed a partnership in 1802. From 1808 to 1810 and again from 1814 to 1816, they were joined by Samuel Hale Parker, who had received training as a bookbinder. The bookselling and publishing firm, which was located on Washington Street and later on Devonshire Street in Boston, published mostly religious and educational works. Munroe and Francis was one of the outlets for the American Unitarian Association. In addition to publishing editions of Scott and other British authors, the firm published Sarah Savage's *The*

Factory Girl (1814) and Samuel Benjamin Herbert Judah's *The Buccaneers* (1827). The firm of Munroe and Francis is best known for its 1827 reprint of Mother Goose rhymes, which was the first to sell well, and for its edition of Shakespeare's *Works* (1810-1812), the first in New England. From 1 January 1814 to 25 February 1815 the company published the *Boston Spectator,* a weekly newspaper. Francis died in 1853, the year the business closed; Munroe died the following year.

—*Earl R. Taylor*

Joel Munsell
(Albany, New York: 1836-1880)
Joel Munsell's Sons
(Albany: 1880-1895)

On 1 May 1834 Joel Munsell entered a partnership with Henry Stone to publish a periodical, the *Microscope,* in Albany, New York. In 1836 Munsell dissolved this partnership, purchased Thomas G. Wait's printing office at 58 State Street, and began publishing books under his own name. The majority of Munsell's output was typical for a small-town printer—law reports, guide books, almanacs, and circulars. Additionally, Munsell published children's literature, including Isaac Taylor's *Scenes in Asia, for the Amusement and Instruction of Little Tarry-at-Home Travelers* (1843) and his own *Select Stories for Children* (1848), as well as fiction, such as Josiah Priest's *History of the Early Adventures of Washington* (1841) and W. H. Bogart's sequel to Scott's novel, *Quentin Durward, the Loser and the Winner* (1869). He also published Richard de Bury's fourteenth-century treatise on the love of books, *Philobiblon* (1861).

Munsell's reputation rests on his fine printing. Like William Pickering in England, Munsell disliked the neoclassical severity of the Didot and Bodoni types. As a result he published a series of historically significant works in limited editions printed with old style types from the Caslon

foundry. His *Papers Relating to the Island of Nantucket* (1856), the first American book printed in old style, led to a revival in fine hand printing. Munsell returned to sixteenth- and seventeenth-century principles of design, using red and black title pages and adopting as his logo the dolphin and anchor of Aldus Manutius, with the motto *Aldi Discipulus Albaniensis.* His interest in printing led him to write and publish works on paper, type, and printing, including his *A Chronology of Paper and Paper-Making* (1856) and culminating in his new edition of Isaiah Thomas's *History of Printing in America* (1874) for the American Antiquarian Society.

Munsell's business suffered in the panic of 1873 and the ensuing depression. After Munsell's death in 1880 the firm continued as Joel Munsell's Sons, specializing in genealogy. Its last significant work was *American Ancestry* (1887); the firm dissolved in 1895.

References:
Bibliotheca Munselliana: A Catalogue of the Books and Pamphlets Issued from the Press of Joel Munsell,

from the Year 1828 to 1870 (Albany, N.Y.: Privately printed, 1872);

David S. Edelstein, *Joel Munsell: Printer and Antiquarian* (New York: Columbia University Press, 1950);

William C. Kiessel, Jr., ed., "The Autobiography of Joel Munsell," *New York History*, no. 37 (1956): 300-309.

—*John H. Laflin*

Frank A. Munsey and Company
(New York: 1882-1925)

See also the Frank A. Munsey entry in *DLB 25, American Newspaper Journalists, 1901-1925.*

In 1882 Frank A. Munsey left his home state of Maine and took with him to New York a pile of manuscripts he had bought for his proposed periodical, the *Golden Argosy*, a magazine of adventure and success stories for boys and girls. Horatio Alger, Jr.'s "Do and Dare; or, A Brave Boy's Fight for Fortune" was one of the manuscripts. Alger's story filled the front page of the first number of the *Golden Argosy* on 9 December 1882. "Munsey himself was an Alger hero," says his biographer, "and with this story he was launching his own fight for fortune." Munsey's first office was at 10 Barclay Street; later he moved to 81 Warren Street and then to 155 East Twenty-third Street.

By 1887 the *Golden Argosy* was selling 150,000 copies each week, netting Frank A. Munsey and Company $78,000 annually; the following year it became simply *Argosy*. Munsey then began his career of founding, purchasing, and absorbing magazines and daily newspapers. In 1889 he launched *Munsey's Weekly*, which became the monthly *Munsey's Magazine* in 1891. By 1907 Munsey claimed that *Munsey's Magazine* was the world's leading magazine in circulation and earnings. *Munsey's Magazine* reserved at least half of its pages for short stories and poems. Yet, with the exception of poems by Edgar Lee Masters in the early numbers and some stories by O. Henry, few of its literary contributors are remembered.

In 1914 Munsey experimented with the idea of publishing full-length novels by popular authors in his magazine prior to publication in hardcover; one such novel was Joseph Conrad's *Victory*, which appeared in February 1915. Anticipating the advertising campaigns for paperbacks of a few decades later, Munsey stressed that his magazine novels sold for a tenth of the cost of a hardcover. Although his idea was not totally new, it alarmed

the book trade; but while the novels helped the sales of his magazine, they started no trend.

Munsey's book production was limited and closely related to his magazine publications. In 1888 he published his own *The Boy Broker*, which was followed by *A Tragedy of Errors* (1889), *Derringforth* (1894), and *Afloat in a Great City* (1897). Two "Carpathian" novels by Robert McDonald appeared in 1897, *In the Reign of Boris* and *A Princess and a Woman*. Matthew White's *The Affair at Islington* (1897) and *A Born Aristocrat* (1898) also appeared under the Munsey imprint.

Munsey bought, discontinued, merged, or renamed the *Scrap Book*, the *Quaker*, the *Puritan*, *Godey's Magazine*, *Peterson's Magazine*, the *Live Wire*, *Junior Munsey*, *Woman*, the *Cavalier*, the *Railroad Man's Magazine*, and the *All-Story Magazine*. He was known as "a dealer in dailies" and "the Grand High Executioner of Journalism," and in his later years journalists used the expression "Let Munsey kill it" to mean financial absorption. At various times he owned eighteen newspapers, including the *New York Daily News*, the *New York Herald*, and the *Washington Times*. He also invested in banks, real estate, and grocery stores. Munsey died in December 1925, leaving instructions in his will that all of his firm's properties were to be sold off.

References:

George Britt, *Forty Years—Forty Millions: The Career of Frank A. Munsey* (New York: Farrar and Rinehart, 1935);

Frank A. Munsey, *The Founding of the Munsey Publishing-House: Quarter of a Century Old* (New York: DeVinne, 1907);

"Obituary Notes: Frank A. Munsey," *Publishers' Weekly*, 109 (2 January 1926): 35;

Erman J. Ridgway, *This for Remembrance: a Tribute* (Chula Vista, Cal.: Denrich Press, 1926).

—*Alan J. Filreis*

John Murphy and Company

(Baltimore: 1836-1943)

Born on 12 March 1812 in Ireland, John Murphy immigrated with his parents to New Castle, Delaware, in 1822. At sixteen he went to Philadelphia, where he apprenticed himself to a printer. In 1833 he went to Baltimore, where in 1835 he became superintendent of a printing plant. After a brief partnership with William Spaulding, in 1836 Murphy went into business for himself as a stationer, bookseller, and job printer at 178 Market Street. Later addresses were 44 and 182 West Baltimore Street and 31 South Howard Street. In 1839 Murphy began publishing books.

Within a few years Murphy became known as a major publisher of Catholic literature in the United States. In 1842 the firm began to publish the *United States Catholic Magazine*, which continued for seven years, and from 1853 to 1859 it published the *Metropolitan* magazine. Murphy also branched out into legal publishing with two volumes of the *Maryland Code* (1860) and the *Constitution of Maryland* (1862). For more than twenty-five years the firm was printer to the Maryland Historical Society.

John Murphy and Company's principal contribution to American literary history was the Catholic novel, including John Delavan Bryant's *Pauline Seward: A Tale of Real Life* (1847), James McSherry's *Pere Jean; or, The Jesuit Missionary* (1847), and three editions of Anna Hanson Dorsey's *The Oriental Pearl; or, The Catholic Emigrants* (1848). After Murphy's death in 1880, his sons Francis K. and Charles Abell Murphy continued publishing in the same vein. The firm was named printers and publishers to the Holy See by Pope Leo XIII in 1887. Juveniles published by the firm included Mrs. Dorsey's *Beth's Promise* (1887) and Mary G. Bonesteel's *Army Boys and Girls* (1895). Murphy's most notable author was Maurice Francis Egan, whose *A Marriage of Reason* came out in 1893. In 1919 the firm moved to 200 West Lombard Street. The company continued publishing Catholic literature until 1943, when P. J. Kenedy and Sons of New York took over much of its line.

References:

"John Murphy & Co.," *Tablet*, 3 (June 1891): 1-2;

Laurence Schlegel, "The Publishing House of John Murphy of Baltimore: The First Forty Years, with a List of Publications," M.A. thesis, Catholic University of America, 1961.

—Everett C. Wilkie, Jr.

First page of an early issue

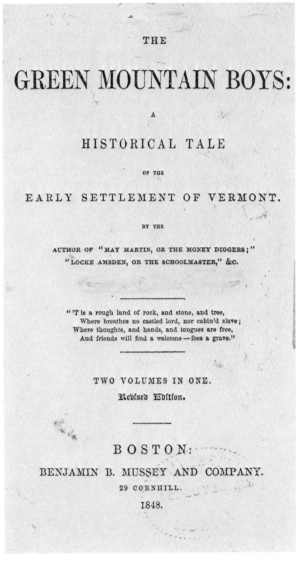

*Title page for a revised edition of Daniel Pierce Thompson's
popular historical novel recounting the adventures of Ethan
Allen in the Revolutionary War*

Benjamin B. Mussey and Company

(Boston: 1848-1855?)

B. B. Mussey

(Boston: circa 1835-1848)

An obscure Boston publisher, Benjamin B. Mussey opened business as B. B. Mussey in the 1830s. His earliest known publication was the anonymous *Six Months in a House of Correction* (1835), followed two years later by John H. Amory's *Old Ironside. First Number. The Story of a Shipwreck.* In the 1840s Mussey published Mrs. A. J. Graves's *Girlhood and Womanhood; or, Sketches of My Schoolmates* (1844) and John H. Warland's *The Plume: A Tuft of Literary Feathers* (1847). Renamed Benjamin B. Mussey and Company, the firm published James Russell Lowell's *Poems: Second Series* (1848).

Mussey's output reached a peak during the 1850s with Cornelius Mathews's *Chanticleer: A Thanksgiving Story of the Peabody Family* (1850), Daniel Pierce Thompson's *The Rangers; or, The Tory's Daughter* (1851), Francis Alexander Durivage's *Life Scenes, Sketched in Light and Shadow from the World around Us* (1853), Mrs. Emma Wellmont's *Uncle Sam's Palace; or, The Reigning King* (1853), William Taylor Adams's *Hatchie, the Guardian Slave; or, The Heiress of Bellevue* (1853), and Isaac W. Scribner's *Laconia; or, Legends of the White Mountains and Merry Meeting Bay* (1854). The firm appears to have ceased operations by 1855.

—*David Dzwonkoski*

Contributors

Susan K. Ahern ....*University of Houston-Downtown*

Gregory Ames ....*University of Rochester*

Phyllis Andrews ....*University of Rochester*

Chris M. Anson .... *University of Minnesota*

Grady W. Ballenger ....*University of North Carolina at Chapel Hill*

Martha A. Bartter .... *Ohio State University*

Nandita Batra...*University of Rochester*

Robert S. Becker ....*University of Pittsburgh*

Margaret Becket...*University of Rochester*

Ruth H. Bennett.. *Rochester, New York*

Robert Bertholf ....*State University of New York at Buffalo*

Ernest Bevan, Jr..*Bates College*

Daniel Borus...*New York, New York*

Deborah L. Brandt..*Indiana University*

Christy L. Brown..*Indiana University*

Judith Bushnell ....*State University of New York College at Geneseo*

Christopher Camuto .... *University of Virginia*

Joan Gillen Conners.. *Rochester, New York*

John R. Conners... *Rochester, New York*

Alma Burner Creek (deceased) .... (formerly *University of Rochester*)

Kathleen R. Davis...*Syracuse, New York*

Linda DeLowry-Fryman..*University of Pittsburgh*

Philip B. Dematteis.. *Columbia, South Carolina*

David Dzwonkoski .... *Virginia Beach, Virginia*

Elizabeth A. Dzwonkoski... *Rochester, New York*

Peter Dzwonkoski ....*University of Rochester*

Neal L. Edgar .... *Kent State University*

Stephen Elwell...*Indiana University*

Nancy Hill Evans...*Carnegie-Mellon University*

Ada M. Fan ....*Phillips Academy, Andover, Massachusetts*

D. W. Faulkner..*New Haven, Connecticut*

Alan J. Filreis .... *University of Virginia*

Margaret W. Fleming.. *Rochester, New York*

Anne Frascarelli ....*University of Rochester*

Christine Garrison...*University of Rochester*

Deborah G. Gorman .... *Philadelphia, Pennsylvania*

Leslie Gossage .... *University of Virginia*

Pamela A. Graunke...*Houston, Texas*

Jon Griffin...*University of Rochester*

Louis S. Gross... *University of Pennsylvania*

Edward J. Hall .... *Kent State University*

John Harrison .... *University of Arkansas*
Gregory M. Haynes .... *University of Virginia*
Joseph Heininger .... *University of Rochester*
Joseph J. Hinchliffe .... *University of Rochester*
Elizabeth Hoffman .... *University of Rochester*
Howard C. Horsford .... *University of Rochester*
Richard Horvath .... *University of Rochester*
Laura Masotti Humphrey .... *Honeoye Falls, New York*
George Hutchinson .... *Indiana University*
Mary M. Huth .... *University of Rochester*
Earl G. Ingersoll .... *State University of New York College at Brockport*
Sharon Ann Jaeger .... *Anchorage, Alaska*
Bruce L. Johnson .... *California Historical Society Library, San Francisco*
Herbert H. Johnson .... *Rochester Institute of Technology*
Karl Kabelac .... *University of Rochester*
Dean H. Keller .... *Kent State University*
Dorsey Kleitz .... *University of Virginia*
Carol C. Kuniholm .... *University of Pennsylvania*
John H. Laflin .... *Purdue University*
Xinmin Liu .... *Beijing, China*
Anne Ludlow .... *Rochester, New York*
Karin S. Mabe .... *Manlius, New York*
Mary Mahoney .... *Boxford, Massachusetts*
Jerre Mangione .... *Philadelphia, Pennsylvania*
Kathleen McGowan .... *University of Rochester*
Robert McNutt .... *Indiana University*
Philip A. Metzger .... *Southern Illinois University*
Carole B. Michaels-Katz .... *University of Rochester*
Theodora Mills .... *Rochester, New York*
Anuradha Mookerjee .... *Cincinnati, Ohio*
Timothy D. Murray .... *Washington University, St. Louis*
Joel Myerson .... *University of South Carolina*
Donna Nance .... *University of South Carolina*
David M. Niebauer .... *University of Michigan*
Bill Oliver .... *University of Virginia*
David Pankow .... *Rochester Institute of Technology*
Elizabeth Ann Peck .... *Brown University*
Vincent Prestianni .... *Monroe Community College, Rochester, New York*
Elizabeth Scott Pryor .... *Atlanta, Georgia*
Linda Quinlan .... *University of Rochester*
David W. Raymond .... *University of Rochester*
Shirley Ricker .... *University of Rochester*
Carmen R. Russell .... *University of Florida*
Lynne P. Shackelford .... *University of North Carolina*
Arlene Shaner .... *Portland, Oregon*
Frank Shuffelton .... *University of Rochester*

Alison Tanner Stauffer...*University of Rochester*

Annie E. Stevens ....*University of Rochester*

Botham Stone..*Columbia, South Carolina*

Christopher Surr..*Columbia, South Carolina*

Earl R. Taylor ....*Brown University*

John Tebbel...*Southbury, Connecticut*

Jane I. Thesing .... *University of South Carolina*

Harry F. Thompson...*University of Rochester*

Ronelle K. H. Thompson .... *Rochester, New York*

Vincent L. Tollers ....*State University of New York College at Brockport*

Gary R. Treadway..*University of South Carolina*

George E. Tylutki.. *Marywood College (Scranton, Pennsylvania)*

Evelyn A. Walker ....*University of Rochester*

Joseph W. Warnick ....*Buffalo, New York*

Everett C. Wilkie, Jr..*Brown University*

Carol Ann Wilkinson ....*University of Rochester*

Jutta Willmann .... *Bloomington, Indiana*

6744

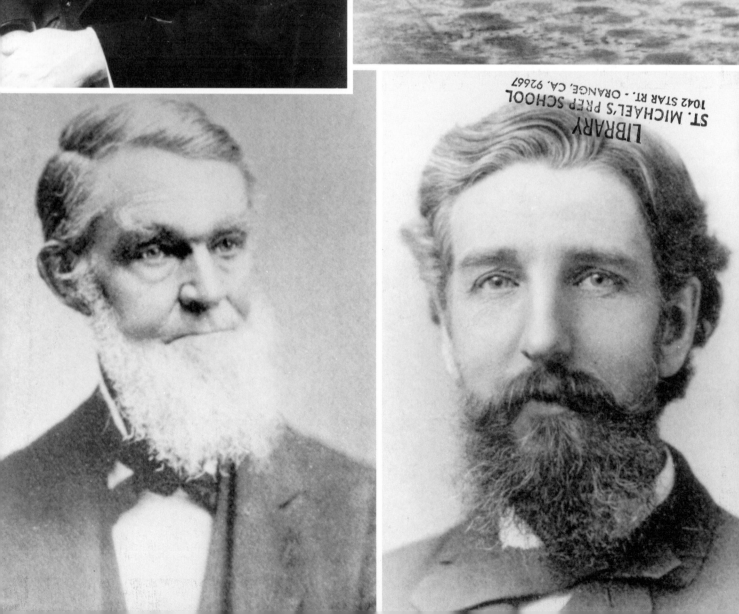